# War and the Art of Governance

# WAR AND THE ART OF GOVERNANCE

## CONSOLIDATING COMBAT SUCCESS INTO POLITICAL VICTORY

### NADIA SCHADLOW

Georgetown University Press | Washington, DC

**Library of Congress Cataloging-in-Publication Data**

Names: Schadlow, Nadia, author.
Title: War and the art of governance : consolidating combat success into
    political victory / Nadia Schadlow.
Description: Washington, DC : Georgetown University Press, 2017. | Includes
    bibliographical references and index.
Identifiers: LCCN 2016024175 (print) | LCCN 2016040666 (ebook) | ISBN
    9781626164109 (pb : alk. paper) | ISBN 9781626164093 (hc : alk. paper) |
    ISBN 9781626164116 (eb)
Subjects: LCSH: United States. Army—Stability operations. | United States.
    Army—Operations other than war. | Postwar reconstruction. | Peace-building.
Classification: LCC U167.5.S68 S33 2017 (print) | LCC U167.5.S68 (ebook) |
    DDC 355.02/80973—dc23
LC record available at https://lccn.loc.gov/2016024175

18 17     9 8 7 6 5 4 3 2
Printed in the United States of America

Cover design by Jen Huppert.

*To Philip, Madeline, George, and Bridget—*
*who waited a long time*
*to see proof of something on the shelf*

# CONTENTS

# PREFACE

REMINISCING about his experiences during World War II, Gen. Douglas MacArthur observed, "Power is one thing; the problem of how to administer it is another." His insight remains true today. Over a decade of war in Iraq and Afghanistan revealed, starkly, that the problem of how to consolidate combat gains into desired political outcomes has cost America lives and, arguably, victory in war.

Eight years into the wars in Iraq and Afghanistan, Secretary of Defense Leon Panetta admitted that there did not appear to be a sustained vision of how to address the political problems of reconstruction. Tellingly, he still saw the problem as essentially distinct from war proper: "The U.S. military was in Iraq to fight a war. They were not USAID. That's not their role." And several years later, recounting his experiences about the US intervention in Libya, President Barack Obama regretfully spoke of the "lesson I had to learn that still has ramifications to this day." While he affirmed that the intervention was "the right thing to do," he acknowledged that he had "underestimated the need to come in full force" and that there had to be a "much more aggressive effort to rebuild societies that didn't have any civic traditions." He explained that that was "a lesson that I now apply every time I ask the question, 'Should we intervene, militarily?' Do we have an answer [for] the day after?"

These examples indicate the difficulty US leaders have had in learning even from the most recent experiences. Despite substantial work on topics such as stability operations and postwar reconstruction and important analyses by the Office of the Special Inspector General for Iraq and Afghanistan, no assessment makes the argument that reconstruction is a central part of war, rather than an optional phase that follows war. Continuing to ignore the need to consolidate military gains has serious ramifications that harm US interests and international security.

The challenge of governance operations—those political and military activities undertaken by military forces to establish and institutionalize a desired political order during and following the combat phase of war—were not new for the United States. This book examines fifteen cases that illuminate the US Army's central role in the reestablishment of political order during and following combat operations. Indeed, the army's conduct of tasks related to the political and economic reconstruction of states has been central to all armed conflicts in which it has fought—from large-scale conventional wars to so-called irregular or counterinsurgency wars. Through a study of the United States' major wars, this inquiry examines the extent to which military and political leaders anticipated at the onset of each conflict the need to reconstruct order, identifies activities common to governance operations, and highlights the recurring operational challenges faced by army forces as they sought to reestablish order. The book uses cases—the Mexican-American War, the Spanish-American War, the Civil War, the Rhineland after World War I, the military governance operations of World War II, the Dominican Republic, Operation Just Cause, and then Iraq and Afghanistan—to show that the army has consistently faced similar governance challenges. Despite this history, there has been a persistent reluctance, rooted in American history and in civil-military relations, to prepare and train adequately for the political dimension of war. The book explains the roots of that reluctance and identifies obstacles to learning from historical experience that continue to impede preparation for armed conflict. This book places the political dimension of war squarely within the nature of war.

The political dimension of war has been considered in the literature on irregular warfare and counterinsurgency (COIN). There is a tendency in ongoing debates to view certain features of COIN as unique, as opposed to so-called traditional war. A look at American military engagements more broadly, however, suggests that politics—and its manifestation of competing groups seeking to gain power—will remain an important operational challenge in any US intervention. The book emphasizes that the need to manage "politics on the ground" in order to establish basic political order during and following combat operations permeates all wars, whether conventional, irregular, or COIN. That requirement is understudied in general army histories.

The book will not only counter the conventional wisdom that recent US military experiences in Iraq and Afghanistan were aberrations; it will also demonstrate that governance operations are and will remain an integral part of the American way of war. The book is not an argument for more military interventions or for so-called nation building. It is about what wars have always entailed and will continue to entail. The American military experience supports the idea that decisions to deploy American troops should be accompanied by operational plans to achieve the desired political end state too. Moreover, it identifies gaps in civilian thinking about the political dimension of war. American political leaders have consistently failed to consider the need to consolidate military gains politically. The book identifies and explains a syndrome rooted in mutually reinforcing civilian and military conceptions of war.

The book's analysis and conclusion are central to ongoing debates (often intense and bitter) about Iraq and Afghanistan and place these recent wars in the context of the American military experience. Regardless of readers' opinions concerning those conflicts, they will learn that the army faced governance challenges in the past and will continue to face them in the future. This conclusion will help military leaders plan better for interventions and help civilian policymakers understand what they are committing American soldiers to do, when US leaders make the decision to send them to war.

# ACKNOWLEDGMENTS

I AM GRATEFUL to so many individuals who have offered their insights and support for this project over the years. This book began as a dissertation far too long ago, while I was a student at Johns Hopkins University's School of Advanced International Studies. I am grateful to my dissertation adviser, Eliot Cohen, and committee members, Thomas Keaney, Bruce Parrot, Andrew Bacevich, and Thomas McNaugher. I am especially indebted to Tom McNaugher, who every year since I finished the thesis would politely, but persistently, inquire about my progress on the book and remind me that, sadly, the issue remained relevant.

*Parameters*, a great outlet for writing about national security issues, published my first article on the topic in 2005. That in turn helped introduce me to thinkers and writers in the US Army, many of whom actually experienced the situations and problems that I merely wrote about. Among those who encouraged me to continue to write on the topic included James Carafano, James Dubik, Tony Echevarria, Richard Lacquement (my coauthor on several articles that addressed topics related to this book), Peter Mansoor, David Johnson, Doug Ollivant, Ty Seidule, and Kalev Sepp. H. R. McMaster, despite the pace of his intellectual and operational activities, managed to find the time to read through the manuscript and offer insights, particularly on the intertwined relationship between war and politics. I appreciate the work of Conrad Crane, a historian who was one of the first to address the issues considered here. And many years ago, Richard Stewart, now retired as the Chief Historian of the US Army Center of Military History, welcomed me as I routed around the old civil affairs archives at Fort Bragg.

Other friends and colleagues whom I would like to thank include Max Boot, my "old" Department of Defense colleagues Ralph Cacci and Karl Pfefferkorn, Janine Davidson (whose book and additional writing on similar topics informed my thinking), Ryan Evans (who offers a great outlet in his *War on the Rocks*), Michelle Fang, Marian Gibbon, Andrea Green, Jakub Grygiel (always willing to listen to my ill-formed ideas), Frank Hoffman, David Kilcullen, Vinca LaFleur, Mac Owens, and Richard Shultz. Laura and Bill Smith helped to sharpen my thinking with their generous glasses of wine and counterpoint arguments! And my daily conversations with my dear friend Samantha Ravich kept me on track and offered a steady and necessary mix of national security discussions and dinner recipes.

I am also grateful to Don Jacobs, the editor at Georgetown University Press who remained interested and responsive throughout the process, despite my many delays, as well as for the helpfulness of Kathryn Owens and the thoroughness of Don McKeon, my copy editor.

All errors in the book are mine alone.

Without the support of my employer, the Smith Richardson Foundation, I could not have completed this book. At critical times, Peter Richardson generously allowed a more flexible schedule so that I could get the writing done. The intellectually stimulating environment at the foundation—driven by my colleagues and friends Marin Strmecki, Mark Steinmeyer (ever patient with my requests to edit this and that), and Allan Song—made my arguments sharper and challenged me to keep up with all of the related literature. In particular, without the advice, unwavering encouragement, and friendship of Marin (who has offered his intellectual guidance to so many) through the years, this book would not have been completed.

Last but not least, I am thankful for my family. The love and support of my husband, Philip, whose writing style I admire and benefited from and who patiently put up with so many weekends (years!) of research and writing, was always there to refine my thinking. And the joyful and easy natures of my three wonderful children, Madeline, George, and Bridget made it possible for me to focus on my work when required. My parents, Alan and Elvira, and sisters, Valerie and Monica, not only encouraged me to write but offered so much critical operational help in juggling commitments at home. Thank you.

# ABBREVIATIONS

| | |
|---|---|
| ACR | armored cavalry regiment |
| AFAK | Armed Forces Assistance to Korea |
| AFE | American Forces Europe |
| AIA | Afghan Interim Authority |
| AMG | American Military Government |
| AMGOT | Allied Military Government of Italy |
| ANA | Afghan National Army |
| ANDS | Afghan National Development Strategy |
| ANP | Afghan National Police |
| ANSF | Afghan National Security Force |
| AQI | al-Qaeda in Iraq |
| CAD | Civil Affairs Division |
| CAMG | Civil Affairs / Military Government |
| CAO | civil affairs officer |
| CATS | civil affairs training schools |
| CATT | Coalition Military Assistance Team |
| CCS | Combined Chiefs of Staff |
| CEB | Combined Economic Board |
| CENTCOM | Central Command |
| CERP | Commander's Emergency Response Program |
| CFC-A | Combined Forces Command–Afghanistan |
| CFLCC | Combined Forces Land Component Command |
| CIA | Central Intelligence Agency |
| CINCSO | commander in chief, US Southern Command |
| CINCUNC | commander in chief of UNC |

| | |
|---|---|
| CJSOTF | Combined Joint Special Operations Task Force |
| CJTF-7 | Combined Joint Task Force 7 |
| CJTF-180 | Combined Joint Task Force 180 |
| COIN | counterinsurgency |
| COSSAC | Chief of Staff to Supreme Allied Commander |
| CPA | Coalition Provisional Authority |
| CT | counterterrorism |
| DDR | disarmament, demobilization, and reintegration |
| DOD | Department of Defense |
| DP | displaced person |
| EAC | European Advisory Committee |
| ECA | Economic Cooperation Administration |
| ECAD | European Civil Affairs Division |
| EROA | Economic Recovery in Occupied Areas |
| ESG | Executive Steering Committee |
| EUSAK | Eighth United States Army Korea |
| FEC | Far Eastern Commission |
| FRUS | *Foreign Relations of the United States* |
| GAO | Government Accountability Office |
| GCU | German Country Unit |
| GPO | Government Printing Office |
| HIG | Hezb-e Islami Gulbiddin |
| IAPF | Inter-American Peace Force |
| IGC | Interim Governing Council |
| IRMO | Iraq Reconstruction Management Office |
| ISAF | International Security Assistance Force for Afghanistan |
| ISF | Iraqi security forces |
| ISI | Inter-Services Intelligence |
| ISIS | Islamic State of Iraq and Syria |
| JAG | Judge Advocate General |
| JCS | Joint Chiefs of Staff |
| JTF | Joint Task Force |
| KCAC | Korean Civil Assistance Command |
| KMAG | Korean Military Advisory Group |
| LOO | line of operation |
| MAAGV | Military Assistance Advisory Group, Vietnam |
| MGA | Military Government Association |
| MNC-I | Multi-National Corps–Iraq |

| | |
|---|---|
| MNF-I | Multi-National Force–Iraq |
| MNSTC-I | Multi-National Security Transition Command–Iraq |
| MOD | Ministry of Defense |
| MOI | Ministry of the Interior |
| MP | military police |
| MSG | Military Support Group |
| NA | National Archives |
| NATO | North Atlantic Treaty Organization |
| NGO | nongovernmental organization |
| NSC | National Security Council |
| OAS | Organization of American States |
| OCCA/MG | Office of the Chief of Staff, Civil Affairs and Military Government |
| OEC | Office of the Economic Coordinator |
| OIF | Operation Iraqi Freedom |
| OOTW | operations other than war |
| ORC | Organized Reserve Corps |
| ORHA | Office for Reconstruction and Humanitarian Assistance |
| ORO | Operations Research Office |
| PCO | Project and Contracting Office |
| PDF | Panamanian Defense Forces |
| PKSOI | Peacekeeping and Stability Operations Institute |
| PMG | Provost Marshal General |
| POW | prisoner of war |
| PRT | provincial reconstruction team |
| PSYOPS | psychological operations |
| RG | Record Group |
| ROE | rule of engagement |
| RSO | regional security officer |
| SAF | Army Security Assistance Force |
| SCAP | supreme commander, Allied powers |
| SHAEF | Supreme Headquarters Allied Expeditionary Forces |
| SIGAR | Office of the Special Inspector General for Afghanistan Reconstruction |
| SIGIR | Office of the Special Inspector General for Iraq Reconstruction |
| SOF | special operations forces |
| SOUTHCOM | US Southern Command |

| | |
|---|---|
| SWNCC | State-War-Navy Coordinating Committee |
| UN | United Nations |
| UNC | United Nations Command |
| UNCACK | UN Civil Assistance Command Korea |
| UNCURK | UN Commission for the Unification and Rehabilitation of Korea |
| UNKRA | United Nations Korean Reconstruction Agency |
| USAFIK | US Army Forces in Korea |
| USAID | US Agency for International Development |
| USAMGIK | US Army Military Government in Korea |
| USASOCOM | US Army Special Operations Command |
| USFET | US Forces, European Theater |
| USFLG | US Force Liaison Group |
| USSOCOM | US Special Operations Command |
| WMD | weapon of mass destruction |
| WPD | War Plans Division |

# INTRODUCTION

You don't dictate end states from the air. You can't control
territory. You can't influence people. You can't maintain
lines of control after you've established them. That will
take a ground force.

—Chief of Staff of the Air Force Gen. Mark A. Welsh III,
responding to comments about the US response to the Islamic
State of Iraq and Syria (ISIS), January 15, 2015

Perhaps the most difficult problem posed by contemporary
warfare, all in all, is the difficulty of achieving a stable,
secure ending to it.

—James Turner Johnson, *Morality and Contemporary Warfare*

SUCCESS IN WAR ultimately depends on the consolidation of political
order, which requires control over territory and the hard work of building
local governmental institutions. In recent years, the challenge of rebuilding
political order in Iraq and Afghanistan dominated national security debates.
The failure to consolidate military gains extended both wars, and as costs in
blood and treasure mounted, Americans engaged in fundamental and ongoing arguments over the structure and purpose of the American military. Since
the emergence of the United States as a global power with global interests,
military and civilian leaders have grappled with the problem of how to link
effectively the destruction and violence that is war to the reconstitution of
new forms of order. Even though US ground forces have engaged in activities
necessary for political consolidation during and following wars for most of the
country's 250-year history, the lessons from these experiences remain elusive.

Despite the recurring operational challenges associated with shaping the political landscape *during* and *following* combat operations, US military and political leaders have consistently failed to devote appropriate attention and resources to organizing for the political requirements of military interventions. For a variety of political, historical, and cultural reasons, the challenge of assessing *whether* and *how* US political objectives could be achieved and the development of an *operational capability* to make those outcomes more likely has eluded the United States. The problem is not just a military one but one rooted in deep-seated civilian ambivalence as well. Because in the United States it is civilian leaders who ultimately drive policy and strategy in wartime, one might expect lessons from those earlier experiences to have shaped US approaches to recent wars. Both our military and civilian leaders, however, consistently overlooked the lessons of past experiences.

Rather than confronting the complexity of how to reconstitute political order following war, the American experience in the post-9/11 period has led to a strong desire to avoid the deployment of ground forces altogether, regardless of the consequences for international order or US interests. Yet the messy interplay of what Thucydides called the "fear, honor, and interests" that combust into war is likely to remain outside the control of leaders who desire to avoid armed conflict. In the disordered world of the twenty-first century, civilian leaders will face decisions about whether to use military force to advance US foreign policy goals or to protect American vital interests. These momentous decisions involving the use of force and the risk to those who fight will require an understanding that war is more than military action and that military efforts must be combined with diplomacy, communications, and economic initiatives to achieve sustainable political outcomes. To wage war effectively, civilian and military leaders must operate as successfully on political battlegrounds as they do on the physical. As the difficulties encountered in Iraq and Afghanistan revealed, integrating efforts across those battlegrounds is essential to success in war.

America's recent experiences in Iraq and Afghanistan were not aberrational. American civilian and military leaders, as they had in the past, vastly underestimated the complexity and criticality of the political dimensions of armed conflict. Indeed, the need to work with local and national actors to restore stability and basic order was consistent with America's experience in virtually all previous conflicts. The political turmoil that followed the collapse of the Taliban and Saddam Hussein regimes and the associated need to consolidate political order were present in the so-called small wars of the 1930s as well as the world wars.

The purpose of this book is to demonstrate that in all of its significant military interventions in the past, the US Army has faced the need to shape the political outcome of a war. Army personnel under the theater commander's operational control supervised and implemented political and economic reconstruction tasks in virtually all of the army's major contingencies. Army personnel who remained in theater overseeing the political transitions were essential to the consolidation of combat gains and victory. With the cases described in this book, I hope to offer a better understanding of the recurring challenges associated with war and, perhaps, bring us closer to what Carl von Clausewitz sought to impress upon his readers: the need to understand the whole of war, whereby "every war must be conceived of as a single whole, and that with his first move the general must already have a clear idea of the goal on which all lines are to converge."[1] That "goal" has always been a political outcome that determines who rules what territory, with what type of institutions. A fuller appreciation of the true character of the American way of war as actually experienced can, in turn, help to inform policymakers of the requirements of war. And ideally, lead to better decisions.

This book is composed of five chapters. Following this introduction, the first chapter introduces the concept of governance operations. It focuses on the idea that throughout American history, the critical operational link shaping the transition from a militarily defeated regime to one more compatible with US interests has been the US Army. The army was, and remains, the only US policy instrument capable of decisively acquiring, holding, and stabilizing territory and deploying enough of a presence throughout a country or territory to provide a foundation for the reestablishment of political order. This chapter summarizes the consistent tensions that have shaped the conduct of governance-related tasks. Chapters 2, 3, and 4 present a historical overview of the recurring debates and challenges relating to the reconstitution of political order that the American army consistently faced—challenges that military and civilian leaders consistently underestimated. Chapter 2 describes the army's early experiences with governance operations in Mexico, California, New Mexico, the American South, Cuba, Puerto Rico, the Philippines, and the Rhineland in Germany following World War I. These cases cover the period in American history characterized by the growth of America into a world power. Despite the absence of formal guidance on how to conduct governance tasks during this period, military personnel repeatedly showed themselves capable of adapting to the challenges posed by the need to establish or reconstitute political order. Chapter 3 focuses on the cases of World War II: Korea, Japan, Italy, and Germany. This period saw the creation of a more institutionalized structure for governance operations, such as a school of military government in Charlottesville, Virginia. Although this period left a legacy of governance-related doctrine and some institutional changes (such as a civil affairs reserve structure), the military governance tasks of World War II remained outside the core responsibilities of the regular army. This separation of functions continued during the Cold War. Chapter 4 focuses on the lesser-known cases of governance operations during the Korean War, the intervention in the Dominican Republic in 1965, and the invasion of Panama in 1989. Despite the successes of the post–World War II military governments, the United States entered the Cold War period with an army that had institutionalized few approaches to consolidating political order during and following combat operations. Chapter 5 considers the recent conflicts in Iraq and Afghanistan. And the last section, "Conclusions," offers some final thoughts and recommendations. It assesses which lessons were learned and which were not.

Although the book is organized chronologically, it reveals common themes and tensions throughout all of America's military engagements. First, political factors and objectives shaped each war. At the outset of each one, political and military leaders anticipated, to varying degrees, the need to reconstruct political order in those states against which US military forces would fight. As US political and military leaders contemplated interventions, they generally also recognized that some level of political transformation in the opposing state would be required. However, the identification of the army as the instrument for this change did not generally occur at the outset of each war. Sometimes, as was the case during World War II, this goal was explicit during war planning. At other times, however, it was several weeks after the outbreak of war that the army was identified as the instrument through which political stability would be restored. In most of the cases studied, there was consistent discomfort among political leaders with giving the army leadership of governance operations. This concern was rooted in American political traditions that go back to the Founding Fathers' determination to prevent the rise of a dictator like the British general Oliver Cromwell, who usurped civilian government during the English Civil War. In addition, the army remained fairly ambivalent about its leadership over such operations but agreed to conduct them, largely owing to military necessity.

Second, the army faced the challenge of developing an organization to conduct governance operations in the wartime theater. The early phase of a governance operation generally involved the need to create an organizational structure amenable to governance challenges and to secure the safety of civilians and American forces. This period of the operation often involved balancing the requirements of "military necessity" due to ongoing combat operations, with the need to stabilize rear areas and prepare for the restoration of law and order. In many cases, this phase involved the simultaneous management of ongoing combat and the restoration of local administrative structures. In virtually all of the cases (including and before World War II), tactical combat officers led this phase, with military government units attached or working alongside tactical officers.

A key challenge for army officers was to decide how to structure the command relationship between military government / civil affairs officers and tactical combat officers. During World War II, a key issue was whether tactical military forces should lead the occupation or whether a specialized military government organization should be created—one for winning the war and one for "winning the peace." Since civilian officials in Washington were so often ill-prepared to provide army officers with guidance for their expected governance tasks, commanding generals were regularly faced with the challenge of gathering as much information about the tasks they faced, as quickly as possible. Governance operations were often "mobile" operations, initially working in tandem with active combat troops in forward areas and then establishing more stable administrative control in rear areas. Governance operations served as more than an extension of traditional combat service support tasks—such as the need to maintain order and ensure that civilians did not interfere with combat operations. They involved broader political, economic, and security tasks as combat ended.

Third, following the creation of an organization for governance operations in the theater, the army undertook specific tasks to restore political and economic stability in order to leave behind institutions compatible with US interests.[2] Soldiers had to determine how to support or reestablish a new governing elite. Army officials established and oversaw new elections, sometimes wrote or oversaw the development of new constitutions, and generally prepared a state or region for independence or the full transfer back to indigenous authorities. Army personnel often had to improve and stabilize the economy of a state or territory. Soldiers helped to reform the legal and judicial systems of states, which often involved the establishment of military commissions to oversee occupying soldiers, as well as new or restructured judicial systems to address crimes in the civilian populace and to restore law and order. Army personnel restored or rebuilt local police and national defense forces and addressed public welfare and health needs. Across all of these tasks, army and civilian officials faced the problem of when and how to transition from military to civilian authority and how to ensure that the state left behind had a functioning, stable economy in order to ensure its future stability.

During World War II, the State Department played a large role in developing plans for the military occupations that unfolded. Other agencies often provided expertise to advise army commanders in a theater. However, no other organization played the extensive role undertaken by the army. The army determined, day to day, how governance plans would unfold, and it implemented these plans. While it seemed to make neither civilians nor military officials happy, the army consistently served as the organization responsible for getting the job done. Because the army remained the main institution charged with implementing key governance tasks, it exerted enormous influence over policy simply because army officers were present in the field, making decisions. Related to this, the cases also reveal that there were consistent tensions among American actors over "who controlled what" when it came to the reestablishment of basic political order. Today these tensions are often reflected in the debate over "unity of command" and "unity of effort" and in debates over the role of civilians in conflict zones.

The themes addressed in this book remain salient today. Firsthand accounts by soldiers and civilians in books, on websites such as the *Small Wars Journal,* and in journals such as *Military Review* flourished, as soldiers, generals, and civilians analyzed, debated, and sought to capture lessons from their experiences in Iraq and Afghanistan. One army officer described the "daunting challenges" facing US soldiers in "navigating Afghanistan's complex labyrinth of local political hierarchies, cultural traditions, and competing powerbrokers" and the way incoming leaders "had to obtain a comprehensive awareness of Afghan politics, culture, and society in order to efficiently operate in this difficult environment."[3] Soldiers described the complexity of marrying up projects that "we think the [Iraqi] locals need but they may not see as a priority" and how important it was to combine US economic assistance with support from the local government because without such support "we risk having facilities that will be unsupported after we leave or function only a few days after their ribbon-cutting."[4]

In addition, for the past decade terms such as "nation building" and "counterinsurgency" have infused if not the popular lexicon then at least the news absorbed by interested audiences. The public saw that in Iraq and Afghanistan problems of political order and organization were as intense as the operational challenges of defeating enemy forces—and, more important, that these components of war were intertwined. Perhaps for the first time ever, the *New York Times* reviewed, as a book, a US Army and Marine Corps doctrinal manual. Debates over the political requirements of winning in Iraq and Afghanistan unfolded on the front page of leading newspapers, with military and political leaders disagreeing over the value of the "surge" strategy that later developed to defeat the insurgents in Iraq and Afghanistan.[5] Articles about the need to restore political order appeared in literary magazines such as the *New Yorker* and the *Atlantic*. These writings reflected on military and civilian experiences with the range of governance-related tasks that had challenged US operators in the past: the need to work with local security forces, the balance between retaining existing administrators or replacing them with new ones, the challenges of rebuilding essential services, and the need to maintain order and reestablish rule of law. Most important perhaps, these experiences again demonstrated the consistent tensions among US military and civilian bureaucracies as they sought to sort out who would lead such activities and how to organize and prepare for them.

In response to the challenges it faced in Iraq and Afghanistan, the army (and the Department of Defense [DOD] as a whole) made some doctrinal, operational, and tactical adaptations. In December 2006, the US Army and Marine Corps published a counterinsurgency manual, *FM 3-24*.[6] That manual, controversial then and now, was written to fill a gap in military thinking and planning. It identified and described the "mix of offensive, defensive, and stability operations conducted along multiple lines of operations" required in a counterinsurgency campaign.[7] The manual set forth, for the first time in decades, the kinds of tasks that US military troops would likely face once they were deployed: the political, social, and economic requirements in an area of operations as combat was under way. It emphasized that in the context of a counterinsurgency operation, support of the people was crucial because insurgents tended to focus on the people. As a result, the doctrine explained that it would likely fall on US soldiers to protect civilians from insurgents' intimidation and to provide basic economic needs and restore essential services such as water and electricity.

Later, many critics excoriated the manual and the effort surrounding it.[8] These critics offered a range of different arguments. Some argued that even if the American military became more adept at fighting insurgencies, "they couldn't make this war acceptable either to the American public or to the people in the lands where it was fought."[9] Other critics maintained that the US approach to counterinsurgency, which focused on obtaining the allegiance of civilians by providing security and undertaking reconstruction and development projects, was fundamentally flawed because insurgencies were defeated by coercion and force.[10] Overall, many of these critics failed to consider two problems: first, how to adapt as a war evolves and, second, the problem of political consolidation. By the summer of 2003 in Iraq, what had begun as a localized, hybrid decentralized insurgency had begun to coalesce and gain strength, and US leaders were unprepared. The national security adviser at the time, Condoleezza Rice, initially believed that after the defeat of the Iraqi army, the institutions there "would hold, everything from ministries to police forces."[11] Because of this failure to assess the political situation accurately from the start, the US Army bore the brunt of the need to develop an operational approach to defeat these insurgents. The COIN manual attempted to address that problem: It developed a combination of military, political, and social measures designed to defeat the insurgency and prevent its reoccurrence. Critics also failed to appreciate that the document provided information about the kinds of activities that soldiers were actually having to conduct, whether or not they wanted to. As former British army officer Emile Simpson observed in his book *War from the Ground Up*, the counterinsurgency doctrine allowed the strategist to access a wide range of tools that had been successfully used in various historical circumstances, but there was still much confusion stemming "from the belief that operational approaches, and in particular counter-insurgency, are comprehensive solutions rather than tools."[12]

The experiences in Iraq and Afghanistan, combined with deep defense budget cuts, have led to a chorus of arguments for "easy" or "antiseptic" approaches to war. There has been a tendency to confuse the tactical utility of advanced technologies—such as drones and remotely piloted vehicles—with their ability to achieve enduring strategic outcomes. Former secretary of defense Leon Panetta described how the growth of special operations forces, unmanned aerial systems, technologies countering improvised explosive devices, and the "extraordinary fusion between military and intelligence" would provide the tools the United States would need to succeed on twenty-first-century battlefields and said that the United States was "closer than ever to achieving our strategic objectives in Afghanistan and Iraq."[13] The vice chairman of the Joint Chiefs of Staff observed that the United States was not "likely to have as our next fight a counterinsurgency" and that the US would need to "avoid the temptation to look in our rear view mirror."[14] Explaining the use of drones in a major speech in 2012, the Obama administration's top counterterrorism official, John Brennan, noted that these weapons were a "wise choice" because they dramatically reduced the danger to US personnel and that their "surgical precision" and "laser-like focus" could "eliminate the cancerous tumor called an al-Qaida terrorist while limiting damage to the tissue around it"—this as Brennan also acknowledged that al-Qaeda and its affiliates deliberately sought to "destabilize regional governments."

Interestingly, that major counterterrorism address did not specifically mention Libya, which by then had been spiraling into chaos following the February 2011 uprisings against the dictator Muammar Qaddafi. Soon after those uprisings, the Libyan leader had warned that his government would have "no mercy and no pity" regarding the rebels. In response to what appeared to be an impending massacre, the United States and the North Atlantic Treaty Organization (NATO) authorized a no-fly zone and air strikes over Libya to protect civilians. The president accepted that violence would likely be on a "horrific scale" but reassured his listeners that America's "unique" military capabilities would be used only on the "front end of the operation" and that the US "would not put ground troops into Libya." Backed by NATO air raids, Libyan rebels initially captured territory but were then forced back by better-equipped pro-Qaddafi forces. Despite the president's optimism that the US had accomplished its objectives of securing "an international mandate to protect civilians, stop an advancing army, prevent a massacre, and establish a no-fly zone" in just thirty-one days, these accomplishments were as fleeting as the rebels' initial successes. Even though then–secretary of state Hillary Clinton spearheaded international efforts to discuss what a political transition in Libya might look like, discussions in London were not enough to shape a political transition. From the air alone, the consolidation of gains is impossible. Indeed, by September 2012, Libya had slid into chaos, with tens of thousands displaced or dead and the American ambassador and three other officials killed by Islamist militants. Today an anarchic civil war continues, with militias of all types running rampant, using torture, rape, and detainment to control populations. Competing groups vie for power, journalists reporting on events are targeted, and electricity blackouts and water shortages occur daily. And Libya's anarchy has created fertile ground for ISIS and related groups who now control and operate from key parts of that disintegrating state.

Moreover, it is hard to consider Libya today without giving consideration to the end state engendered by the use of a particular course of military action. As two scholars of just war theory, Dan Caldwell and Robert Williams, have pointed out, "What happens following a war is important to the moral judgments we make concerning warfare, just as the intentions going in and the means used are."[15] They write that it is inconsistent to go to war for the defense of human rights if such a war is likely to result in the deaths of extraordinary number of civilians.

With *jus ad bellum* and *jus in bello* theories, theorists and policymakers have pondered the morality of going to war as well as the ethical conduct of combatants in war. But an emerging literature points out the need to consider *jus post bellum* too—that is, a judgment about what is likely to happen when the fighting stops, since "what we intend to do after we have fought must be part of the moral calculus in determining whether or not we may justly go to war." Caldwell and Williams urge a consideration of specific policy problems, to include how a victor restores order and how to restore the rights to basic sustenance, such as economic reconstruction. And as others have noted, there is a need for clearer thinking about the postbattle considerations of war and the operational concerns of postcombat operations that stabilize and restore order.[16]

Few relish the challenge of making predictions, and it adds little to policy debates to "call" policymakers on the wrong ones. But to delink the political motivations that drive conflict from the use of military force is shortsighted. It deliberately eschews history, ignoring that the use of force is not an end in and of itself and that decisions to use force require a consideration of how to achieve desired political goals. It is shortsighted to undervalue the lessons of the past ten years and to advance a view that the capabilities developed over the past decade will be *less* relevant to future conflict. As one prominent military thinker and practitioner, Lt. Gen. H. R. McMaster, contended, "it is wishful thinking that makes the future appear easier and fundamentally different from the past," and "the belief that new technology had ushered in a whole new era of war was applied to the wars in Afghanistan and Iraq, which clouded our understating and delayed the development of effective strategies."[17] He continued that the "best way to guard against a new version of wishful thinking" was to understand three age-old truths about war: (1) that it is political; (2) that it is human, grounded in the fears, interests, and sense of honor that drives social, economic, and historical factors; and (3) that it is uncertain, "precisely because it is political and human."

As the end of 2016 approaches, these are not necessarily welcome observations. There is a consistent and growing argument from many civilian policymakers, politicians, and military experts that the United States will never again face the difficult operational challenges of trying to turn interventions into politically sustainable outcomes. In contemplating the most recent violence in the Middle East, from Libya to Iraq to Yemen and Syria, the president of the United States has repeatedly emphasized that any US engagement would be very limited. For example, his requests to Congress to authorize the use of military force against ISIS deliberately excluded the use of ground forces. Yet, as we glance at the newspapers today, it is clear that our enemies understand the value of control over territory. The desire to control territory—*and to establish political order over territory*—is evident in the tribal areas of Pakistan, which remain bastions of violence; in Europe, where the post–Cold War political order has been upended by Russia's de facto dominance over parts of Ukraine; and in Mesopotamia, where ISIS battles to overtake key cities and areas.

Indeed, ISIS's vicious and genocidal campaign against "nonbelievers" in Iraq and the region has repulsed much of the world. Despite calls for action, developing a policy response to this violence posed a particular problem for the United States. Although ISIS from the start recognized the importance of establishing control and governance over territory, the US remains challenged in its ability to reconstitute political order in conflict environments. Top American officials consistently emphasized that any efforts in the region would be "different from the wars in Iraq and Afghanistan" and would not "involve American combat troops fighting on foreign soil."[18] Others, including the chairman of the Joint Chiefs of Staff, linked any decision to put boots on the ground to the articulation of a desired political end state. Yet, operationally, this remains a serious challenge for the US, leading to efforts to deliberately narrow the problem of ISIS to one of terrorism. President Obama described it as a "terrorist organization, pure and simple," an interpretation that seemed to detach its activities from the politics and ideology that drive its leaders. With ISIS "just" a terrorist organization, the application of a "sustained counter-terrorism strategy" could suffice, and the US could thus avoid the problem of how to connect the deployment of ground forces to a desired political outcome. In this case, the desired outcome was a narrow weakening of a terrorist movement, not the shaping of a political landscape to counter that movement.

The United States continues to lack the operational capabilities to consolidate combat gains in order to reconstitute political order. Certainly, after a decade and a half of conflict in the Middle East and South Asia, many key military and political leaders now openly discuss and debate the lessons of the need to connect the use of ground forces to a desired political end state. This book is not about *whether* the United States should intervene in other states—whether for humanitarian purposes or to protect its vital interests. This book is about how such interventions consistently involve the need to consolidate combat gains and restore political order and hopes to encourage decision makers to consider that "what we intend to do after we have fought must be part of the moral calculus in determining whether or not we may justly go to war."[19]

Certainly the recent literature, as well as the doctrinal and training changes instituted by the US Army over the past several years, reflects considerable institutional and individual learning. That large volume of writing offers important insights, captures lessons from the recent wars, and continues to inform planning for current and future military engagements. This book hopes to contribute to that work by reinforcing insights with historical examples and by highlighting the political and bureaucratic sensitivities that have historically shaped the US conduct of governance-related tasks and that remain relevant today. Until the United States accepts the political challenges that are integral to any use of force, it will continue to have mixed results using its military forces. The purpose of this book is to elucidate an enduring Clausewitzian observation that "the war of a community—of whole nations and particularly of civilized nations—always starts from a political condition, and is called forth by a political motive. It is therefore a political act."

The United States still requires a concept of operations and the organizational and command structures to allow US military forces to conduct the governance operations that will inevitably fall to them during war and that are necessary to link military actions to political outcomes. When civilian and military leaders debate the use of force, they must also determine whether the US has the will, organizations, and resources to go from combat successes to achieving political outcomes. They should decide if this burden is too great and therefore decide against military action. This is an enduring problem with the American way of war and must be part of any calculus to use force. This book, by exploring what has unfolded in America's experiences with war, hopes to contribute to smarter deliberations about the decision to use force.

# NOTES

1. Clausewitz, *On War*, 582–83.

2. Sometimes elements of the reconstruction phase took place concurrent with combat, before a country was defeated or brought under American authority. In Italy and Germany, for example, fighting between the Allied and Axis powers continued as civil affairs officers were simultaneously working to establish political and economic order in defeated rear areas.

3. Wright, *Vanguard of Valor*, 86.

4. Craig Collier, "Observations from a Year in the Sunni Triangle," *Small Wars Journal*, April 13, 2008.

5. Elizabeth Bumiller, "West Point Is Divided over a War Doctrine's Fate," *New York Times*, May 27, 2012.

6. US Army and Marine Corps, *Counterinsurgency Manual*, FM 3-24 (Chicago: University of Chicago Press, 2007). The original was issued in December 2006.

7. Similarly, several years later, on September 16, 2009, the DOD issued Instruction 3000.05, "Stability Operations," which affirmed that stability operations activities would occur through "all phases of conflict and across the range of military operations, including in combat and non-combat environment." http://www.dtic.mil/whs/directives/corres/pdf/300005p.pdf.

8. See, for example, Bumiller, "West Point Is Divided," and Gentile, *Wrong Turn*.

9. Kaplan, *The Insurgents*, 365.

10. Gentile, *Wrong Turn*, 8.

11. Gordon and Trainor, *Cobra II*, 463.

12. Simpson, *War from the Ground Up*, 153.

13. Secretary of Defense Leon Panetta, Opening Statement, House Armed Services Committee, No. 112-76, 1st sess., October 13, 2011, https://www.gpo.gov/fdsys/pkg/CHRG-112hhrg71447/html/CHRG-112hhrg71447.htm.

14. Colin Clark, "U.S. Military to Scrap COIN," *AOL Defense*, November 17, 2011.

15. Williams and Caldwell, "Jus Post Bellum." Their quotes in this paragraph are from pages 309, 318, and 319.

16. Rear Adm. Louis V. Iasiello, Chaplain Corps, US Navy, "Jus Post Bellum: The Moral Responsibilities of Victors in War," *Naval War College Review* (Summer/Autumn 2004): 37.

17. McMaster, "Pipe Dream of Easy War," A12.

18. "Statement by the President on ISIL," White House, Office of the Press Secretary, September 10, 2014. https://www.whitehouse.gov/the-press-office/2014/09/10/statement-president-isil-1. See also Ambassador Samantha Powers, US permanent representative to the United Nations, "Remarks on Syria at the Center for American Progress," Washington, DC, September 6, 2013, in which she stated that given Iraq and Afghanistan, Americans were "ambivalent" and that thus any "any use of force will be limited." http://usun.state.gov/remarks/5793.

19. Phrase is from Williams and Caldwell, "Jus Post Bellum," 310.

# ONE

# AMERICAN DENIAL SYNDROME

## FAILING TO LEARN FROM THE PAST

HISTORICALLY, the United States has gone to war with the implicit or explicit assumption that the desired end state should favor US regional or strategic interests. US forces have fought against the armies of opposing states, as well as against less well-organized irregular military forces. In all armed conflicts except those in which political objectives were narrowly constructed, the US Army has served as the critical operational link in shaping transitions from a militarily defeated regime to one more compatible with US interests. A common feature in all of the conventional wars fought by the United States has been the army's leading role in the establishment of political and economic order in states or territories in which it has fought.[1] Although the US Marine Corps has also played a key role in developing thinking about small wars and executing limited expeditionary operations, the larger size of the army means that it is the only service capable of decisively acquiring, holding, and stabilizing territory and operating in sufficient scale for ample duration to provide a foundation for a transition to the reestablishment of political order. American political and military leaders have consistently avoided institutionalizing and preparing for the military and political activities that are associated with the restoration of order during and following combat operations.

Before the wars in Iraq and Afghanistan, few if any official or unofficial military histories paid much attention to the army's conduct of these kinds of operations.[2] Military governance, a term stemming from World War II, was "not sufficiently military to fit into the military history genre and too military to be treated as general history."[3] The absence of a sustained discussion of governance operations in official and unofficial army histories reflected the prevailing view that such operations were separate and distinct from the prosecution of war as a whole.[4] Many of the problems related to the reconstruction efforts in Operation Iraqi Freedom and Operation Enduring Freedom in Afghanistan demonstrated the consequences of this denial of governance operations as integral to war and, thus, of the need to prepare for and set aside resources for them. As the United States went into Iraq, the prevailing view among top civilian leaders—such as the national security adviser—was that the US forces would defeat the Iraqi army and that the "institutions would hold, everything from ministries to police forces." The top civilian official in Iraq at the time, Jay Garner, later admitted that he had not anticipated the need to take on the physical and political reconstruction of Iraq.[5] This denial of operational challenges and requirements of achieving a desired political end state was not new but, rather, was a prevalent feature of America's approach to war.

There are several plausible explanations for this denial. They are rooted in history, and many endure today. One explanation relates to concerns about the appropriate role of the military in a democratic society and maintains that it is dangerous to give the military governing authority—even if abroad. Since military government is so overtly a political activity, states committed in principle to civilian control of the military are reluctant to place officers in charge of local governments.[6] Influential Harvard University political scientist Samuel Huntington observed that "liberalism does not understand and is hostile to military institutions and the military function."[7] Although most of the army's experiences with governance operations have occurred outside the United States, the creation of an army capable of accomplishing these governance missions (albeit abroad) may have worried those who thought that such forces could be used at home as well.[8]

Civilian and military leaders have been unwilling to assign the army a lead role in governance operations owing to such reservations. During the Mexican-American War, Gen. Winfield Scott observed that the American authorities were "evidently alarmed at the proposition to establish martial law, even in a foreign country, occupied by American troops."[9] As that war ended, General Scott hesitated to get involved in the debate about "annexation v. occupation" since it was "impertinent as a soldier to inquire about such things."[10] In the aftermath of the Civil War, President Andrew Johnson expressed deep concern about the army's role in the political reconstruction of the South, fearing that such power in the hands of the army was in "palpable conflict" with the Constitution and a formula for "absolute despotism."[11] At the turn of the century, Secretary of War Elihu Root observed that the American soldier's experience as a self-governing American citizen could inform and shape his ability to conduct varied tasks in the interests of American foreign policy.[12] Contemporary scholars have observed that the resistance to the idea of military officers "governing" in any capacity—even abroad—is rooted in the ambivalent relationship Americans have had toward their military.[13]

Indeed, domestic concerns about the role of the military and about what it should, or should not, be doing have always shaped decisions about how to organize and train US forces. The Founding Fathers, debating America's first Constitution, sought to separate politics from the military and to create barriers to the military's acquisition of an overtly political role in American civic life. Their goal, for the most part, was the subordination of military to civil power. Opponents of a standing, regular army argued that a citizen-based militia was adequate to safeguard America and would also prevent the acquisition of too much power by one organized group. Alexander Hamilton described the tension between these two viewpoints: To be safer, he wrote, countries "become willing to run the risk of being less free."[14] Another member of the Continental Congress observed that "there was not a member in the federal Convention, who did not feel indignation at the prospect of a standing Army." Thomas Jefferson argued that the defense of the United States would rest in a citizen-based military force and that civilian supremacy would be maintained by eliminating a professional and permanent military force.[15] Eventually, the Constitution granted the federal government the right to raise a standing army for no more than two years.

A second reason for this denial syndrome is rooted in America's ambivalence about "governing" others, which stems from its anticolonial legacy. During the Spanish-American War, US military and political leaders referred to governance operations as colonial matters.[16] Although Secretary of War Root expressed great pride in American soldiers' reconstruction efforts in "poor bleeding Cuba" and "devastated" Puerto Rico, he was also careful to placate critics and reassure them that no American army would "make itself a political agent" or a "Pretorian [sic] guard to set up a President or an emperor."[17] He worked to assuage political concerns about the army's role in the Philippines by stating, "No one knew of the American Army seeking to make itself a political agent. . . . No one knew of the American army seeking to throw off that civil control of the military arm which our fathers inherited from England."[18] Similar concerns over soldiers serving as administrators continued through World War II. President Franklin Roosevelt and many in his administration shared the view that "military government was . . . a repulsive notion, associated with imperialism, dollar diplomacy and other aspects of our behavior we had abandoned."[19] President Harry Truman, following one of his first briefings on occupation plans, said that civil government was "no job for soldiers" and that the War Department should begin planning to turn over occupation responsibility to the State Department as soon as possible.[20] Later, in contemporary debates about "nation building," some of these earlier concerns about colonialism reemerged—most famously during presidential candidate George W. Bush's statement that US troops should not be used for "what's called nation building."

Related to these two characteristics of American denial syndrome is a third: the persistent belief that civilians could and should be taking the lead in undertaking governance operations during war. This view contributed to the lack of development of an institutionalized capacity for governance tasks in the army but never prevailed enough to succeed in creating an effective standing civilian capability within civilian agencies such as the State Department. This problem became especially apparent in Afghanistan and Iraq. Despite the creation in 2006 of a State Department office to grow a civilian capacity to undertake reconstruction tasks, continual funding problems, as well as organizational culture tensions, prevented a strong capability from emerging. Throughout the wars in Afghanistan and Iraq, US military and civilian leaders cited the need deploy or "uplift" more civilians to both theaters. Yet it was found that in addition to significant infrastructure and security costs, it cost the US government between about $410,000 and $570,000 to deploy one employee to Afghanistan for one year.[21] And overall, US civilian employees to Afghanistan topped out at just over 1,000 by 2011. (It has been about 300 in 2009 and less in previous years.) Given that the State Department consistently struggled with requirements to send civilians to work on reconstruction and development projects, the United States tended to turn to military reservists to fill the gap. In 2009, when former secretary of defense Robert Gates expressed concern that the government would not "get the civilian surge into Afghanistan as quickly as we are getting troops into Afghanistan," he asked the US Marines and other services for volunteers who had specific skills "who might serve as a bridge, getting them out of there quickly, and then bringing them back when their civilian replacements are hired." This lack of civilian capacity, combined with the policy preference to adhere to unity-of-effort as opposed to unity-of-command models, further complicated US efforts and was consistent with past problems in deploying an adequate civilian capacity to conduct governance operations.

The army's traditional view of war, which has emphasized the centrality of battle and the defeat of enemy military forces over the achievement of broader strategic outcomes, is a fourth explanation for Washington's reluctance to develop and institutionalize a robust governance capability. One military scholar observed that the army had essentially focused on "defeating an adversary tactically" rather than approaching war with a "holistic view of conflict, one that extends from prewar condition setting to the final accomplishment of national strategic objectives."[22] The prominent military historian Russell Weigley observed that the American way of war has been characterized predominantly as one that emphasized strategies of annihilation and attrition.[23] This more narrow approach to war failed to pay attention to the political consolidation and operational steps required to achieve strategic victory in war. As the military strategist Antulio Echevarria more recently pointed out, Weigley's analysis did not address how useful military strategies might be in turning tactical victories into policy successes.[24]

This approach to war perpetuated the separation between governance operations and the regular army. Before and after World War II, the army treated governance operations as problems of military law or as part of those tasks taken to minimize civilian "interference" on the ground. Army leaders did not embrace governance functions but recognized that they would have to keep civilians apart from combat operations, manage refugee flows, and restore law and order since control over these tasks allowed officers to protect their forces and minimize interference with combat operations. This theme first emerged in the mid-1800s. Official army documents described Gen. Winfield Scott's governance operations during the Mexican-American War as having saved the "combat commander problems with the civilian populace."[25] During the Civil War, the provost marshal general had purview over governance tasks, reinforcing the view that they were problems associated with military law as opposed to serving as the operational link to broader political objectives. This perspective continued after World War I, when the army's judge advocate general retained oversight over governance tasks and the provost marshal general retained jurisdiction over training and doctrine related to civil affairs and military government through the early 1940s, with later graduates of the military government course at Camp Gordon reminded of "the importance of assuring that our military operations are not impeded by civil disturbances."[26]

This separation from core army war-fighting priorities and the reluctance to institutionalize governance activities continued after World War II—despite the fact that governance operations were crucial to strategic victory in that war. Initially following the war, the army dismantled its civil affairs division, not heeding the advice of Col. Irwin Hunt, the officer in charge of civil affairs for the Third Army and American forces in Germany during World War I, who later observed that it was "extremely unfortunate that the qualifications necessary for a civil administration are not developed among officers in times of peace."[27] Only through active lobbying by former military government personnel was the new Civil Affairs Division (CAD) created. One of the early division chiefs of the CAD, Maj. Gen. William Marquat, observed that there was "an alarming lack of appreciation" for civil affairs activities, even though they had become "important functions of the Department of the Army."[28]

A broader consideration of governance tasks developed during the early Cold War years, but this shift took place within the context of *unconventional* war. In the 1950s and 1960s, two interrelated trends—revolutionary upheaval in the third world and the need to develop a way of thinking about war below the nuclear threshold—led to discussions about low-intensity conflict. Low-intensity conflict focused on the destruction of the enemy's political and social fabric and the subsequent rebuilding of a state in a manner consistent with US objectives, but these were activities viewed as apart from "regular" warfare.[29] The concept of nation building also gained prominence. Today the term tends to be used in a broader context, but in the 1960s nation building focused on the training of other nation's military forces so that they could resist Communist aggression themselves—as opposed to relying directly on US military forces.[30] The creation of the Military Assistance Advisory Group, Vietnam (MAAGV) in 1955 was one example of this approach. The MAAGV sought to improve the military capabilities of the Republic of Vietnam's armed forces through planning, developing, and administering military assistance.[31] Later in Vietnam, the army's pacification program included elements of traditional governance operations, such as civic action, land reform, and political reform. These tasks, however, were considered a part of the army's "other war."[32]

A central problem in Vietnam was the US failure to understand how broader pacification efforts fit into the war as a whole. This debate continues today, with arguments over the degree to which two kinds of wars were pursued simultaneously: a conventional war of attrition combined with a more sophisticated counterinsurgency strategy designed to reduce support for the Vietcong among the populace.[33]

The political and economic challenges posed by low-intensity conflict situations did result in a shift in thinking about governance operations as primarily combat-support tasks. An emerging community within the army began to view civil affairs assets as instruments for undercutting the political support behind an enemy's forces and mobilizing the support of indigenous populations.[34] However, the army still viewed such activities as a side category of warfare, distinct from conventional war and the tasks of regular troops. The inclusion of civil affairs in the newly created US Special Operations Command (USSOCOM) in 1987 essentially codified this view.[35] Civil affairs was one of several special missions assigned to the new command, and at the time many of its advocates—most of them reservists—argued that the move was positive, would increase awareness of civil affairs, and would "sensitize" other commands to their capabilities.[36] Some, however, expressed concern that including civil affairs in this new command would reinforce its separation from the "regular" army and, thus, from conventional war.[37] Adding to this idea of separateness was the fact that most of the civil affairs structure remained in the US Army Reserve, which is often considered distinct from the professional heart of the military.[38]

The separation of governance-related tasks from conventional warfare intensified after the collapse of the Soviet Union. In the early 1990s, a burgeoning discourse on peace operations and operations other than war (OOTW) emerged. Analysts argued that large-scale conventional war would be less likely and that more attention should be paid to "new" forms of military engagement, the requirements engendered by the "new security environment," and the challenges posed by weak or failing states.[39] The kinds of military activities referred to in this discourse were very broad, ranging from policing activities to the use of military troops in peace operations to the deployment of army forces to prevent the outbreak of conflict—what was called at the time "preventative diplomacy."[40]

Civil affairs became a catchall term to describe the many activities that a commander must undertake to "facilitate military operations and help achieve politico-military objectives derived from U.S. national security interests."[41] Civil affairs assets were useful in such a wide range of operations that their relationship to war had been obfuscated. The 1990s debate about peace operations and OOTW focused on the use of army forces in noncombat roles in situations *other than war, short of war,* or *after war.* This distinction reaffirmed the army's tendency to consider governance-related activities apart from conventional war. Army personnel might be used to monitor a cease-fire, to rebuild a city after a natural disaster, to deliver humanitarian aid, or to police streets in areas of instability. While these tasks might pose similar tactical and operational challenges to governance operations, they are not, for the most part, conducted within a wartime theater.

The fact that former civil affairs personnel undertook much of the advocacy for civil affairs issues within the army tended to reinforce the separation of governance-related tasks from the "real army." Their emphasis on the "specialness" of civil affairs strengthened the prevailing view of governance operations as separate and distinct from conventional war and the regular army.[42] This line of argument tended to ignore the fact that regular army officers conducted governance missions throughout the army's previous wars. Since the army's governance capabilities resided in its reserve, reserve civil affairs personnel focused on perfecting certain functional tasks, hoping to establish reserve branch status for military government and civil affairs—since they had lost the battle to create a corresponding branch in the active army. These efforts often clashed with the army's view that officers should be fit for general service, since "despite specialization . . . they cannot expect tours of duty restricted to military government duties only."[43]

This separation might be traced partly to Carl von Clausewitz, whose influence on the US Army has been, and remains, pronounced. Clausewitz was a Prussian general whose book *On War* explains the character of war and the characteristics of combat. Some of his most enduring observations relate to the relationship between politics and war. He observed that people tended to "separate the purely military elements of a major strategic plan from its political aspects, and treat the latter as if they were somehow extraneous."[44] Clausewitz wrote that no one started a war, or "no one in his sense ought to do so," without clearly understanding what he intended to achieve and "how he intends to conduct it."[45] However, he did not explore the problems posed by the destruction of an enemy's forces, which often leaves a vacuum of power in a state. His discussion of the relationship between politics and war focused on the "why" of war (politics explain *why* wars are fought) but not on the "how" behind this linkage.

Governance tasks were distinct from what Clausewitz called "war proper." Clausewitz identified a dichotomy between the "gray area" of activities that were "preparations for war" and "war proper," reinforcing the US Army's view of governance operations as external to war.[46]

Huntington made a similar distinction in his classic study, *The Soldier and the State.* That book played a central role in developing the idea of the military as a distinct profession. Huntington argued that the military profession was set apart from other professions by its focus on "the management of violence." Since governance operations do not explicitly involve "the management of violence," they would at best be considered "auxiliary vocations."[47] The tasks associated with governance operations involve inherently "civilian" concerns—such as writing new constitutions, preparing for new elections, or restoring civic infrastructure and educational systems.

An additional factor contributes to army "denial" as well—the tendency to view war through the lens of technological prowess, whereby innovations in weapon systems would afford the United States an unprecedented level of situational awareness and the ability to apply force rapidly and accurately. As former army chief of staff Gen. Raymond Odierno explained, there was a "thought process out there that technology can solve our problems, it's a clean way to conduct war" and that if we "stand off and we throw precision missiles and rockets, that will cause the enemy to capitulate and solve all of our problems."[48] And army historian Conrad Crane has written that an increasingly important part of the new American way of war has been a reliance on stand-off technology to project power. Crane pointed out that the "lure" is minimal friendly casualties and short, inexpensive wars with only limited land-power commitments.[49]

The four themes that shape this denial syndrome—discomfort in a democracy with the idea of the military taking the lead in political activities, American concerns about colonialism, the view that civilians could take the lead in governance operations, and traditional views about what constituted war and the military profession—created continuous tensions as the United States planned for and executed its major wars. At certain times, this syndrome dominated, weakening American efforts and having negative impact on strategic outcomes. During other times, the syndrome or parts of it were less pronounced, facilitating better actual outcomes.

The cases that follow in this book reveal that regular army conventional forces faced the operational reality of Clausewitz's dictum about war and politics: They could not escape the "politics of war" and its military implications. Once deployed into a wartime theater, army forces consistently faced the need to reestablish some semblance of political order as conflict unfolded. Tactical combat forces—not just specialized civil affairs forces—often played key roles in political and economic reconstruction. Despite the frequent requirement for governance tasks, US military and civilian leaders did not appreciate the operational complexity of this challenge and did not institutionalize lessons from past contingencies. The problem is not just rooted in military culture and ideas about war—which are, in fact, changing—but also in civilian views about the appropriate role of the military in a democratic society. The wars in Iraq and Afghanistan brought many of these debates to forefront again, with many of these same issues appearing, sadly, familiar. Despite the central truth of Clausewitz's observation that war is an extension of politics by other means, he did not draw out the operational steps taken by military forces to consolidate strategic victory as combat ends. Decades later, in his classic book about how wars end, the strategist and scholar Fred Iklé recognized the "intellectual difficulty of connecting military plans with their ultimate purpose."[50] This problem is the theme of this book.

## NOTES

1. The weakest victories were arguably the Rhineland (1919), Korea (1948), and, later, Operation Desert Storm, since in these cases a new political order did not take root, causing continued problems for the United States.

2. By official histories, I mean books such as Matloff, *American Military History*. Prominent histories that contain almost nothing on governance operations include Millet and Maslowski, *For the Common Defense*; Weigley, *American Way of War* (1977); Weigley, *History of the United States Army* (1984); and Millis, *Of Arms and Men*.

3. Ziemke, *U.S. Army in the Occupation of Germany*, 450.

4. There is an unpublished monograph by William E. Daugherty and Marshall Andrews that could be considered an overview of such operations. See Daugherty and Andrews, "Review of U.S. Historical Experience." During the 1950s and 1960s, the army had a special relationship with the Operations Research Office (ORO). Under a project called Legate, the ORO produced many monographs on civil affairs for the army. Andrew Birtle's book *U.S. Army Counterinsurgency* addresses governance operations within the context of counterinsurgency warfare. There is also a RAND Corporation study by James

Dobbins et al., *America's Role in Nation-Building*, which does not focus on wars specifically and addresses cases that range from war to broader peacekeeping missions.

5. Quote is from Condoleezza Rice in Gordon and Trainor, *Cobra II*, 532.

6. This theme is contained in Ziemke, "Military Government," 290, 299.

7. Huntington, *Soldier and the State*, 167.

8. The English philosopher James Harrington observed that an army's structure—the way it was organized and the tasks that it could do—could have domestic political repercussions. See Charles Blitzer, *Harrington: His Writings* (New York: Bobbs-Merrill, 1955), 97, 160, cited in William Odom, *The Soviet Volunteers: Modernization and Bureaucracy in a Public Mass Organization* (Princeton, NJ: Princeton University Press, 1973), 31.

9. Scott, *Memoirs*, 394.

10. Scott Report No. 41, December 25, 1847, reprinted in ibid., 560.

11. "Veto of the First Reconstruction Act," in Bergeron, ed., *Papers of Andrew Johnson*, 12:84. Johnson was wary of the military usurping too much power. See also pages 85 and 89.

12. Root, "American Soldier," 3–15.

13. For a discussion of these views, see Eliot Cohen, *Citizens and Soldiers: The Dilemmas of Military Service* (Ithaca, NY: Cornell University Press, 1985), 121–25.

14. Hamilton, "The Federalist VIII," 334–35.

15. Huntington, *Soldier and the State*, 168–69.

16. Root, "American Soldier," 13.

17. Ibid., 11, 18.

18. Root, "Character and Office of the American Army," 18.

19. Quoted in Millis, *Of Arms and Men*, 124.

20. Clay, *Decision in Germany*, 88. See also discussion of this view in Gimbel, "Governing the American Zone," 95–97.

21. *The U.S. Civilian Uplift in Afghanistan Has Cost Nearly $2 Billion, and State Should Continue to Strengthen Its Management and Oversight of the Funds Transferred to Other Agencies*, SIGAR Audit-11-17 and State OIG AUD/SI-11-45 Civilian Uplift, September 8, 2011, https://oig.state.gov/system/files/172019.pdf.

22. Echevarria, "Transforming the Army's Way of Battle," 367.

23. Russell Weigley persuasively documented this in his *The American Way of War*. This book is often required reading at service and command schools and has appeared on several army chief of staff reading lists. See also Linn, "American Way of War Revisited," 502.

24. Echevarria, *Reconsidering the American Way of War*, 11.

25. Headquarters, Dept. of the Army, Field Manual 41-10, *Civil Affairs Operations* (Washington, DC: Department of the Army, January 11, 1993), 1–11.

26. "Address by BG Patrick H. Tansey, Chief of the Supply Division, Department of the Army, to 7th Military Government Group," *Military Government Journal and News Letter* 4, no. 4 (April 1952): 1. A publication of the Military Government Association.

27. In 1920 Hunt wrote that it was "extremely unfortunate that the qualifications necessary for a civil administration are not developed among officers in times of peace." See Hunt, *American Military Government in Occupied Germany*, 56–57.

28. "Memo to the Secretary General General Staff [*sic*]; Subject: Briefings of Newly Assigned Officers by the Chief of Staff; 20 January 1954; From Major General W. F. Marquat, Chief, Civil Affairs and Military Government Division, DCSOPS, Dept. of the

Army," National Archives (NA), Record Group (RG) 319, box 11 (300.6–310.1), folder 300 CAMG Administrative Files.

29. Blaufarb, *Counterinsurgency Era*; Robert E. Osgood, *Limited War: The Challenge to American Strategy* (Chicago: University of Chicago Press, 1957); and Callwell, *Small Wars*. See also the US Marines, *Small Wars Manual* (Washington, DC: Government Printing Office [GPO]: 1940; reprint 1987, Dept. of the Navy, Headquarters Marine Corps): 1.

30. Jones, "Nation Builder," 64.

31. Collins, "Development and Training of the South Vietnamese Army," 3.

32. This is a central argument in Krepinevich, *Army and Vietnam*, 215–17. He argued that the army focused on a strategy of attrition as opposed to pacification.

33. Blaufarb, *Counterinsurgency Era*, 101–7. He discusses the US plan to garner more internal support for the Ngo Dinh Diem regime.

34. Barnes, "Civil Affairs, A LIC Priority," 39.

35. For a good description of the debates surrounding the creation of this new command, see Marquis, *Unconventional Warfare*.

36. Lord et al., *Civil Affairs*, 40.

37. Fred Iklé, the undersecretary of defense for policy at the time, was one individual making these arguments. See Marquis, *Unconventional Warfare*, 156–59.

38. Lord et al., *Civil Affairs*, 44.

39. See *A National Security Strategy of Engagement and Enlargement*, White House, February 1996, which is available at on the web at http://www.fas.org/spp/military/docops /national/1996stra.htm.

40. This discourse does not distinguish between operations conducted in the aftermath of war and operations that use military troops to provide humanitarian aid. Governance operations do *not* include the latter. See De Pauw and Luz, *Winning the Peace*. See also Chayes and Raach, *Peace Operations*, 5.

41. *Joint Doctrine Encyclopedia*, July 16, 1997, 97. Later updated to *Joint Doctrine for Civil-Military Operations*, Joint Publication 3–57 (Washington, DC: Joint Staff, February 8, 2001), 1–4.

42. Sen. Strom Thurmond was a key ally of the civil affairs community in the early 1950s. His views seemed fairly typical: Civil affairs reservists were "uniquely" qualified owing to their civilian job expertise due to their regular roles in civilian life. See his report on the subject: NA, RG 319, box 11 (300.6–310.1), folder OCAMG 310.1, Administration and Organization, 1952–54.

43. "Address to Washington Chapter of the Military Government Association by Franklin L. Orth," NA, RG 319, box 5, folder 080.

44. Clausewitz, "Two Letters on Strategy," 126–27.

45. Clausewitz, *On War*, 579.

46. Ibid., 128–31.

47. Huntington described a military specialist as "an officer who is peculiarly expert at directing the application of violence under certain prescribed conditions." Huntington, *Soldier and the State*, 11–12.

48. Paul D. Shinkman, "Army Chief Chafes at New Reliance on Technology," *U.S. News and World Report*, October 23, 2013. See http://www.usnews.com/news/articles/2013 /10/23/army-chief-chafes-at-new-reliance-on-technology.

49. Crane, "Lure of Strike," 5.

50. Iklé, *Every War Must End*, 1. Army doctrine from the post–Cold War period did call for collaboration between political and military leaders and cautioned that before the first shot was fired, the theater commander must understand the desired end state and the means to achieve it: Failure to do so could result in a military victory that fails to achieve strategic objectives. See Dept. of the Army, *FM 100–5: Operations*, 6–1.

# TWO

# THE EARLY YEARS

## IMPROVISATION

THE AMERICAN ARMY served as the principal instrument for the extension and consolidation of the US government's control over much of the North American continent, with governance operations serving as the operational link by which the army completed this task. As the army engaged in combat and governance operations to consolidate the political and geographic boundaries of the United States, debates about the army's appropriate role in American society shaped its organization and doctrine, including its approach to governance tasks.

The army conducted governance operations in Mexico, California, New Mexico, the American South, Cuba, Puerto Rico, the Philippines, and Germany's Rhineland. The army that accomplished these early governance operations was mainly a frontier force that had been focused on building and manning fortifications across the country to supplement a defensive system of coastal fortifications designed to deter an enemy attack.[1] This army managed to conduct constabulary duties in the American West, fight against Native Americans, build towns and railroads, and de facto, serve as government representatives on the frontier. Some historians argue that the army was so busy "nation building" that it did not take the Native American threat seriously enough.[2] Military governments were the instruments through which the territories of Louisiana and Florida, and then California and New

Mexico, transitioned into states.[3] This frontier army, perpetually under-manned and resource poor, improvised on the scene—a skill (or requirement) that would surface again and again. While some guidance from Washington officials existed, for the most part the War Department issued few guidelines to direct the army's efforts related to governance tasks.

Following the Revolutionary War, the army grew in fits and starts, pulled in various directions by Congress's ambivalence about creating and sustaining a regular, standing force. Many argued that a standing army could pose a danger to a liberal society—a view that shaped the size and character of the army. Others believed that the defense of the United States required the creation of a more professional, standing force. President George Washington had advocated a small standing army backed by a well-trained and federally controlled militia, explaining that if the United States desired to "avoid insult, we must be able to repel it; if we desire to secure peace, one of the most powerful instruments of our rising prosperity, it must be known that we are at all times ready for war."[4] Later Alexander Hamilton argued that a militia alone was not enough to protect the country and that war, "like most other things, is a science to be acquired and perfected by diligences, by perseverance, by time, and by practice."[5] Nonetheless, during the Revolutionary War period many in Congress preferred a state-controlled, militia-based force, arguing that "the principles upon which our armies have been raised and organized have been denounced by professional soldiers in every generation, beginning with Washington, as wasteful, extravagant, inefficient and wrong."[6]

Despite some states' efforts to improve the quality of their forces, there was little standardization or coherence across military units. Eventually a cadre of military professionals, determined to reduce the bloodshed caused by ill-prepared volunteers, grew. Supported by early strategic thinkers such as Emory Upton, a Civil War officer considered to be one of the army's most important innovators, these reformers argued that only a standing force could improve America's military effectiveness and, in turn, save American lives. Upton saw "glaring defects" in the volunteer system that had cost Americans "treasure and blood."[7] This small group was determined to improve the organization of the War Department, particularly in the areas of logistics and supply, so that it could better serve the army in the field. Although Congress had voted in June 1784 to create a regular army, it had left it to states and individual officers to recruit men. Thus, by the late 1780s a mere 40 officers and some 700 men constituted the US Army.[8] Formal training for officers barely existed before the War of 1812.

The creation of a military academy at West Point in 1802 marked an important victory for advocates of increased professionalization, though it was not without controversy. The Ohio General Assembly passed a resolution to abolish West Point, arguing that the institution was at odds with the "spirit and genius of our liberal institutions."[9] The emergence of a more professional army, however, had a limited impact on its conduct of governance operations. West Point emphasized tactical skills and the military sciences, rather than political-military issues or strategy, since the prevailing view held that science made the profession "real."[10] The early army was organized around managerial functions, and little thought was given to training for broader political-military roles. The study of the Native American campaigns was viewed as interesting history "rather than as case studies from which lessons of immediate relevance might be drawn."[11] The army's Native American war experiences, however, revealed the need to balance repression with pacification and, years later, formed a foundation for the Lieber Code (also known as General Orders No. 100), which established rules of war during the Civil War. The Lieber Code was one of the first official documents to reflect the understanding that non-combat matters could have a direct influence on the course of a war. Only following the occupation of the Rhineland did doctrine more specific to governance functions emerge.

The appointment of Elihu Root as secretary of war in 1899 influenced governance operations more than any doctrinal developments. Arriving in office on heels of the army's experiences in the Philippines, Cuba, and Puerto Rico, Root showed a keen appreciation for the strategic importance of governance operations, setting him apart from those who had focused on the tactical utility of these tasks. Secretary Root recognized that he would likely have to spend much time thinking about the difficulties of occupation duty and, upon first taking office, compiled a list of books that covered "in detail both the practice and the principles of many forms of colonial government under the English law"; he was determined to study his collection as much as time would permit.[12] He spent the first three years of his tenure examining the problems of colonial administration and trying to improve the army's ability to address these tasks. According to his main biographer, Root's files contained fifteen books dealing with English colonial policy and practice. Root believed that although the army had succeeded during the Spanish-American War, its organization made completing these "colonial missions" almost impossible. He had been appalled by the conditions the army faced in Cuba, which the Dodge Commission of 1898 had documented. And with the help of

Judge Charles Magoon, a lawyer who later served as military governor in the Philippines, Root developed approaches to applying US laws to overseas territories. Root believed that people in the islands had a "moral right to be treated by the United States in accordance with the underlying principles of justice and freedom which we have declared in our Constitution." His attention to this issue reflected a recognition of the connection between governance operations and war and provided a foundation for thinking about the continued presence of US troops in a region following combat operations.

On December 13, 1898, the United States created the Division of Customs and Insular Affairs, and a young army officer, John Pershing, served as its first chief. Secretary Root assigned to the new division all matters related to the customs and civil affairs of the Philippines, Puerto Rico, and Cuba. He believed that "questions of government" in areas such as the Philippines and Puerto Rico were "constant and imperative" for the War Department and that the United States had few precedents when it came to the complicated responsibilities associated with overturning old laws and writing new ones, "save the simple and meager proceedings under the occupation of California and New Mexico."[13] The secretary realized that the War Department had "no machinery" for doing the thousands of tasks involved with the islands and thus, "of necessity," created the new division. In 1902 this office became the Bureau of Insular Affairs and ended up performing "with admirable and constantly increasingly efficiency the great variety of duties which in other countries would be described as belonging to a colonial office, and would be performed by a much more pretentious establishment." Four commissioned officers and forty-four civil employees served in the bureau, and the attorney general at the time interpreted its work as that of making the government of the Philippines Islands a "branch of the War Department."[14]

Root reassured his counterpart, Secretary of State John Hay, that the bureau would transition out of the War Department "as soon as practicable," but he stood firm in his view that as long as military troops were deployed, they should be part of the same department. This highlighted a recurring theme in virtually all of the governance operations undertaken by the army—that unity of command in a wartime theater was desirable. Root was sensitive to the bureaucratic inefficiencies and problems that could result without central control and was wary of "introducing an element of double control, which would be quite intolerable."[15] The War Department position was that, given its myriad responsibilities, the bureau could not have been located anywhere else.[16] Overall, through the early 1900s, several pieces of legislation reaffirmed

War Department control over matters related to the civil affairs of the Philippines and Puerto Rico.

In the 1920s, US officials engaged in a broader debate about the reorganization of its governmental departments. As part of these discussions, Congress created the Joint Commission on Insular Reorganization to study matters related to the insular possessions of the United States and whether these islands should be placed under one entity.[17] President Theodore Roosevelt believed that in the interest of efficiency, one executive department should control all insular possessions, including the Philippines and Puerto Rico.[18] As the government considered these reorganization options, debate ensued over whether the War Department should retain the Bureau of Insular Affairs, whether the bureau should be transferred to the Department of the Interior (which dealt with other territorial possessions, such as Hawaii and the Virgin Islands), or whether the bureau should be moved to the State Department, but most of the discussion seemed to focus on the move to the Department of the Interior.[19]

Several views shaped the War Department's position that the bureau should remain within it. Some wanted to preserve a clear chain of command and take advantage of the expertise already accumulated through the army's work in the Philippines and Cuba. The War Department contained a wealth of information regarding the islands, since many of the officers who had supervised schools, governed the provinces, created and directed the constabulary, organized the health departments, and served as judges in the courts were simply not available to any other US government agency.[20] Secretary of War John Weeks believed that it was not possible to separate civil and military problems, given that they "interlocked" and that a separation of the issue would "handicap the Department in meeting its responsibilities."[21]

The War Department maintained that not only did there exist "a material portion of the United States Army" in the bureau, but that there was also a direct link between the military and civil activities. By the same token, Weeks acknowledged that policy officials would likely hesitate about appointing "Army officers to all those places which are civilian in character." Appearing before Congress, Weeks explained that the War Department was most effective in the Philippines and Puerto Rico because it was best organized and equipped to run civil governments and had already set up the appropriate organizations, such as legal, finance, and public health departments.[22] In addition, accounts of the transfer of control of the civil government of Puerto Rico to the Department of State and then to Department of the Interior refer to the experience as unsatisfactory, and many argued that the War Department would have done a better job at civil administration. These descriptions rein-forced the War Department's view that the Bureau of Insular Affairs should retain control of the Philippines and Puerto Rico. The governor of Puerto Rico actually complained about the transition, which contributed to an eventual reversal, with the governor again allowed to report to the War Department.[23]

War Department officials also cited the advantage accrued by having sta-bility among personnel on the ground, noting that it would avoid "frequent and unnecessary changes in the incumbents" (i.e., military personnel) and cited the desirability of employing personnel with experience in the region, both situations that "in no similar degree" applied to any other government department.[24] Finally, they argued that the department was the only agency capable of restoring order in the event of disturbances. Memoranda explained that there were "numerous past occasions when the War Department has, as the result of unforeseen contingencies, been suddenly called upon to exercise civil control in occupied or disturbed areas."[25] Despite these arguments, in 1939 President Franklin Roosevelt approved a plan to transfer the bureau to the Interior Department's Division of Territories and Island Possessions, citing the move as one of "obvious desirability."[26]

Although Secretary of War Root paid considerable attention to the rela-tionship between governance and war, he is better known for his efforts to create an army general staff. This may be because, as his main biographer observed, Root found "little popular interest" when he tackled issues of colo-nial governance. Many citizens were apathetic, and those who did care were concerned about imperialism.[27] Much of the literature about the Spanish-American War centers on the occupation as evidence of America's imperialist intentions.[28] The tasks of occupation were viewed as imperial instruments of the United States, not as part of the problem of the consolidation of political order during and following war. Still, many of the problems associated with the occupations during the Spanish-American War spurred Root to under-take the broader War Department reforms of 1903, which had implications for army planning as a whole.[29]

From the Mexican-American War until the early 1920s, American political leaders expressed concerns about the implications of the military's involve-ment in political tasks. When conducted internally, governance operations sparked concerns about the use of the military for civilian tasks. When con-ducted abroad, governance operations spurred debates about imperialism. The army itself appeared ambivalent about retaining control over these missions and argued for it mainly owing to a desire for greater control over its soldiers and for efficiency. During the Mexican-American War, Secretary of War William Marcy warned his commanding generals that those tasks related to civil administration would be the least pleasant part of their duties.[30] Writing from Mexico, Maj. Gen. Winfield Scott expressed concern that it was "impertinent" for a soldier to "inquire about such things [as] annexation and military occupation." During the period of military government in California, to offset tension among civilians, the military governor worked hard to assure them that he was more of a *civil* governor.[31] One military historian later explained that the military governments were never really popular owing to the "natural odium felt against military authority by civilians."[32] During the initiation of military government in Cuba, President William McKinley made an effort to explain that military government was being established for "non-military purposes."[33] And following the passage of the Reconstruction Acts just after the Civil War, Gen. Ulysses Grant grew increasingly uncomfortable with the acquisition of so much power by the army.[34] President Andrew Johnson argued passionately against the acts, believing that such power in the hands of the army was in "palpable conflict" with the Constitution and a formula for "absolute despotism."[35]

Concerns among Washington policy officials regarding the army's role in governance operations were offset by the absence of alternatives. For several years *after* the peace treaty was signed with Mexico, army military government continued in California and New Mexico until Congress took final action to admit the territories as full states into the Union. During the Civil War, commanding generals naturally focused on combat operations and were resistant to diverting their troops to meet the requirements of the military governors. As one historian of the period explained, "Fighting generals believed that military objectives should come first: win the war and then worry about the political ramifications later."[36] In the late 1920s, President Calvin Coolidge explained that Maj. Gen. Leonard Wood, who had served as governor-general of the Philippines, had little choice but to rely on the army to do work that might be better suited to civilian experts.[37] US military officers and soldiers entered this period with little guidance on how to conduct governance tasks. As World War I ended, after the substantial governance experiences in the Rhineland, there was still relatively little appreciation for these tasks within the army. In these problems of the 1920s, there are clear echoes of the later problems in Afghanistan and Iraq, as officials sought to find more civilians to fill key reconstruction-related positions. These themes of army reluctance and civilian ambivalence, as well as the fact that the army was simply the only government agency that could fulfill the personnel requirements for such tasks, reappear through World War I and beyond.

## THE MEXICAN-AMERICAN WAR

James K. Polk won the 1844 presidential election on a platform of expansion.[38] Upon assuming office, he announced his intention to extend the boundaries of the United States to the Pacific and to "reacquire" Oregon, Texas, California, and New Mexico. Army forces served as the instrument of this expansion, first through combat operations to secure these territories and then through the establishment of administrative and political structures to provide a foundation for the absorption of these territories into the Union.

Tensions over the Texas-Mexico border had become a major source of friction between the United States and Mexico. President Polk initially tried to resolve the issue diplomatically, but the special mission failed. War between the United States and Mexico broke out on April 26, 1846, following Mexico's deployment of a force of approximately sixteen hundred men across the Rio Grande, which killed over a dozen of Maj. Gen. Zachary Taylor's four thousand men. Polk's declaration of war blamed Mexico, stating that it had violated US borders and had "shed American blood on American soil."[39] President Polk envisioned a short war without a major military commitment, but the army's eight thousand regulars proved to be inadequate, and Congress ended up authorizing an increase to fifty thousand volunteers and a doubling of the regular army's authorized strength of privates.[40]

In the early period of the campaign, tensions between Polk and his commanders resulted in several changes of command. Polk first appointed General Scott to lead an army of regulars and volunteers to the Rio Grande, but owing to growing tensions with Scott (whom he distrusted for political reasons), Polk subsequently ordered General Taylor "to occupy, protect, and defend the territory of Texas" and reinforce the mouth of the Rio Grande as the Texas border with Mexico.[41] Eventually, as the operation in Mexico became more complex, Polk again placed Scott in command, uncertain of whether Taylor was capable of undertaking the more complex campaign and believing that he had few, if any, other competent choices besides Scott.

There is some debate over when Polk's broader territorial aims became clear, although there is evidence that by the end of May he sought the acquisition of Upper California, New Mexico, and some northern provinces of

Mexico.[42] Polk resisted making statements that would reassure Mexicans that the United States did *not* intend to annex territory. The president believed that "though we had not gone to war for conquest, it was clear that in making peace we would if practicable obtain California and such other portion of the Mexican territory as would be sufficient to indemnify our claimants on Mexico." At the very least, the United States would "hold California permanently." Polk sought to establish permanent governments for the conquered territories, as opposed to more temporary ones "which had been [initially] established by our naval and military commanders according to the laws of war." In early May, he directed the governor of Missouri to raise troops for the conquest of New Mexico, and the governor then appointed Col. Stephen Watts Kearny, commander of the Army of the West, to lead this mission.

A few weeks after the war had begun, Secretary of War Marcy issued what were probably the earliest formal instructions regarding the conduct of governance operations. Secretary Marcy's guidance provided a framework for the establishment of the military governments in New Mexico, California, and Mexico, affirming the political objectives of the war as outlined by President Polk and recognizing that army and navy forces would in effect be responsible for the establishment of a new political order in New Mexico and Upper California.[43] The instructions directed Kearny to establish temporary civil governments in the conquered areas of New Mexico and California and warned that what related to "civil government will be a difficult and unpleasant part of your duty and much must necessarily be left to your own discretion." Marcy's instructions reaffirmed the US objective of providing a "free government" to the people of the territories.

This guidance also included the first reference to "indirect rule," a principle that would emerge in virtually all of the army's future governance operations. Marcy stated that it would be "wise and prudent . . . to continue the employment of officers friendly to the United States" and to obtain their oaths of allegiance. Marcy anticipated that eventually the "freemen" of the territories would elect their own representatives to new territorial legislatures. While this principle of indirect rule may have reflected a degree of optimism about the desire of local leaders to work with US soldiers, it also reflected reality: It was unlikely that there would be enough soldiers to take on the full administration of a particular state or territory. Aside from this broad guidance, army officers created a framework for the administration of the new territories themselves, by clarifying the US rationale for the creation of a military government organization and explaining US intentions to the region's inhabitants. The secretary of war's guidance was helpful, but it left virtually all of the operational details to the army commanders—a pattern that persisted in the future.

The army's two main objectives during this period of governance were to provide information to local inhabitants and establish a basis for the rule of law. Army officers first issued a series of proclamations throughout the new territories that clarified the military's authority, proclaimed the good intentions of the United States, and explained that US officials would allow most indigenous civil administrators to retain their positions. In New Mexico, Colonel Kearny explained that the "wish and intention" of the United States was to provide a "free government" for New Mexico and that the people of New Mexico would likely "be much gratified" by US rule.[44] Kearny announced that he would establish a civil government, appoint officers for it, and then march to Upper California.[45] As instructed, he also clarified that officeholders could remain in place as long as they were in good standing with the United States and took an oath of allegiance.[46] As Colonel Kearny headed to California, Maj. John Frémont and the navy's Cdre. Robert Stockton also issued proclamations to the inhabitants of California. These statements informed the region's inhabitants that they would enjoy the same privileges and protections as US citizens and that officeholders could retain their positions "at least until the government of the territory can be more definitely arranged."[47] Commodore Stockton announced the establishment of a military government, appointed himself governor, and provided for a territorial governor, secretary, and legislative council.[48] Arriving at Vera Cruz in Mexico in April 1847, General Scott spoke directly to the Mexican people, reassuring them that "Americans are not your enemies, but the enemies for a time of the men who . . . misgoverned you."[49]

The little guidance from Washington regarding the details of how to restore political order resulted in tensions between army officials in the theater and political leaders in Washington. Kearny initially overstepped his bounds by promising the inhabitants of New Mexico annexation to the United States and the rights of US citizens.[50] General Scott reprimanded him, reminding the colonel that the incorporation of the territory "must depend on the government of the United States."[51] President Polk also complained that Kearny had promised too much and had made statements without presidential or congressional approval.

In Mexico, General Scott also lacked guidance from Washington. Although US political leaders aimed to create new governments in California and New

Mexico, they were less certain about US objectives toward Mexico, and this lack of guidance often seemed to frustrate General Scott, who tried to solicit instructions from Washington but was continually rebuffed. The secretary of war issued "nary a response," giving only a "startle" to his requests for more instructions.[52] The secretary actually returned Scott's orders, viewing them as "too explosive for handling." Scott later recalled that the attorney generals also appeared to be "stricken with legal dumbness" on these issues, with Scott observing that political leaders in Washington appeared to be "alarmed at the proposition of establishing martial law, even in a foreign country, occupied by American troops," thus leaving him alone in "darkness on the subject."

General Scott took matters into his own hands, setting the stage for the conduct of basic reconstruction by developing a framework for maintaining law and order in the country. He showed determination to rein in his own troops, believing that "men free at home must maintain the honor of freed men when abroad."[53] Absent guidance from Washington, he developed his own orders for martial law, General Order 20, which established rules for the conduct of American troops and created military commissions to try those who failed to abide by these rules.[54] These commissions had jurisdiction over cases involving *both* Americans and Mexicans, but military authorities permitted some Mexican courts to retain control and jurisdiction over Mexican citizens, and commanding generals tried to support Mexican police when possible.[55] Another aspect of Scott's initial efforts to establish rule of law included addressing the repercussions of the decision by Mexican leader Antonio López de Santa Anna to release thousands of criminals from prisons. Scott took immediate actions to quell the resulting violence, warning local administrators that whole blocks of homes would be destroyed if the looting were allowed to continue.[56] One author notes that "nearly all infractions of good behavior were quickly and severely punished."[57]

General Scott appeared sensitive to winning the "hearts and minds" of the Mexican people. Although officials in Washington ordered him to levy taxes on Mexicans in occupied areas, he was reluctant to comply, believing that such actions could destroy efforts to win the friendship of the inhabitants.[58] Overall, throughout the Mexican-American War, military leaders in California, New Mexico, and Mexico worked to establish stricter controls over American troops (e.g., he prohibited the sale of liquor to soldiers) in an effort to foster peaceful relations between the military governments and the populace.

The absence of guidance also produced tensions among American officials.[59] When Colonel Kearny arrived in California, he had assumed that he would control the territory as military governor, since Secretary Marcy had made him responsible for the establishment of "temporary civil government."[60] However, US Navy forces had actually arrived in the region first. Cdre. John Drake Sloat raised the American flag on July 7, 1846, and prepared to establish a civil administration in Upper California.[61] President Polk resolved the issue of control in favor of Colonel Kearny, maintaining that a military officer on land should deal with the administration of the territory.[62] Kearny served as military governor until May 1847. Upon his departure Kearny appointed the senior military officer, Col. R. B. Mason, as his replacement.

The establishment of law and order in Mexico and the new territories allowed Colonel Kearny and General Scott to focus on rebuilding key political and economic structures. In New Mexico and California, the army sought to abolish Mexican levers of control and replace them with new institutions to prepare for the integration of these territories into the United States. In Mexico, Scott established military governments in key cities *before* he signed a peace treaty with Mexico. His goal was not the absorption of Mexico into the US, but the restoration of stability and the creation of conditions to promote the emergence of a Mexican leader to replace Santa Anna. Such a change of political leadership in Mexico would ostensibly force Mexico's hand to accede to a transfer of New Mexico and Upper California to the US. As he conquered specific cities and established order, Scott provided a framework for improved civil government by creating new export and import laws, judiciary systems, and tax systems.[63] In all three regions, army officials sought to keep indigenous administrators in place.

The army oversaw varying degrees of political change in each territory. The most fundamental took place in the two territories slated to become a part of the Union. In New Mexico and California, army officers established temporary governments that, in turn, provided the foundation for transforming these territories into permanent states.[64] Secretary Marcy wanted to ensure that changes were undertaken with "the presumed consent of the governed," as opposed to military fiat.[65] Thus, the military governments in New Mexico and California created territorial legislatures and organized and held elections. They also supervised local officials to ensure the application of relevant US laws to the region and worked with local officials as long as they swore loyalty to the Constitution.[66]

The establishment of a new legal system to govern each soon-to-be state was central to preparing each territory for accession to the Union. This task fell to army officers as well. In New Mexico, a volunteer colonel, Alexander

Doniphan, produced a territorial constitution, a bill of rights, provisions for trial by jury, and other laws.[67] Doniphan's work culminated in the "Kearny Code," which provided the foundation for New Mexico's statehood in 1912.[68] In California, military officials oversaw the election of municipal officials, and the military governor appointed municipal officials when necessary. In addition, the military government in California took full control over the local magistrates (the *alcaldes*), who had exerted significant power in California under Mexican rule. In Mexico, General Scott did not undertake wholesale political reform, but he did exert influence over the shape and character of local governments in cities under his control. In certain Mexican cities, local Mexican officials retained their power, but in others Scott dissolved stubborn city councils and appointed new ones. As would be the case in future governance operations, the United States sought to transfer the burden of maintaining law and order from its own soldiers to local forces. Scott worked with Mexican authorities to create indigenous Mexican police forces of some twenty-five armed and mounted men to work with American military police and to protect their towns against robbers; Mexicans were also permitted to arrest drunken American soldiers.[69]

Army officials also dealt directly with economic matters, often on their own because orders from Washington took so long to arrive. Owing to concerns about financing the occupations, the military governments in New Mexico, California, and Mexico focused on issues related to the revision of duties and taxes and adjusting the import and export systems.[70] Secretary of War Marcy's instructions allowed the imposition of only light duties on the inhabitants, since he hoped to win over locals. But President Polk eventually supported an increase in duties to shift the burden of the occupation away from the army. Military officers assumed control over civil tax collectors and continued to supervise their accounts even after the final peace treaty with Mexico was signed. In California, the military governor created a special "civil fund" from customs duties that was used to defray some government expenses. In Mexico, General Scott also created a new system of taxation for the occupied areas, allowing military government officials to collect revenues from tobacco, gold, and silver. There was insufficient time for Scott to develop a long-term reform plan for the economy, although his efforts suggested that he sought to do so: In some Mexican cities, the military government created chambers of commerce. Scott's troops also undertook projects to improve public health, mainly by cleaning water supplies and streets to reduce the spread of disease.

By the spring of 1847, US domestic political pressure to end the Mexican-American War and transition away from military government to a civilian one was growing. President Polk appointed an emissary, a State Department official and former law clerk, Nicholas P. Trist, to begin negotiations to end the war.[71] Polk's decision to send a civilian emissary was not surprising, given his negative views of many of his top military commanders in the region. Polk wrote that General Taylor seemed to "act as a regular solider, whose only duty it is to obey orders . . . [without possessing] the resources and grasp of mind suited to the responsibilities of his position."[72] Trist's arrival sparked tensions with General Scott, who had requested that the president spare him "the personal dishonor of being again required to obey the orders of the chief clerk of the State Department."[73] Scott was wary of Trist's close relationship with the president and of anyone who might degrade his authority in the theater, believing that operations in hostile environments should be left to the military commander. Scott disagreed substantively with several of Trist's positions, and when Trist arrived in the theater, Scott initially refused to see him. Eventually, however, the two developed a working relationship and managed, through military coercion and diplomatic persuasion, to bring the Mexicans to the negotiating table. The United States and Mexico signed the Treaty of Guadalupe Hidalgo in February 1848. It required the withdrawal from Mexico of the remaining US forces, ceded Upper California and New Mexico to the United States, and recognized US claims over Texas. Scott departed Mexico in February 1848, turning over command to Maj. Gen. William Butler, who served until June 1848, which was when the new Mexican president, José Joaquín de Herrera, entered office.

Following the treaty, the military governments in New Mexico and California remained in place to serve as transitory organizations until the territories could become part of the Union. Tensions relating to civil-military coordination also emerged and proved to be similar to the kinds of coordination problems that would emerge in future governance operations. The problem was that as new civil administrators gained power and as elections were held, their relationship to the existing military government became unclear. In California, given the absence of a "properly appointed civil governor, the commanding officer [remained] *ex officio* civil governor of the country."[74] Colonel Mason, who was the military governor and tactical commander of all military forces in the territory, tried to preserve unity of command but also wanted to avoid tensions with civilians. He thus ordered military commanders to assist civil administrators, although he made clear that final authority should rest with the military. Until Congress accepted these states into the Union, the military governor had to balance the wishes of the inhabitants with his desire to retain authority.[75] Mason's successor, Brig. Gen. Bennet Riley was also operating without clear instructions regarding his authority in the region and called himself an "executive of the existing civil government" in order to offset concerns about military authority.[76] As military governor, however, he played a central role in the creation of a civil government and the organization of elections to prepare California for statehood. Riley made it clear that the people "were now called upon to form a government for themselves."[77] Following his oversight of the development of a new state constitution in November 1849, the military governor yielded his authority to the first elected governor of the state, Peter Burnett.[78]

In New Mexico, instability unfolded after the peace treaty until one unified government could be established among the various factions vying for power. A new territorial government was created there in March 1851, followed by the cessation of the civil-military functions of the commanding officer.[79] The new legislature adopted many parts of the original Kearny Code, and once the US Congress resolved its concerns about admitting a new nonslave state into the Union, New Mexico officially became a part of the Union. Although the situations differed among Mexico and the territories, all three cases involved the challenge of establishing new authorities and revealed tensions over the transition from military to civilian control. The governance operations conducted as part of the Mexican-American War consolidated military gains by shaping the transition to a stable civil order. Some military and civilian leaders seemed to recognize this. General Kearny's comments to his troops about how to treat the inhabitants of California, as well as the secretary of war's instructions to his generals, reflected an appreciation of President Polk's broader strategic purpose—the hope that by treating noncombatants as friends and transforming these territories to reflect the principles that governed the United States, the chances of going to war again would be reduced, and stability along America's borders would be improved. American political leaders were sensitive to the idea that the new territories represented conquests and took steps to achieve local buy-in from the inhabitants, suggesting that the goal was not merely combat victory, but a broader strategic victory rooted in the transformation of these regions into political systems compatible with democracy and, ultimately, US interests.

The longer-term presence of US Army forces in New Mexico and California consolidated President Polk's strategic goals at the outset of the war.

Although General Scott's goals and accomplishments were more limited, many of his experiences with governance operations in Mexico would reoccur in subsequent operations. Scott recognized the link between rule of law and stability and reconstruction, and his orders to keep his troops under control and to be sensitive to the concerns of local inhabitants were important in establishing this link. He also applied the principle of indirect rule, allowing Mexican civil administrators to remain in place, overseen by US Army personnel.

## THE CIVIL WAR AND RECONSTRUCTION

In addition to preserving the Union, President Abraham Lincoln's political objectives in the Civil War aimed to change the political, social, and economic character of the South. The US Army's conduct of governance operations served as the critical operational link for achieving this objective, not only through the defeat of Confederate forces but also through the creation of new governments that would form the foundation for a new political and economic order. President Lincoln's electoral victory in 1860—achieved without the electoral votes of the Southern states—put the North and South on a collision course. In his first inaugural address, the president reiterated his view that the US Constitution did not permit secession and that the Union must remain whole. Lincoln believed that the "central idea of secession is the essence of anarchy," and he warned against the "destruction of our national fabric." On April 15, 1861, years of increasing tensions between the North and South culminated in the first battle between federal and Confederate troops at Fort Sumter in South Carolina.

Three phases of governance operations took place during the Civil War.[80] The first period coincided with the appointment of Lincoln's war governors, from about 1862 to 1865, and occurred in tandem with intensifying combat operations. The second period of governance took place from 1865 to 1867, after combat operations between the North and South had formally ended. This period was characterized by the appointment of President Johnson's provisional governors throughout the South. The third period began after Congress passed the Reconstruction Acts in 1867, largely as a reaction to the perceived leniency of Johnson's provisional governments. Many argued that Johnson's soft policies would undermine the combat victories of the war by endangering the nascent Unionist governments in the South. In this last period, the congressional acts directed the military to institute harsh military governments, and federal forces were used to enforce political, economic, and social change on an unrepentant and militarily defeated South.

In the first period, as federal troops advanced south in 1862, Lincoln appointed war governors in Arkansas, Tennessee, Louisiana, and North Carolina to protect Union troops, reestablish order, and create new governments. Despite the emergence of the Confederate States of America, President Lincoln continued to believe that most Southerners would not support the Confederacy and that only a few leaders were responsible for steering Southerners onto the wrong path. As a result, he believed that the establishment of military governments in a few strategic states could provide Unionists in the South with focal points around which to rally for new state governments.[81] The president's decision to give the army governance tasks was a strategic one: The pressure and direction provided by military forces could reshape local governments and undercut political support for the Confederacy. Thus, federal forces entered the South in 1862 with two roles: as agents of political change through the conduct of governance operations and as coercive instruments of military force to use as necessary.

Several army leaders shared Lincoln's view that military governments in the South could help to "reeducate" the populace and convince it to rejoin the Union.[82] Although Maj. Gen. George McClellan would later advocate overwhelming force against the South, his early hope was to avoid unnecessarily antagonizing civilians.[83] McClellan believed that Union troops should treat unarmed inhabitants in a way that would not widen "the breach existing between us and the rebels."[84] Maj. Gen. Henry W. Halleck, then the commanding general in Missouri, also initially favored a conciliatory approach, issuing strict orders against the destruction of private property by Union troops, urging them to "show our fellow-citizens . . . that we come merely to crush out rebellion and to restore peace and the benefits of the Constitution and the Union."[85] Maj. Gen. Benjamin Butler, commanding general of the Department of the Gulf, believed initially that many in the South were "tired and weary" and would "gladly return their allegiance" if their acts could be forgiven.[86]

Many of the military governors during this phase were civilians who had been given the rank of brigadier generals. President Lincoln appointed Andrew Johnson military governor of Tennessee just two weeks after Maj. Gen. Don Carlos Buell's troops entered the city. The president also appointed John Phelps military governor of Arkansas, Edward Stanley military governor of North Carolina, and George F. Shepley military governor of Louisiana. Lincoln and his war governors tried to explain the political aims of the military governments with the hope that further conflict could be avoided. Secretary of War Edwin M. Stanton's instructions to one military governor were to "re-establish the authority of the Federal Government [in the state of North Carolina] and provide the means of maintaining the peace and security to the loyal inhabitants of that State until they shall be able to establish a civil government."[87] In early 1862 General Buell issued a general order that reflected his view that the Union's occupation in Nashville would spur Unionist sentiments throughout the state. He reminded people that we were "in arms, not for the purpose of invading the rights of our fellow-countrymen anywhere, but to maintain the integrity of the Union and protect the Constitution under which its people have been prosperous and happy."[88]

Two broad sets of instructions guided the war governors and the military commanders in this early governance period. First, the Lieber Code included rules and regulations regarding the treatment of civilians in the theater. Second, Lincoln's Proclamation of Amnesty and Reconstruction, also known as the "10 percent plan," offered some strategic direction by outlining the steps required of each state for readmittance into the Union.[89] In the second period of governance, during the early Johnson years, the president's proclamations of 1865 also included instructions on allowing amnesties and overseeing oaths of loyalty and pardons. Army personnel played a key role guiding the transition to new civil authorities during the 1861–67 period, with the war governors and the tactical commanders responsible for developing many of the specific operational details of implementing measures. Some officers were uncomfortable with these tasks. General Butler in New Orleans complained that he had not heard from anyone in the War Department since he had left Washington and that while "leaving me to my own discretion is sufficiently complimentary, it [was] embarrassing enough [given] all the responsibilities of my position."[90]

As during the Mexican-American War, a recurring issue that shaped the military governments of 1862–65 was the problem of how to establish a balance of power between the theater commander and the leader of the civil governments (first the war governors and then the provisional governors). Although Lincoln's war governors were civilians, they exerted control over federal forces and could direct federal troops to support the new government and protect themselves. This often led to clashes with the military theater commander because in effect two sets of federal troops existed—one under the military governor's authority and the other set reporting to the theater commander. The division of authority in the theater, creating two chains of command over troops, was not popular. Commanding generals understandably preferred to focus on combat and resisted the diversion of troops to meet the requirements of the military governors. One historian observed that "fighting generals believed that military objectives should come first: win the war and then worry about the political ramifications later."[91] Overall, Union commanders believed that competing jurisdictions adversely affected the war effort.[92]

General Halleck had "always opposed the origination of civico-military [sic] government, under civilians," as it merely embarrassed the military government "without effecting any good."[93] In Tennessee, friction emerged between military governor Johnson and Buell, the commanding general. Johnson had received few specific instructions on how to create a new civil government, and he insisted on having some troops at his command, including his own "governor's guard."[94] Although Buell reassured Johnson that Buell's troops would comply with Johnson's requests, the commanding general made it clear that any troop movements "must of course be dependent on the plan of military operations against the enemy."[95] Only Secretary of War Stanton's intervention managed to resolve the matter. The secretary reassured Johnson that he had instructed the army to place adequate military forces under Johnson's command.[96] Buell continued to protest against this division of authority and argued that the establishment of the civil government might not be necessary at all. Tensions continued between Johnson and Buell's successor, Maj. Gen. William S. Rosecrans, and the army decided to divide responsibilities between Rosecrans, who would manage military matters, and Johnson, who would have oversight over most other civil affairs.[97]

As the war progressed, problems stemming from crossed chains of command continued, with inconsistencies in the way that disputes were resolved. An ad hoc approach emerged, with military officers clarifying lines of authority through negotiation or by appealing to officials in Washington directly. In Louisiana, the authority of General Butler eventually supplanted George F. Shepley's authority as military governor.[98] Because he had not received specific guidance from the War Department, Butler used his discretion and succeeded in building a political party in Louisiana that formed the basis of a civilian government.[99] Similar tensions resurfaced when Maj. Gen. Nathaniel Banks replaced Butler. Banks, as the new commanding general of the Department of the Gulf, reminded the military governor, Shepley, that powers between the two should be clearly divided. He believed that although Shepley had jurisdiction over matters related to the state government, the commanding general should have control over military appointments and matters of military policy. Banks thus rejected Shepley's appointment of a provost marshal, since the provost marshal was "an officer of purely military character."[100] Banks relieved Shepley's choice and, with Lincoln's support, managed to shift more power to himself. Governor Shepley subsequently resigned. In Tennessee, Maj. Gen. William Tecumseh Sherman, the commander of the Army of Tennessee, disputed the rationale behind the creation of separate civil governments. He argued that the organization of civil governments merely "complicates the game" and that "all the Southern States will need a pure military Government for years after resistance has ceased."[101] Sherman gradually tried to increase military jurisdiction over the city, and Banks's successor, Maj. Gen. Stephen Hurlbut, transferred local judicial functions to a military commission in February 1863.[102]

These types of disputes over unity of command persisted after 1865. Andrew Johnson assumed the presidency determined to preserve direct presidential control over Reconstruction. Through June 1865, he issued a series of proclamations for provisional governors, launching a complicated program for Reconstruction by executive fiat.[103] With the support of military commanders, Johnson's provisional governors would oversee the election of state and federal officials. The president believed that since eight states had ratified the amendment to abolish slavery, the South was showing its desire to renew its allegiance to the federal government. The president and his supporters, such as the commanding general of the army, Ulysses Grant, believed that reform was progressing fairly well.[104]

Maj. Gen. John M. Schofield hoped to preserve unity of command by allowing the military governor and the provisional governor to be the same person. President Johnson, however, chose a divided system, with a civilian serving as governor and a military commander aiding the governor.[105] Not surprisingly, disputes continued. In South Carolina the provisional governor, Benjamin F. Perry, assumed office hoping to restore power to all civil and municipal officers in the state. However, the tactical commander, Maj. Gen. Quincy Gillmore, was unclear about the extent of Governor Perry's authority and voiced his objections to the War Department, complaining that Perry had abolished martial law.[106] Eventually the secretary of war was forced to resolve the issue and did so in favor of the civil authorities. The provisional governor and military commander tried to resolve future disputes by themselves, eventually achieving, according to Maj. Gen. George

Meade, "a harmonious cooperation of the civil and military authorities of the State."[107]

The creation of yet another new authority in the South, the Provost Marshal General (PMG), further complicated the chain of command.[108] The PMG became a new bureau in the War Department in 1863. Its initial focus was on enforcing new national conscription policies and administering loyalty oaths. Col. James Fry served as the first provost marshal general, and his representatives throughout the South—provost marshals of a town or a city—reported directly to him, bypassing the tactical commanders. The provost marshal in a town was an important and powerful figure, responsible for administering laws and exercising all law enforcement duties, including that of judge and sheriff. The PMG maintained internal security with special cavalry and infantry detachments, which were sometimes augmented by Union military troops. Some Civil War experts believed that the PMG represented a new cadre of politicians in the South. Overall, the powerful provost marshals, existing civil administrators, and tactical forces created competing lines of authority in the theater.

The provost marshals in the South played a large role in dealing with one of the army's central governance challenges—how to deal with existing Confederate administrators and how to administer oaths of loyalties. It would have been impracticable to force all Confederates out of power. The challenge was to balance between federal supervision and conciliation and real change in the political character of the Southern governments. From 1863 to 1865, there were many debates about the way to handle Confederate administrators and no consistent policies. While the principle of indirect rule did, in a sense, prevail during the early Reconstruction period, it was a difficult policy to administer. General Butler in New Orleans oversaw an oath policy that treated those who refused to express loyalty to the Union as enemies of the United States, and he exiled them behind rebel lines.[109] In Tennessee, the war governor (then Andrew Johnson) and the theater commander (General Rosecrans) undertook new elections, with Union officers overseeing oaths of loyalty. Under elections for a new constitutional convention, slavery was outlawed, and acts of the previous secessionist governments were declared void.[110]

During the 1862–67 period, the theater commanders wielded great discretion over policy matters. As during the army's earlier experiences in the Mexican-American War, they exerted a great deal of power over policy issues largely because Washington did not provide much guidance. Indeed, this was a reflection of divisions in Washington over how to treat the South. President Lincoln preferred to avoid direct interference with his commanders in the field, informing General Banks in Louisiana that while he knew "what I would be glad for Louisiana to do, it is quite a different thing for me to assume direction of the matter."[111] Lincoln stated, "My policy is to have no policy."[112] Conservative Northerners believed that the full rights of a belligerent should be extended to the South, while radicals argued that Confederates should be treated as criminals.

Military authorities navigated between these divergent viewpoints about the appropriate character of the military governments. Generally, Andrew Johnson in Tennessee agreed with those advocating softer policies, while General Butler in New Orleans implemented harsher rule. Union officers also had wide latitude in administering the Lieber Code. General Halleck believed that the application of Lieber's principles should be left to the judgment of commanders, since they had the most local knowledge.[113] General Sherman agreed, believing that it was virtually impossible to "lay down rules," and thus, he also left "the whole subject to the local commanders."[114] When Maj. Gen. Philip Sheridan requested an authoritative decision on who could register to vote, General Grant advised him to provide his own interpretation of the law until the attorney general could offer an opinion.[115] One historian summarized that it was more appropriate to think of this period as a "constellation of policies rather than a single policy" guiding federal troops.[116]

After 1865, several features of Reconstruction in the South emerged. First, Union forces engaged in much harsher measures to transform the political and economic systems there, following the passage of Congress's Reconstruction Acts in 1867. Second, various War Department agencies played active roles in the theater in overseeing Reconstruction. Third, Congress passed the Reconstruction Acts as a response to President Johnson's relatively lenient approach to the South after 1865. Many congressional Republicans demanded a tougher line, arguing that the president's efforts at reconciliation risked abandoning the fruits of victory. Congress asserted its power over the president by passing the First and Second Military Reconstruction Acts in March 1867, which installed much harsher versions of military governments than those that had existed previously. The acts voided the legality of governments in the ceded states (except Tennessee), placed the South under military rule, and specified how states could be readmitted to the Union.[117]

The first act divided the ten Southern states into five military districts, with a general officer appointed by the president to command each district. This officer would maintain order, protect individuals, and establish a military commission to administer justice if civil tribunals proved ineffective. The second act outlined the mechanics of registering voters and holding constitutional conventions. A third act in July allowed district commanders to remove civil officials if necessary. Congress also passed the army appropriations bill, which marked an unprecedented effort to require the president and the secretary of war to transmit all orders through the commanding general of the army. The bitter debate over the Reconstruction Acts suggested that differing views over how to administer the South would no longer be acceptable and that Washington would now demand adherence to a more consistent policy to shape the character of the newly emerging governments.

Three main War Department agencies in the theater controlled and oversaw various aspects of Reconstruction: the PMG, the commanders of each military district, and the War Department's Bureau of Refugees, Freedmen, and Abandoned Lands (the Freedmen's Bureau). The Freedmen's Bureau, created in March 1865, became a symbol of the Union army's role in the dismantling and rebuilding of political life in the South. The bureau's mission was to assist black refugees in the wartime South.[118] Its commissioner, Brig. Gen. Oliver O. Howard, oversaw the administration of relief, hospitals, and medical aid, as well as the administration of educational and justice systems.[119] Though controversial, the bureau gave the army a central role in implementing and consolidating some of the strategic objectives for which the war was fought. The bureau's relationship to the War Department and theater commanders was complicated. On paper, bureau commanders were senior to most occupation forces, but in reality military officers were pulled between tactical commanders and their obligations to the bureau.[120] Overall, there was little centralized control over the bureau, which was staffed by a mixture of military (predominantly) and civilian officials. Some officers and personnel pursued more radical agendas, and others chose to focus on preserving a baseline of law and order.[121]

The Freedmen's Bureau also sought to improve and reform educational opportunities for blacks by improving literacy and, ultimately, their employment opportunities.[122] In Florida, Maj. Gen. John Pope oversaw the imposition of a special tax to improve educational opportunities for blacks and even worked to ensure that the state's education superintendent was a qualified administrator.[123] In New Orleans, occupying forces ensured that its public school system continued operations and imported Northern textbooks so that schools would no longer serve as "nurseries of treason."[124] Results were decidedly mixed, but Union troops were deeply involved in this task.

Under the Reconstruction Acts, federal troops in the South protected civilian populations, oversaw and administered new courts, undertook police functions, and regulated trade. Although the acts provided some guidance for federal troops, as in previous governance experiences, the preferences of individual military governors played a large role in the implementation of specific tasks.[125] Overall, two tasks dominated political reform after 1867: the installation and the protection of the new governments. Union troops administered, supervised, and installed Republican governments in the South and then tried to protect them from violence, as opponents of the governments sought to subvert the new leaders.[126] About 40 percent of the army was involved in Reconstruction-related activities.[127] Although federal forces had undertaken these types of tasks before the Reconstruction Acts, the intensity of their involvement in political and economic reconstruction increased, as did the South's resentment.

Federal forces also oversaw the reconstruction of the region's judicial system. Military authorities established military commissions, provost courts, and civil courts, advancing some judicial reforms.[128] Commanding generals exerted almost full control over occupied areas, including the punishment of civilians. Three types of court systems emerged, creating confusion due to overlapping authorities.[129] The court-martial system focused on offenses committed by Union forces and was guided by articles of war and army rules and regulations. It did not have jurisdiction over civilians. Military commissions were similar to courts-martial but not guided by statute law. The authority of military commissions derived from the theater commander, and he could decide to try civilians if they had committed offenses within the martial law system. In addition to these two types of courts, the Union army created provost courts. These provost courts fell under the PMG staff that was attached to each Union army corps. As noted, the PMG focused on internal security and oversaw the creation of new police structures.

As new civil governments emerged, federal troops sought to improve the general welfare and infrastructure in the region. Many structures and utilities that had been built initially for use by the Union military governments were transferred back to civilian authorities. To address health-related problems, Union troops instituted rules to control communicable diseases such as smallpox by prohibiting large assemblies of people, instituting strict cleanliness regulations, and in some places overseeing compulsory vaccination programs.[130] Union troops also tackled economic issues related to labor, trade, and finance.[131] Part of this was necessary because before the Reconstruction Acts, trade with the South had been prohibited. Union troops had to institute and enforce new taxation systems and establish rules for the employment of large numbers of freedmen, ensuring that labor contracts for them were fair.[132] Union generals also oversaw banks in the South and forced those that had been paying debts in Confederate currency to switch to US coins. In addition, during the Reconstruction period, the War Department became very involved in land-reform issues and worked to improve the ownership of land by blacks, although successes in this area were limited.[133]

The American Civil War marked the army's most extensive experiences with governance operations, a situation that would remain true until World War II. Despite almost fourteen years of governance operations in the South, from 1862 to 1877, the results of Reconstruction were decidedly mixed. Although by 1870, Republican governments had emerged throughout the South, virtually all of these governments were replaced by Southern Democratic governments. The Freedmen's Bureau was abolished in 1872. One historian of the period wrote that after the departure of Union troops, Republicans were "abandoned to their own meager devices against the overwhelmingly and increasingly impatient white Democracy."[134] Despite the efforts of the Union army to implement the political goals of the war—the transformation of Southern society through the election of new governments and the inclusion of the eleven Confederate states into the Union—the staying power of this new system was weak. When Ulysses Grant became president, he continued to aim for this objective and believed in the need to implement the laws set forth by Congress in the Reconstruction Acts.

During Civil War, the US Army was an army pulled by two divergent political viewpoints. The Reconstruction Acts that were passed by Congress over the president's opposition required Union troops to pursue policies opposed by their commander in chief. This weakening of the president's authority upset some army officers. General Butler believed that the attempt "to degrade the Executive, by transferring his duties to subordinate military Commanders, must open the eyes of the people to the intolerable usurpations of a factious and fanatical Congress."[135] The secretary of the navy believed "almost the whole of the Military officers have, under the manipulation of the war department, been persuaded that the administration is in Congress—the Executive is of little account."[136] The broader transformation of society in the South involved more than the military alone could manage or implement. While federal forces implemented many of the laws passed by political authorities, supporting political, social, and economic changes took much longer to evolve. Reconstruction did not protect blacks in the South in the near to medium term. Indeed, many argue that violence against blacks increased as Southern whites became threatened by their liberty.

In judging the final outcome of governance operations in the South, a central consideration is whether the army was tasked to implement policy that required much longer-term social change than the limited presence of US military forces could ever accomplish. Southern Democrats were determined to weaken the new governments, and although federal forces were enforcing federal laws, they could not do so indefinitely. Moreover, opponents of Reconstruction became increasingly willing to use violence, particularly after 1870, when it became clearer that federal forces would depart.[137]

A central issue was whether the failures of Reconstruction were due to a failure in implementation or a failure to understand the political forces that Reconstruction had unleashed and to develop a strategy to deal with these forces. Governance operations were central in trying to achieve President Lincoln's strategic objectives vis-à-vis the South, even if in the end, they fell short. Several themes related to governance operations emerged during this period and would return in later operations. First, the army's extensive role in politics generated controversy and concern among both military and civilian leaders. This issue would emerge again during the Spanish-American War and World War II, when political leaders also gave the army broad powers of governance. The Reconstruction Acts created two governments: military and civil. Both were considered provisional until new state constitutions were framed, and each state was admitted to representation in Congress. Part of Johnson's deep opposition to these acts stemmed from his concern that such power in the hands of the army was in conflict with the Constitution.[138] Individuals such as Attorney General Henry Stanbery argued that the Reconstruction Acts meant "military officers were not required to obey the opinion of any civil officers of the United States."[139] Some army leaders shared these concerns about the military's involvement in politics. When Maj. Gen. Winfield Scott Hancock assumed command in New Orleans in November 1867, he issued General Order No. 40, stating that the "the military power should cease to lead and the civil administration [should] resume its natural and rightful domination."[140]

Thus, Johnson tried to separate the offices of the provisional governors and the military governors, rejecting the military's advice to unite the two for the sake of efficiency.[141] This duality created tensions throughout the war. Governance operations revealed the need to balance "military necessity"—the requirements of the tactical commander—with those of the military governments, which were focused on political and economic reconstruction. During the 1862–65 period, President Lincoln's military governors and commanding generals sparred often over appropriate priorities. The "fighting generals believed that military objectives should come first: win the war and then worry about the political ramifications later."[142] This view persisted throughout the war, and some of Lincoln's military governors resigned because of frustration. Third, during the Civil War, governance operations took place alongside combat operations—a development that would unfold in subsequent wars.

Following the Civil War, the army demobilized to such an extent that supplies and material were reduced to minimum levels. The War Department reported that much of its transportation and equipment was "insufficient for any important military operation."[143] Secretary of War Russell Alger wrote that for thirty years before the Spanish-American War, the army had "become quite fixed in the narrow grooves of peace."[144] By early 1898, the War Department's primary focus shifted to improving its capacity to mobilize, train, and equip its regular and volunteer forces. The army numbered about twenty-eight thousand men, officers and enlisted, with most scattered in regiments around the nation.[145]

## THE SPANISH-AMERICAN WAR

On the eve of the war against Spain, US political leaders anticipated that a political transformation of the Spanish territories would be required, although it was several weeks after the outbreak of war before specific discussions about the army's role in achieving this objective took place. Initially US officials did not contemplate the need for a large expeditionary army to invade the Spanish colonies. Although the newly elected president, William McKinley, supported the growing independence movement in Cuba, he assumed office in 1898 reluctant to challenge Spain's control over the island. US recognition of the Cuban insurgents risked the involvement of other European powers.[146] President McKinley tried to mitigate growing internal tensions in Cuba through diplomatic channels, still hoping to avoid the "terrible calamity" of a war against Spain. The president's efforts did not succeed, and eventually congressional pressures spurred him to consider more decisive action.[147]

The publication of the infamous "De Lôme letter" and the sinking of the battleship *Maine* in February 1898 undermined the possibility of a diplomatic solution to the crisis.[148] Following the destruction of the *Maine*, the navy instructed Cdre. George Dewey to prepare to destroy the Spanish fleet in Philippine waters. Congress passed the 50 Million Dollar Act to raise appropriations for the army and navy and authorized an increase in army strength.[149] In April 1898, it passed the Teller Amendment, which declared Cuba independent, called for the withdrawal of Spain, and authorized steps to expel the Spanish if needed. The Teller Amendment explicitly noted that the United States would undertake the political transformation of Cuba but forbade the annexation of the island, stating that the US would liberate Cuba and that once "pacification" was achieved control of the island would transfer back to its inhabitants.[150] Although McKinley disavowed any intentions to exercise sovereignty or jurisdiction over the island, he believed that Cuba would likely have to pass through a period of American tutelage. In addition, the president's special envoy to Cuba acknowledged that the US would probably "have to accept the ownership and responsible management of Cuba in order to establish permanent peace in the island."[151] There seemed to be less explicit discussions among political and military leaders about what would likely unfold in the Philippines. In the event of a war against Spain, the navy planned to concentrate its forces on Spain's outlying possessions in order to give the army time to mobilize its strength for campaigns in Cuba and the Philippines.[152] Naval planners believed that the war would be fought for the independence of Cuba and that command of the sea would be critical for victory.[153]

On April 25, 1898, Washington formally declared war on Spain, and a series of cabinet meetings took place to consider campaign plans. The army's commanding general, Nelson Miles, believed that the army should focus its support on the navy by placing artillery to command the harbor of Santiago de Cuba.[154] General Miles argued that troops should move west along the Cuban coast, capture ports along the way, supply the insurgents, and eventually move the large American cavalry into Cuba's interior. Miles initially sidestepped planning for a longer-term role of the army in Cuba because his primary focus was on avoiding the deployment of troops there during the summer "sickly season." His main concern was to protect army soldiers from tropical diseases, and he argued consistently that deploying troops during the summer would be "extremely hazardous."[155] On April 15, the mobilization of troops began in New Orleans, Tampa, and Mobile. Following the navy's relatively quick victory over the Spanish fleet in Santiago harbor, Brig. Gen. William Shafter received instructions to sail with his troops to Cuba.

Governance operations began before Spain formally surrendered in August 1898 because US Army personnel faced the challenge of reestablishing political order in Cuba, Puerto Rico, and the Philippines while engaged in varying degrees of combat. In the preliminary protocol signed by the United States and Spain at the end the war, Spain agreed to cede Puerto Rico to the US and relinquish its sovereignty over Cuba. Peace talks would seek to resolve the status of the Philippines, but in the interim army forces conducted combat as well as governance tasks. Army commanders in all three places issued proclamations to explain the purpose of US forces there. These proclamations were based on guidance issued by President McKinley on May 19, which was the first clear guidance related to governance operations in the Spanish-American War.[156]

Although the army benefited from this general guidance regarding the establishment of new governments in Cuba, Puerto Rico, and the Philippines, army commanders were responsible for its implementation, which left them much leeway. Similar to Secretary of War Marcy's guidance during the Mexican-American War, President McKinley's guidance provided a framework for governance operations but left the operational details of managing the transition away from the Spanish administrations in Cuba and Puerto Rico to army officers in the theater. His instructions explained that the army of occupation would have a "twofold purpose": first, to reduce Spanish power and, second, to provide "order and security to the islands while in the possession of the United States." Governance operations served a strategic purpose for McKinley, since the president believed that "the first effect of the military occupation of the enemy's territory is the severance of the former political relations of the inhabitants and the establishment of a new political power."

In Cuba the Spanish surrendered to General Shafter on July 14, 1898. President McKinley's instruction clarified that the US military commander's power would be "absolute and supreme." This statement of intentions was consistent with the army's previous governance experiences, when it was quite common for the theater commander to clarify the intentions and expectations of the occupying forces. The army was reluctant to commit large numbers to Cuba. General Miles hoped that twenty-five thousand men would suffice—in his view the "smallest number that may be required for the preservation of order and the maintenance of military and civil government."[157]

Perhaps sensing the difficulty of the task, Miles asked the secretary of war for an auxiliary force of native troops for service in Cuba, the Philippines, and Puerto Rico, to assist US troops in the manner of "British forces in Egypt and India."[158] Miles remained very concerned about the health of his troops, writing to the War Department that there was "not a single regiment of regulars or volunteers with General Shafter's command that is not infected" with disease.[159] In November 1898, Secretary of War Alger appointed three volunteer regiments as an army of occupation.[160] About a month later, the president appointed Maj. Gen. John R. Brooke as military governor and commander of the War Department's new Military Division of Cuba. Brooke was "dual-hatted" as the supreme civil authority (military governor) and the commander of tactical troops on the island. Following Brooke's assumption of power, the president again provided guidance for the occupation. He clarified that Brooke served as the president's direct representative, that the military government in Cuba had been established for "non-military" purposes, and that it would be temporary, lasting until there was "complete tranquility on the island and a stable government [was] inaugurated.[161] He also made it clear that the military government would give "aid and direction" to Cubans to form their own government.[162]

Guided only by McKinley's general instructions, General Brooke developed an organization for military government and a system of civil administration. First, he clarified the purpose of the military government to the inhabitants of Cuba. His proclamation of January 1, 1899, inaugurated the US Military Government of Cuba and described its goal as giving "protection to the people, security to person and property, to restore confidence, to encourage the people to resume commercial traffic and to afford full protection to the exercise of all civil and religious rights."[163] Second, Brooke established an organizational structure for the military government. He developed two parallel structures—a civil administration and a military division.[164] The civil administration consisted of four departments, each headed by a Cuban secretary and composed of both Cuban and American personnel. The military governor exerted control over local municipalities through his appointments of local Cuban officials. Brooke's military government was organized along territorial lines, dividing into seven departments that corresponded to the six Cuban provinces and Havana; later it was consolidated into four.[165]

Not surprisingly, and as before, this dual structure resulted in tensions over the appropriate chain of command. At various points during his tenure, General Brooke reduced the functions of his subordinate military commanders and placed them under the four civil departments, which resulted in tensions between the civilian provincial governors and the military commanders. Nevertheless, the immediate tasks of the military government were accomplished—the maintenance of order and the provision of relief for the starving.[166] As Brooke consolidated the military government organization, Brig. Gen. Leonard Wood, the newly appointed military governor for the Santiago region, focused on the problem of establishing law and order as a first step toward the improvement of public health.

As the army consolidated political stability in Cuba, President McKinley inquired when it could prepare an expeditionary force to "take and hold" Puerto Rico.[167] By July the War Department was ready to transport there some twenty-five thousand men. General Miles sailed to Puerto Rico, landed at Guánica on July 25, and without resistance, occupied the port city of Ponce. Miles issued a statement that the purpose of the military government in Puerto Rico was to sever the "former political relations of the inhabitants" and improve the functioning of municipal laws, criminal court systems, transportation, churches, and public funds.[168] He explained that the military occupation would be beneficial for the island, using language similar to President McKinley's May 19 message. General Miles remained military governor of Puerto Rico until October 1898, when General Brooke succeeded him.

Governance operations in the Philippines developed in an ad hoc manner and were complicated by the growth of a strong insurgency against the presence of US troops.[169] Admiral Dewey's naval victory over the Spanish fleet had opened another front in the war against Spain, and Maj. Gen. Wesley Merritt, commander of the Eighth Army in the Philippines, admitted that he did not know if it was McKinley's "desire to subdue and hold all of the Spanish territory in the islands, or merely to seize and hold the capital."[170] Military leaders initially disagreed about the number of troops required for an expedition to Manila, which suggested uncertainty about the army's longer-term presence in the region. Dewey argued that five thousand men would suffice to retain possession of Manila and consolidate victory, with Miles agreeing that relatively few troops would be needed because it was unlikely that "at this time [the army would need to] carry on a war to conquer an extensive territory."[171] General Merritt disagreed and believed that the army would face extraordinary difficulties.[172] Merritt's position eventually prevailed, suggesting that McKinley was beginning to recognize the longer-term implications of the United States' expanding political goals. After the defeat of the Philippine general Emilio Aguinaldo's conventional forces, US policy toward the islands became clearer. The president declared that the future control and government of the Philippines should be ceded to the United States, and he instructed the Eighth Army's new commander, Maj. Gen. Elwell Stephen Otis, to inform Filipinos that US troops had arrived "not as conquerors" but "as friends" and that Otis should extend the US occupation "with all possible dispatch to the whole of the ceded territory." The president clarified that until the situation in the Philippines stabilized, Otis would retain authority.

General Merritt initially issued a proclamation informing the people of the Philippines that the military commander's power was "absolute and supreme" but that municipal laws could remain in force unless they interfered with the occupation. Merritt's message also clarified that operational decisions would be left to the commanding general, who "must be guided by his judgment and his experience and a high sense of justice." In addition to establishing the basic parameters for the occupation, Merritt immediately confronted the need to manage the complex political situation on the ground. One historian of the period observed that General Merritt had been entrusted with "the greatest administrative responsibilities that had ever fallen to an American soldier."[173] When US troops captured Manila, Aguinaldo's forces had also entered the city, and the Philippine leader used this as leverage to insist that Manila remain jointly occupied. Merritt requested instructions from Washington on how to respond to the insurgents' demand for joint occupation. Washington responded that "there must be no joint occupation of the city . . . and that [the insurgents] and all others must recognize the military occupation and authority of the United States."[174] Aguinaldo's demands continued to occupy General Merritt's successor, General Otis, for months.[175]

Governance operations conducted by the US Army in Cuba, the Philippines, and Puerto Rico were among the most comprehensive in its history. Tactical combat units established city governments, created constitutions, rebuilt sanitation and health services, and established educational systems. The army initiated all of these operations without advance preparation and without specialized forces. Although political leaders had anticipated the need for US political control over the islands, Washington did not issue explicit instructions and guidance to the army until troops were actually in Cuba and a naval victory had been achieved in the Philippines. The political guidance that did emerge set forth the longer-term goals of the United States (such as the support for democratic forces) but left the operational details to army leaders. No manual existed to guide officers on how to organize a military government headquarters, nor did staff sections or specialist teams exist.[176] The army's reestablishment of political order in Cuba, Puerto Rico, and the Philippines revealed its flexibility and resourcefulness, qualities that allowed the army to successfully meet the governance challenges it faced.[177]

In the Philippines, political and economic reconstruction through the establishment of stable local governments was a critical part of the army's strategy in fighting the Philippine guerrillas. The United States tried to establish a series of functioning civil governments but faced many difficulties, given a populace unused to civil administration and the increasing attacks by guerrillas against nascent government structures.[178] General Otis faced two central challenges as he undertook governance operations: managing ongoing combat against the insurgents and creating functioning governments throughout the countryside.[179] By February 1899, the army was fighting a difficult counterinsurgency campaign while also trying to reestablish civil order in the countryside, improve public works, and manage revenue collection. Governance operations served as a key instrument for trying to secure the allegiance of Filipinos and assuring them that, in President McKinley's words, the US aim was "benevolent assimilation."

Governance operations were to remain squarely under the command of combat officers, and General Otis organized the army's garrisons along geographical lines.[180] This was, in effect, a territorial form of military government that would remain under his control. Otis and his successor, Maj. Gen. Arthur MacArthur Jr., served as commanding officers as well as military governors. This civil and military integration of occupation duties occurred throughout, with colonels and majors ruling provinces and serving as customs collectors, judges, and mayors.[181] Under this system, Otis's field and company officers had significant civil-military responsibilities, including educational reform. Army commanders took the job seriously; in Northwest Luzon in six month of occupation, the army established schools attended by over ten thousand children.[182] Under General Otis's supervision, some fifteen hundred public schools were reopened.[183]

In 1900 President McKinley decided to create a civil commission under the leadership of William Howard Taft, which introduced, unsurprisingly, civil-military tensions to reconstruction efforts. The president believed that although military commanders should remain supreme during combat operations, civil commissioners could undertake certain governance tasks and eventually should take over from the military.[184] With the military fighting a tough guerrilla campaign and also leading governance operations in the countryside, McKinley gave the new commission the authority to overhaul the Philippine government. Initially, the president allowed the commanding general full control over civil administration and the military campaign, but the commission's mandate was to legislate, appropriate funds, and appoint the military governor's civil subordinates.[185] Commissioner Taft believed the army should transfer as many provinces as possible to his authority, a demand that generated serious tensions with General MacArthur, who had taken over as military governor. MacArthur was upset at his loss of power and wanted a clearer division of authority.

As the war progressed, provinces were declared pacified and turned over to the commission, and eventually to its enforcement arm, the Philippine Constabulary. In 1901 the police force had been created under the leadership of American army colonel, Henry T. Allen. (Allen would later become the military governor of the Rhineland following World War I.) The constabulary was supposed to maintain control of provinces after they had been pacified by US forces and transferred back to the civil Philippine Commission. It was an effort to create an indigenous police force in order to shift some of the burden for law and order away from army forces and onto native troops.[186] The military governor, General MacArthur, urged commanders to develop local constabulary forces, although many disagreed with his view and argued that such forces would become too politicized.

In Cuba, the military government established conditions for political and economic reconstruction through a combination of tactical and territorial control.[187] When General Brooke was appointed military governor of the island, the War Department also appointed Brig. Gen. Leonard Wood to serve as military governor of the city of Santiago. The latter's success in that job, his political power, and the confusing system that General Brooke had instituted eventually led to Wood's promotion to military governor of the entire island in December 1899. McKinley had instructed Wood to prepare Cuba, "as rapidly as possible, for the establishment of an independent government, republican in form; to arrange for an efficient administration of justice; and a good school system." Wood reorganized the four civil departments set up under Brooke and established clearer chains of command. In the provinces he established four military districts, each headed by a general officer, but also with military governors heading the provinces under these districts. Military officers controlled Wood's new chain of command, and Cuban civil officials reported through them. Wood described his task as involving maintenance of order, reestablishment of municipal governments, reorganization of the courts, and doing "the thousand and one things incident to re-establishing the semblance of government in a stricken and demoralized country."

The military government in Cuba tried to prepare Cubans for self-government, but this goal was complicated owing to the disappointment of Cuban insurgents, who had fought alongside American troops against the Spanish and had expected the United States to hand the country over to them. Before the US intervention, most Cuban separatists had aligned themselves with the United States, but there were soon tensions with the Americans when it became clear that Cuban commanders (not surprisingly) "expected to be placed in command" and the towns turned over to them. Many Cubans, however, were willing to work with the military government, offering their services to the War Department as guides, translators, navigators, and pilots.

By early 1900 the military government in Cuba had developed general election laws providing for suffrage and the conduct of elections throughout the island.[188] The military government also oversaw the operational details of holding elections, from the preparation of ballot boxes, to the distribution of information, to the oversight of the elections themselves. It contributed to the development of a constitution and the convening of a constitutional convention. In addition, army officers helped with town governance, often working on town budgets. General Wood's government in Cuba undertook a complete revision of the tariff and customs system and created an independent treasury on the island. Col. Tasker S. Bliss organized a new customs service that included US Army personnel. In addition, industry was revived, and army personnel tried to increase the amount of arable land.

General Wood observed that sanitary conditions in Cuba were "as unfavorable as can be imagined," with little or no clean water and sick soldiers and civilians everywhere.[189] Troops resupplied hospitals, organized the training of nurses, and improved facilities for orphans and the mentally ill. Army personnel also created a new school system based on US laws and improved infrastructure, established procedures for enforcing attendance, helped to produce new textbooks, and initiated teacher training. By the end of the war, public school enrollments had dropped dramatically; one year later, enrollment increased sixfold. The military government also undertook extensive public works projects, rebuilding roads, repairing and constructing buildings, and fixing bridges, sewers, and waterworks. General Wood's government in Cuba also dealt with public safety issues, since the military government was eager to shift some responsibilities for the maintenance of law and order to indigenous forces. Army personnel organized a rural guard composed of Cubans to maintain order in rural areas.[190]

General Wood also instituted important changes in the Cuban judicial and penal systems.[191] The military government worked through hundreds of cases of prisoners being held without trial and released many deemed to have been held unlawfully. Wood established a new system of judicial appointments and abolished trials by juries. Overall, the military government introduced the idea of a separation of powers and improved legal protections by instituting the writ of habeas corpus.

In Puerto Rico, an August protocol between the United States and Spain, as well as Spain's evacuation from Puerto Rico, paved the way for the subsequent military occupation of the island.[192] As previously noted, Secretary of War Root had given some attention to the type of government for Puerto Rico and the problem of how to deal with existing laws and reestablish economic relationships. His goal was to create "the best government [of] which we are cable" to prepare Puerto Ricans for self-rule. By the fall of 1898, some 87 officers and 2,855 enlisted men of the regular army were on the island administering the civil government and instructing people in "the rudiments of self-government."

When General Brooke left for Cuba, Maj. Gen. Guy Henry became military governor in 1898. General Henry worked to reestablish schools, create municipal governments, improve sanitation, establish a taxation system, and restore public order. The military government approved the appointment of key officials, such as the governor, as well as other officers in Puerto Rico's civil administration. The principle of indirect rule held, with Secretary Root encouraging the use of "capable" Puerto Ricans when possible. The military government also encouraged minority groups to participate in government, recognizing that such participation could contribute to the development of democracy. Although the military government tried to create a body of Puerto Rican laws, in the interim it aimed to retain law and order.[193] US policy advocated the use of existing laws when possible, though, if necessary, relevant US laws could be applied to situations on the island. The military government created a Puerto Rican supreme court composed of judges appointed by the US president, as well as trial courts throughout the island. Regarding economic issues, the military government oversaw complete reform of the old taxation system, which was viewed as regressive and as penalizing to industry and development.[194] The military government also rebuilt roads as well as the island's entire telegraphic system.[195] Army personnel also administered an inoculation program, succeeding in vaccinating practically the entire population of the island.

In Cuba and Puerto Rico, the military government period ended relatively smoothly, with a transfer of authority back to the islands' inhabitants and the departure of US Army forces. In Cuba, elections were held, a constitution was adopted, and authority was transferred from Military Governor Wood to the new Cuban president, as opposed to a US civilian official. The transfer of the island back to its inhabitants occurred in May 1902, following an act of Congress and pursuant to Cuban agreement to adopt the constitution.[196] Although a small number of artillery troops were to remain on the island, Secretary Root clarified that they were not to be considered an occupying force and that the commander of these remaining forces was to refrain "from even the appearance of interference in governmental or political affairs."[197] As General Wood prepared for his departure, he wanted to ensure that the United States would continue to provide some form of economic assistance to Cuba, so that the gains of the military government would not be lost. Wood believed that "a reasonable degree of reciprocity" in terms of economic arrangements should be made.[198]

In Puerto Rico, the transfer of authority occurred relatively smoothly. With the passage of the Foraker Act in May 1900, Charles Allen became the first civil governor. By the time the Puerto Rican government resumed control, US Army personnel had organized and overseen elections throughout the country. Prisons and jails had been improved, roads had been rebuilt, schools had been expanded and extended to more children, and taxation laws had been improved. The departing military governor believed that "the trust confided to the Army by the President and the people had not been abused but instead has been wisely and justly exercised in the interest and for the benefits of the inhabitants of this beautiful island."[199] In the Philippines, given the growing insurgency following the initial military government period and the decision to divide authority in the theater between the military governor, General MacArthur, and the Philippine Commission, conflict continued.

Although the Philippine Insurrection formally ended in July 1902, in reality the conflict dragged on for years. Henry Stimson, as secretary of war in 1912, warned against leaving the Philippines too soon. He believed Americans had made great progress there, that the success of "increasing native participation in the native government has been accomplished only because every step has been carefully checked and watched by Americans," that, if the United States left, "the great mass of people" would be subject to oligarchic rule rather than self-government, and thus that the US should not leave until "our work there was completed."[200] Later Stimson was very critical of the reversal of the policy of slowly expanding self-government; he criticized Governor-General Francis Burton Harrison for succeeding in "permanently disbanding the experienced and disinterested cadre of American officials."

Governance operations in the Spanish-American War revealed several themes and trends that would reemerge in future operations. First, a key problem was whether and how to introduce US civil authorities into a theater and the nature of their relationship to the theater commander. In Cuba, General Brooke introduced tensions by creating two parallel structures, resulting in confused lines of authority between civil administrators and military officers. In the Philippines, President McKinley established a civil commission while combat operations were still under way and gradually transferred control to this commission, also generating tensions between General MacArthur and William Taft. In addition, the Spanish-American War revealed that when called upon, tactical combat troops could govern. Given that volunteers called up for war would be available for only one year of service, this would de facto leave any longer-term governance operation to be conducted by regular army troops. In Cuba and Puerto Rico, the army also faced the problem of dealing with existing civil administrators, mostly Spanish, and filling positions with indigenous administrators while supervising new programs.

The Spanish-American War marked a turning point in the army's history: The army had transitioned from a constabulary force to an instrument of global power. The war represented the third time that the army tackled the complex problem of reestablishing political order following war. As the war against Spain began, President McKinley and his advisers realized that political transitions in Spain's former colonies would be required. They did not necessarily believe that the United States should annex these territories permanently, but they did believe in the value of preparing the inhabitants of Cuba, the Philippines, and Puerto Rico for self-government. Governance operations were a critical element for completing the political objectives set forth by McKinley during the course of the war.

As noted earlier, the governance challenges that emerged were a key impetus to the 1899 appointment of Elihu Root as the new secretary of war. For the first three years of his tenure, he spent time on the problems of colonial administration. By 1900 the army had become the main instrument of political and economic change in the three key former Spanish colonies. In recognition of the import and burdens of these new duties, the War Department reorganized in December 1898 to handle new responsibilities of civil administration by creating the Division of Customs and Insular Affairs. The division was given bureau rank in 1902 and for two generations was a central part of the government's machinery for administering overseeing overseas possessions.[201] Root's biographer later wrote: "It was not for Root to decide whether or not the United States should embark upon a policy of expansion of empire. The die was already cast, the islands had been acquired, the era of colonial administration had already begun."[202]

# WORLD WAR I

When the United States entered World War I, President Woodrow Wilson's political objectives did not directly suggest that the US Army would end up occupying a portion of Germany.[203] However, many of Wilson's statements in 1916 and 1917 suggested that the political transformation of key countries involved in the war would be required, since only through such change would US objectives, such as the elimination of "militarism and navalism," become attainable.[204] As the war progressed, it became clearer that a longer-term presence of Allied forces in Germany would be required in order to shape a desirable peace.

In April 1918, President Wilson asked Congress to accept "the status of belligerent" formally "thrust upon" the United States. He called for the establishment "among the really free and self-governed peoples of the world such a concert and purpose of action as will henceforth ensure the observance of [democratic] principles," denounced crimes of the German government, and argued that the US should fight for the liberation of the world's peoples.[205] The president's "Peace without Victory" speech in January 1917 explained that *how* the war ended would matter a great deal.[206] He hoped to garner support for the League of Nations and the maintenance of a democratic postwar political environment. Wilson's famous Fourteen Points called for the transformation of the political character of key states—such as Poland, Russia, and Belgium—and the creation of new states in Austria-Hungary and the Ottoman Empire. The content of these documents focused on transforming the character of existing or newly formed states, and as major combat operations ended in Europe, Allied occupying forces would play key roles in finalizing these political objectives.

President Wilson established a US Commission of Inquiry in 1917 to prepare for eventual peace negotiations as well as the reconstruction of Germany and other states. Commission members researched the political, military, and economic situation of states in order to prepare for the reestablishment of governments.[207] Diplomatic and political representatives, rather than military officers, dominated this process.[208] A December 1917 inquiry commission memo noted that the democratization of Germany "would include legal changes and changes in leadership" and involve economic improvements.[209] Another commission document foresaw that "reform and reconstruction" of "embittered areas" would need to be undertaken, and by December 1918, commissioner Walter Lippmann had observed that "neutralizing the left bank of the Rhine" had become an issue of "first class importance."[210]

Despite the Allies' broader political objectives and the commission's work in this area, detailed discussions about the character of an occupation of Germany began only after the armistice agreement was signed on November 11, 1918. Several months after the Third Army arrived in Germany, key issues such as the longevity and cost of the occupation, French security concerns, and contingency plans if Germany refused to sign the treaty were discussed during the Paris peace negotiations in April 1919.[211] During these negotiations, the United States spent a great deal of time managing divergent French and British positions on Germany. President Wilson commented that "the problem of occupation [looks] almost insoluble, because the British are at one extreme, and the French at the opposite."[212] The French demanded a permanent occupation of the left bank of the Rhine and the bridges crossing the river. The Americans and the British were opposed. As a compromise, they agreed to the demilitarization of the Rhineland and an Allied occupation of the region until 1935. Britain believed that a long occupation was unnecessary and that German support for occupying forces would result in reduced reparations payments. The Americans shared this view, arguing that the occupation could place too great a strain on Germany, because nothing would be left to be applied to indemnities. The US and Britain viewed occupying forces as a means of shaping a postwar balance of power in Europe, namely, by mitigating French aspirations regarding Germany.

The November 1918 armistice agreement established that Allied troops would occupy parts of Germany and assigned control of the left bank of the Rhine to the United States, France, Great Britain, and Belgium.[213] However, details about how this occupation would unfold developed only as US troops marched to Germany and as Allied leaders met in Paris to discuss a final peace with Germany. As late as July 1919, military representatives still questioned the proportion and number of troops designated for the occupation.[214] Eventually negotiators agreed that the final size of the occupying army should be decided after the Treaty of Paris was concluded.[215]

President Wilson's Fourteen Points revealed US concern about the character of the postwar political environment, suggesting that combat victory alone would not be sufficient to address these concerns. Nevertheless, it was left to army officers on the ground to make operational decisions about the structure of the occupation and the mechanisms for the supervision of the German government in the Rhineland. As the army advanced to the Rhine, Col. Irwin Hunt, an army officer who would later play a key role in the occupation, observed that "investigations of the local situation began . . . in order to frame intelligently an American policy."[216] The only information distributed to soldiers that focused on "the organization, government, and laws of the country" that they were called on to govern was a general War Department pamphlet, *Notes on German Local Government.*[217]

Gen. John Pershing created the American Third Army on November 15, 1918, for the express purpose of occupying parts of Luxembourg and Germany. Maj. Gen. Joseph T. Dickman, a highly regarded soldier-scholar who had served in Cuba and the Philippines, commanded the Third Army. Early in his career, he had been an instructor at West Point and at Fort Leavenworth, and he wrote the army's *Field Service Regulations*, which described the conduct of units in the field. Dickman spoke German and had translated several major German military works into English. According to General Pershing, he had the "tact and discretion" necessary to command occupying forces in Germany.[218] The army of occupation consisted of about two hundred thousand troops—two corps, each with three divisions.[219] Command of the Third Army then passed to Maj. Gen. Hunter Liggett, who was also a highly regarded veteran of past wars and who General Pershing had promoted rapidly. US forces occupied the region around the Coblenz bridgehead on the Rhine River until the summer of 1923.

In November 1918, Allied forces entered a German nation that had been significantly weakened by four years of war; it had lost all of its overseas colonies (and investments) as well as significant parts of its territory, including Alsace-Lorraine to France and its eastern regions to Lithuania and Poland. The port of Danzig became a part of Poland, splitting East Prussia from the rest of Germany. The Republic of Austria was prohibited from joining with Germany. These changes reduced Germany's population by 13 percent, and there was a significant loss of natural resources such as coal and iron. Germany was also required to pay reparations to Allied governments and their citizens. In November 1918, Otto von Bismarck's state collapsed, replaced by the Weimar Republic. One prominent historian of Germany argued that the Allied occupation was a key force behind the formation of a new government that would impress the Allies "by its representative character and its liberal philosophy."[220]

Several key issues shaped early governance operations in Germany. First, the German government remained virtually intact, with US occupying force supervising existing German civil administration. Article 5 of the Rhineland Agreement declared that civil administration would remain in the hands of the German authorities, reaffirming the principle of indirect rule, which had always been a preference for the United States in its conduct of governance operations.[221] Second, the Third Army assumed a dual mission of both occupying the Rhineland and preparing for a possible resumption of hostilities. Allied forces arrived in Germany amid continuing uncertainty that the war was not necessarily over and that the German government would not necessarily sign the peace treaty. If Germany refused, the Allies were to prepare to march to Berlin.[222] Maj. Gen. Robert Bullard, who commanded the First Division and had made the first American divisional offensive of World War I against Cantigny, later wrote, "Nobody was sure that peace had come with the armistice" and "Waiting requires the highest discipline."[223] Because the Third Army was also preparing for the possibility of resuming offensive operations against Germany, it remained organized along tactical lines as opposed to being organized for military governance per se.[224]

The army's structure for governance operations was complicated and divided. Two organizations in the American sector oversaw the German civil government: the Advanced General Headquarters of the American Forces Europe (AFE), which included the Office of Civil Affairs and an officer in charge of civil affairs, and the Third Army, which reported to the AFE headquarters. The AFE officer in charge of civil affairs was Brig. Gen. H. A. Smith, who also served as the supreme civil authority in the American zone. He controlled all civil affairs in the occupied territory through five departments: public works and utilities, fiscal affairs, sanitation and public health, schools and charitable organizations, and legal affairs.[225] Col. Irwin Hunt served as General Smith's deputy and as representative to the Third Army. Smith had three primary duties: to draw up ordinances relating to the civilian population, to supervise orders issued by unit commanders of the Third Army, and to administer the city of Trier.

In reality, Third Army division commanders, through their attached civil affairs officers in various towns, were the true administrators of local government. The Third Army headquarters required each of its subordinate major units to designate a civil affairs staff officer to handle governance tasks in each town or *Kreis* (district).[226] Unit commanders, who had authority over towns and villages, "were in no sense members of any separate hierarchy of military government" and supervised the execution of orders.[227] The Third Army's tactical formations implemented most of the military government's day-to-day tasks.[228] Given that two Third Army organizations were involved with civil affairs, it was not surprising that confusing lines of authority emerged between General Smith at the Advanced General Headquarters and General Dickman, the Third Army's commanding general.

The dual structure of American control over German civil governments "caused a double type of thinking and organization to prevail. . . . [The combat divisions] . . . looked down just a little on the new duties which their former comrades were beginning to take over in long range military government."[229] Adding to some of this confusion was the fact that the Third Army's formations did not parallel the German civil administration that they were supposed to supervise. On the other hand, the French and British, "possibly due to their better knowledge of the German system," modeled their military governments along lines paralleling the German civil system.[230] To reduce tensions in the theater, officials in Washington eventually decided that General Dickman, the Third Army commander, should supervise civil affairs in the field. In practice, his newly appointed officer in charge of civil affairs, Colonel Hunt, exercised this supervision.[231] In June 1919, the Advanced General Headquarters was disbanded, and the Third Army became the sole administrator over civil affairs. The Third Army organization shifted from tactical control to one emphasizing a more territorially focused organization. Each territorial unit in Germany was placed under an officer in charge of civil affairs. At times, these civil affairs officers lacked information about local conditions and the "future codes of laws being drawn up" by the Third Army headquarters.

In addition, tensions among the Allies were another challenge for US occupying forces. Consistent tensions with the French, who had longer-term designs on the region, complicated the Allied occupation. As noted previously,

Paris had hoped for outright annexation of the Rhineland. Marshal Ferdinand Foch, commander in chief of the Allied forces, believed that the occupation should serve as "a mortgage in the hands of the Allies" in order to "guarantee the payment of the indemnities" by Germany.[232] When General Liggett assumed command of the Third Army in April 1919, he found that "owing to certain misunderstandings the feeling existing between our people and the French was not as cordial as it should have been."[233] US officials tried to carve out areas of unilateral control, hoping to ensure that each ally had a well-defined territory of occupation. Consistent with past and future operations, the US Army wished to retain full control over all of its forces on the ground. President Wilson had earlier ordered Maj. Gen. Tasker Bliss, the army's representative to the Commission of Inquiry, not to allow the US Army to take direction from Marshal Foch regarding "the future occupation of Germany" unless instructions came from Wilson himself.[234]

As the Rhineland occupation began, army officials issued a series of statements to the German people informing them of the occupation's objectives. Marshal Foch issued the earliest set of instructions to guide occupying armies on November 15, 1918.[235] The guidance stated that German officials could continue in office, affirmed that criminal codes would be enforced, and called for the creation of military tribunals and provost courts. The commanders of each occupying army approved the instructions separately.[236] During the Allies' advance to the Rhine, their armies issued three subsequent proclamations: Two focused on relations with the civilian population, and the third provided instructions for officers and men.[237] This last proclamation outlined tactical and operational steps to keep occupying forces secure and to maintain stability in the area but did not describe longer-term political objectives regarding the occupation. Overall, the proclamations basically reaffirmed that occupying forces would respect German persons and property, "adhere to the laws of civilized warfare," and respect existing laws and regulations as long as they "did not interfere with the duty and security of American troops."[238] Despite this general guidance regarding the relationship between military forces and German civilians, as the Third Army crossed from Luxembourg into Germany on December 1, 1918, many issues related to the occupation remained unresolved.

US political objectives for the occupation in the Rhineland were limited. Governance operations there focused on the restoration of order and on shaping Germany's larger response to the peace treaty, rather than an outright replacement of the German government. Leaders such as President Wilson and British prime minister Lloyd George viewed the continuing presence of Allied troops on German soil as a means of weakening the German government and pressuring it to sign the peace treaty. If Germany refused to sign a treaty, the allies would consider a more extensive occupation.[239] By the fall of 1919, only about 18,000 enlisted and 850 officers remained in Germany as the occupying force.[240]

As combat troops began to leave Germany in the summer of 1919, a shift to a more formal military government structure took place. Maj. Gen. Henry T. Allen, who had served in the Philippines in 1901 as military governor of one island and as the chief of the Philippines Constabulary for five years, was appointed military governor. General Allen believed that with the removal of American combat troops from the region, the military government improved and the "machine was at its best."[241] This shift to a "purer" military government meant that subordinate military governors in each German district no longer functioned as tactical commanders but could focus primarily on governance issues. In addition, some of the earlier restrictions on Germans were relaxed as the occupation expanded and the goal of rebuilding the German economy and political structure took over.

Broad guidance shaped US and Allied efforts at political and economic reconstruction in the Rhineland. The November 11, 1918, armistice agreement and the Paris peace negotiations, which resulted in the Treaty of Versailles, provided basic parameters for the character of the occupation. The armistice agreement ended the fighting and set the stage for the Allied occupation, with the armistice agreement setting forth several protocols that addressed the initial movement of Allied troops into the Rhineland.[242] Subsequently, the June 1919 Versailles Treaty stated that the Rhineland could be occupied for fifteen years or more, depending on German compliance with reparations and other Allied demands. An annex to the Versailles Treaty, "Agreement with Regard to the Military Occupation of the Territories of the Rhine," developed the main objectives for the occupation. The first thirteen articles of the agreement focused on the logistical issues, such as payments, troop lodging, and communications, rather than strategic guidance on the long-term purpose or objectives of the occupation.[243] The Versailles Treaty also established the Inter-Allied Rhineland High Commission, which was the body through which the Americans, British, and French coordinated their occupation policies in their respective zones. Different issues addressed by the commission included problems such as the maintenance of roads and the distribution of food.[244]

Although civilians oversaw reconstruction activities, they were implemented by military forces. The French feared that two systems would lead to confusion, while the British believed that occupying armies should retain power over civil matters, partly to ensure their safety. In the end, a two-tiered system emerged, with civil authorities supreme over policy matters.[245] The Versailles Treaty affirmed that a civil High Commission would be responsible for all directives in the occupied territory. The fact that the United States did not ratify the Treaty of Versailles only added to this challenge. In General Allen's words, this left him in "an extremely peculiar position."[246] The Senate's rejection of Versailles meant that the High Commission could not issue orders to the Americans, and thus, army commanders in the occupied zone reissued Allied orders as American ones.

Army officials needed to understand politics in the Rhineland. Each civil affairs officer was required to submit an essay on the organization of his *Kreis*, proving that he was thoroughly familiar with the laws and politics of the country. Since Germany was "recovering" from the political dislocation following the November revolution (which had overthrown the monarchy), occupying forces helped determine the circumstances under which new elections could be held. German authorities had to seek Allied approval for elections, and US forces ensured that elections were fair. A great deal of coordination took place between the US Army's officers in charge of civil affairs and German officials. In the early period of the occupation, there was little desire to change local government officials, since they were regarded as experienced and capable. Eventually, however, occupying forces allowed local elections to take place. Army personnel also tempered the political movement that emerged for the creation of a separate Rhenish republic in the Rhineland. While it was favored by the French, the Americans did not support the creation of an autonomous new state and negotiated among German and Rhenish political leaders, as well as the French, to find an acceptable compromise.[247]

US Army officers also supervised some reform of the German police. They oversaw German police arrests and actions in towns, in some cases overruling police decisions, and prohibited the police from carrying certain types of weapons. As American combat troops began to return to the United States, leaving fewer numbers of military police in localities, the army turned increasingly to German civil police to assist with keeping order. The Third Army hoped to reduce its burden of keeping the peace and at the same time encourage a more "democratic" approach to policing to offset the traditional centralization of German police structures in Berlin. Army personnel oversaw the creation of police reserves, on a New York City model, to be established in German towns. The army also established a fairly extensive system of provost courts, with military commissions trying individuals for offenses against the laws of war or the military government.[248]

Soldiers also tackled the problem of health and public welfare, by working to prevent the spread of disease among troops.[249] Army specialists worked to improve the health and sanitation of the populace and to control epidemics such as influenza and pneumonia. They conducted surveys on communicable diseases and established new requirements to report them. In addition, since venereal disease was a problem among soldiers, various legal and health measures were instituted to reduce these cases. Although there was no orga- nized relief work until April 1920, when a larger system of child relief came into existence, General Allen's military government oversaw physical exam- ination of children by German physicians and the shipment of food and its distribution.

Occupying forces strained the Rhineland's already weak infrastructure, and this too required attention by army troops.[250] Plants supplying water and electricity to key cities were in poor shape, and there was a coal shortage. When Third Army forces arrived in Germany, they exerted full control over all utilities, with the rationale that utilities directly affected the well-being of army forces. As time passed, full control was relinquished, and the military government actively supervised German administration of public utilities. An officer in charge of public utilities and roads and a chief engineer assisted German managers in operating key plants. In addition, the military govern- ment became very involved in water management, working to ensure that certain cities were not deprived of water at the expense of others. The chief engineer also worked to increase the capacity of key electrical plants and to run them more efficiently. Plans for coal and gas conservation were also drawn up, with American teams requiring that German plants complete daily reports on the amount of coal consumed and the amount of gas generated.

Allied leaders and occupying generals also played a large role in economic issues, largely in the interest of securing reparations and payments. For instance, to pay for food imports to feed the population, Allied leaders needed to arrange payment through foreign securities. In addition, decrees promulgated by occu- pation officials regulated the activities by German banks. Furthermore, in US-occupied areas, US military leaders had the right to control budgets and the collection of taxes, as well as to make determinations about what would be taxed.[251] American forces also became involved in mediating labor disputes, and when necessary, army personnel worked to diffuse labor unrest and to deport labor agitators.[252]

The US Senate's refusal to ratify the Treaty of Versailles left the United States technically at war with Germany until the summer of 1921, when the two countries signed a separate peace agreement. During this period, the Senate began to debate the purpose of keeping US troops in the Rhineland, and by 1922 pressure had grown to reduce the American presence there. In March 1922, President Warren Harding signed an agreement providing for the departure of American troops by July, although it was not until the summer of 1923 that the last American troops left. Through the ongoing presence of US troops in Germany, the US had reshaped the balance of power on the continents by tempering French demands, by keeping Germany's power in check, and by influencing the ongoing negotiations to determine the final economic issues related to Germany. As in previous governance operations, a key issue regarding the timing and departure of US forces was the objective of leaving behind a reasonably stable economic and political order. In the case of Germany, its economic stability was of particular importance, given France's continued determination to extract the severest possible reparations. The United States believed that economic conditions in Europe had to be addressed and that a failure to do so would have "injurious consequences."[253] Washington believed that a "prostrate Germany" would result in no economic recuperation in Europe. Thus, from 1921 to 1923, the US engaged in heated discussions and conferences with the Allied powers over the reparations issue.[254] These conferences resulted in the Dawes Plan, which developed arrangements for Germany's payment of reparations.[255] These negotiations sought to link economic growth in Germany with security arrangements such as the Locarno Agreement of 1925; the aim was to create a web of interlocking agreements to keep Germany and France balanced.

Not everyone welcomed the withdrawal of US forces. Many Germans hoped for their continued presence, believing that the United States could prevent a change in the Rhineland's status and serve as a buffer against competing French, British, and Belgian interests. Perhaps more so than in the army's previous governance operations, from the outset of the occupation of the Rhineland, US occupying forces played a very important strategic role by balancing French power and aspirations on the continent.[256] The occupation of the Rhineland served as an instrument by which the final aspects of German settlement could be enforced.

The occupation of the Rhineland and the governance experiences of the Spanish-American War and Reconstruction reaffirmed the need for military forces to consolidate key political objectives following combat in war. Although American occupying forces did not install a new German government—occupying armies ruled through existing German civil administration—this government was shaped by Allied policies and rule, and the Allies used their occupying forces to reinforce a desired political settlement. Army training manuals later recalled the World War I experience as having "firmed down legally and spelled out in detail many of the principles, policies and practices, and techniques which had only been sketched out in the earlier pattern of our history."[257] Furthermore, the occupation and the consolidation of some stability in at least a part of Germany contributed to the longer-term goal of the United States—strengthening Germany to counter the growing threat of Bolshevism, which concerned a number of American leaders at the time.[258] The occupation played a clear policy purpose, with France and Belgium hoping to offset German control of the Rhineland and the United Kingdom and the United States determined to circumscribe French power. The very fact that the occupation was limited in its aims—for example, that it sought to work through the German government—was to some the root of its ultimate failure. A prominent historian of the period argues that by failing to replace the German bureaucracy, the seeds of World War II had been sown.[259]

## CONCLUSIONS

> Belief was indulged in many quarters that armies could
> occupy enemy soil and yet dispossess themselves of most
> of the responsibility of government.
>
> —Henry Allen, *The Rhineland Occupation*

The US Army conducted governance operations in virtually all of its major wars from the Mexican-American War to World War I. Despite the virtual absence of formal guidance on how to conduct governance tasks during this period and the fact that these operations occurred during a period of expansion and contraction within the army, military personnel repeatedly showed themselves capable of adapting to the challenges posed by governance operations. The Civil War marked the end of governance operations on the territory of the

United States. The Spanish-American War, which marked America's emergence as a world power, illustrated that governance tasks would continue to be required to consolidate the political objectives of war.

The cases examined in this chapter posed different challenges for the US Army. The governance operations were not mirror images of each other; some cases involved the complete creation of new governments (such as in the occupations of California and New Mexico and during and after the Civil War), while others worked through existing governmental structures. All of the cases, however, involved the conduct of governance operations by tactical forces rather than specialized troops, and they all required the involvement of the army in political issues in a particular theater. The operations conducted during the Spanish-American War and Reconstruction were perhaps the most extensive, but those in the Mexican-American War and the Rhineland also required army involvement in "overtly political tasks" and demanded the day-to-day implementation of governance-related tasks by army personnel. In some of the cases, civil authorities wielded more power over governance tasks and issued directives related to governance policies, such as Taft's civil commission in the Philippines and the High Commission during the Rhineland. Even in these cases of more direct civil involvement in day-to-day implementation of governance tasks, army personnel made an effort to retain unity of command. Overall, two general arrangements can be identified: political oversight versus political reconstruction. These general categories appeared in these early cases of governance and would reappear in the future.

General Scott's experiences in Mexico combined looser control and reconstruction. Army forces controlled all of Mexico City and undertook administrative functions, but a Mexican government existed until Santa Anna resigned and an interim president took over. General Scott ably balanced American authority on the ground with sensitivity regarding how Mexicans would perceive the actions of US troops. His efforts to improve life in Mexico City played a strategic role: winning hearts and minds. At the same time, while managing governance operations in Mexico City, Scott also waged war against Santa Anna's troops, thus reinforcing the link between the two types of operations in war. During the Civil War, governance operations were conducted through a range of circumstances. First, in the earlier period of the war, they were conducted while combat raged in the South and were viewed by President Lincoln as important tools to persuade Southerners to rethink their steps toward secession. Later, they were designed to enforce a political and economic system on the South—a "right" won by the combat victories of the Union army. During the Spanish-American War, full-fledged military governments were established in Cuba and Puerto Rico, where Spanish administrators essentially departed the islands, leaving the United States to fill in for governments and find indigenous civilian replacements. In the Philippines, the challenges were greater because the political situation was not stabilized, and the United States fought challenges to its political authority—Aguinaldo's forces—while establishing a foundation for a government that would be more compatible with longer-term US interests. In the Rhineland, an oversight arrangement emerged, with the army supervising existing German administrative organs.

The recurring themes and challenges that surfaced during these periods—whether full-fledged military government or the "looser" arrangements—suggest that governance operations contained fairly regular phases and patterns. Army officers developed organizations to balance the requirements of combat operations with governance tasks. They had to create tactical organizations that could handle ongoing combat along with organizations more suited to governance operations. Second, from the beginning of each of these wars, political leaders anticipated, albeit often reluctantly, that army personnel would need to undertake fairly extensive civil administrative duties. Army officers received varying degrees of political guidance once a war began, but most managed to respond well to the challenges. During the Mexican-American War, Secretary of War Marcy announced that a power conquering a territory had "the right to establish a civil government . . . as a means of securing the conquest."[260] In the Mexican-American War, governance operations created the foundations necessary for the absorption of two new states—California and New Mexico—into the United States. In Mexico, General Scott established a framework for fair governance in key cities. During the Civil War, President Lincoln sought to transform the political character of the South, with Union forces playing a key role in this task. In the Spanish-American War, governance operations dismantled Spanish institutions and replaced them with new administrative structures, contributing to the consolidation of Washington's broader aims in the war. In the Philippines, the US Army engaged in combat, occupation, and administration of hostile territory. Finally, the occupation of the Rhineland during World War I contributed to Woodrow Wilson's broader aspirations for political change in Europe. While the occupation did not go far enough in changing German political structures, it provided a foundation for more systematic thinking about governance operations within the army and foreshadowed the extensive governance operations conducted during World War II.

Third, tensions related to civil-military issues continued to surface. The use of army forces in political roles raised concerns within the American polity, driven by worries about the impact of military government on liberalism at home and abroad. Charles Sumner, a key supporter of Lincoln's war effort who later supported the idea of creating a colonial department in the Department of War, nevertheless expressed concern about the role of federal forces in political matters. He justified the creation of military governments in Mexico and California because they were not yet part of the Union; thus, it might be "proper to set up military government for a conquered country beyond our civil jurisdiction."[261] He believed, however, that it was "questionable" to set up "such governors in States which we all claim to be within our civil jurisdiction." Sumner was concerned that the creation of military governors reversed the "policy of the republic" by subjecting civil to military authority. In World War I, Pierrepont Noyes, a key member of the armistice talks, expressed concern about military control of the occupation and argued for civil control.[262]

Fourth, all of these cases also revealed tensions related to unity of command. Commands were often divided between combat-oriented tasks and reconstruction tasks, and the army tended to resist such divisions—not owing to their interest in governing but owing to concerns about maintaining control over events in a wartime theater. In 1864 General Sherman was eager to find a way to "free the hosts of [army] guards and officers whose time has heretofore been absorbed in civil matters."[263] General Miles believed that it was a pleasure to be relieved of governance-related responsibilities.[264] Secretary of War Root recognized this issue in his arguments during the Philippine engagements. He believed that the military should control all personnel until the area was ready for transition to the State Department. In the Rhineland, the army issued the civil High Commission's ordinances as its own. President Lincoln's establishment of interim civil governments under the authority of civilian military governors not only divided the command of military authorities but also created a gray area between these governments and the elected civil governments in the South. Concerns about unity of command would also appear during World War II. For the most part, the principle of military necessity prevailed, with tactical commanders controlling activities in the theater as long as the possibility of combat existed. The issue of unity of command remains a problem today. It has strategic significance because the existence of divided commands continues to reveal a fundamental uncertainty about the appropriate role of the military in governance operations and, as such, about the relationship between governance operations and war. As later chapters in this book will show, the replacement of unity of command with unity of effort during the wars in Afghanistan and Iraq revealed a failure to understand the fundamental differences between the two. This replacement was arguably one of the most important operational failures in the post-9/11 wars. Fifth, the principle of indirect rule—balancing the need to introduce change with the reality of needing to rely on indigenous administrators— emerged during these contingencies as well. As previously noted, during the Mexican-American War, Secretary of War Marcy directed that the United States should work with indigenous personnel whenever possible. This guidance stemmed largely from necessity, since a dearth of personnel meant that that the army could not completely take over governments and had to focus on supervising existing administrative structures.

The cases examined in this chapter cover the period in American history characterized by the growth of America as a world power. By 1898, with the Spanish-American War, America's role in the world had grown dramatically. While previous wars were fought to defend territory and to expand and consolidate power internally, now America focused abroad. Yet, in both types of contingencies, governance operations were required. With the acquisition of new territories overseas, governance operations were required to exert US political control over them. Combat victories alone were not enough; the steps needed to retain and shape the political contours of those territories proved to be equally important. US troops remained in a theater at the direction of US civilian leaders in order to help realize the political objectives that drove each intervention in the first place. Despite the diversity of challenges and the range of operations, army personnel showed adaptability and flexibility and the requirements that we seek in strategic leaders today. Today the army calls this skill "mission command." In the past, it was simply responding to what needed to be done, with limited resources and limited guidance.

# NOTES

1. For discussion of the army in 1820s, see Weigley, *American Way of War*, 59–61. See also Coffman, *Old Army*, 42–103.

2. Utley, *Frontiersmen in Blue*, 46, cited in Robert Wooster, "The Frontier Army and the Occupation of the West, 1865–1900," paper presented at the Combat Studies Institute conference Armed Diplomacy Two Centuries of American Campaigning, August 5–7,

2003, p. 8. Available at http://usacac.army.mil/cac2/cgsc/carl/download/csipubs/Armed Diplomacy_TwoCenturiesOfAmericanCampaigning.pdf.

3. A military government was established following the Louisiana Purchase in 1803 and then during the process of acquiring parts of Florida in the 1818–21 period. Grivas, *Military Governments in California*, 19–21, 29.

4. See his *Fifth Annual Message to Congress*, Philadelphia, December 3, 1793, and his *Sixth Annual Message*, November 19, 1794, both reprinted as part of Yale University's Avalon Project, Annual Messages of the Presidents, http://www.yale.edu/lawweb/avalon/presiden/sou/sou.htm.

5. Statement is from Federalist Paper 25, December 22, 1787, in Alexander Hamilton, James Madison, and John Jay, *The Federalist Papers*, ed. Ian Shapiro (New Haven: Yale University Press, 2009): 127.

6. Francis Vinton Greene, *The Revolutionary War and the Military Policy of the United States* (New York: Charles Scribner's Sons, 1911), 285.

7. E. Upton to James H. Wilson, James Wilson Papers, Library of Congress, cited in Fitzpatrick, "Emory Upton and the Citizen Soldier," 365.

8. Coffman, *Old Army*, 5.

9. Ibid., 46.

10. Ambrose, *Duty, Honor, Country*, 24–35. Cadets focused heavily on mathematics, and the majority of those who flunked out of the academy did so because of the tough math curriculum. See Morrison, *Best School*, 117.

11. Utley, *Frontier Regulars*, 45.

12. Root to Charles F. Maclean, July 27, 1899, cited in Jessup, *Elihu Root*, 218. The rest of the citations by and about Root in this paragraph are from this source, 222, 300.

13. Information from this paragraph is from "Memorandum for the Secretary of War, Subject: Relations of the War Department to the Civil Government Affairs of Puerto Rico, From F. LeJ. Parker, Chief, Bureau of Insular Affairs, March 17, 1931," located in NA, RG 350, box 1022, file 24983–116.

14. "Letter to the Honorable Hiram Bingham, Chairman, Joint Commission on Insular Reorganization, United States Senate, from the Secretary of War, May 6, 1929," p. 3, NA, RG 350.

15. "Secretary of War Elihu Root, Statement to Congress, January 22, 1902, cited by Memorandum for the Secretary of War from Chief, Bureau of Insular Affairs F. LeJ. Parker, December 27, 1930," NA, RG 350, box 1022, file 24983–114.

16. "Memo to Senator Bingham from Secretary of War Weeks, February 9, 1924," NA, RG 350, box 1022, file 24983/84.

17. Public Resolution No. 108, 70th Cong., Joint Resolution to Establish a Joint Commission on Insular Reorganization, NA, RG 350, file 24983–90.

18. "Comments by President Theodore Roosevelt, Special Message to Congress, December 3, 1906," which can be found online at the American Presidency Project, http://www.presidency.ucsb.edu/ws/index.php?pid=29547&st=&st1.

19. A reference to moving the bureau to the State Department can be found in "Senate Document No. 302, 67th Congress, 'Reorganization of the Executive Departments,' Letter from the President of the United States to Walter F. Brown, February 13, 1923," located in NA, General Records Relating to More Than One Island Possession, RG 350, box 1022, file 24983–79, part I.

20. "Memo to Senator Bingham from Secretary of War Weeks, February 9, 1924."

21. Quotes from Secretary of War Weeks here and in the next paragraph are from his testimony before the Joint Committee on the Reorganization of the Administrative Branch of the Government of the United States, 68th Cong., 1st sess., January 7–31, 1924, copy of which is located in NA, RG 350, box 1023, file 24983–84, 108–16. See also "Memo to Senator Bingham from Secretary of War Weeks, February 9, 1924."

22. "Memorandum to the Honorable Hiram Bingham from Patrick Hurley, Chairman, Joint Commission on Insular Reorganization, United States Senate, Secretary of War, December 30, 1929," NA, RG 350, box 1022, file 24983–97.

23. "Memo to the Secretary of War from F. Lej. Parker, Chief, Bureau of Insular Affairs, March 17, 1931," NA, RG 350, box 1022, file 24983-AF-116.

24. "Memo to the Secretary of War from F. Lej. Parker, Chief, Bureau of Insular Affairs, March 17, 1931," NA, RG 350, box 1022, file 24983-AF-116. These themes are included in this memo and the one dated December 30, 1929.

25. "Memo of December 30, 1929," p. 2.

26. Franklin D. Roosevelt, "Message to Congress on Plan II to Implement the Reorganization Act, May 9th, 1930," located at the American Presidency Project, http://www.presidency.ucsb.edu/ws/index.php?pid=15760&st=insular&st1=1939.

27. Jessup, *Elihu Root*, 241.

28. See, for example, Harvey Rosenfeld, *Diary of a Dirty Little War: The Spanish-American War of 1898* (Westport, CT: Praeger, 2000), and Langer, "Critique of Imperialism," in which Langer argued that "military and official classes" had an interest in territorial acquisitions because such acquisitions provided jobs. Also Joseph Freeman and Scott Nearing, *Dollar Diplomacy: A Study in American Imperialism* (New York: Viking, 1925).

29. Root was appalled by the wretched conditions facing occupying troops in Cuba. See Jessup, *Elihu Root*, 241. Millett and Maslowski, *For the Common Defense*, 327–28, argue that Root's goal was to reduce bureaucratic rivalries, which he believed contributed to military ineffectiveness.

30. US Congress, Executive Document No. 60, and Scott, *Memoirs*, 560–61.

31. Grivas, *Military Governments in California*, 223.

32. In California, opposition seemed to be less against the military government per se and more against specific political decisions, such as retaining the power of the local magistrates (*alcaldes*). See Grivas's description of opposition to the *alcaldes*. Ibid., 193–96.

33. Healy, *United States in Cuba*, 55

34. Dawson, *Army Generals and Reconstruction*, 57.

35. "Veto of the First Reconstruction Act," in Paul H. Bergeron, ed., *The Papers of Andrew Johnson*, vol. 12, *February–August 1867* (Knoxville: University of Tennessee Press, 1995), 84. Johnson was wary of the military usurping power. He wrote that military law had no application to citizens "[or] even to the citizen soldier enrolled in the militia in time of peace." See pages 85 and 89.

36. Maslowski, *Treason*, 20.

37. Calvin Coolidge, "4th Annual Message to Congress, December 7, 1926," located at http://www.presidency.ucsb.edu/ws/index.php?pid=29567&st=&st1.

38. Some studies relating to the military governments in this period include Grivas, *Military Governments in California*; Twitchell, *Leading Facts of New Mexican History*; Thomas, *A History of Military Government*; Bauer, *Mexican War*; Dawson, "American Civil-Military Relations"; Eisenhower, *Agent of Destiny*; Scott, *Memoirs*; McCaffrey, *Army*

*of Manifest Destiny*; Smith, "American Rule in Mexico"; and US Congress, Executive Document No. 60.

39. Polk, *Polk*, May 11, 1846, 87.

40. Millett and Maslowski, *For the Common Defense*, 149.

41. Marcy to Taylor, May 28, 1845, reprinted in US Congress, Executive Document No. 60, 60–79. The message of June 15, 1845, is on pages 82–83.

42. Polk, *Polk*, May 30, 1846. Heated debate took place throughout the summer over these aims, but it seems that by late May Polk knew what he wanted. See Schroeder, *Mr. Polk's War*, 161–63. Later, Polk decided to take Upper and Lower California too. See Polk, *Polk*, December 17, 1846, 177. Quotes from this paragraph are from his diary entries from May 13, 1846, 91; July 7, 1846, 130; July 26, 1846, 132; and December 1, 1846, 175.

43. Marcy referred to a series of messages on the occupation of Mexico as "all the orders and instructions which have issued from this department" related to the establishment or organization of civil government. "Marcy to President, December 21, 1846," in US Congress, Executive Document No. 60, 150–51. The rest of the quotes in this paragraph are from his instructions, which are reprinted in Ward McAfee and Cordell J. Robinson, *Origins of the Mexican War: A Documentary Source Book*, vol. 2 (Salisbury, NC: Documentary Publications, 1982), 166–67.

44. "Letter from Gen. Kearny to General Wood, Aug. 22, 1846," in US Congress, Executive Document No. 60, 171.

45. "Message from Kearny to Adjutant General, August 24, 1846," ibid., 169.

46. House Executive Document No. 19, 29th Cong., 2nd sess., 20, cited in Thomas, *History of Military Government*, 104.

47. The July 7 statement is reprinted in House Executive Document 30, 30th Cong., 2nd sess., no. 1, 1010, cited in Thomas, *History of Military Government*, 161. See also Grivas, *Military Governments in California*, 82.

48. "Stockton, Los Angeles, to Bancroft, Washington, August 28, 1846, in Commodore Stockton's Correspondence, June 1846–February 1848, Letters Received by the Secretary of the Navy from Commanding Officers of Squadrons," NA, microfilm 89, roll 33, cited in Grivas, *Military Governments in California*, 56.

49. Proclamation at Vera Cruz, April 11, 1847, reprinted in Dept. of the Army, *Military Government: An Historical Approach*, 30.

50. Dawson, "American Civil-Military Relations," 561; "Polk Message to Congress, December 22, 1846," in Richardson, *Compilation of the Messages*, 506–7.

51. "Winfield Scott, Washington, to Kearny, November 3, 1846, US Government Document Service 499," 14, cited in Grivas, *Military Governments in California*, 37. See also Executive Document 19, 29th Cong., 2nd sess., 14, cited in Thomas, *History of Military Government*, 106.

52. Quotes from General Scott are from his *Memoirs*, 394.

53. General Order 395, cited in Smith, "American Rule in Mexico," 297. See also Dept. of the Army, *Military Government under General Winfield Scott*, 2, and Scott, *Memoirs*, 392–93.

54. "General Orders 20, Tampico, Mexico, February 19, 1847," reprinted in Dept. of the Army, *Military Government under General Winfield Scott*, handwritten date, October 1960.

55. Thomas, *History of Military Government*, 113.

56. Eisenhower, *Agent of Destiny*, 301.

57. Wallace, "United States Army in Mexico City," 160.

58. Bauer, *Mexican War*, 335–36. Scott did end up complying and levying assessments on Mexicans.

59. For full discussion of the Kearny-Stockton dispute, see Grivas, *Military Governments in California*, 64–70, and Clarke, *Stephen Watts Kearny*, 256–87.

60. "Marcy to Kearny, War Department, June 3, 1846," in US Congress, Executive Document 60, 244. Also, Clarke, *Stephen Watts Kearny*, 258, and Singletary, *Mexican War*, 140–41.

61. "Secretary of the Navy George Bancroft to Commodore Sloat, July 12, 1846," in US Congress, Executive Document 60, 238–39. Polk mentions the Bancroft message in his diary, on January 11, 1847, *Polk*, 185.

62. Orders had existed since November, which would have resolved the dispute, but neither Kearny nor Stockton had received them until months later. "Message from Department of the Navy to Stockton, Nov. 5, 1846," in US Congress, Executive Document 60, 245. See also Grivas, *Military Governments in California*, 75–76.

63. Many orders are reprinted in US Dept. of the Army, *Military Government under General Winfield Scott*, 3.

64. Thomas, *History of Military Government*, 110.

65. Ibid., 132–33.

66. Grivas, *Military Governments in California*, 123, and Marcy's June instructions, US Congress, Executive Document No. 60.

67. Dawson, "American Civil-Military Relations," 559–60.

68. The code established the executive power of a governor for two years; he also served as commander in chief of the militia in the territory and could appoint all military and civil officers. US Congress, Executive Document No. 60, 177. As *alcaldes* faded out in the late 1800s, many were elected mayors of towns and cities. Grivas, *Military Government in California*, 175, 185.

69. "Memo from Adjutant-General's office, 'Office of the Civil and Military Governor,' Puebla, 22nd January, 1848," cited in footnote 11 in Smith, "American Rule in Mexico," 295–96. See also Berge, "Mexican Dilemma," 239.

70. Information about customs duties from Thomas, *History of Military Government*, 196–201; from US Dept. of the Army, *Military Government: An Historical Approach*, 37–38; and from Grivas, *Military Governments in California*, 129–31.

71. There were initially bitter personal disputes between Trist and Scott, though these were eventually resolved, and they worked together fairly well. See Connor and Faulk, *North American Divided*, 161–62. See also "Marcy to Scott, April 14, 1847," in US Congress, Executive Document No. 60, 940, cited in Bauer, *War with Mexico*, 282.

72. Polk, *Polk*, entry September 15, 1846, 148.

73. Scott, *Memoirs*, 578.

74. US Congress, House, California and New Mexico, 31st Cong., 1st sess., House Executive Document 17 (Washington, DC: 1849), serial no. 573, cited in Thomas, *History of Military Government*, 211–12.

75. Grivas, *Military Governments in California*, 6–9, 110, 116.

76. "Proclamation to the District of San Francisco, Riley, Monterey, June 4, 1849,"cited ibid., 140–41. General Kearny served as governor until May 31, 1847. He was succeeded by Col. Richard Barnes Mason and then by Brig. Gen. Bennet Riley, who served until the state government went into operation. Thomas, *History of Military Government*, 195–96.

77. US Congress, House, California and New Mexico, 31st Cong., 1st sess., House Executive Document 17 (Washington, DC, 1849), serial no. 573, 861–62, cited in Grivas, *Military Governments in California*, 217.

78. Grivas, *Military Governments in California*, 79, 148.

79. Thomas, *History of Military Government*, 147.

80. There is a disagreement about this in the literature. James Sefton argues that the army's role in Reconstruction began in 1867 after the passage of the Reconstruction Acts. See his *United States Army and Reconstruction*. Others argue that Reconstruction began in 1861–62, when Army troops tried to consolidate the political situation following early Union victories. Peter Maslowski argues that Reconstruction was part of the war, "not just a postwar phenomenon." See his *Treason Must Be Made Odious*, xiii. James McPherson also believes that Reconstruction began in December 1863. See his *Ordeal by Fire*, 391. John Hope Franklin argues that Reconstruction began in 1862, with Benjamin Butler's occupation of New Orleans. See his *Reconstruction after the Civil War*. Since Lincoln gave the army direct tasks to secure the Union's victory in states as early as 1861, I believe these latter interpretations to be more accurate.

81. McPherson, *Ordeal by Fire*, 402; Ash, *When the Yankees Came*, 29, 115. See also Maslowski, *Treason Must Be Made Odious*, 28.

82. Ash, *When the Yankees Came*, 34. Grimsley argues that there were two policies at work. By early 1862, armies marching into Virginia, the Carolinas, and Tennessee were advocates of conciliation, while troops farther West were less so. See Grimsley, *Hard Hand of War*, 7–22, 24–25, 48.

83. McClellan memo to the "Army of the West," July 16, 1861, in US Dept. of War, *War of the Rebellion*, 236. Hereafter referred to as *Official Records*.

84. *Official Records*, 4, 342, 355–56, cited in Grimsley, *Hard Hand of War*, 35.

85. *Official Records*, 8, General Order No. 8, November 26, 1861, 380–81, and General Orders No. 46, February 22, 1862, *Official Records*, series II, vol. 1, 563, both cited in Grimsley, *Hard Hand of War*, 49, 51.

86. "Correspondence, Memo to the Secretary of War Stanton from Butler, June 10, 1862," in *Official Records*, series I, vol. 27, chap. 39, part III, 466.

87. E. G. Scott, *Reconstruction during the Civil War* (Boston, 1895), 323, cited in Carpenter, "Military Government of the Southern Territory," 478.

88. General Order No. 13a, February 26, 1862, *Official Records*, series II, vol. 7, 669–70.

89. The plan offered amnesty to all but a few Southerners, as long as each took an oath of loyalty to the Union and promised to abide by wartime measures on slavery. When a number equal to 10 percent of the voters in the 1860 presidential election took the oath, the nucleus of a new loyal state government could be formed. Once the local government abolished slavery, the state would be considered reconstructed. Provisional governors would be appointed to new states, and these governors would register voters and guide states through the adoption of a new constitution abolishing slavery, repudiating Civil War debts, and voiding the ordinance of secession. See Richardson, *Compilation of the Messages*, 310–14.

90. "Correspondence, Memo to the Secretary of War Stanton from Butler, June 10, 1862," in *Official Records*, series I, vol. 27, chap. 39, part III, 466.

91. Maslowski, *Treason*, 20.

92. Futrell, "Federal Military Government," 191.

93. "Letter from Halleck to Sherman, October 1, 1863," in "War Department HQA, Letter Book," vol. 13a, 372, NA, cited in Futrell, "Federal Military Government," 184.

94. Maslowski, *Treason*, 26 and 27. Maslowski also noted that "Lincoln made a serious error when he failed to provide Johnson and Buell with explicit instructions on their respective responsibilities."

95. "Buell to Andrew Johnson, March 19, 1862," *Official Records*, 47 cited in Maslowski, *Treason*, 38. Rosecrans later echoed Buell's opinion, stating that he wanted Nashville in the hands of an "able and experienced officer" who could exercise a "most rigid military policy." See "Rosecrans to Halleck, 4 April 1863," *Official Records*, part I, vol. 23, 2, 208, cited in Maslowski, *Treason*, 48.

96. "Stanton to the Honorable Edward Stanley, Military Governor of NC, 20 May 1862," *Official Records*, part I, vol. 9, 397, cited in Maslowski, *Treason*, 38.

97. Hesseltine, *Lincoln's Plan of Reconstruction*, 63.

98. Hesseltine described Shepley as a "mere clerk for Butler [whose] actual role was circumscribed by Butler's whims." Ibid., 66.

99. Capers, *Occupied City*, 74.

100. "HQ Dept. of the Gulf, Nineteenth Army Corps, New Orleans, January 27, 1865, N. P. Banks, Major General, Commanding, to Brig. General George F. Shepley, Military Governor of Louisiana," in *Official Records*, series I, vol. 26, part I, 1097–98.

101. Letter from Sherman to his brother, Lancaster Ohio, December 29, 1863, reprinted in Thorndike, *Sherman Letters*, 219.

102. Futrell, "Federal Military Government," 185.

103. McKitrick, *Andrew Johnson and Reconstruction*, 7.

104. General Grant returned from a tour of the South convinced that the North should display leniency toward the region, though he predicted that "small garrisons" throughout the region would remain necessary. "Grant to Johnson, December 18, 1865," in Simpson et al., *Advice after Appomattox*, 212–13.

105. Sefton, *Army and Reconstruction*, 17.

106. Exchanges between Perry, Gillmore, and Stanton cited in Simpson et al., *Advice after Appomattox*, 229, and 237n4.

107. Meade to Stanton, September 20, 1865, ibid., 230. Then head of the Military Division of the Atlantic, Meade was touring South Carolina, North Carolina, and Virginia at the time.

108. These provost marshals were different than the military's own policing provost marshals, which predated the PMG and were more narrowly focused. See also Hyman, "Deceit in Dixie," 65.

109. Ibid., 74.

110. Ibid., 39

111. Quote is from Hesseltine, *Lincoln's Plan for Reconstruction*, 68. Another example was General Butler's efforts in Louisiana to get guidance on how to deal with slaves, since Louisiana had been exempt from the Emancipation Proclamation. Lincoln reportedly told Butler he had to "get along" with the problem as best he could. See Capers, *Occupied City*, 55, 95.

112. Grimsley, *Hard Hand of War*, 35

113. "Letter from Halleck, General in Chief, HQ Army to Major General S. A. Hurlbut, Memphis, TN, June 22, 1863," in "US War Department, HQ, Army, Letter Book," vol. 16, 326–27, NA, cited in Futrell, "Federal Military Government," 181.

114. Thorndike, *Sherman Letters*, 65.

115. Dawson discusses Grant and Sheridan's conversation in *Army Generals and Reconstruction*, 48. Attorney General Stanberry's view on the Reconstruction Acts is in "Letter from Attorney General Henry Stanberry to Andrew Johnson, June 12, 1867," cited in Bergeron, *Papers of Andrew Johnson*, 320.

116. Grimsley, *Hard Hand of War*, 35.

117. McKitrick, *Andrew Johnson and Reconstruction*, 13.

118. James Alex Bagget, "Emancipation, Freedmen, and the Freedmen's Bureau," in *The American Civil War: A Handbook of Literature and Research*, ed. Steven E. Woodworth (Westport, CT: Greenwood, 1996), 580.

119. Elizabeth Bethel, "The Freedman's Bureau in Alabama," *Journal of Southern History* 14, no. 1 (February 1948): 49.

120. Sefton, *United States Army and Reconstruction*, 47.

121. Randy Finely, "The Personnel of the Freedmen's Bureau in Arkansas," *The Freedmen's Bureau and Reconstruction: Reconsiderations*, ed. Paul A. Cimbala and Randall M. Miller (New York: Fordham University Press, 1999), 93.

122. Govan and Livingood, "Chattanooga under Military Occupation," 45. See also Robert C. Morris, *Reading, 'Riting, and Reconstruction: The Education of Freedmen in the South, 1861–1870* (Chicago: University of Chicago Press, 1981).

123. Sefton, *Army and Reconstruction*, 124

124. Elizabeth Joan Doyle, "Nurseries of Treason: Schools in Occupied New Orleans," *Journal of Southern History* 26 (1960): 161–69, cited in Ash, *When the Yankees Came*, 88.

125. "In carrying out the Reconstruction Acts, army generals played political chess, improvising the rules as the game progressed." See Dawson, *Army Generals and Reconstruction*, 75.

126. Ibid., 4.

127. Wooster, "Frontier Army and Occupation," 2.

128. Unless otherwise noted, information about courts is from Futrell, "Federal Military Government," 186–87.

129. Sefton, *Army and Reconstruction*, 30–32.

130. Govan and Livingood, "Chattanooga under Military Occupation," 43, and Futrell, "Federal Military Government," 191.

131. Unless otherwise noted, the source for this section is A. H. Carpenter, "Military Government of Southern Territory, 1861–1865," *Annual Report of the American Historical Association for the Year 1900*, 2 vols., vol. 1, submitted to the House of Representatives, 56th Cong., 2nd sess., Document No. 548 (Washington, DC: GPO, 1901): 489–93.

132. Bethel, "Freedmen's Bureau in Alabama," 54–55.

133. Claude F. Oubre, "Forty Acres and a Mule: The Freedmen's Bureau and Black Land Ownership," in *The African American Experience in Louisiana: Part B; From the Civil War to Jim Crow*, ed. Charles Vincent (Lafayette: Center for Louisiana Studies, University of Louisiana, 2000), cited in Bagget, "Emancipation, Freedmen, and the Freedmen's Bureau," 582.

134. See Melinda M. Hennessey, "Reconstruction Politics and the Military: The Eufaula Riot of 1874," *Alabama Historical Quarterly* 38 (Summer 1976): 112–25.

135. "Edward G. W. Butler to Johnson, July 30, 1867," in Bergeron, *Papers of Andrew Johnson*, 12, 441.

136. "Gideon Welles to Andrew Johnson, August 4, 1867," in ibid., 455.

137. Joseph G. Dawson III, "The US Army in the South: Reconstruction as Nation Building," paper presented to the Combat Studies Combat Studies Institute conference Armed Diplomacy: Two Centuries of American Campaigning, US Army Command and General Staff College, Fort Leavenworth, KS, August 5–7, 2003, 15, http://usacac.army .mil/cac2/cgsc/carl/download/csipubs/ArmedDiplomacy_TwoCenturiesOfAmericanCam paigning.pdf.

138. "Veto of the First Reconstruction Act," in Bergeron, *Papers of Andrew Johnson*, 84. Johnson was wary of the military usurping too much power.

139. Quoted in Dawson, *Army Generals and Reconstruction*, 55.

140. Ibid., 69.

141. Sefton, *Army and Reconstruction*, 16. See also Bergeron, *Papers of Andrew Johnson*, "Veto of the First Reconstruction Act," 82.

142. Maslowski, *Treason Must Be Made Odious*, 20.

143. US Dept. of War, *Annual Reports of the War Department for the Fiscal Year Ended June 30, 1898*, 4. Hereafter cited as *ARWD, FY June 30, 1898*.

144. Russell Alexander Alger, *The Spanish-American War* (New York: Harper & Brothers, 1901), 7. Alger was secretary of war during the war.

145. Cosmas, "From Order to Chaos," 106. See also Alger, *Spanish-American War*, 7. The National Guard numbered around 114,000 men, but no legal machinery existed to enlarge the army to use it for an invasion of Cuba, nor was it prepared even if it could be called upon. Cosmas, "From Order to Chaos," 107. The matériel needed to clothe and equip large armies was not even manufactured at the time, reported the army's commanding general. *ARWD, FY June 30, 1898*, 8.

146. Not all historians agree with this characterization. Walter LaFeber argued that US expansionists had targeted Cuba since the 1800s. LaFeber, *American Search for Opportunity*, 149.

147. Trask, *War with Spain*, 11–12. Part of this may be attributed to US investments in Cuba, which ranged from $30 million to $50 million; the import-export trade had reached $100 million. Ernest May also wrote about how the disruption in the sugar trade affected Congress. See his *Imperial Democracy* (New York: Harcourt, Brace & World, 1961), 114–66. See also Trask, *War with Spain*, 13, 21. Trask also notes that shortly after his election, McKinley sent a special envoy to Spain to try to find a diplomatic solution to the problem.

148. The Spanish ambassador to Washington wrote the letter, which contained harsh words about McKinley and the United States, inciting congressional hawks.

149. Cosmas, *Army for Empire*, 81–82. There is some dispute over whether the act allowed for offensive preparations or was primarily a defensive measure to deter Spain. See also Alger, *Spanish-American War*, 14.

150. "Teller Amendment in Proclamation No. 301, Headquarters, Division of Cuba, Habana, July 25, 1900," reprinted in US Dept. of War, *Five Years of the War Department following the War with Spain, 1899–1903*, 108.

151. "Woodford to McKinley, March 18, 1898, Foreign Relations of the United States, 1898," 720, cited in Healy, *United States in Cuba*, 21.

152. Crawford, Hayes, and Session, *Spanish-American War*, 9.

153. Millett and Maslowski, *For the Common Defense*, 288; Matloff, *American Military History*, 322.

154. *ARWD, FY June 30, 1898*, 13–14.

155. "Message from Miles to the Secretary of War, April 18, 1898," ibid., 7.

156. "Message from William McKinley to the Secretary of War, May 19, 1898," in US Dept. of War, *Correspondence Relating to the War*, 676. Quotes from the message in the rest of this paragraph and the next are from this guidance.

157. Quoted in Cosmas, "Securing Fruits of Victory," 86.

158. Miles report in *ARWD, FY June 30, 1898*, 25.

159. "Miles Memo to Secretary of War, July 21, 1898," in *ARWD, FY June 30, 1898*, 27. See also the series of cables between Miles, Shafter, and Alger, ibid., 23–27.

160. Cosmas, *Army for Empire*, 300, and Cosmas, "Security Fruits of Victory," 86.

161. See transcript of President William McKinley's Second Annual Message, December 5, 1898, http://millercenter.org/president/mckinley/speeches/speech-3770.

162. Quoted in Healy, *United States in Cuba*, 50.

163. US Dept. of the Army, *Military Government: An Historical Approach*, 64–65.

164. A good discussion of these two divisions is in Healy, *United States in Cuba*, 56–57. The departments were (a) finance; (b) agriculture, commerce, industry, public works; (c) sanitation and public instruction; and (d) state and government.

165. US Dept. of War, *Five Years of the War Department following the War with Spain*, Report for 1899, 17.

166. Ibid.

167. "Telegram from Alger to Miles, Washington, DC, June 6, 1898," in *ARWD, FY June 30, 1898*, 12, and "Telegram from Alger to Miles, Washington, DC, July 14, 1898," in *ARWD, FY June 30, 1898*, 24.

168. Ibid, 32–33. As in Cuba, Miles was very concerned about the health of his troops. See Miles's report in *ARWD, FY June 1898*, 25.

169. See Linn, *U.S. Army and Counterinsurgency*, 163–69.

170. "Message to McKinley from W. Merritt, Major-General, U.S. Army, HQ Department of the East, May 15, 1898," cited in US Dept. of War, *Correspondence Relating to the War*, vol. 2 , 645–46.

171. "Nelson A. Miles, Commanding, to the Secretary of War, HQ of the Army, Washington, May 18, 1898," in US Dept. of War, *Correspondence Relating to the War*, vol. 2, 648–49.

172. "Major-General Commanding, W. Merritt to H.C. Corbin, Adjutant General, HQ Department of the East, May 17, 1898," in US Dept. of War, *Correspondence Relating to the War*, vol. 2, 648. Merritt's wider political aims also discussed in Gates, *Schoolbooks and Krags*.

173. Leech, *In the Days of McKinley*, 212.

174. See "Annual Report of Maj. General E. S. Otis, Commanding the Department of the Pacific and Eight Army Corps, and military governor of the Philippines Islands, covering the period August 29, 1898 to August 31, 1899," cited in US Dept. of War, *Annual Reports of the War Department for the Fiscal Year Ended June 30, 1899*, 4.

175. See exchange of letters between Otis and Aguinaldo, ibid., 4–10. See especially the letter of September 8, 1898, 6–7.

176. US Dept. of the Army, *Military Government: An Historical Approach*, 76.

177. Brian McAllister Linn also makes this argument his *US Army and Counterinsurgency*, 168, first and last chapters.

178. Ibid., 126–29.

179. US Dept. of War, *Five Years of the War Department following the War with Spain*, Report for 1900, 407.

180. Linn, *US Army and Counterinsurgency*, 21.

181. Linn, *Guardians of Empire*, 13.

182. Linn, *US Army and Counterinsurgency*, 21, 111.

183. US Dept. of the Army, *Military Government: An Historical Approach*, 88

184. US Dept. of War, *Five Years of the War Department following the War with Spain*, Report for 1900, 408, 409.

185. For this point and the next, see Rowland T. Berthoff, "Taft and MacArthur, 1900–1901: A Study in Civil-Military Relations," *World Politics* 5 (January 1953): 200.

186. US Dept. of War, *Five Years of the War Department following the War with Spain*, Report for 1900, 135.

187. Information about the organization Wood created and his quotes in this paragraph and the next are from Wood, "Military Government of Cuba," 153, 156, 157.

188. Unless otherwise noted, information is from ibid., 8–10, 25, 115–16.

189. Ibid., 153. The rest of the information in this paragraph is from US Dept. of War, *Five Years of the War Department following the War with Spain*, Report for 1899 and 1900.

190. Wood, "Military Government of Cuba," 2.

191. Information from ibid., 5–8, and US Dept. of War, *Five Years of the War Department following the War with Spain*, Report for 1900, 114.

192. The information contained in this introductory paragraph is from US Dept. of War, *Five Years of the War Department following the War with Spain*, Report for 1899, 22–24.

193. Information about judicial and legal issues is from ibid., 37–38.

194. US Dept. of War, *Five Years of the War Department following the War with Spain*, Report for 1900, 119.

195. Information is from Dept. of War, *Five Years of the War Department following the War with Spain*, Report for 1899, 23–24, and Report for 1900, 116–21.

196. Information about transfer in cables from Secretary Root to General Wood. See appendix A, Appendixes to the Report for 1902, in Dept. of War, *Five Years of the War Department following the War with Spain*, 419–25.

197. "Memo from Elihu Root to General Wood, War Department, March 27, 1902," in ibid., 422.

198. Wood, "Military Government of Cuba," 28–29.

199. Statement by the last military governor of Puerto Rico, Brig. Gen. George Davis, reprinted in Dept. of War, *Five Years of the War Department following the War with Spain*, Report for 1900, 120–21.

200. Quotes from reprint of portion of secretary of war's report from 1912, in Stimson and Bundy, *On Active Service*, 120–21.

201. For more, see Pomeroy, "American Colonial Office," 521–32.

202. Jessup, *Elihu Root*, vol. 1, 221.

203. Few World War I studies are focused on the occupation. The most comprehensive treatment is Hunt, *American Military Government of Occupied Germany*. Other works include a memoir, *The Great Crusade*, by Gen. Joseph T. Dickman, who commanded the Third Army when it became the Army of Occupation, and a memoir by Henry T. Allen, military governor of the Rhineland in 1920, *The Rhineland Occupation*. There is also US Dept. of the Army, *United States Army in the World War, 1917–1919*, vol. 10, *The Armistice Agreement and Related Documents*, and a dissertation by Rasmussen, "American Forces in Germany and Civil Affairs, July 1919–January 1923."

204. Walter Millis, *Road to War: America 1914–1917* (Boston: Houghton Mifflin, 1935), 230.

205. Ibid., 439.

206. *Congressional Record*, 64th Cong., 2nd sess., 1741–43, cited in May, *Imperial Democracy*, 34.

207. US Dept. of State, *FRUS, 1919: Paris Peace Conference*, vol. 1 , 19–21. One American participant, the chief of the Territorial Section, suggested that US ability to tackle many of the commission's questions was weak; he believed that the United States was at a disadvantage in understanding the politics of the countries because it did not have the experiences of the colonial powers. See Mezes, "Preparations for Peace," 5.

208. One account suggests that in the fall of 1918, only one military officer—a low-ranking major who contributed to geographical questions—was involved. Ibid., 7.

209. US Dept. of State, *FRUS, 1919: Paris Peace Conference*, vol. 1, Inquiry Document No. 887, December 22, 1917, "Memo on The President Situation: The War Aims and Peace Terms It Suggests," 44. In November 1917, the secretary of war told Walter Lippmann that "every energy must be combined to make Germany livable after the war." US Dept. of State, *FRUS, 1919: Paris Peace Conference*, vol. 1, 39.

210. Ibid., vol. 1, 56–57 and 287.

211. For example, on this last point, see the memorandum of conversation between Marshal Foch and General Pershing, April 28, 1919, "HS Secret Documents: Vol. H-1, Memo," reprinted in US Dept. of the Army, *United States Army in the World War, 1914–1919*, vol. 10, part 2, 1056.

212. Wilson to Lansing, US Dept. of State, *FRUS, 1919: Paris Peace Conference*, vol. 11, 219.

213. Article V is reprinted in Hunt, *American Military Government of Occupied Germany*, 267. The armistice agreement can also be found on the web, at sites such as http://www.firstworldwar.com/source/armisticeterms.htm.

214. US Dept. of State, *FRUS, 1919: Paris Peace Conference*, vol. 7: 308, 311. Foch wanted about 150,000 occupying forces.

215. See notes from May 5, 1919, meeting with Wilson, George, Clemenceau in *FRUS, 1919: Paris Peace Conference, 1919*, vol. 5, 471.

216. Excerpt from the Hunt Report reprinted in US Dept. of the Army, *United States Army in the World War, 1914–1919*, vol. 11, 152.

217. Allen, *Rhineland Occupation*, 18.

218. See Pershing's introduction to Dickman, *Great Crusade*, vii–viii.

219. Ibid., 198–99. See also Hunt, *American Military Government of Occupied Germany*, 27.

220. Craig, *Germany, 1866–1945*, 396–97.

221. A copy of the Rhineland Agreement can be found in "Agreement between the United States of America, Belgium, the British Empire, and France of the One Part, and Germany of the Other Part, with Regard to the Military Occupation of the Territories of the Rhine," *American Journal of International Law* 13, no. 4, Supplement: Official Documents (October 1919): 404–9.

222. Field orders developing a plan for the Third Army's advance to Berlin are contained in the appendix to Liggett, *Commanding an American Army*, 182–83.

223. Bullard, *Personalities and Reminiscences*, 316. Bullard had also served as a member of Cuba's provisional military government.

224. Pershing said that Allied armies need to be prepared to resume offensive operations against Germany. See US Dept. of the Army, *United States Army in the World War, 1917–*

*1919: Occupation*, vol. 11, 144. The Third Army included a G-1 through G-5, as well as administrative and technical services such as an adjutant general, an inspector general, etc.

225. Rasmussen, "American Forces in Germany," 21.

226. See US Dept. of the Army, *Military Government: An Historical Approach*, 104–5.

227. Excerpt of the Hunt Report in US Dept. of the Army, *United States Army in the World War, 1917–1919*, vol. 11, 161.

228. US Dept. of the Army, *Military Government: An Historical Approach*, 107. Hunt believed this was a "grave" error because it did not take into account the "minutely and carefully organized system of German government." Excerpt of chapter 4 of the Hunt Report in US Dept. of the Army, *United States Army in the World War, 1917–1919*, vol. 11, 158.

229. US Dept. of the Army, *Military Government: An Historical Approach*, 107.

230. Hunt, *American Military Government of Occupied Germany*, 67.

231. Information in this sentence and in rest of paragraph is from the Hunt Report excerpt in US Dept. of the Army, *United States Army in the World War, 1917–1919*, vol. 11, 157–59, 168.

232. Foch, *Memoirs*, 490.

233. Liggett, *Commanding an American Army*, 136.

234. "Memorandum for the Chief of Staff, May 17, 1919," in US Dept. of the Army, *United States Army in the World War, 1917–1919*, vol. 10, 1198.

235. Hunt Report, chapter 3, in "Inter Allied Control," ibid.

236. Fraenkel, *Military Occupation and Rule of War*, 23.

237. The proclamations were Foch's "Proclamation to the Inhabitants of the Occupied Territory" and General Pershing's "Proclamation to the Inhabitants." These are reprinted in Hunt, *Military Occupation of the Rhineland*, 30–32. Later an expert observer noted that "without any preparations made by the Army prior to the armistice and without clear policy instructions from the American government thereafter, the army of occupation could hardly have done more." Holborn, *American Military Government*, 2–3.

238. Hunt, *American Military Government in Occupied Germany*, 31.

239. This point is supported by the memorandums of conversation between the US, British, and French leaders during the Paris Peace negotiations. See US Dept. of State, *FRUS, 1919: Paris Peace Conference*, vol. 6, 501–2, 506.

240. "American Forces in Germany, HQ," *Historical Report, July 1919–January 1920*, in American Forces in Germany Collection, cited in Rasmussen, "American Forces in Germany," 26.

241. Allen, *Rhineland Occupation*, 47–48.

242. See, for example, "Memorandum of the Permanent International Armistice Commission, Control of Occupied Territory, December 3, 1918," in US Dept. of the Army, *United States Army in the World War, 1917–1919*, vol. 10, part 1, 225.

243. See annex in *FRUS, 1919: Paris Peace Conference*, vol. 13, 762–68.

244. Many of the regulations proved ineffective because lines of authority were not well established. See Hunt Report excerpt in US Dept. of the Army, *United States Army in the World War, 1917–1919*, vol. 11, 146–243.

245. Ordinances by the Rhineland High Commission were to be communicated to army commanders, although if they directly affected the armies, the commission was supposed to consult beforehand with commanders. Notes from meeting on June 13, 1919, in US Dept. of State, *FRUS, 1919: Paris Peace Conference*, vol. 5, 385–86.

246. Allen, *Rhineland Occupation*, 119.

247. Hunt Report excerpt in US Dept. of the Army, *United States in the World War, 1917–1919*, vol. 11, 234.

248. On courts, see Hunt Report excerpt, ibid., 170.

249. "American Forces in Germany, Assistant Chief of Staff (G-2), *American Representation in Occupied Germany*," no page number, cited in Rasmussen, "American Forces in Germany," 116–26.

250. Ibid., 173–79.

251. Marshal Foch wanted to exempt the military's purchase of wine from taxes.

252. Rasmussen, "American Forces in Germany," 213. See also Hunt Report excerpt in US Dept. of the Army, *United States Army in the World War, 1917–1919*, vol. 11, 194–95.

253. Quotes from this sentence and the previous one are from "Address of Charles E. Hughes, Secretary of State, before the American Historical Association at New Haven, Connecticut, on December 29th, 1922," reprinted in appendix of Dawes, *Journal of Reparations*, 239.

254. A good discussion of these is contained in Ronald E. Powaski, *Toward an Entangling Alliance: American Isolationism, Internationalism, and Europe, 1901–1950* (New York: Greenwood, 1991), 39.

255. For a discussion of these talks about reparations, which provided a foundation for the end of the occupation, see Dawes, *Journal of Reparations*, preface.

256. As noted, the French wanted to create an independent Rhineland with a new government. See "Action of Third Army on Political Agitation in Rhineland, AGO, GHQ, AEF: 20376-B-104: Telephone Message, May 22, 1919," in US Dept. of the Army, *United States Army in the World War, 1917–1919*, vol. 10, part 2, 1129.

257. US Dept. of the Army, *Military Government: An Historical Approach*, 100.

258. "Suggestions toward Fostering Stable Government in Germany, G-3, GHQ, AEF: Fldr. 1223: Letter from American Section, Permanent International Armistice Commission, April 1, 1919," reprinted in the US Dept. of the Army, *United States Army in the World War, 1917–1919*, vol. 10, part 2, 943.

259. Craig makes this argument in *Germany*, 396.

260. "Marcy to Kearny, January 11, 1847, U.S. Congress, House, California and New Mexico," 31st Cong., 1st sess., *House Executive Document 17* (Washington, 1849), serial no. 573, 44, cited in Grivas, *Military Governments in California*, 48.

261. Quotes are from "Honorable Charles Sumner, 'Our Domestic Relations: Or How to Treat the Rebel States,' Entered According to Act of Congress, in the Year 1863 by Ticknor and Fields, in the Clerk's Office of the District Court of the District of Massachusetts," 508. Electronic document available through the Making of America project at the University of Michigan: http://quod.lib.umich.edu/m/moa/ABJ5672.0001.001/1?g=moag-rp;rgn=full+text;view=image;xc=1;q1=our+domestic+relations.

262. Pierrepont Noyes, *While Europe Waits* (New York: Macmillan, 1921), 42–47, cited in Fraenkel, *Military Occupation and the Rule of Law*, 71.

263. Ash, *When the Yankees Came*, 84, and *Official Records*, vol. 32, series 1, 179–80.

264. Miles cited in Birtle, *U.S. Counterinsurgency and Contingency Operations*, 58.

# THREE

# WORLD WAR II

## BUILDING AN ORGANIZATION

THE INTERWAR YEARS, while relatively quiet for the US Army in terms of military engagements, were full of change regarding its doctrine and organization. By the end of World War I, a massive demobilization had taken place, and only about 130,000 soldiers remained in the regular army, including those occupying the Rhineland.[1] As after every war, debate ensued over the army's appropriate size, composition, and organization. This debate essentially culminated in the National Defense Act of 1920, which codified one of the first major agreements regarding the appropriate mix of army forces. The act reflected an agreement to create a relatively small regular army of 280,000 that would be supplemented by a citizen army drawn from a new organized reserve and a national guard. It balanced Emory Upton's hope of creating a more regular professional army with the views of others who argued that the bulk of America's defenses should rest with its citizen soldiers.

Despite the army's civil affairs experiences in the Rhineland, almost two decades passed before it developed its first real guidance related to military governance. In his assessment of the Rhineland experience, the officer in charge of civil affairs for the Third Army, Col. Irwin Hunt, remarked that it was "extremely unfortunate that in the qualifications necessary for civil administration [were] not developed in times of peace" and that despite the army's earlier experiences, lessons of governance "seemingly have not been learned."[2] Colonel Hunt's report was one of the first comprehensive examinations of the army's occupation experiences as a strategic problem, rather than one, predominantly, of military law and order. During the interwar period, however, the War Department only periodically referred to the Hunt Report.[3] And the army's Bureau of Insular Affairs, created by Elihu Root in 1903, was disbanded in 1939 and absorbed into the US Department of Interior, which shifted its focus from occupation duties abroad to issues related to the management of Native Americans in the United States.[4]

World War I ended with military government being the ad hoc responsibility of the theater commander, with few efforts to systematize thinking about the issue strategically. In 1940 the army's Judge Advocate General (JAG) published *FM 27-10: The Rules of Land Warfare*, but this document focused on the rights and obligations of occupation forces, reiterating the Lieber Code tradition of focusing on rules of conduct and military law. It reflected the prevailing tendency of the Army War College in the 1920s to treat civil affairs and military government as elements of military law.[5] Despite this inclination, on the eve of World War II, some advocates within the army staff and in the army's personnel and operations directorates (called G-1 and G-3, respectively) believed that the broader role of governance functions deserved some attention. They argued that since "American forces [were] now serving in a number of bases in foreign countries . . . there is the possibility of future service of military government by the United States Army. These facts indicate the need of competent personnel for such duties. Their detail from combatant units will deplete the officer strength of such units."[6] Thus, in the years immediately before America's entry into World War II, some staff officers were thinking about broader strategic problems, and the army began to take its first significant steps to formalize civil affairs–related organization and training.

In the midst of this shifting strategic environment, the army's personnel section eventually prevailed on the JAG to write a field manual specifically for military government.[7] The JAG had initially resisted this, arguing that the office had already produced *FM 27-10: The Rules of Land Warfare*, which contained a section on civil administration.[8] The JAG's view reflected the tension between broader governance problems and military law. Nevertheless, in June 1940, the JAG produced *FM 27-5: Military Government*, drawing on many of the army's past experiences, particularly in the Rhineland.[9]

*FM 27-5* illustrated the army's view of the dual role of military governance. On one level, the document reflected a "tactical" understanding of civil affairs—the need to prevent civilians from interfering in combat operations and the need to preserve military security. On the other hand, the document attached strategic importance to governance tasks, noting that the goal of "any war is to obtain a favorable and enduring peace" and that the "just, considerate, and mild treatment of the governed by the occupying power will convert enemies into friends."[10] The 1943 version of *Military Government* contained a more explicit recognition of the strategic value of military government.[11] It maintained that military government could promote military and political objectives "in connection with future operations" and that it could extend beyond combat operations until it achieved "the ends of national policy toward which the operations are directed."[12] FM 27-5 viewed military government as an instrument of American policy and an instrument for the consolidation of political order in defeated countries.

FM 27-5 also clarified several key principles that had actually emerged in previous operations.[13] First, it reiterated the army's preference to vest full authority in the commanding general in the theater. Second, it reaffirmed the army's preference for retaining existing civilian personnel, institutions, laws, and customs "when practicable." The manual also offered a clear role for tactical forces in military governments. It described scenarios in which an occupying power would need to exercise the functions of civil government, noting, "military government is the organization through which it does so." The manual also noted the role that tactical forces could play in governance operations, explaining that personnel could be reassigned from combat units to military government duties when hostilities subsided, since civil affairs activities could "in the long run prove an economy" by lessening the need for garrison forces. It supported the use of tactical units as "organs" of military government and specified that each tactical unit would have a civil affairs section corresponding to the unit's size. When a tactical unit was moved, its civil affairs section could remain behind to provide some continuity.[14] The manual discussed the use of tactical forces for civil affairs duties, recognizing that they could play an important role in governance tasks.

FM 27-5 recognized the importance of military necessity and of retaining flexibility in a theater.[15] Although the manual noted that the commanding general's staff could include up to nine specific departments,[16] it let civil affairs officers prioritize among departments, allowing situational decisions to override formal guidance. While the practical utility of these field manuals is debatable, FM 27-5 provided a basic template for planning specific operations in Germany, Japan, Italy, Korea, and North Africa. Furthermore, it was the most comprehensive document to date regarding civil affairs and military government and, more important, seemed to have incorporated some of the key lessons from past operations. The publication of this guidance, however, still left most of the operational decisions in the hands of the theater commander. Indeed, FM 27-5 clearly stated that the exercise of military government was a "command responsibility," with full "legislative, executive and judicial authority" vested in the commanding general of the theater.[17]

The publication of guidance related to military government suggested that the army officially recognized that it would likely conduct governance operations in the future. This in turn spurred the development of a more formal training apparatus for such operations. FM 27-5 allotted responsibility for the planning of military government and the training of personnel to the G-1 section of the War Department General Staff.[18] Nevertheless, practical considerations determined that the provost marshal, who already controlled training for military policing, should receive the responsibilities for military government instruction. The army's G-1, as well as the representatives from its G-3, disagreed with the placement of military government functions under the provost marshal because he traditionally focused on the narrower area of military policing.[19] While the army grappled with the issue of where to locate governance functions within its broader organization, it began to recognize that such tasks could affect operations in the wartime theater and thus deserved more serious consideration. In the fall of 1942, civil-military coordination problems encountered by Lt. Gen. Dwight D. Eisenhower during Operation Torch in North Africa were a key impetus toward a reconsideration of civil-military relationships in a theater of war. These problems spurred arguments within the army about the appropriate direction and administration of military government. Operation Torch, initiated because of Great Britain's desire for early action against the Axis powers, created confusion among civil and military officials over the appropriate administration of the region. Many argued that such activities should belong "wholly to the military command" and that if there was "one outstanding lesson to be gained from prior American experiences in military government, it is the unwisdom of permitting any premature interference by civilian agencies with the army's basic task of civil administration in occupied areas."[20] Documents from this period reveal that military and civilian authorities debated the appropriate chain of command over civil matters. In the 1942 invasion of North Africa, General Eisenhower had been frustrated by the system of divided control.[21] Before the invasion, Gen. George C. Marshall anticipated that civil affairs would be an important part of the mission, so he created a civil administrative section on his staff to coordinate political matters.[22] Robert M. Murphy, a former political officer in France, assumed leadership of this new section in North Africa. General Eisenhower wrote to Marshall, stating that he wanted a single staff authority over all of the representatives of the various agencies that would soon descend "like locusts" on the region.[23] Army officials were determined to rise above the morass of civilian planning efforts. Eisenhower complained about the potential problems of dividing authority in the theater and made it clear that Murphy should work through him, as the commanding general in the theater: "I hesitate to raise an issue which might cause you embarrassment . . . [but] as I am responsible for the success of the operations I feel that is it essential that final authority in all matters in the theater rest in me, . . . with Mr. Murphy as my operating executive and advisor for civil affairs."[24] Eisenhower's view reaffirmed the point in the army's 1940 manual: Military necessity required military control of civil affairs in the theater.[25] This theme, which had emerged in earlier governance operations, suggests that the army was less concerned about governance operations per se and more concerned with ensuring control over activities that could affect events in the military theater as a whole.

During this period, the assistant secretary of war, John J. McCloy, traveled to North Africa and returned with the recommendation to create the CAD to advise the secretary of war and the chief of staff on nonmilitary matters "in areas occupied as the result of military operations."[26] The CAD was one of five new special staff divisions on the General Staff created during the General Marshall reorganizations of 1942–43 and marked the War Department's first effort to centralize thinking and control over occupation-related activities and to consider the central role that the army would play in occupation-related tasks. With the creation of the CAD, primary responsibility for civil affairs and military government shifted from the personnel section of the General Staff to a separate military government staff section, G-5.[27] The new section issued instructions to the theater commanders, though the provost marshal still ran civil affairs training.[28] Maj. Gen. John H. Hilldring, the former army personnel chief, became chief of the CAD and remained in that position throughout the war.

This decision addressed General Eisenhower's concerns by establishing the army's first organization for dealing with civil affairs matters. The creation of the new CAD also helped to overcome a previous obstacle to the army's assertion of greater control over civil affairs, which was that jurisdiction over such matters had spanned across many offices—for example, the PMG, its personnel sections, and its operations division. More unified control within the War Department would help the army exert control over civil affairs in the theater by creating "a central clearing house on civil affairs."[29] The creation of the new division recognized that these functions were not being adequately addressed by existing organizations, since the G-1 focused on personnel issues and requirements, while the PMG focused on training and military police issues. The creation of the G-5 and the CAD recognized that the planning function for governance-related activities needed attention as well.

The creation of a separate CAD also marked an important departure from the tendency to consider civil affairs within the military-policing functions of the army.[30] The new division superseded the small military government section within the PMG and was outside the purview of the PMG. This development suggested a growing appreciation for the broader role of civil affairs and military government and for the role of governance tasks outside military-policing functions. Until 1940 policing duties and governance tasks were often intermingled. This tended to reaffirm the approach to civil affairs as a "law and order" function within the military and a consideration of governance-related tasks within the army's constabulary functions. Before World War II, civil affairs and policing functions were conducted mainly by tactical forces anyway, and the nature of the tasks—from keeping law and order to establishing new authorities over a region—often overlapped.

This separation had also occurred during the Civil War, with the creation of a separate PMG staff. These specialized provost marshal units served as law enforcement officers charged with ensuring that new laws in the South were followed and to control raiding and marauding.[31] Following the Civil War experience with provost marshals and the army's experiences during World War I, it retained the provost marshal position and functions, with provost marshals overseeing some civil affairs and police tasks. As noted previously, however, some in the army began to argue that civil affairs and governance involved broader duties than policing.

In the spring of 1942, the War Department established a training school specifically for civil affairs (though this training still fell under the PMG's purview). The School of Military Government, located in Charlottesville,

Virginia, trained individuals in the new CAD who "may reasonably be expected to operate a military government."[32] Some on the army staff resisted this diversion of soldiers from combat responsibilities to what they believed was a postwar mission.[33] By early 1943, the school had graduated only two classes, with army civil affairs officers numbering around 130.[34] The debate surrounding the creation of the school revealed the army's uncertainty about governance tasks. Equally important, it revealed that civilian concerns over military government played a role in shaping the army's conduct of governance operations. Although some argued that military government was essentially a variant of the army's existing police functions, others, such as the assistant army chief of staff, argued that military government was broader in scope than military police activities and that training should remain distinct.[35]

A broader view of military government began to gain adherents. Officers from existing army units attended the Charlottesville school, as did officers commissioned from civilian life. The army also developed a month-long training course at Fort Custer, Michigan, and created civil affairs training schools (CATS) on university and college campuses around the country.[36] The CATS program lasted about eight weeks, and the courses specialized in a particular region and language. Much of this training was fairly general, resembling "basic university courses dealing with history and civilization of Western Europe." They included courses on army regulations, policing, military law, general principles of military government, histories of previous occupations, public administration, and general information about countries. The army's philosophy was to train personnel so that they could lay the groundwork for the restoration of political and economic life in the occupied territories. A principle behind the programs was that "military government is best which governs least." This approach was consistent with the kind of administration that evolved on the ground in countries before, during, and even after World War II. Secretary Marcy's instructions regarding "indirect rule" had established the US preference for using local officials when possible, and the army's governance philosophy emphasized supervision rather than detailed administration unless absolutely necessary.

## CIVIL-MILITARY TENSIONS

The creation of a War Department organization to conduct civil affairs and military government sparked significant civilian concerns. Two somewhat contradictory viewpoints emerged. First, some argued that military government was a dangerous notion, as it placed too much power in the hands of the military. At the same time, many of these very same individuals acknowledged that no other organization in a theater of war was well suited to conduct such tasks. President Roosevelt believed that military government was "both strange and somewhat abhorrent,"[37] but he also realized that if "prompt results" were desired, the army would "have to assume the initial burden" of military government.[38]

After the opening of the Charlottesville school, a prominent official wrote, "No task undertaken by the Army produced more misunderstanding at the high levels of the government."[39] Some accused the army's JAG of being "fascist," and others warned that army planning for military government would be a threat but that since civilians seemed to "lack a comprehensive plan and a unified purpose," they were in danger of "of losing the postwar world by default."[40] Presidential adviser Harold Ickes noted that the army's "ambitious" plans filled him with "grave misgivings" and that "if a stop is not put to them . . . we are headed for the worse kind of trouble."[41] President Roosevelt continued to maintain that governance was a civilian task and civilian administrators should be installed in occupied areas.[42] Even by the end of World War II, President Truman expressed misgivings about the military's acquisition of governmental responsibilities.[43]

Despite the reluctance of US political leaders to give the army too much control over administrative matters, military necessity prevailed. Secretary of State James F. Byrnes maintained that while the State Department should retain policy oversight and control, the army should control administrative and logistical matters.[44] He believed that the State Department did not have the capacity to run an occupation and that trying to do so would degrade its ability to "define wisely important foreign policies."[45] Secretary of War Henry Stimson agreed that military government was a "natural and inevitable" result of military operations in areas where friendly governments did not exist, and he viewed the army's experiences as a "bright page in American history."[46] During the 1942 debate about civil affairs in North Africa, Secretary Stimson argued that the military governor's authority stemmed from the power of the president as commander in chief and that the War Department's past successes with military government suggested that it was well suited to accomplishing such tasks. Stimson argued vigorously to allow General Eisenhower control over civil affairs in the theater, stating that the State Department's primary role was that of diplomatic adviser to the military governor, since it was not up to the task of administering territory.

Despite Stimson's view, there were few indications that the army was eager to assume governance duties. General Eisenhower's experiences in North Africa merely reaffirmed the view that military necessity drove the army's efforts to control governance tasks. The general argued that because he was responsible for the success of overall operations, he should retain "final authority in all [other] matters" in the theater.[47] The North African experience revealed that it was difficult to exert both civilian and military authority over the same territory.[48] General Eisenhower's chief of staff, Brig. Gen. Walter Bedell Smith, believed that Americans would not accept the idea of government exercised by military officers.[49] Later, before his appointment as military governor of Germany, Lt. Gen. Lucius Clay believed that it would be difficult to convince officers there that the army's civil functions would soon become "its primary mission."[50]

It is important to avoid confusing the army's objective of retaining unity of command with a desire for political control per se, as there is little evidence of the latter. The chief of the War Department's CAD expressed his views unequivocally: The army was not a "welfare organization," and its "interest and activities in military government and civil affairs administration [was] incidental to the accomplishment of the military mission. . . . [A lack of] social stability in an occupied area would be prejudicial to the success of the military effort."[51] This reasoning seemed to be behind the army's insistence that the tactical commander retain control over all operations in the theater. The army believed that leadership over military government was a short-term necessity,[52] essential to ensuring unity of command because it was the "sole agency capable of initiating the reconstruction process."[53] The prevailing view among military and civilian leaders was that civilian agencies would eventually take over governance functions.[54] General Clay wrote that he and Eisenhower intended to build an organization that could "be transferred bodily to a civil branch of government."[55] Months after the establishment of military government in Germany, Clay informed army commanders that the War Department believed military government was not a job for soldiers and should be turned over to the political side as soon as possible.[56]

As the Allies won their first combat victories in Europe, the United States began to consider the likelihood that military occupations would be a key part of the war, since US leaders believed that combat victory would not be complete unless it was accompanied by the political transformation of key states. Consistent with the army's earlier experiences, two basic schools of thought regarding military government emerged. First, some emphasized that governance operations in each theater would play a critical combat-service-support role by keeping lines of communication open, ensuring that civilians did not interfere with combat operations, and consolidating combat victories in rear areas.[57] Second, some US leaders believed that governance operations could have lasting strategic value. General Marshall felt that military government could transform individuals in liberated countries into "fighting allies."[58] An army instruction manual at the time noted that occupation was considered a "natural consequence of conflict" and a "burden or a privilege, depending upon the philosophy of the conqueror."[59]

As the army embarked on its governance experiences during World War II, it had emerged from the interwar period with several important views that guided its approach to governance tasks in the wartime theater. First, the army believed that it should retain control over military government tasks, owing to military necessity. Second, although the army sought control over the implementation of governance tasks, military leaders did not assume that they could be the sole repository of expertise required for governance operations. Instead, they sought the advice of other agencies and intended to transition governance activities to civilian control as soon as possible. Third, for the first time, with the creation of a separate planning and training structure for civil affairs, military government was separated from the policing structure within the army organization. This suggested the emergence of a broader strategic appreciation for the role of governance tasks.

Overall, through the reconstruction of governments in Italy, Germany, Japan, and Korea, the army served as a critical instrument of political change in Europe and Asia, as well as a key instrument for shifting the strategic landscape to favor US interests during the Cold War. Although each of these operations involved different degrees of planning and differences in execution, all four, as will be seen, could be broken down into two main categories: political oversight and political reconstruction. In some cases, such as Korea and Japan, the army worked through existing civil administrative structures, shaping developments to favor US interests. In others, such as Italy and Germany, more concerted efforts to replace government personnel took place.

The military governments established in Italy, Germany, Japan, and Korea following World War II became synonymous with the army's governance experiences. Given the extensive nature of these operations, they tended to overshadow previous and subsequent army governance operations. While critically important, the consolidation and reconstruction tasks undertaken by army forces during World War II in Italy, Germany, Japan, and Korea actually *reinforced* many of the army's past experiences and highlighted problems and issues that would reappear in *future* operations. Furthermore, they illustrated that in cases of conventional war such operations were integral parts of strategic victory.

# ITALY

US policymakers viewed an Allied victory over Italy as a step toward eliminating a key Axis power from the war and reducing the overall burden on the Allies. Although the Mediterranean operation was a "sideshow" compared to the priority of a cross-Channel invasion,[60] it involved planning for long-term stability and the transformation of Italy into a democratic state. General Eisenhower recognized that the imposition of a friendly regime in Italy would be necessary but was concerned about the timing of an occupation and whether it should be done from the outset or after German forces had been defeated.[61] He appreciated that the Italian operation would set an important precedent and recognized from the outset that "the period of occupation will be much longer than the period of the assault." Other army officials also seemed to appreciate the importance of an occupation of Italy, believing that "the character and efficiency of the civil administration of the area will influence the will of the Italian people and armed forces to resist in subsequent operations."[62] American planners also hoped to develop a system of administration that would take advantage of the "good will" they believed most Italians had for Americans.[63]

In late 1942, the State Department had conducted a study of Italy examining what a postwar interim government would look like. Eventually, the United States agreed that the Italian monarchy, the House of Savoy, could be allowed to form an interim government under Allied supervision. By March 1943, a basic plan for the occupation existed, drafted primarily by US Army lieutenant colonel Charles Spofford, who had studied previous American and British operations and existing army field manuals and produced an "Appreciation and Outline Plan for Military Government in Sicily."[64] The plan advocated joint Anglo-American responsibility and administration by military personnel, with the commanding general also serving as military governor.

The Spofford plan envisaged that civil affairs personnel would arrive in the theater early but that as long as combat continued, the commanding general would retain control. The plan excluded civil political representatives (such as Robert Murphy in North Africa), which meant that the Combined Chiefs of Staff would be the primary channel of communication to the American and British governments.

A key issue in planning for the Italian operation was how to balance US and British concerns over the development of appropriate command-and-control arrangements for the occupation. British and American officials eventually agreed to the establishment of a joint military government, whereby one British and one American would head the occupation, but each would remain under the overall control of the commanding general, Eisenhower. Unlike most of the army's previous governance operations, a basic operational organization for governance existed before the actual arrival of American forces in Italy. On May 1, 1943, three months before the invasion, the Allied Military Government of Italy (AMGOT) was created. A British officer, Maj. Gen. Lord Rennell, served as AMGOT's chief, with Colonel Spofford serving as his deputy. On one level, AMGOT served a tactical purpose to ensure the security of occupying forces and lines of communication, relieve combat troops of the need to provide for civil administration, restore law and order, and provide economic resources to Allied troops as needed. It was also, however, charged with the broader goal of promoting the "overall political and military objectives of allied forces."[65] Although these objectives and some preparations existed before the arrival of US forces in Italy, several key uncertainties remained. US political leaders had not agreed on what the final Italian government should look like, and many believed that the character of the government (e.g., whether it would remain a monarchy) could be settled after the war by the Italians themselves.[66]

### Developing an Organization for Governance

Army leaders faced two separate but related challenges as they arrived in Sicily. First, they needed to organize command-and-control relationships between civil affairs officers and combat units. In Italy, as in subsequent occupations, army leaders wanted tactical commanders to remain in control through the assault and combat phases of the war. Army officials were wary of repeating the coordination problems experienced in North Africa and aimed to keep the chain of command in military channels.[67] General Marshall did not want a situation that would "deprive" Lt. Gen. George S. Patton Jr., commander of the Seventh Army, and his tactical commanders of any authority over civil affairs, "as long as their troops are present in the area."[68]

Second, army officers needed to create an organization that would allow civil affairs officers to provide adequate support to combat units while also beginning the administration of defeated territories in rear areas. About one hundred military government / civil affairs officers landed with the First, Third, and Forty-Fifth Divisions, the Seventh Army, and the Eighth Army.[69] The civil affairs officers who accompanied the Eighth Army undertook civil affairs functions in areas of fighting but were also expected to administer rear areas even though the skeletal staff made this requirement virtually impossible to accomplish.[70] During the first few days of the invasion, the numbers of military government personnel were small: Just sixteen officers were assigned to the Seventh Army and thirty to the Eighth Army.[71] These spaces were viewed as "luxuries" by the commanding officers, who did not want military government officers there at the expense of tactical combat troops.

The pressure of managing mobile military governments while keeping an eye on governance needs in expanding rear areas resulted in the division of AMGOT. While military government was in place in the south, fighting continued to engulf much of northern Italy until Germany's surrender in April 1945. Officials argued that one headquarters could not handle both jobs, and thus, a dual structure emerged, with AMGOT dividing into two headquarters in October 1943. A mobile American Military Government (AMG), attached to the Fifteenth Army Group, accompanied field armies through Italy and could be more responsive to the needs of military combat units. A static AMG headquarters in Palermo administered rear areas.[72] This division balanced the needs of combat with those of reconstruction challenges.

Army personnel faced two broad sets of challenges during the reconstruction phase in Italy. First, combat troops needed to begin to address the requirements of the civilian population. Second, as the situation in Italy stabilized, army commanders came under pressure to consolidate all military government functions back under one organization. The dual structure that had emerged was a reflection of Eisenhower's insistence that military government units adapt to the needs of combat troops, but it also bred confusion, with civil affairs officers from the mobile military government teams and from the static headquarters promulgating different policies around the country. Pressure grew in late 1943 to unify control over military government and promote more uniform policies. The chief civil affairs officer of the Fifteenth

Army Group, General Lord Rennell, believed that the decentralized situation was "intolerable." Eisenhower, however, argued that as long as combat continued, mobile military government units should remain under tactical control to "insure that civil affairs are so conducted as to meet military requirements on the spot."[73]

Eventually, the Allied Control Commission was established in November 1943 in an effort to coordinate governance-related policies.[74] Because the president of the council was also the Allied commander in chief and the military governor, General Eisenhower's concerns about unity of command were addressed. The military governor delegated most of the civil affairs functions to a chief civil affairs officer (CAO). A territorial type of military government emerged, following the patterns of local Italian governments. A CAO assigned to one of Italy's six regions supervised local officials and worked with them to implement reconstruction goals. In some areas, CAOs from across various regions would try to meet to coordinate activities and maintain uniform policies.[75]

### Political and Economic Reconstruction

Military government in Italy essentially implemented the objectives set forth in the 1943 Moscow Declaration, which called for the removal of Fascist elements from Italian life, the creation of democratic organs and constitutional reforms, the arrest of war criminals, the reestablishment of a judicial system, and the creation of a new educational system. President Roosevelt outlined US goals in Italy in his July 1943 fireside chat, when he called for Italy's unconditional surrender and announced that Americans would help the Italian nation "reconstitute herself." Following Benito Mussolini's resignation and the reconstitution of a new government headed by Marshal Pietro Badoglio, who had the support of the Italian king, the United States hoped to establish a broad coalition government that balanced competing factions—anti-Fascists, Fascists, and Communists—so that they could all participate in a future government.[76] As the United States considered the character of this new government, it was also negotiating with the interim government over the terms of the armistice. In September 1943, Marshal Badoglio signed the Long Armistice agreement with the United States, which placed Italy under Allied military control and set the stage for Italy's declaration of war against Germany.

The removal of Fascists from Italian political institutions was a central element of political reconstruction in Italy. This process was sometimes referred to as epuration and was subject to criticism.[77] Allied military officers created new regional governments in Italy, staffing them with new administrators, but as they did, they sought to find an appropriate balance between purging former Fascists and avoiding complete administrative breakdown.[78] Army officers issued proclamations ordering the dissolution of the Fascist Party and its affiliated organizations and established procedures to screen out Fascist officials. In practice, epuration proceeded in an uncoordinated manner, with no centralized guidance, and thus, the process unfolded differently across Italy's regions.[79] Army personnel made efforts to develop a nuanced policy, to take into account the situation of specific individuals, and to give officers involved some leeway in making final judgments regarding individuals.[80]

While the military government succeeded in removing some elements of the old regime, it was later criticized for conducting a policy that was not well developed and lacked the authority of a single controlling agency.[81] The United States hoped that the interim government would take charge of the purge to establish its legitimacy and to offset the criticism of those who blamed the US for problems related to defascization.[82] Through 1943 and 1944, a broader political spectrum of Italians became involved in political life, and by January 1944, Italians were permitted to participate in political activities as long as they were orderly. In early 1944, six parties existed and had formed coalitions to function until national elections could take place. In the fall of 1945, a consultative assembly met in Rome, allowing Italian politicians to begin participating in politics again.

Despite initial American reluctance to become deeply involved in Italian political life, from the start of the occupation US military and political leaders grappled with choices about which type of government to support in Italy, particularly as the power of the Soviet-backed Communists grew. From 1943 to 1944, the United States and Britain debated which post-Mussolini government to support. Prime Minister Churchill advocated support for a regime that could bring the war in Italy to an end quickly, stating that he would support any Italian authority that could "deliver the goods" and "make the Italians do what we need for our war purposes," even if it meant dealing with the Italian king.[83] The United States agreed to support Marshal Badoglio's government (and the Italian king) temporarily, since President Roosevelt was still committed to self-determination for the Italians as soon as the situation on the ground stabilized.[84]

The political transition in Italy required not only the removal of former Fascists, but also minimizing the growing power of the Italian Communist parties and ensuring the creation of a broad-based government. The growing tensions between the Italian Communist movement, supported by the Soviets, and the emerging Christian Democratic and Socialist groups forced US military and civilian leaders to reassess earlier reluctance to become deeply involved in Italian politics. And a central part of the longer-term success of any newly elected Italian official would be the strength and stabilization of the Italian economy. Initially, army officials approached the problem of economic stabilization from the perspective of relief and rehabilitation—their objective was to minimize conditions that could result in civilian unrest and interfere with military operations.[85] In the fall of 1943, Assistant Secretary of War McCloy wrote to Harry Hopkins, one of President Roosevelt's closest advisers, that "so far as Army responsibility for relief is concerned it should be confined to subsistence levels."[86] As noted earlier, army officials had hoped that civilian relief agencies would take over, although Secretary of War Stimson expressed frustration that the War Department was expected to develop long-range plans without clear guidance. He urged the State Department to offer guidance so that the military would know US objectives. Stimson reiterated his view that the military's purpose should be immediate rehabilitation.[87]

However, as the occupation unfolded, pressure grew for the military government to implement a longer-term program of economic aid. The Allied Control Commission believed that if the military government continued to consider "only what is essential to the interests of the war effort, [it might] lose the opportunity of ensuring the creation of a reasonably prosperous and contented postwar Italy."[88] The State Department now argued that Italy had become a US government "responsibility," and Assistant Secretary of State Dean Acheson urged the army to "broaden its views on the relief problem . . . until some other international relief agency could take over the job."[89] As the army worked out these broader policy issues, it was also engaged in more specific day-to-day tasks to reestablish a functioning Italian economy. The military supervised the creation of a central bank, reorganized the Ministry of Finance, and attempted to streamline the Italian tax-collection system. The military government also became involved in price-control issues, and officials developed programs to control inflation.[90] Military government officials also worked to repair the shattered Italian transportation system, which was central to long-term economic stabilization.

The Allied military government also sought to reform Italy's judicial system.[91] The military government's objective of replacing Fascism with democracy required not only changes in Italian institutions but also its laws. It accomplished this task with relatively few personnel and drafted proclamations and general orders, some of which formed the basis for new legislation.[92] The overall goal was to return the bulk of court cases to the Italian courts and lay a foundation for restoring the Italian government. As in previous governance operations, the military government also created special military courts to try civilians charged with offenses against the military government. Judicial officers of the military government served on these courts. Special courts were also established to deal with more complicated cases and the sequestering of property. Allied military government officials also worked to improve prison conditions and to ensure that prisoners received timely trials or were released; Italian police were directed to discontinue the practice of holding civilians in jail pending investigation. A key question for the military government was the extent to which it should rely on existing Italian law enforcement structures to preserve law and order. Complicating this judgment was the poor level of intelligence about existing Italian police organizations. Initially, many Italian paramilitary organizations, such as the Carabinieri, were targeted as military entities and their members jailed.[93] Eventually, the military government's public safety division worked with the Carabinieri, which led to a shift of their initial views of the national policemen as "useless" to "sufficiently improved" so that "their worth [was] now deemed invaluable."[94]

Army officers also developed food-production and agricultural policies. In combat zones, military government officers focused on the immediate needs of the populace. As the rear areas stabilized, they worked to revise the existing policy of relying on food imports to meet Italy's needs and instead devised ways to increase Italian food production. One CAO remarked that the food situation in Sicily was "the most serious preoccupation of the administration."[95] CAD guidance urged the military government to rehabilitate agriculture production in the theater in order to reduce demand on US and UK food supplies.[96] Although little advance planning had taken place in the area of educational reform, once in place army officials became deeply involved in this area as well.[97] They opened schools as quickly as possible, improved the safety of buildings, revised the content of school curricula, and checked the political background of teachers. Similar to what would occur later in Japan, army personnel also encouraged more local involvement in education through the establishment of provincial educational committees.

After the retirement of the Italian king in June 1944 and the establishment of a new republic in June 1946, a general amnesty was declared, allowing the transfer of control from the military government directly back to the newly elected Italian government. The emergence of the new republic, however, did not mean the disengagement of the United States. The withdrawal of American occupying forces only heightened the need for continued American economic and political engagement in Italy in order to ensure that the gains of the war would not be lost to the increasing strength of the Italian Communist Party.

Throughout the spring of 1946 and into the spring of 1948, US political leaders debated the appropriate amount of aid to Italy. Many US policymakers, as well as activists in the Italian American community, argued that unless the Italian economy was strengthened, the country would fall to the Communists.[98] George Kennan argued that if the "Communists were to win election there our whole position in Mediterranean, and possibly in western Europe as well, would probably be undermined."[99] These arguments were countered by those who believed that the United States could not afford the diversion of assistance to Italy.[100] Overall, however, with the Truman administration's growing concerns about the intentions of the Soviet Union and unrest in Greece (which sparked the announcement of the Truman Doctrine), many in the policy community viewed Italy as a bulwark against the growing Soviet threat. Policy officials in Washington argued that Italy needed assistance before the Marshall Plan began. These arguments prevailed, and Congress voted for interim aid to Italy in December 1947.[101] In addition to continued economic support for Italy, the United States decided to actively back the Christian Democrats there, hoping to create a government that could withstand Communist pressure.[102] In April 1948, in the aftermath of the Communist coup in Czechoslovakia, a Christian Democratic government led by Prime Minister Alcide De Gasperi won electoral victory against the Popular Front, an alliance of the Communist and Socialist Parties. Eventually, as concerns about Soviet power and intentions over Western Europe grew, the Popular Front parties in Italy were excluded from the Italian government.[103]

Although some believed that the military government in Italy was too limited in its aims, it accomplished a great deal.[104] Occupation forces in Italy were the key instrument through which many of the objectives set forth in the 1943 Moscow Declaration were realized.[105] They removed many Fascist elements from the Italian government, created more democratic administrative structures, reestablished a judiciary and educational system, arrested war criminals, and provided the foundation for new democratic elections. Governance operations in Italy revealed the importance of stabilizing rear areas while combat in forward areas continued and forced the army to manage political concerns and the pressures of combat simultaneously.

## GERMANY

Well before America's formal entry into World War II, US military and political leaders anticipated that a change in Germany's political and economic order would be required. The United States conducted extensive planning for governance operations in Germany,[106] anticipating that the United States would be responsible for Germany's reconstruction.[107] Planning within diplomatic and military channels took place. US civilian and military officials debated the character of an occupation at meetings of War and State Department committees such as the State-War-Navy Coordinating Committee (SWNCC), the European Advisory Committee (EAC) in London, and at the series of foreign minister conferences throughout the war.[108] In addition to these political discussions, several different military planning organizations— the Joint Chiefs of Staff (JCS), the War Department's CAD, and Supreme Headquarters Allied Expeditionary Forces (SHAEF)—developed operational plans for an occupation of Germany.

At the 1943 Moscow Conference, the United States presented an early plan for the postwar treatment of Germany. At the conference, President Roosevelt had instructed Secretary of State Cordell Hull to explore "the question of what our plan is to be in Germany and Italy during the first months after Germany's collapse."[109] Hull described a shared US-British-Soviet occupation, with a commission to enforce Allied policies. The plan anticipated the emergence of new political parties in Germany, elections, and the reestablishment of a central German government. It also assumed that eventual responsibility for the administration of Germany would be transferred from military to civilian institutions.

These earlier conferences did not result in agreement about the character of a German occupation, and civilian and military planners continued to debate this issue through 1944.[110] At the September 1944 Quebec Conference, Secretary of the Treasury Henry Morgenthau presented a plan to punish Germany by prohibiting its reindustrialization and to transform it into an agricultural state, thus undercutting the possibility of a resurgent German war potential.[111] The State Department, supported by some War Department officials, opposed Morgenthau's approach, arguing that some self-sufficiency for Germany should be permitted.[112] This disagreement set the stage for the development of an alternative plan produced by the JCS and known as JCS 1067.[113] Approved by the president in late 1944, JCS 1067, "Directive to the Commander in Chief of US Forces of Occupation Regarding the Military Government of Germany in the Period Immediately following the Cessation of Organized Resistance," reflected an effort to tone down some of the harshest elements of the Morgenthau Plan.[114] In JCS 1067, the army assumed that Germany would require extensive administrative control.[115] It contained guidance about preventing the resurgence of German power, demilitarizing Germany's military, and dissolving the Nazi Party. Relief supplies would be permitted to prevent disease and disorder.[116] JCS 1067 was an important planning document for the army's occupation of Germany and contributed to the development of the Eclipse operational plan that emerged later that year.[117] Furthermore, it revealed that military officials were involved in thinking about the broader strategic objectives of a proposed occupation, not merely its operational details.

Several competing tensions shaped the development of JCS 1067. President Roosevelt was reluctant to make too many concrete decisions regarding the postwar treatment of Germany.[118] He disliked "making detailed plans for a country which we do not yet occupy [since the details] were dependent on what we and the Allies find when we get into Germany, and we are not there yet."[119] To a certain degree army leaders endorsed this position, since they wanted flexibility and control once in the theater. The War Department's concerns about retaining military control over operations in the theater drove its CAD to oppose the State Department plan to create zones of occupation in Germany. The War Department argued that such zones were a "military matter" that should be determined by the location of troops at the time of Germany's collapse.[120] Through 1943 civil affairs representatives in the War Department had reportedly been given "strict instructions to agree to nothing."[121] Since the JCS directive focused on the "initial post-defeat period," it was not considered an "ultimate statement" of policy and thus safeguarded the army's goal of retaining flexibility in the theater. Thus, JCS 1067 managed to satisfy the War Department's desire for guidance while balancing Roosevelt's view that detailed policy should not be developed until the country was actually occupied.[122] The document hedged against both demands by giving military government staffs a "long-awaited basic statement of policy for the post-hostilities period."[123]

Although army organizations in Europe underwent many changes, through all of these various transitions a group of staff officers planned for occupation.[124] The Allied strategic planning agency Chief of Staff to Supreme Allied Commander (COSSAC) studied the possibility of an unconditional surrender and developed an occupation plan called Rankin.[125] Rankin focused on securing areas of Germany and provided basic instructions to army groups and other tactical units on how to prepare for the occupation. A Post-Hostilities Planning Section in COSSAC and its CAD (which evolved into a G-5 staff division) considered problems related to Germany's surrender. When SHAEF replaced COSSAC, it absorbed the latter's governance-planning functions, and by the spring of 1944 SHAEF had completed some seventy posthostilities studies.[126] A special staff to SHAEF, the German Country Unit (GCU), included some 150 British and American officers who produced functional manuals on public safety and education, local and regional government, and other administrative issues.[127] In February 1944, a civil affairs training apparatus emerged in Europe to prepare troops for occupation duties.[128] The European Civil Affairs Division (ECAD) was created to administer civil affairs personnel in the European theater and to serve as their "parent organization."[129] It was considered odd because it had no field command functions, and personnel assigned to the ECAD received orders through the tactical units to which they were attached.[130]

Following the cross-Channel invasion in June 1944, the Rankin plan evolved into Operation Eclipse. Eclipse considered issues such as terms of surrender, disarmament, treatment of police and paramilitary organizations, arrest of war criminals, establishment of law and order, administration of military government, and treatment of displaced persons (DPs) and prisoners of war (POWs).[131] Eclipse envisioned a clear division between the combat phase and the beginning of the occupation: Eclipse would be implemented after certain conditions were met.

The extensive army planning, supplemented by political-military planning in Washington, suggests that political and military leaders considered the reconstruction of Germany an integral part of the war effort. By early 1945, many of these political and military plans for the occupation of Germany coalesced at the Yalta and Potsdam Conferences.[132] At Yalta the allies agreed to partition Germany into four zones, and at Potsdam they developed details for the administration of each zone. The Potsdam agreements set forth economic objectives, including measures to prevent a rebuilding of Germany's war potential, to develop agriculture and peaceful domestic industries, to maintain a "balanced economy" to encourage a reduction in imports, to enlarge coal production, to maximize agricultural output, and to repair transportation networks.

Each zone commander had the power to disarm and demilitarize Germany, destroy the Nazi Party and its institutions, and "prepare for the eventual reconstruction of German political life on a democratic basis." A commission composed of the supreme commanders of each zone would coordinate policies of the four occupying powers. At the Potsdam Conference, Allied leaders essentially endorsed the conduct of an extensive political reconstruction program by military forces.

### Developing an Organization for Governance

The Potsdam Agreement provided general guidance for military officers, but the major issue facing army officers in theater was how to manage combat and governance operations simultaneously. Because army governance operations in Germany began while combat was still under way, *tactical units* from the army's Twelfth and Sixth Army Groups began to undertake administrative tasks as they entered Germany.[133] General Eisenhower showed flexibility by recognizing that conditions for the occupation might arise sooner than anticipated and that therefore Eclipse might need to be implemented in parts of Germany as combat operations continued.[134] Some of the army's earlier plans had developed the idea of "pinpointing" specific military government detachments to German *Stadt* and *Landkreise* (urban and rural districts). These plans anticipated deploying military government detachments throughout the occupied territories.[135] But since American troops moved into Germany so swiftly, there were not enough military government detachments available in rear areas, leaving tactical units to set up military governments and administer towns before the collapse of Berlin.[136] It is important to note that the G-5 staffs of the armies joined them late, which meant that they had limited opportunities to integrate with regular army staffs or to develop detailed organizational arrangements.[137] As a result, tactical officers played a large role in developing and implementing aspects of governance tasks.

Following Germany's unconditional surrender, the commanders in chief of each sector retained supreme authority.[138] The US Forces, European Theater (USFET) replaced SHAEF, and the commanding general of the USFET, General Eisenhower, became the military governor of Germany, enjoying "supreme legislative, executive and judicial power."[139] As in virtually all of the army's previous governance experiences, Eisenhower faced the immediate challenge of developing an operational organization for military government. This task fell in practice to the then deputy military governor, General Clay. A West

Point graduate and engineer, Clay had served as a deputy to Eisenhower and as deputy director for war programs in the Office of War Mobilization and Reconversion. President Roosevelt had "handpicked" Clay to head the German occupation.[140] Although eager to get back to Germany, Clay had hoped for a field command and was initially "horrified" at the prospect of returning as military governor.[141] He had experience in engineering and war mobilization but not in political planning. After assuming the post of military governor in 1947, he was considered an effective, if sometimes imperious, leader.[142]

The American zone in Germany was divided into an eastern and western zone, with an army group assigned to each. As military governor, Eisenhower first created coordinating bodies under the three German states of Hessen, Württemberg-Baden, and Bavaria in order to administer the territory more uniformly.[143] In addition to providing for coordination within the American zone, US officials tried to coordinate Allied policies multilaterally through the US Control Council, which reported to the quadripartite Allied Control Commission. In practice, however, the commission functioned on directions from national governments, with serious differences in national policies often preventing agreement.[144]

The first military government detachments arrived in Germany while combat was still under way, and they thus remained under the control of tactical units.[145] In 1944 a new level of organization under the army's "G" staff was created, with civil affairs becoming the G-5 at the theater, army group, army, corps, and division levels, and military government field detachments in Germany reported to the G-5 of each tactical unit.[146] A G-5 was created at SHAEF in order to allow the supreme headquarters to have a "small high powered section" that would be "responsible for policies and directives, for long range outline planning and for general co-ordination" of civil affairs–related matters.[147] The theater also established a civil affairs pool so that personnel could be assigned as needed. As tactical troops moved into an area, military government detachments followed and identified requirements in the area. Military government staffs at the divisional level had direct contact with field military government detachments, and command channels flowed through the division.[148] Thus, orders for the military government detachments came from the armies, not from the ECAD.[149] As noted, tactical forces, through corps, divisions, regiments, and even companies, had great input into administrative matters, with some civil affairs specialists characterizing this influence as interference.[150] One frustrated military government officer observed that there was "no way to disseminate an order from the top and have it get down to the bottom except through the military chain, and of course, that was not built for that type of communication."[151] Given that army tactical units retained responsibility for governance functions during the initial occupation period, SHAEF argued for retaining control over military government. General Clay recalled that fights between himself as deputy military governor and the Chiefs of Staff "over control" had gotten to the point "that it was almost unbearable."[152] SHAEF believed that military government was a command responsibility and that only later, in permanent form, should military government shift to a territorial form of organization.[153]

As combat operations ended, however, the governance organization in Germany shifted from a tactical to a territorial organization. This was consistent with General Clay's view that military government should be run separately from the staff activities of the army.[154] In January 1946, the Office of Military Government for Germany replaced the US Group, Control Council as the main controlling element for military government. A deputy military governor oversaw each German state in the American zone, and military government detachments and teams were assigned to cities and counties within each state. A key impetus behind this push by General Clay to restructure the military government organization (e.g., his desire to remove the G-5s from the tactical chain of command) was his belief that it would be easier to convert a stand-alone military organization to civilian control.[155]

This reaffirmed the army view that it did not want indefinite control over governance functions. Army leaders consistently emphasized that their role was temporary and that a transition to civilian control should occur as quickly and smoothly as possible.[156] Assistant Secretary of War McCloy believed that the military government of Germany would be the "immediate responsibility" of the War Department, but not a long-term one.[157] The War Department had also emphasized that military government was "not a job for soldiers" and should be turned over to civilians as soon as practicable.[158] President Truman and General Eisenhower agreed.[159] General Clay tried to integrate civilians into G-5 theater staff positions and encouraged officers in certain military government jobs to convert to civilian status.[160] As the demobilization of the USFET began, Eisenhower continued to press for shifting more governance responsibilities to the State Department.[161]

Despite the broad objectives set forth in the Potsdam and other conferences, as well as the guidance included in JCS 1067, statements by the army at the time suggest that it hoped to minimize long-term costs and commitments associated with such operations. SHAEF maintained that military government was not necessarily a means of transforming Germany and urged military government personnel to be "disabused" of the notion that they were to make "Germany a 'happy land' again."[162] Eisenhower shared this outlook, clarifying that "the true function of the Army in [Germany] was to provide for the United States that reserve of force and power, that can insure, within our Zone, the prompt enforcement of all laws and regulations."[163] The army's priority seemed to be to ensure law and order, particularly while combat continued. Shortly after Germany's surrender, Secretary of War Stimson warned Generals Clay and Eisenhower not to put too much effort into carrying out JCS 1067 "the way [it was] written" because their main job "was to bring about law and order and the ability of the people in this country to live."[164]

Flexibility was paramount. JCS 1067 had emphasized the need for flexibility and adaptability in the theater, recognizing that occupation tasks would likely evolve and that the military governor would need to continuously survey "economic, industrial, financial and social conditions" and adapt policies as needed.[165] Once in Germany, General Clay and others became very critical of JCS 1067 for failing to anticipate actual conditions in the theater.[166] One financial expert noted that "economic idiots" had written the directive.[167] Overall, Clay did not believe that JCS 1067 met the needs of Germany, and he began to "slowly wipe out" its key provisions. He believed, for instance, that its provisions relating to currency reform merely prohibited him "from doing anything to improve the German economy," and he consistently showed his determination to improvise as needed, emphasizing how military government organizations and policies evolved and were shaped by commanding officers.[168]

Although the Allied Control Council had existed since the summer of 1945, "it met and argued but never agreed."[169] General Clay rarely received formal briefings and later approvingly recalled that his men on the ground controlled policy development and "made recommendations back to the department instead of vice-versa almost during the entire occupation."[170] He recalled how he was often drawn into situations in which there was "no boss . . . other than the President and obviously you can't draw the President into everyday administrative problems." The parts of JCS 1067 that Clay liked were implemented, while other aspects were modified or dropped.

American tactical and military government personnel, guided by the objectives of denazification, democratization, and decentralization, created new political authorities, organized and held elections, and encouraged the development of more democratic ideals through the reform of Germany's judicial and educational systems. Initially army personnel took almost complete control of the collapsed German government, but as Germany began to rebuild key administrative structures, the army's role shifted to one of oversight and supervision. Eventually army officials permitted lower levels of the German government to assume more autonomy, with military government detachments ensuring that German governments below the *Land* level functioned as required.[171]

Through an active program of denazification, army officials oversaw the removal of Nazis from positions of power. Denazification was directly linked to the development of new political parties, since it was through the removal of old leaders and the vetting of new political candidates that a foundation for a new Germany government was established. Although JCS 1067 had maintained that "democratization" was an important US objective in Germany, it left most of the details regarding denazification to military officers in the theater. Military government detachments included special branches to weed out Nazi incumbents and candidates from influential positions. Through interviews and the use of thousands of detailed questionnaires, army personnel made judgments about which German officials to trust and whom to remove.[172] The military government came under criticism for inconsistencies in implementing denazification.[173] General Clay strove for more consistency, issuing a law in October 1945 that excluded Nazis and Nazi sympathizers from all government and private employment above the level of common laborer. As a part of the army's effort to emphasize supervision rather than direct administration, the military government shifted responsibility for drafting denazification laws to German officials. In March 1946, a new law to liberate Germany from Nazism went into effect, and German organizations were held accountable for its enforcement. Clay later observed that although denazification had been difficult to implement, "we came out better by getting an entirely new and different group of people into the political life of Germany."[174]

The military government also prepared for new elections, with General Clay eager to "get the machinery [of elections and government] going."[175] In September 1945, military district commanders were given four months to prepare for elections in smaller towns and about eight months in larger cities. Clay believed that with earlier elections, the United States would be able to get local governments "back in the hands of Germans [and] the better off they would be and we would be."[176] Running elections involved intensive work for military government personnel. They oversaw all necessary paperwork and investigated each candidate. During October 1945, the average military government detachment dispatched over three hundred reports a month.[177] By November 1945, political parties began to form. In addition, military government soldiers oversaw the creation of a constitutional convention and elections for representatives to a new constitutional assembly, after which it was "in [Germans] hands."[178]

As local governments became more self-sufficient, US military government detachments around the country were reduced in size.[179] Eventually more and more responsibilities related to the reconstruction of German political life shifted to Germans. The military government detachments of each *Land* exerted supervisory rather than operational control, and more responsibility devolved to *Land* governments.[180] In addition, by early 1946, General Clay began to "civilianize" or transfer more military government to the German civil service.[181]

As in Italy, army units also played a central role in the reestablishment of German educational institutions. The military government's education branch rebuilt buildings destroyed in the war, redrafted textbooks, screened old teachers, and selected new ones. After lower-level schools opened, attention turned to higher schools, and by the spring of 1946, most of these were up and running. Once the more "mechanical processes" of school rehabilitation were completed, attention shifted to the broader goal of introducing democratic ideals and methods into teaching processes. One practitioner estimated that some 80 to 85 percent of teachers were removed.[182] Much of the work of reforming Germany's educational system was done by officers "without training or experience" in this field, since there were only a small number of educational specialists available and few positions open in field detachments to allow someone to devote his time only to education.[183]

Military government specialists were also involved in all aspects of rebuilding the German economy, including supervising the administration of public finance and banks, controlling properties of the German government, and introducing new currency. As was the case in Italy, part of the army's interest in this task stemmed from its desire to reduce the costs borne by the occupying troops.[184] The military government, however, also shared the broader US goal of establishing a foundation for the economic unification of Germany and leaving Germany a viable and functioning state. General Clay played a key role in overall economic policy development and in supporting Germany's unification by refusing to dismantle more German industries for reparations until he knew that Germany would be treated as an economic unit by the other occupying powers.[185] He played a key role in currency reform, which was opposed by the French. Clay's view was that "only military government could have made a currency reform as drastic and as effective as currency reform in Germany."[186] Clay also stopped the payment of reparations from the American zone out of frustration that other powers were not accounting for the reparations they were taking. Political leaders in Washington did not oppose Clay's actions, which he believed was "entirely within [the military government's] purview."[187] The army also exerted control over financing for imports and exports. At Potsdam, President Truman had directed the army to assume this responsibility, even though the army had to go to Congress to request funds for this purpose. The military government encouraged German export production in order to balance agricultural imports. By encouraging progress in this area, the army reduced its own budgetary request for this purpose.[188] Overall, the military government in Germany oversaw a transition toward a more self-sufficient German economy and implemented policies that supported Washington's objective of creating an economically unified German state.

In Germany, the "problem of food was to color every administrative action," and the military government strove to prevent famine and to "keep the German people alive and able to work."[189] Occupying forces managed and rationed thousands of tons of seed and began a sustainable planting program. Planting eventually rose to about 90 percent of normal levels.[190] General Clay worked hard to reduce malnutrition in the country and spent much time negotiating with Washington over the problem of food shipments and relief. The military government also undertook a children's feeding program and a land reform program that provided small farms to resettled refugees. By 1946 German public health organizations had been reorganized and were considered competent to "assume local responsibility." By 1948 Clay believed that public health agencies were "functioning satisfactorily, medicines [were] in adequate supply, and hospitals [were] repaired."[191]

As in previous governance experiences, army personnel worked to rebuild local police forces to assist with the maintenance of law and order. US policy respected the authority of local forces unless they revealed themselves to be "unworthy of such support."[192] German police had been centralized under the Nazi government, and American military personnel aimed to create a more decentralized organization. Initially the military government had wide powers to arrest not only high-level Nazi officials but also lower-level personnel—persons who held commissions down to and including the rank of major, for instance.[193] The Allied Control Council had also mandated the complete abolition of all German land, naval, and air forces.[194]

The approach to law and order in Germany worked on two levels. One system of military government courts focused on prosecuting offenses related to the occupation. A second effort focused on a broader restructuring of Germany's judicial system, with input from legal experts in the United States.[195] Following denazification, local courts were returned to local control. In addition, military government officials removed Nazi additions to the German administrative code and, by January 1948, extended the writ of habeas corpus to most Germans. US soldiers inspected prisons and reviewed cases of prisoners. On a broader level, military government detachments in the field were responsible for ensuring that laws were carried out, but they did so in conjunction with German authorities who were responsible for operational planning to implement the laws. Often, the military government laws were reissued as German *Land* laws.[196]

## Departure

In September 1949, four years after the establishment of a military government in Germany, control passed to the new Federal Republic of Germany. The military government established in 1945 had developed the main framework to allow a relatively smooth transition. General Clay had worked with Germans to establish elections for a constituent assembly whose delegates would draft a democratic constitution that could then be approved by the occupying powers. Once the new constitution and electoral procedures were approved, Germans would elect a new federal government.[197] In August 1949, Germany's first national postwar elections took place. Germans elected Theodore Heuss as the Federal Republic's first president.

A month after these elections, President Truman appointed John McCloy as the civilian high commissioner for Germany, replacing the military governor. As noted previously, army officials had been eager to pass control to a civilian. One of Truman's special envoys observed that US military leaders felt that "the administrative machinery of the Army [was] not well adapted to the tasks of governing a foreign population."[198] As McCloy took over, he was aware that General Clay had already accomplished much of the hard work.[199] He told President Truman that Clay had been a "real constitutional innovator," had "real political acumen," and had been responsible for key laws. Overall, McCloy appreciated that Clay had "gotten things moving up to a point where the so-called high commission had quite a good base upon which to operate." It is interesting that when McCloy had first been approached to take the job in Germany, as major combat operations were ending, he refused. He believed that it was too early for a civilian to take over governance tasks and that not only would generals and soldiers "be marching and counter-marching at that time," but that problems in Germany were not a "matter of the reconstitution of a constitution at that point. It was something in the nature of what I call a 'Mississippi River disaster.'" Thus, he believed that "you have got to put the military in charge because a civilian would be lost that quickly after the close of hostilities." McCloy thus oversaw Germany's transition away from military control and continued the process of integrating Germany into Western Europe. He worked to ensure that the new German government carried out the Marshall Plan and continued to reform German industrial interests. His efforts resulted in a 1951 antitrust treaty that formed the foundation for the future European Economic Community. In addition, the founding of NATO in 1949 provided a basis for reintegrating Germany back into Western Europe by reassuring the West against Germany's future rearmament.

By 1949, when McCloy arrived in Germany, both the principles and specifics for the foundation of a German state and its future integration into Western Europe had already been established by General Clay's military government. Clay had played a pivotal role in creating a responsible government that could be returned to German control. The reporting and analysis done by army military government personnel contributed to the view in Washington that a more positive policy toward Germany was needed, and Clay's active involvement in policy development (as discussed previously) shaped the restructuring of the entire German state. Through his leadership, the bizonal territory that was created to mesh the US and British zones in Germany, which eventually included the French zone, was sometimes called Bizonia, and it coalesced to become West Germany despite continuing Soviet objections.[200]

There was a growing view that as military government wound down, a continuing program of economic support for Germany would be necessary to consolidate American accomplishments. Secretary of State George Marshall's June 1947 speech, as well as a revised directive, JCS 1779 (published in July 1947), broadened the military government's goals to include the explicit promotion of economic unification and popular self-government. It acknowledged that the creation of a central government would be a "constructive" development.[201] The continuing presence of US troops in the country served as important leverage to back ongoing US negotiations with France and the Soviet Union. As in the cases of Japan and Korea (which will be discussed later), the presence of US troops in Germany beyond the end of combat operations played a critical role in shaping a final, desirable political order in Europe. The growing threat posed by the Soviet Union shaped US objectives in Europe as well as US support for the reunification of Germany—which might not have been realized absent the presence of military government personnel. The Soviet threat, combined with concessions from the French, allowed for the establishment of a central West German government, which, owing to the efforts of the US military government, was in strong enough shape to withstand pressure from Moscow.[202]

# JAPAN

Well before Japan's surrender, US military and political leaders gave serious thought to the possibility that US forces would restructure Japanese society and administer a defeated state.[203] US political and military leaders had considered the possibility of an occupation of Japan since 1942.[204] Secret advisory groups in the State Department studied postwar issues and produced papers setting forth basic principles—such as demilitarization and democratization—that would eventually be applied to Japan and other states.[205] Following the 1943 Cairo Declaration, which called for Japan's unconditional surrender, the War Department began considering the implications of a total collapse of the Japanese government and the possibility of an occupation by American military forces. In the summer of 1944, the War Department began planning in earnest for an occupation of Japan and Japanese-held strategic positions.[206] The SWNCC also established a special subcommittee on the Far East to deal with posthostility problems.[207] Military and civilian planners on the SWNCC considered a range of problems, from Japan's future economy, its political organization and form of government to the appropriate role of occupying forces. Several times during this period, the War Department took the lead as military planners worked to draft initial terms of surrender for Japan.[208]

In the summer of 1945, the General Headquarters of the American Forces in the Pacific produced Operation Blacklist, a plan for the occupation of Japan and Korea.[209] Blacklist called for the progressive occupation of fourteen areas in Japan, using all available US forces in the region. It anticipated immobilizing Japan's armed forces, establishing control over major political centers, and securing food supplies and communications. US military planners considered the need to manage combat operations *and* reestablish political order. This pattern of securing rear areas as combat continued elsewhere in the theater was repeated in other governance operations, including Germany, Italy, and in 1950, Korea.

As in previous operations, the War Department expressed concern regarding its proposed governance responsibilities and pressured political leaders for more guidance.[210] Its CAD requested instructions from the State Department regarding the extent, duration, and character of the occupation of Japan. Eventually the State Department provided preliminary answers to most of the War Department's requests.[211] As with Germany, debate took place on the character of the occupation and the appropriate level of toughness toward Japan. Some believed that harsh terms should be imposed, while others maintained that a viable Japanese economy should be preserved.[212] A key issue was whether the United States would recognize any existing central authority. As in previous governance operations, the limited numbers of military personnel constrained the possibility of a complete takeover of the Japanese government.

By the fall of 1945, policymakers had developed several key documents that would shape the occupation: the July 1945 Potsdam Declaration, the August 1945 "U.S. Initial Post-Surrender Policy for Japan" (which emerged from the SWNCC's work), and a November 1945 JCS paper, *Basic Initial Post Surrender Directive to the Supreme Commander.*[213] Together, they outlined specific tasks for occupying forces, such as establishing control over Japanese trade and financial institutions, extracting reparations, conducting trials of war criminals, restituting property, resuming peaceful economic activity, and creating democratic political parties.[214] The guidance called for the demilitarization of Japan, the democratization of Japanese politics and society, the reconstruction of Japan's economy, and the evolution of Japan into a peaceful, democratic state.

### Developing an Organization for Governance Operations

Following Japan's surrender in August 1945, General MacArthur became supreme commander, Allied powers (SCAP) and began to implement Blacklist.[215] Advance planning for the occupation of Japan had specified the main principles and objectives that would guide the military government, but as in previous governance operations, army commanders on the ground became responsible for operationalizing these policies.[216] As in previous cases, War Department planners initially believed that their role would be much more limited than would in fact be the case.

The War Department's earlier planning had focused on the development of broad parameters to guide the occupation, but the army was tasked with actually organizing an occupation force rather quickly.[217] The War Department designated the Sixth and the Eighth Armies for the occupation of Japan, with the Eighth Army controlling the Tokyo-Yokohama area and northward and the Sixth Army controlling areas to the south.[218] The army and navy had over two thousand officers and four thousand enlisted men available for occupation duty in Japan. Troops collected at the civil affairs staging area in Monterey, California, and were organized into tactical military government units attached to the Sixth and Eighth Armies' invading forces.[219]

In the fall of 1945, trained military government units began to arrive and take over for tactical units,[220] and a two-layered occupation organization emerged. The SCAP headquarters included twelve special military government staff sections, which exerted overall policy responsibility for military government and developed directives to oversee the Eighth Army's reconstruction efforts.[221] In theory, the supreme commander issued policies and directives that were passed on to the commanding general of the Eighth Army, Lt. Gen. Robert L. Eichelberger. The Eighth Army headquarters also included a special military government staff section and a field organization based on two corps headquarters, with special military government units attached to tactical army units.[222] Eighth Army occupation troops worked through normal command channels.[223] Military government units were organized to correspond to Japanese prefectures, although initially there were not enough military government units for the forty-six prefectures.[224] Some units were thus broken up into detachments and reorganized into teams to parallel Japan's governmental organization. Eight regional headquarters oversaw these military government teams.[225] The military government prefecture teams were organized to meet the needs of particular regions. For example, although prefectures varied in size and population, initially a standard military government unit was assigned to all prefectures. Thus, initially Tokyo received the same number of military government personnel as much smaller cities.[226] A year into the occupation, however, a reorganization deployed military government units more tailored to the specific needs of prefectures.[227]

A combination of a tactical/territorial control emerged through the Eighth Army,[228] resulting at times in a "long and devious" channel of communication between SCAP and the prefecture military government teams.[229] The prefecture military government teams reported through corps and regional military government teams rather than directly to the Eighth Army.[230] This prevented direct communication between the Eighth Army's special staff sections and their opposite numbers in the field. Furthermore, specialists on the regional and prefecture military government teams did not always have counterparts on the special staff sections of the SCAP headquarters, which often resulted in overlapping jurisdictions and confusion.[231]

Technically, the occupation of Japan was an Allied endeavor. The Far Eastern Commission (FEC), representing the eleven countries that had fought against Japan, was created at the December 1945 Moscow Conference. The commission was a means of allowing Allied states some input into policies related to the occupation. In theory, the FEC made recommendations to the US president. Following his approval, directives would flow from the JCS to the supreme commander in Japan.[232] In practice, however, there were few Allied personnel represented in the supreme commander's headquarters, and no Allied government was permitted to work with the Japanese government except through SCAP.[233] Thus, the FEC's decisions tended to confirm policies already followed by SCAP.[234] As far as the Japanese were concerned, "the occupation [was] primarily a MacArthur operation, secondarily an American occupation and only remotely an Allied operation."[235]

### Political and Economic Reconstruction

Upon his arrival in Japan, General MacArthur reflected that his professional military knowledge "was no longer a major factor," since he "had to be an economist, a political scientist, an engineer, a manufacturing executive, a teacher, even a theologian of sorts . . . [and he had to] rebuild a nation completely destroyed by war."[236] By the fall of 1945, the United States hoped to create a peaceful and responsible government in Japan and to shape developments there so that the country did not become a future threat to US interests.[237] To accomplish this, MacArthur modernized Japan's constitution, held free elections, and built a representative government.

Political reform in Japan required the military government to dismantle old political organizations and create new forms of authority, while preserving elements of Japan's basic administrative structures. The United States reaffirmed the principle of indirect rule.[238] Given the dearth of American forces, a complete takeover of Japan's government was not possible. The emperor, although stripped of his authority, still commanded respect and cooperated with occupation authorities.[239] Thus, existing Japanese administrative structures implemented reconstruction under the direction and oversight of SCAP.[240] Although able to exercise direct control if necessary,[241] SCAP issued directives through the Japanese government agency, the Central Liaison Office.[242]

As in previous experiences, army leaders balanced elements of the old regime, worked through existing administrative structures, and initiated reforms. Military government personnel tried to ensure that SCAP directives were properly implemented. Civil affairs teams were instructed to "observe, investigate and report" compliance with SCAP instructions by the Japanese government.[243] SCAP's Government Section initially reviewed and issued approvals for all Japanese cabinet orders.[244] A central committee of Japanese and American officials issued directives to the Japanese government.[245] This system did not work perfectly, since there was a tendency among military government field officers to get the job done themselves. Although army units in the field were not permitted to issue instructions to local Japanese governmental structures without first receiving permission from headquarters, one military government officer later noted that "a common attitude among field administrators is pride in the fact that they report as little as possible to headquarters and solve their own problems."[246] As a result, a "subtle transfer in responsibility" to military government personnel in the field took place.

Given that few military government teams received instructions in the fall of 1945, this proactive attitude was probably good. Often teams were unaware of the directives that they were supposed to enforce. Some army officers reportedly became aware of directives only by reading the English-language press, which often included reprints of SCAP directives.[247] In the spring of 1946, SCAP sent its directives to Eighth Army military units in an effort to improve the flow of information, and army leaders also tried to increase uniformity among military government field personnel by assisting them with planning and reporting frameworks.

Military government officials tried to create safeguards to ensure that individuals associated with the old order were prevented from retaining power. Military government directives prohibited the retention or selection of individuals associated with "militant nationalism" or "aggression," and in January 1946 SCAP's Directive 550 dissolved all organizations considered harmful to democratization and pluralism.[248] As a result of this purge, some thirteen hundred organizations were dissolved.[249] Nine out of ten high officials became ineligible to hold office.[250] Army officials replaced key personnel throughout the Japanese government, encouraged the decentralization of administrative structures (and the development of more local autonomy), drafted a new constitution, and supported the creation of more political parties. Previously, the imperial government had appointed many local officials, but SCAP soon issued laws forcing the election of local officials by direct vote.[251] By December 1945, sixty new political parties had been organized,[252] and within a year the number of polling places doubled, from twenty thousand to over forty-two thousand.[253] In April 1946, the first general elections took place, with Japan's two conservative parties—the Liberals and Progressives—capturing 139 and 93 seats, respectively, of the Diet's total of 466 seats.[254] Local elections followed one year later.[255] General MacArthur believed that holding elections was a necessary means of allowing "free and untrammeled expression of the people's will."[256]

MacArthur's team also wrote an entirely new constitution for the country.[257] Less than two months into the occupation, he liberalized the existing Meiji Constitution, abolished certain advisory organs, strengthened the Diet's powers, and created an independent judiciary. The new constitution created a constitutional monarchy, and the Diet became Japan's highest organ of power. SCAP also drafted a bill of rights removing restrictions on civil, political, and religious liberties and, overall, improving the rights of the Japanese people. The emperor presented the bill of rights to the public for approval, and it came into force in May 1947.[258]

SCAP also developed new laws. The military government sought to balance its policy of indirect rule and its preference for relying on local structures to maintain law and order, with the need to reform Japan's powerful security organs. As with political reforms, MacArthur emphasized decentralization and supported measures to allow local entities with more power over security organs.[259] SCAP's October 1945 Bill of Rights stripped Japan's police organs of their power over censorship and other forms of control. By 1947 SCAP had dissolved Japan's Home Ministry, which had been one of Japan's most powerful institutions, and enacted new police laws limiting the number of police personnel and also their jurisdiction.[260] The Japanese government abolished its secret police forces, police departments charged with censorship, and other police agencies concerned with control of thought, speech, religion, and assembly. About five thousand members of the Japanese police system, including one hundred top-ranking officials, were removed from office.[261]

Military government officers also instituted broader judicial reforms, including the introduction of a new civil code that provided women with greater legal rights and reduced elements of Japan's highly patriarchal system.[262] Military government officers developed a system to arrest and try Japanese military personnel for offenses against the laws of war and established the International Military Tribunal for the Far East, which included justices from eleven countries who held hearings on major Japanese war criminals.[263] SCAP established provost courts under the Eighth Army's control in February 1946,[264] and for years after the election of a new Japanese government, SCAP oversaw the trials of thousands of accused Japanese war criminals.[265] By allowing the Japanese government key authority, many SCAP directives evolved into Japanese law.[266]

Demilitarization was also a central element of reconstruction in Japan. In June 1946, the United Kingdom, China, and the Soviet Union signed a draft treaty that announced their intention to disarm and demilitarize Japan. Demobilization of Japan's armed forces was actually handled through Japan's War and Navy Departments, although this oversight was then transferred to civilians in the Japanese government.[267] The 1947 Constitution prohibited the development of land, sea, and air forces.[268] However, by the end of the Allied occupation, growing concern about the Soviet Union contributed to support for the creation of a self-defense force of about seventy-five thousand members.[269]

SCAP also focused on economic reforms, primarily through the decentralization of power.[270] The military government facilitated a "reasonable restoration" of Japan's economy so that the "peaceful requirements of the population [could] be satisfied."[271] Occupation authorities sought to weaken the economic base of Japan's military strength by decentralizing economic power through the deconcentration of Japan's large family combines—the zaibatsu. The zaibatsu were closely associated with Japan's war effort and held a monopoly over Japan's main industries. The United States believed that a reduction in the zaibatsu's power was necessary to promote democracy. Thus, a year into the occupation SCAP developed a plan to dissolve zaibatsu holding companies.[272] The Diet later reviewed a law, promoted by General MacArthur, to eliminate the "excessive concentrations of economic power."[273]

MacArthur's focus on deconcentration was challenged in mid-1947, when policymakers in Washington began to reassess the wisdom of SCAP's focus on reform at the expense of creating a more robust Japanese economy. George Kennan, a member of the State Department's policy planning staff, briefed MacArthur in Japan and argued for a shift from reform to recovery.[274] Kennan and his colleagues, including top army officials, such as the undersecretary of the army, argued that MacArthur's determination to decentralize and reduce the power of key Japanese economic entities would weaken Japan too much and leave it vulnerable to Soviet pressure.[275] MacArthur strongly resisted pressures to change course.[276] Many believed that his refusal to take guidance from Washington and his overall stubbornness regarding policies toward Japan was a result of his interest in asserting his power over President Truman in order to set the stage for an eventual run for the presidency.[277] Eventually, however, the State Department prevailed, and a "reverse course" began in early 1948.

Regarding fiscal reform, the JCS's original Basic Initial Post Surrender Directive to Supreme Commander for the Allied Powers for the Occupation and Control of Japan (JCS 1380/15) had instructed General MacArthur to curb inflation, since it could "retard" broader economic goals.[278] MacArthur also believed that tax reform was a fiscal necessity, and he invited US experts to completely revise Japanese tax laws and methods of collection. SCAP also shaped labor policies in Japan, and special directives allowed for the establishment of labor unions, which had previously been banned.[279] SCAP's policies encouraged the creation of labor unions as a part of the general US effort to increase the number of politically active bodies in Japan. A trade union law of December 1945 was passed, allowing workers the right to strike and organize, and eventually a labor ministry was created to oversee labor rights.[280]

Army occupying forces also conducted extensive land reform programs in order to increase agricultural output and democratize a system in which most Japanese farmers functioned essentially as serfs. Around 47 percent of the Japanese population that lived on farms were barely able to survive.[281] Through a large-scale program of buying large tracts of land from landlords and reselling smaller tracts to farmers, SCAP's Natural Resources Section hoped to increase owner-operated farms and improve farming so that the agricultural sector would contribute to and not burden the economy.[282] By 1950 more than five million acres had been redistributed.[283] In addition, MacArthur tried to address the problem of famine by fixing some prices and, when necessary, importing huge amounts of foodstuff and fertilizer from the United States.[284]

Reform of Japan's educational institutions formed another component of building a stronger democratic polity. SCAP developed an educational policy based on the Potsdam principles early in the occupation and succeeded in making significant changes in this area. General MacArthur requested a visit by a special educational mission to propose how the reorganization and reorientation of Japan's educational system might take place.[285] A joint War and State Department mission examined ways to eradicate militarism, encourage decentralization, and encourage more independence among teachers; it also endorsed a purge of teachers.[286] MacArthur took much of its advice and revised the existing system of central control over education by instituting more measures for local control. By the end of the occupation, compulsory school attendance had been raised, textbooks rewritten, and teachers purged, with new ones hired. MacArthur later wrote that there had been "a complete reorientation in the outlook of Japanese children," and a prominent historian later wrote that Japan's Ministry of Education had been transformed into one of the country's "most zealous proponents of democracy."[287]

Occupation forces also reformed Japan's health system and raised health care professional and educational standards. SCAP oversaw the transition from a wartime system to one that could meet civilian health needs and tried to improve data collection related to public health issues so that it could better assess the extent of the problems throughout the country.[288] It decentralized the health system by encouraging more local autonomy over health resources, improving the quality and number of hospitals and placing more responsibility on local government agencies. In addition, occupation forces oversaw vaccination programs and assumed control of medical supplies throughout the country, returning them to civilian use.[289]

## Departure

Two main issues shaped the end of the US occupation in Japan: First, the United States wanted to ensure that Japan was economically stable enough to withstand Soviet pressure; second, there was disagreement over the nature of America's sustained military presence in the region. The US policy community was divided over how and when to depart Japan. By the summer of 1947, the strategic situation had shifted, requiring that attention to Japan's internal political and economic development be balanced with emerging strategic concerns about Soviet intentions in Asia and the world as a whole. The departure of occupying forces from Japan was closely tied to the ability of the United States to sustain a presence in the region and ensure that Japan remained a viable state after the withdrawal of US forces.

As US policymakers planned the withdrawal of American forces, they balanced concerns about a continued presence in Japan with the strategic ramifications of a quick departure. By mid-1947 General MacArthur believed that Japan was almost ready to sign a peace treaty with the United States and that the "spiritual revolution" that he had presided over would insulate Japan from internal or external threats, eliminating the need for an expensive recovery program.[290] Following Japan's adoption of its new constitution in May 1947, MacArthur argued that the "political phase" had approached completion and that a sufficient framework for democracy had been established.[291] However, others in Washington believed that signing a formal peace treaty with Japan too early could reduce the US presence in the region and result in greater Soviet influence. As noted earlier, some in the State Department and the Department of the Army warned that an early peace would leave Japan vulnerable to Communist influence, and they advocated for a type of "Marshall Plan" for Japan.[292]

Debate about the departure of American forces from Japan unfolded in tandem with discussions about how to ensure that Japan remain strong economically. President Truman's adoption of a "reverse course" for Japan (as noted earlier) in the fall of 1948 endorsed the State Department view that the United States should shift to promoting production and boosting exports, rather than focusing on industrial reform. This basic plan was codified in National Security Council (NSC) Directive 13/2 in October 1948 and Congress's passage of the Economic Recovery in Occupied Areas (EROA) bill, which provided Japan with substantial amounts of capital and raw materials.[293]

In 1949 SCAP abolished prefecture-level military government teams and directed local Japanese officials to take over completely, subject to oversight by the highest government levels in Tokyo for the remainder of the occupation. MacArthur believed that the character of the occupation had shifted from the "stern rigidity of a military operation" to more of a protective force.[294] Negotiations for a final peace treaty with Japan began in 1949, culminating in the Treaty of San Francisco, which went into effect in 1951 and formally ended the occupation.

A central issue at the peace conference was how to balance the US desire to retain long-term basing rights with Japan's desire for sovereignty and rearmament.[295] The JCS wanted to retain control over islands in the entire region, to allow American bases in Japan to form "staging areas" from which the United States could project power.[296] The DOD hoped for unilateral control over bases in Japan, which the Japanese government, not surprisingly, opposed. Eventually, the JCS agreed to a security treaty, as opposed to a "collective self-defense treaty," which would allow US forces to "contribute to the maintenance of international peace and security in the Far East and to the security of Japan against armed attack from without."[297] The Pentagon would lease bases on Japan and retain authority over US forces.

With the intensification of the Cold War, US leaders began to recognize the value of retaining Japan as a new ally in the region. The occupation goals had evolved as US strategy broadened—Japan was now considered an important state in creating a bulwark against Communism in Asia. The occupation of Japan, initially driven by a desire to punish and disarm a wartime enemy, was replaced by the desire to implement reforms to strengthen Japanese society against the rising tide of Communism and create a new strategic partner for the United States in Asia.[298]

# KOREA

From 1943 to the summer of 1945, War and State Department officials considered a US military occupation of Korea.[299] They also considered the need to rebuild Korea after its many years as a Japanese colony.[300] At the December 1943 Cairo Conference, Allied leaders discussed political settlements following an Axis defeat and announced that in "due course Korea shall become free and independent."[301] Strategically, the United States believed an occupation could be important in offsetting Soviet domination of the region. Army chief of staff George Marshall advocated landing a division in Korea to prevent complete Soviet domination of the region after Japan's collapse and to establish US control over the area.[302]

Korea had been a Japanese colony since the Russo-Japanese War, when in 1905 Japan had established a protectorate over the peninsula and controlled and shaped Korea's industry and educational systems.[303] The northern part of the peninsula retained heavy industry and hydroelectric power, while lighter industry in the southern part was supplemented by irrigation, agriculture, and research facilities. Korea also had a solid rail and road transportation network. While the decent infrastructure greeted US Army forces upon their arrival, the United States faced an uncertain political climate. Internally, thousands of Japanese administrators ran Korea, and collaborators were hated by the majority of Koreans.[304] Externally, the presence of Soviet troops on the peninsula complicated US goals, and following the Soviet Union's entry into the Pacific war in July 1945, Korea was roughly split along the thirty-eighth parallel into North Korea and South Korea.

Given the relationship between Korea and Japan, US planning for a Korean occupation took place within the broader framework of planning for the occupation of Japan. The JCS had assumed that responsibility for an occupation of

Japan and Korea would fall to US Army forces, and they directed the Joint War Planning Committee to plan for the occupation of those territories held by Japan in the event of Japan's surrender.[305] A month before Japan's surrender, Operation Blacklist was approved. Blacklist was primarily a plan for the occupation of Japan but included a portion, called Baker-Forty, that focused on Korea.[306] For both countries, US forces would rely on existing governmental machinery. Baker-Forty assigned American troops the mission of establishing a military government in Korea.[307] The plan instructed the military government to seize control of all Japanese military forces and governmental and private institutions, disarm the Japanese military, suppress activities that might be harmful to occupying forces, maintain law and order, recover and repatriate Allied prisoners of war, and facilitate peaceful commerce.[308]

As in previous governance operations, War Department officials requested specific guidance from the State Department on political contingencies that might arise in the region.[309] The War Department's CAD requested information about the kind of governmental machinery that would need to be established in Korea, the role of army and navy administrators, and the policies to be followed regarding Japanese nationals.[310] Political leaders debated the character and longevity of an occupation. At Yalta, Washington backed the creation of an international trusteeship that would eventually progress to self-government, independence, and United Nations (UN) membership for Korea.[311] This position remained the basis of US policy well into the occupation. Later, at Potsdam, the United States committed to sending an occupation force to Korea, although many details regarding the character of the occupation remained unresolved.[312] Thus, although the broad outlines of an occupation policy for Korea policy existed by August 1945, US officials believed that the challenges of combat and the difficulty of finalizing the outlines for a postwar settlement would make it impossible to produce "complete blueprints" for occupation activities in Korea.[313] Planners on the SWNCC expressed concern that there was still no agreed view "as to the character of administration of civil affairs in Korea."[314] Just two weeks before the arrival of US troops in Korea, it was still uncertain which forces would serve as occupiers, and the army's original intention of assigning occupation responsibilities to the Tenth Army shifted to XXIV Corps.[315]

## Developing an Organization for Governance Operations

For at least two years before the arrival of US forces in Korea, US military and civilian leaders recognized that an occupation of that country was likely, but when American troops landed in Korea on September 8, 1945, no detailed operational guidance existed for the establishment of a military government.[316] US planners were still debating the duration of the proposed occupation and questioning whether a military government was suited to "cope with difficult and complex problems bound to arise in the transformation of a colonial territory into an independent state."[317] There was also concern over whether the American people would support a military government that extended "beyond military necessity."[318]

Japan's unexpected surrender caught military and civilian planners by surprise and necessitated making quick arrangements to get XXIV Corps to Korea. Because of its proximity, General MacArthur had assigned XXIV Corps to Korea and selected Lt. Gen. John R. Hodge to serve as commanding general of US Army Forces in Korea (USAFIK). General Hodge had no prior occupation experience.[319] The corps consisted of the Sixth, Seventh, and Fortieth Infantry Divisions, and no civil affairs troops landed with these forces. President Truman declared that the United States was mindful of the "difficult tasks" that lay ahead and that it would require "time and patience" before Koreans could "assume themselves the responsibilities and functions of a free and independent nation."[320]

Instructions had been issued to XXIV Corps just days before its arrival in Korea.[321] Baker-Forty, as well as Field Order No. 55, advised troops to be "prepared to assist in the establishment of a separate post-war government and Army of Occupation and to transfer responsibilities to these agencies when established and as subsequently directed."[322] Additional broad instructions toward Korea emerged a month after the arrival of General Hodge's troops with the Basic Initial Directive to the Commander in Chief, US Army Forces, Pacific, for the Administration of the Civil Affairs in Those Areas of Korea Occupied by U.S. Forces (SWNCC 176/8), produced by the SWNCC in October 1945.[323]

General MacArthur directed General Hodge to occupy the southern part of the peninsula in three phases: the Seoul-Inchon area, the Pusan area, and the Kunsan-Chongju area.[324] Hodge was to destroy hostile elements, suppress activities unfriendly to occupation forces, and take measures to facilitate law and order.[325] As in previous governance operations, one of the first steps taken by the theater commander was to issue proclamations announcing the intention of the United States, which was to help Korea operate under more democratic rule. The statements, made by MacArthur, also explained that governmental authority was to be "assumed by the United States Army," that the security of American forces was to be safeguarded, and that certain types of currencies would be considered legal.[326]

Despite the existence of this broad guidance regarding the occupation, details related to the implementation of specific tasks were left to General Hodge. Soon after Hodge's appointment, General MacArthur requested that Washington provide guidance to Hodge on the occupation, as Hodge was concerned that unless he received such guidance, US policy would fail.[327] An officer attached to the headquarters of XXIV Corps recalled that its "instructions consisted primarily of a MacArthur directive based on the principle that for our purpose Korea was to be considered an integral part of Japan."[328] However, the policy statements provided to Hodge were so "sparse, vague, and ambiguous, he was required to feel his way at every step."[329]

In the first few weeks of the occupation, General Hodge faced two challenges. He needed to gather more information about the specific situation and to organize occupying forces into a functioning military government. Hodge worked to collect more information about the situation, with the XXIV Corps intelligence section (G-2). It gathered information by interrogating Korean POWs, conducting air reconnaissance, and contacting Japanese officials still in Korea.[330] The G-2 assessed the political situation, determining that two opposing political groups (right and left) operated in the South and recommended that US forces remain aloof from these divisions since the North-South division would likely continue.[331] To improve his understanding of the situation in the North, Hodge dispatched a small group of military officers to gather information. A party was sent to make direct contact with Soviet troops there, and representatives from XXIV Corps arrived in Pyongyang on September 11, 1945,[332] though no substantive discussions with the Soviets resulted.[333]

Although it would later evolve, army officers established a military government organization within a few weeks of landing in Korea. Consistent with MacArthur's instructions, Hodge, as commander of XXIV Corps, retained overall responsibility for the occupation. However, in a departure from the previous governance experiences, a separate military governor was appointed right away. Hodge's deputy, Maj. Gen. Archibald V. Arnold, commanding general of the Seventh Division, became the military governor of what was now being called South Korea.[334] Arnold established a separate command within the USAFIK headquarters, and a civil administrator was appointed to assist him.[335] The military government structure initially mirrored the organization that the Japanese had put into place.

On paper, there was ostensibly a separate military government chain of command, but in reality there were several reasons why the combat organization still dominated.[336] First, there was a dearth of qualified administrative personnel to staff the separate military government headquarters.[337] Second, Hodge did not have civil affairs units to undertake governance tasks and relied on combat troops for these jobs. Third, although General Arnold, as military governor, commanded all civil affairs personnel *not* attached to tactical units, his oversight was effectively limited because most *were* attached to combat units.[338]

The duality of the command arrangements in Korea created some tensions between combat forces and the military government teams charged with the administration of Korean provinces.[339] Civil affairs teams in the field remained under tactical control and had to report through "tortuous army channels" as opposed to reporting directly to the military government.[340] Initially combat units would arrive in a town, expel a former Japanese head of government, and replace him with a military government officer until a Korean was prepared to take over the position.[341] Further complicating arrangements, the boundaries of combat division areas did not always correspond to Korean territorial/governmental divisions.

In addition to developing the details of a military government organization, General Hodge tackled the immediate need of securing the safety of US troops by demobilizing existing Japanese forces in Korea. He devoted a "considerable number of troops" to guard arms and ammunition stores against saboteurs.[342] And in order to stabilize the situation on the ground, XXIV Corps also undertook a huge repatriation program.[343] From August 1945 to September 1946, the US Army oversaw the movement of some 2.6 million people in Korea.[344]

General Hodge faced two main challenges in the political and economic reconstruction of Korea. First, the military government there sought to reduce Japanese control and oversight and rebuild independent Korean economic, political, and social institutions.[345] Second, Hodge needed to focus on external considerations to ensure that any final transition would preserve the South's political integrity. Thus, Hodge spent months and months working to develop an arrangement with the Soviet Union to establish a provisional government for a unified Korea. The official history of the period noted that Hodge had received little or no instructions "on thorny questions" such as the eventuality of Korean independence, methods of handling various political factions, or the severance of Korea from Japanese influence.[346] Hodge nevertheless played an active role in resolving these issues throughout the occupation.

During reconstruction, a transition from tactical to a predominantly territorial organization occurred in January 1946. General Order 1 created the US Army Military Government in Korea (USAMGIK), which transferred control over military government units from tactical commanders to the separate military government command.[347] USAMGIK installations were removed from tactical commands, thus allowing these teams to communicate directly with their headquarters on problems related to governance. Provincial military government teams were responsible for civil affairs in their area, and they were to report directly to the military governor.[348]

Army officers confronted the recurring problem of how to transition from the use of the existing Japanese-controlled administrative machinery to governmental structures controlled by Koreans. A key difference between the military government in Japan and Korea was that in the latter case the United States was forced to reassess its initial decision to rely on existing governmental structures. Early in the occupation, Washington had instructed General Hodge to rely on Japanese personnel as much as possible, with President Truman announcing that Japanese administrators should be retained "as servants of the Korean people and of our occupying forces [because] they are deemed essential by reason of their technical qualifications."[349] However, the ensuing controversy forced a reappraisal of US policy. Hodge appreciated the implications of the Koreans' growing opposition to keeping Japanese administrators in place, and he lobbied Washington to rethink its policy. Shortly after, the JCS allowed the removal of Japanese administrators,[350] and within a year Koreans headed all major departments in their government.[351]

The arbitrary geographic division of Korea complicated reconstruction.[352] While army military government officers worked out the details of political and economic reform in the South, they were also forced to develop the details of an international trusteeship for Korea, since that remained the official US position as long as negotiations with the Soviet Union continued. However, since Moscow had not yet agreed to the trusteeship formula, there remained much uncertainty regarding the duration of the US occupation. Discussions among SWNCC planners in the fall of 1945 suggested that many believed that the army's occupation would be limited in time and that the trusteeship would then take over. Thus, as the occupation unfolded, little effort was made to transition from military to civilian authority. In fact, Secretary of State Byrnes encouraged President Truman to do just the opposite, arguing that administrative efficiency and policy coordination would be more certain if the military retained authority.[353] War Department efforts to end the occupation in early 1946 were also rejected by President Truman.[354]

After the US decision allowing the removal of Japanese administrators from Korea, General Hodge worked to develop a democratically oriented, independent Korean government. Initially, policymakers in Washington prohibited Hodge from recognizing the "so-called Korean provisional government" at Chongqing.[355] Washington wanted Hodge to remain "neutral" and treat all political parties alike—including disciplined Communist groups financed from Moscow.[356] However, it was difficult for Hodge to ignore the overtures of the provisional government, and in the end he played a key role in pressing for a change in policy to allow the use of "exiled Koreans" to help establish order and undermine Communist elements in the South.[357] He also played an important role in developing plans to counter Soviet-inspired Communist activities, which were hampering his efforts to provide the foundations for an independent government in the South.[358]

Now immersed in South Korean politics, Hodge also dealt with the politics of trying to create a joint provisional government for the peninsula. Some still believed that the Americans and the Soviets could work together and establish a foundation for the eventual independence of a whole Korea. A joint US-Soviet commission had been established at the December 1945 Moscow Conference to work on the development of a provisional government for Korea and encourage US and Soviet commands to cooperate in "administrative-economic matters."[359] However, after 1946, US-Soviet talks grew increasingly futile and eventually collapsed following Moscow's refusal to accept any specific proposals.[360] Hodge was more than willing to forgo Soviet agreement and instead focus on developments in the South, with the goal of supporting greater political pluralism in Korea and establishing the foundations for a future independent state.[361]

A main objective of the military government was to reform Korea's national Bureau of Justice. SWNCC 176/8 instructed Hodge to remove Japanese judges and court personnel and establish military courts as needed. Korean courts could remain intact, but they were to be supervised and could operate only on cases not of direct concern to the occupation.[362] Two types of military courts were created: provost courts and military commissions.[363] The Bureau of Justice was reorganized, and an American was appointed as its head. Once Japanese personnel were removed, a lack of qualified personnel in the bureau became a problem, and as a result American civil affairs officers who were attorneys in civilian life were admitted to the Korean bar.[364] Overall, reform in this area proceeded quite rapidly. By December 1945, except for the director, all military government officers in the Bureau of Justice had transitioned to adviser status, and Koreans were integrated into positions of responsibility.[365]

As in previous governance cases involving the reform of security forces, the army dismantled existing structures and created new ones. In Korea, the presence of Soviet forces in the North only intensified the military government's need to create strong new police and national defense forces. The military government assumed control over the Bureau of Police and appointed an American as head of the bureau.[366] Within two months after US troops had landed in Korea, the military government appointed a new director of national defense who asserted jurisdiction over the Bureau of Police and the new Bureau of Armed Forces. Army officers supervised the removal of Japanese and other "collaborationist" elements from Korean police agencies, allowing the retention of some only under appropriate supervision.[367] Initially US military police (MP) officers replaced Japanese police, although eventually civil affairs officers entering the region took over from MP officers.[368] Occupying forces dissolved the Thought Control, Economic Control, and Censorship Police,[369] and they recruited and trained Koreans to for the new force. At the time, Koreans made up a mere 30 percent of the police force.[370]

In addition to reforming Korea's police forces, army personnel oversaw the development of what would become the nucleus of South Korea's national defense forces.[371] As the United States began to transfer more authority to the South Korean government, the Department of the Army requested that General Hodge evaluate South Korea's national defenses.[372] Some in Washington advocated limiting aid to the creation of a police-type constabulary force. Others, including Hodge, urged the development of more substantial defense forces (of about a hundred thousand troops) in order to provide stability when US troops withdrew.[373] Opposition to the creation of strong defense forces was due to concerns that a strong South Korean army could jeopardize reunification talks with the Soviets.[374] In the end, the United States agreed to create a fifty-thousand-man constabulary force to supplement Korean police forces and relieve US tactical troops from some of their police functions.[375] Active recruiting and training for a constabulary began, and an American was appointed its first chief.[376]

US occupation forces in Korea also restructured the complicated system of property rights, without specific guidance other than general instructions to maximize the production of foodstuffs. The Japanese had established a rigid system of economic controls over the sale of food in Korea. Occupation authorities created a bureau of agriculture, and the military government lifted some price controls and administered surveys to gauge attitudes about Japanese- and Korean-owned lands.[377] Overall, military government officers became immersed in complex land reform, price-control issues, and efforts to undercut the black market.

SWNCC 176/8 had ordered the creation of a financial division within the military government to promote economic stability and minimize strains on occupying forces. Similar to the military government's goals for political reform, the overall objective for economic reform was to reduce Korean dependence on Japan. This required detailed involvement by army personnel in the economic affairs of the country. Occupation officials severed relationships between banks in Korea and those in Japan, oversaw all aspects of currency reform and control, and introduced a new supplemental yen currency. The directive had ordered the closing of specific banks by name and instructed the military government to exercise control and supervision over the expenditure of public funds. A key objective in Korea was to control inflation and to protect plants and property; in addition, occupation authorities worked to adopt measures to constrain Korean firms from participating in monopolies or cartels.

Occupation forces in Korea created a new central agency for public health.[378] One of the few doctors assigned to the military government became head of the department of public health and welfare, which reported to the new bureau of public health. He faced considerable challenges because there were few non-Japanese doctors in Korea and there were serious problems with infectious diseases. To try to control their spread, the military government established rodent-extermination teams and special "case finding" committees to determine the extent of epidemics in various regions of the country. The military government also started inoculation programs. The bureau of public health also oversaw the repatriation of Koreans from other countries (mainly Japan). And as in Germany and Japan, army personnel tackled the restructuring of Korea's educational system.[379] The military government sought to replace the Japanese-imposed system with an American system. A provisional educational office was established, with a Korean head. Korean textbooks were rewritten, schools reopened, and teachers were fired and hired. The military government oversaw the restoration of school buildings and the replacement of stolen or destroyed property and instituted compulsory education for the first time in Korea's history.

### Departure

By 1947 Washington's original aim of establishing a unified administration in Korea with US and Soviet commanders acting jointly had become untenable, given Moscow's determination to dominate the peninsula.[380] This failure to reach an agreement with the Soviet Union left Korea much weaker than Japan, Germany, and Italy. Thus, two main concerns shaped the end of the US military government in Korea and the withdrawal of US troops. First, many policymakers in Washington believed that a US presence in Korea could not be sustained owing to limited resources and that, given limited resources, Korea was less important than Europe in the emerging Cold War with the Soviet Union.[381] Second, to ensure that US gains in Korea were not lost, State Department and Defense Department officials argued for a withdrawal to be accompanied by sufficient political, economic, and military aid to give the South a chance of withstanding pressures from the Soviet-backed North. NSC 8, approved by President Truman in early April 1948, outlined two policies to shape the US withdrawal: completion of the buildup of South Korea's constabulary forces and the provision of US economic aid to offset the chance of an economic collapse.[382] President Truman requested that Congress continue economic assistance to Korea through 1950, formalizing the policy outlined in NSC 8.[383]

General Hodge was particularly concerned that the departure of US forces could undermine many of the important gains made by his military government. Through 1947, he tried to convince Washington that US-Soviet negotiations were failing and that US policy would also fail unless the Truman administration had definite plans "to establish South Korea quickly and confidently."[384] Hodge lamented that the State Department tended to ignore recommendations sent from the field, and he pressed for a US policy that would show Moscow Washington's "determination" and its readiness to "stick it out" in Korea for as long as needed.[385] At the same time, Hodge was acutely aware of the delicate political situation in Korea and Koreans' growing impatience for their own provisional government.

Debate over how to handle South Korea's internal political problems intensified, particularly as officials in Washington began to reevaluate its strategic importance for the United States. In the fall of 1947, the JCS notified Secretary of State Marshall that the US had "little strategic interest in maintaining the present troops and bases in Korea" and that the forty-five thousand troops in Korea "could well be used elsewhere."[386] This opinion reflected the growing concern about the overextension of US resources. Such views increased pressure on individuals such as General Hodge, who wanted to be sure that when a withdrawal did take place, it would be done on American terms, in such a way as not to undermine the South.[387] In the spring of 1947, the SWNCC recommended that a withdrawal be accompanied by the provision of limited military assistance and supplies to Korea in order to keep its emergent constabulary force strong.[388] Others echoed this view, adding that elections should first take place and that programs for economic stabilization should be instituted.[389]

Growing doubts about Korea's strategic value to the United States, coupled with increasing frustration over Moscow's intransigence toward developing a workable solution to the Korea problem, led Washington to bring the Korean case before the UN.[390] A special UN mission to Korea, the United Nations Temporary Commission on Korea, arrived in January 1948 to oversee elections. Members of the military government and the UN commission developed election details, such as the appropriate voting age, the day of the election, and methods to ensure that elections were free and fair. Over 90 percent of Korean voters went to the polls to elect a new National Assembly, and on May 31, 1948, it chose Syngman Rhee as president of the newly established Republic of Korea (ROK).

The US military government in Korea formally ceased to exist on August 15, 1948, following the inauguration of the Korean president and his government. President Rhee and General Hodge signed an agreement whereby the ROK government would gradually assume command over Korean national security forces.[391] The United States also appointed a special representative of the president, John J. Muccio, who would negotiate with the Rhee government over the transfer of authority over national defense forces and the future status of US troops.[392] General Hodge supported the departure of US occupying forces but continued to express concerns over the North's ultimate intentions and the need to handle the withdrawal properly so that a South Korean government was "backed strongly" by the United States.[393] As the US military occupation ended, civil affairs personnel were transferred to a civil affairs section of USAFIK to assist with the transfer of governmental responsibilities and provide some continuity as the transition to Korean officials took place.[394] By January 1949, the lingering regimental combat team of seventy-five hundred troops was withdrawn. As the last US troops departed, Koreans assumed full control of their armed forces in June 1949.[395]

As in the cases of Italy, Japan, and Germany, the United States was concerned about Korea's vulnerability once US troops departed. In this case, given Korea's proximity to the Soviet-supported North, security concerns were especially acute, and President Truman approved continued US military assistance to Korea through the creation of a Korean Military Advisory Group (KMAG) in March 1949.[396] This group continued training Korea's defense forces through the Korean War, since during that war the United States hoped to supplant its forces with functioning, capable Korean troops. KMAG worked with the new ROK government and the US embassy in Seoul to develop a military aid program. From 1949 to 1950, KMAG worked toward this difficult task, with mixed results. Probably the most comprehensive study of KMAG's role in Korea concluded that before the invasion, the team had begun to improve and strengthen the ROK army and its organization. KMAG established training and military educational programs to improve the quality of the army's leadership. It also worked to link the ROK army's logistics to the country's economy. Unfortunately, this study also noted that "time ran out and the first effort by KMAG was doomed to failure."

The US military government in Korea undertook political reconstruction and helped to create a functioning Korean government. The departure of US troops from Korea involved transitioning authority from the military government to a newly elected Korean government, negotiations to establish the parameters for a final withdrawal of US troops, and a consideration of options to bolster the new republic against a stronger, Soviet-backed North. Strategically, the US withdrawal from the divided peninsula signaled that the United States was abandoning its hope of creating a unified country and accepting the division of the peninsula. As in previous governance cases, as the military occupation wound down, policy officials in Washington believed that Korea would need support—economic, political, and military. Overall, however, Korea was still beset by too many internal weaknesses for limited assistance to succeed. The US provision of limited aid was insufficient to overcome an inherently weak and unstable political situation.

## CONCLUSIONS

The four occupations of World War II succeeded in transforming key states into more democratic and liberally oriented political and economic systems.

The governance operations did so through political supervision and political reconstruction. In addition, the military occupations in these countries served as key instruments for the consolidation of US power during the early years of the Cold War. At the start of each of these occupations, the broader strategic role eventually played by US occupying forces was not, for the most part, anticipated. Only as the occupations in Europe and Asia unfolded and as the Soviet threat became more apparent did this broader role become clear. The reform and stabilization of Japan, Italy, Germany, and South Korea changed the character of these states, and they became important strategic outposts for the United States in a world divided by the Cold War.

The occupation of Italy helped to avoid a political vacuum of power in Europe once a key Axis state was defeated. A political transition there could transform that state into an ally—or at least less of an impediment—as the war in Europe progressed. In a sense, military government in Italy was a means of protecting and bolstering the Allied rear in Europe. Just as governance operations served, during a particular conflict, to protect rear areas as American forces fought *within* a state, the occupation of Italy served a similar role in the broader strategic conflict (until the war ended). As Allied troops moved into Italy, they were faced with the need to reestablish order and manage an interim political government before the complete surrender of Italy or the signing of the armistice. Allied forces succeeded in managing a complicated political transition while engaged in various degrees of combat against German forces in Italy. Political reconstruction occurred in Italy as the Allied military government there worked to bring a new Italian government to power and remove officials from the old government. The character of this government directly affected the role Italy would play in the West. The transition in Italy was a direct one—from the military government to the newly elected Italian government. No interim US civilian authorities were created.

The occupation of Korea, similar to that of Italy, also formed part of a strategy to protect America's strategic rear given the arrival of Soviet troops on the peninsula. Officials in Washington wanted to ensure that American troops arrived less to transform Korea and more to serve as a counterweight to the possibility that Soviet troops would reach the southern tip of the peninsula first.[397] The United States had few choices—apart from seeing the entire peninsula fall to Soviet control—other than to establish a presence on the peninsula. The occupation of Korea involved little planning and a great deal of on-the-scene decision making by General Hodge. His military government essentially engaged in political supervision there, replacing Japanese administrators with Koreans but essentially working through existing governmental structures. Hodge's goal was to restore the legitimacy of the Korean government and establish a basis for the future evolution of democracy. In addition to the challenge of reconstructing a society in a country that had been a Japanese colony for decades, Hodge also had to broker with the Soviets and the UN over Moscow's role in the region. In Korea, the external pressures associated with North Korea made a final settlement difficult to reach, ultimately foiling the US goal of creating a stable and secure state. Although the United States provided South Korea with substantial economic aid and although US political and military leaders established a program to strengthen South Korean military forces, this assistance was not enough to deter an eventual attack by the North.

Unlike the occupations of Italy and Korea, a central driving force from the start of the occupations of Germany and Japan was transformation of the political and economic character of these states. Because Germany and Japan were key protagonists in the war, America's stake in their transformation was a central issue from the start. The success of these transformations was paramount, given the role that each state played in Europe and Asia, respectively. Despite the different challenges in Germany and Japan, the army faced many similar challenges in both states, including the purging of government officials, dismantling and rebuilding security forces, organizing and conducting new elections, and writing new constitutions.

As in previous experiences, elements of American denial syndrome emerged during the World War II occupations. In all of these cases, the army did not vie for these jobs. Rather, it was the only organization in each theater capable of restoring order and stability in the midst of ongoing combat and then, once combat wound down, the only institution with the personnel, organizational structure, and geographic reach to implement reforms throughout each country. These steps were essential to finalizing the end of the war in each theater. As General Clay later observed, there was nobody "of requisite size that would volunteer to take the job or would take it, except an army officer whom you could tell to take it."[398]

Army leaders in Europe were anxious to receive more concrete guidance regarding the probable form of an occupation, but in all of the cases, although US policymakers had developed broad plans and goals for the occupations, the details of implementation were left to officers on the ground. The US military implemented key economic and political decisions, although to varying degrees they were advised by civilian experts from the UN or the State Department.

Despite the US ambivalence (understandably) about the military's role in society and the initial hesitancy among civilian and military leaders to engage deeply in shaping the political character of the states in question, in practice all four occupations revealed the inevitability of "taking sides" politically. In Italy early instructions directed military government personnel to refrain from politics, clarifying that "your job is to administer and not to frame policy or talk politics."[399] In Korea, General Hodge was forced to make decisions regarding newly emergent political parties there. Despite the desire to avoid the nitty-gritty of politics, in each of the occupations US military leaders brokered among many competing political groups, realizing that a failure to strengthen democratically oriented political factions—at the expense of the Communist- and Soviet-supported factions—would have undermined key US strategic goals in the region. Regarding economic reform efforts, the US officials were keenly aware that a stronger economy in each country would reduce the costs of the occupation to the United States, as well as bolster the new governments against internal and external political pressures. Thus, army officers lobbied internally for continued US economic and often military assistance in order to preserve the gains made during the occupation period.

Although advance planning for governance operations took place during World War II, many specific command-and-control issues remained unresolved, and army officers in the theater were required to manage both combat operations and the administration of conquered territories. Theater commanders were often forced to balance the requirements of military necessity with the reality that governance tasks often necessitated different sorts of command channels. The military government organizations that emerged during World War II mirrored the two basic frameworks that had evolved in earlier governance operations: *tactical* and *territorial* organizations.[400] A tactical organization afforded tactical and civil affairs control to the theater commander. This organization aimed to ensure that all activities in a zone would be fully coordinated in support of the military commander; the theater commander was also the military governor. A tactical organization offered the advantage of unity of command. However, it also forced small-unit commanders to focus on the tactical employment of their troops and civil affairs functions, often leaving less attention to the latter functions. In addition, since tactical combat units were more likely to change locations, civil affairs activities were often disrupted. Under a tactical organization, a unit's operating area might span several geographical or political subdivisions, which meant that one military government officer might have to interact with officials from different cities or take orders from more than one military commander.

A territorial organization was based loosely on existing political and geographic divisions of an occupied area. This type of organization sought to assign civil affairs teams more permanently to towns and cities, to encourage continuity in policies. In Italy a territorial organization emerged relatively quickly; in Japan one eventually evolved as well. A territorial organization separated the chain of command for governance operations from regular combat channels and made it independent of military commanders below the theater level. Civil affairs teams reported to the military governor, who in turn reported to the theater commander. The benefits of this type of organization included fewer burdens for a military staff focused on combat issues. General Clay believed that army military government succeeded because it could run apart from the army's regular chain of command. He later observed that the army's military governments in Cuba, the Philippines, and other areas had succeeded because the military government had been removed from the ordinary chain of command and that they would not "have worked" if the army had to "follow the ordinary chain of command."[401]

In practice, a combination of tactical and territorial types of organizations existed in most governance operations, both before and during World War II. During the earlier stages of an invasion, a tactical organization was often created, and as the battle pushed deeper into enemy territory, a territorial type of organization evolved in rear areas, paving the way "for the transition from military government to control by civilian agencies."[402] In the early phases of combat, staff from the theater headquarters had a civil affairs section set up as G-5 on the general staff.[403] As regiments moved into an area, spearhead civil affairs detachments also moved in, and on the basis of the requirements they identified, additional detachments might arrive as well. These detachments then came under division control and, in turn, under corps and army control.[404]

In all four of the cases to varying degrees, the army's approach to indirect rule prevailed. In Italy and Japan this was easier since existing administrative structures existed, while in Germany and Korea it was more problematic. In Italy the army's principle of indirect rule guided the military government's approach to the occupation. From the start of the occupation there, army officials realized that only a very limited number of Allied military personnel would be available for administrative duties, thus virtually negating the possibility of a complete "takeover" of existing governmental structures.[405] Eisenhower argued that if military government had to be established in all of Italy, it would require "heavy commitments" of men.[406] Thus, throughout the military government period, he advocated working through existing Italian leaders once Mussolini had fallen.

Despite the development of more specialized civil affairs personnel, throughout World War II combat units remained in the theater and served as occupying forces, often manning borders and checkpoints, enforcing curfews, and retaining order while military government detachments worked to get up and running. In addition, tactical personnel continued to play key administrative roles in the reconstruction of political and economic systems. In Japan official reports on the progress of the occupation barely mentioned military government teams and instead focused on the tactical forces of the Eighth Army as the designated occupation force.[407] The military government section of the Eighth Army was "an appendage" to its regular headquarters. Indeed, in terms of the army's internal organization, during World War II the army created, for the first time, an organization to employ more specialized forces to undertake governance tasks. In addition to specially training those already in its ranks, the army recruited civilian specialists to fill key administrative slots in the governments in Germany, Japan, Korea, and Italy. At the onset of World War II, the army began training for civil affairs. Nevertheless, it is important to keep in mind that despite the formal emergence of an army civil affairs organization and the tendency of civil affairs advocates to view their World War II experiences as illustrations of the importance of specialized civil affairs units, much of the work of the occupation was accomplished by tactical units working in tandem with military government specialists.

Notwithstanding the central role of tactical combat forces in occupation duties during World War II, uncertainty remained about the role that such operations played in the American way of war. As the occupation in Germany came to an end, the War Department dissolved its CAD and reassigned its functions to several other army agencies. This arguably diluted attention to these tasks. The army's plans and operations division on its general staff assumed most of the planning functions for civil affairs and military government.[408] Despite this move, individuals such as Maj. Gen. John H. Hilldring, the former head of the wartime CAD, lobbied the active army to restore a military government / civil affairs component to the army staff.[409] Hilldring worked closely with the Military Government Association (MGA), which had emerged after the war, to improve the army's "understanding of and need for MG/CA in the national military establishment."[410] The association believed that the army would benefit from the creation of a centralized civil affairs division to integrate the disparate civil affairs activities scattered throughout the army. A consultant to the secretary of the army, Daniel Fahey, echoed this view in early 1951. His report examined the army's civil affairs and military government organization, and among its many recommendations, the report advocated the creation of a central army office to coordinate civil affairs / military government activities.[411] In November 1951, the secretary of the army directed the chief of staff to implement key aspects of the so-called Fahey Report.[412] A few months later, the army chief of staff created the Office of the Chief of Staff, Civil Affairs and Military Government (OCCA/MG), thus integrating key civil affairs–related functions.[413] In reality, however, control over civil affairs was still divided, since the PMG retained oversight over training, mobilization, and personnel issues.[414]

An active group of reservists were determined that the army not lose its expertise in governance-related tasks. They hoped to heed Col. Irwin Hunt's warnings after World War I that it was "extremely unfortunate that the qualifications necessary for civil administration [had not been] developed among officers in times of peace."[415] Despite these efforts, the army did not give branch status to civil affairs in the active force. The prevailing army view held that branch status was "hardly warranted," given the few numbers of such officers needed in the field.[416] Proponents of active-branch status, such as Sen. Strom Thurmond, who had been a military government officer in Germany before he was elected to Congress, argued that without it, civil affairs and military government officers would remain loyal to their primary branches, diluting their dedication to civil affairs.[417] In 1949 the army created seventy peacetime reserve civil affairs / military government units based on an official table of organization and equipment.[418] Three active army units—the Ninety-Fifth Group and the Forty-First and Forty-Second Civil Affairs Companies—were also established at this time. Only in 1956 did the army create a civil affairs / military government branch, but it was in the reserve.

There is little systematic data on recruitment for civil affairs units both during and immediately after World War II, an absence that continued for many years. The general perception that emerges from reading reports, articles, and other documents from the mid-1940s to the early 1950s suggests that while there was some World War II training to allow high grade administrators to occupy key positions, there was also a sense that training for these occupation positions could only accomplish so much and that the best training would come from on-the-ground experiences: "Hence each area in which we establish a military government will become a training ground in itself where able and experienced administrators can be developed for use in other areas."[419]

After the war, there seemed to be a certain prestige attached to the civil affairs community and the kinds of jobs the reservists held.[420] One prominent civil affairs reservist, interviewed some twenty years later, recalled that many of his colleagues held top-notch jobs in the civilian world. Describing one individual in Germany, the interviewee noted that his friend went on to become the State Department's chief legal adviser, a "Harvard, New England Brauman [sic] who had a mansion on Foxhall Road [in Washington, DC]."[421] This interview also referred to former city managers who had been reservists, as well as an assistant director of the budget under Truman and various state senators and judges. Another prominent civil affairs official at the time referred to the "bank presidents, industry executives, school superintendents," and others who were civil affairs reservists in the 1950s.[422] A strong sense of pride among the civil affairs reserve community existed—understandable pride in their World War II accomplishments and an ongoing sense of cama-raderie that was helpful in lobbying the army to appreciate better the importance of civil affairs tasks.[423]

Nevertheless, after World War II, the army leadership placed much of the institutional knowledge for governance operations in the reserve. As the Cold War intensified, civil affairs tasks and units were considered specialized and distinct, not part of the conventional army. Increasingly civil affairs came to seen as important mainly within the emerging areas of low-intensity conflict. In fact, despite the importance of governance tasks during World War II and the strategic role played by governance operations, most of these experiences came to be overshadowed by the new forms of warfare that took hold during the Cold War.[424] With the pressures of the Soviet nuclear buildup and the threat of nuclear war, the active army was hesitant to fully embrace civil affairs–related missions as a core competency, despite the best efforts of the civil affairs community. Nevertheless, with the wars in Korea, the Dominican Republic, and Panama, they emerged as important once again.

# NOTES

There is a fairly extensive literature related to World War II civil affairs and military government. This includes Holborn, *American Military Government*; Charles Hyneman, "The Army's Civil Affairs Training Program," *American Political Science Review* (April 1944): 342–53; Ralph Gabriel, "American Experience with Military Government," *American*

*Political Science Review* 37, no. 3 (June 1943): 417–38; Daugherty and Andrews, "Review of U.S. Historical Experience"; Friedrich, *American Experiences in Military Government*; and Coles and Weinberg, *Civil Affairs*. The latter contains copies of memos from archival sources and mainly focuses on operations in Italy.

1. Weigley, *History of the United States Army*, 396–271. See also Watson, *Chief of Staff*, 23–26.

2. Hunt, *American Military Government of Occupied Germany*, 56–57.

3. Ziemke, *U.S. Army in the Occupation of Germany*, 3.

4. United States Code, Title 48, Territories and Insular Possessions, Section 1. A copy of the code is available at http://caselaw.lp.findlaw.com/casecode/uscodes/48/chapters /1/sections/section_1.html.

5. Hayward, "History of the Civil Affairs Division," 4, cited in Ziemke, *U.S. Army in the Occupation of Germany*, 3.

6. "Letter, Col. Harry A. Auer, JAGD, for BG Wade H. Haislip, 5 September 1941," cited in Coles and Weinberg, *Civil Affairs*, 8.

7. Hayward, "History of the Civil Affairs Division." See also US Dept. of War, *Military Government and Civil Affairs: Field Manual 27-5* (1940). A revised version was published in 1943.

8. Ziemke, *U.S. Army in the Occupation of Germany*, 4.

9. Dept. of War, FM 27-5 (1940). See also Swarm's discussion of this manual in "Impact of the Proconsular Experience," 398.

10. Dept. of War, FM 27-5 (1940), 4.

11. There are several differences between the two versions. One is that the 1940 version had a "softer" view of civil affairs, stressing the "welfare of the governed" as the second objective of military government. The 1943 version described the primary objective of military government as that of military necessity, whereby the just treatment of civilians facilitated military operations. The 1943 version also included principles to guide the subsequent establishment of military government in Germany. See US Dept. of the Army and Dept. of the Navy, *Manual of Military Government and Civil Affairs: FM 27-5* (1943), 5, 7.

12. Ibid., 3, 4.

13. Ibid., 36. Also see Swarm, "Impact of the Proconsular Experience," 399.

14. Dept. of War, FM 27-5 (1940), 11.

15. Dept. of War and Dept. of the Navy, FM 27-5 (1943), 6–9.

16. Departments include public works and utilities, fiscal, public health, education, public safety, legal, communication, public welfare, and economics. See Dept. of War, FM 27-5 (1940), 7–9.

17. Ibid., 1.

18. Ibid., 1–3. This later shifted to the G-5 (Military Government) section, created in 1943.

19. See "Memo Major General Myron C. Cramer, JAG to ACofs, G-1, 23 Dec 1941," in Coles and Weinberg, *Civil Affairs*, 9.

20. "Memo, Miller for Col. Edward S. Greenbaum, OUSW, July 23, 1942," in Coles and Weinberg, *Civil Affairs*, 15. North Africa is considered a test of the theory of civilian control over civil matters in a wartime theater. See chap. 2 in Coles and Weinberg, *Civil Affairs*, 30–62.

21. See messages in Coles and Weinberg, *Civil Affairs*, 31–43.

22. "Memo, Gen. George C. Marshall for President Roosevelt, 3 September 1942," in Coles and Weinberg, *Civil Affairs*, 31. Information for the rest of the paragraph is from the same source.

23. "Eisenhower to Marshall, 4 December 1942," ibid., 59.

24. "Msg. Eisenhower to Marshall, September 19, 1942," ibid., 32.

25. Dept. of War, *FM 27-5* (1940), 5. The manual states, "It follows from the basic policy of military necessity . . . that the commanding general . . . must also have full control of military government therein." See also Coles and Weinberg, *Civil Affairs*, 19–20.

26. Hayward, "History of the Civil Affairs Division," cited in James E. Hewes Jr., *From Root to McNamara: Army Organization and Administration*, Special Studies (Washington, DC: Center of Military History, US Army, 1975), 114. See also Stimson and Bundy, *On Active Service*, 553–59.

27. When Gen. John Pershing became chief of staff in 1921, he recommended a reorganization resulting in a "G" system, similar to that of the French and British armies. This resulted in the creation of a G-1 (Personnel), G-2 (Intelligence), G-3 (Operations and Training), G-4 (Supply), and War Plans Division (WPD). G-5 (Military Government) was also added at the theater, army, corps, and division levels.

28. Ziemke, *U.S. Army in the Occupation of Germany*, 113–14.

29. Neff memo to Patterson, in Coles and Weinberg, *Civil Affairs*, 66–67.

30. In an effort to shift some control over planning back to the army, the War Department had created the Division of Military Government under the PMG in 1942 to "silence any claims by civilian agencies to leadership in the military government program." See "Memo, Miller, Associate Dir, MGD, for Greenbaum, OUSW, 30 July 1942," in Coles and Weinberg, *Civil Affairs*, 17. See also "Gullion Memo to Under Secretary of War, 25 July 1942," ibid., 16. The PMG office for military government was relatively low on the totem pole. See comments by Harold Neff, an assistant to the secretary of war, ibid., 66.

31. The very first Military Police Corps emerged as part of a provost unit in the Continental Army. See Robert K. Wright, *Military Police*, Army Lineage Series (Washington, DC: Center of Military History, US Army, 1992), 2. However, the extensive use of provost marshal units really occurred during the Civil War.

32. "Memo, Assistants Chief of Staff, G-1, for ACofs (WPD), September 10, 1941," in Coles and Weinberg, *Civil Affairs*, 8.

33. Ziemke, "Military Government," 294.

34. Eric James Bohman, "Rehearsal for Victory: The War Department and the Planning and Direction of Civil Affairs, 1940–1943," PhD diss., Yale University, 1984, 307, and Coles and Weinberg, *Civil Affairs*, 45.

35. See "Memo, Major General Myron C. Cramer, JAG, for Army Chief of Staff, G-1, 23 Dec 1941," in Coles and Weinberg, *Civil Affairs*, 9.

36. The following discussion of the CATS program relies on the account by Col. Joseph P. Harris, "Selection and Training of Civil Affairs Officers," in *Public Opinion Quarterly* (Winter 1943): 694–706. This whole issue is devoted to issues related to occupied territory.

37. Ziemke, "Improvising Stability," 59. See also Stimson and Bundy, *On Active Service*, 556.

38. Ziemke, *U.S. Army in the Occupation*, 22.

39. Stimson and Bundy, *On Active Service*, 553.

40. Ibid. See also "Memo, Saul K. Padover, Dept. of the Interior, for Ickes, 8 Jan 1943," cited in Coles and Weinberg, *Civil Affairs*, 26.

41. Coles and Weinberg, *Civil Affairs*, 27, and Sherwood, *Roosevelt and Hopkins*, 668.

42. Ziemke, "Military Government," 294.

43. Ziemke, "Improvising Stability," 59.

44. "Statement by John H. Hilldring, Assistant Secretary of State for Occupied Areas," *American Policy in Occupied Areas*, US Dept. of State, Publication #2794, 1.

45. James Byrnes, *Speaking Frankly* (New York: Harper & Brothers, 1947), 244.

46. Stimson and Bundy, *On Active Service*, 556.

47. "Msg. Eisenhower to Marshall, 19 Sept 1942 OPD Msg files, CM-IN8213," cited in Coles and Weinberg, *Civil Affairs*, 32.

48. "Memo, Miller for Col. Edward S. Greenbaum, OUSW, 23 July 1942, PMGO Files, O14.13, MG," cited in Coles and Weinberg, *Civil Affairs*, 15–16.

49. "Memo, W. B. Smith for Byron Price, October 14, 1945, in USFET SGS 014.113," cited in Ziemke, "Improvising Stability," 64.

50. Clay, *Decision in Germany*, 53.

51. "Hilldring to Asst Secy of State Acheson, 9 Nov 1943," cited in Coles and Weinberg, *Civil Affairs*, 153.

52. Coles and Weinberg, *Civil Affairs*, 95, 70, 71, 120–21. At Potsdam, Eisenhower urged a civilian takeover of military government as soon as possible, noting that though Secretary Byrnes agreed with this idea, Byrnes had changed his mind owing to his concern about the administrative burden on the State Department. See Eisenhower, *Crusade in Europe*, 443–41.

53. "Memo, Wickersham, Commandant, School of Military Government, for PMG, 17 June 1942, PMGO files, 321.19, MG," cited in Coles and Weinberg, *Civil Affairs*, 12.

54. Roosevelt's statement to Stimson cited in Ziemke, "Military Government," 295.

55. Clay, *Decision in Germany*, 53.

56. "Min US Gp CC Staff Meeting of Division Directors, June 22, 1945, in OMGUS 12–1/5, V60–12/1," cited in Ziemke, "Improvising Stability," 59.

57. Marshall believed that military government could help mobilize resources in liberated and occupied territories and secure lines of communication and supply channels. George C. Marshall, "Biennial Report of the Chief of Staff of the United States Army, July 1, 1943–June 30, 1945," in Millis, *War Reports*, 247.

58. Ibid. See also US Dept. of the Army, US Army Infantry School, "Theory and Operation of Military Government," 140.

59. Ibid., 161.

60. Murphy, *Diplomat among Warriors*, 91. See also Stimson and Bundy, *On Active Service*, 427.

61. Comments in this paragraph about Eisenhower's thinking are from "Msg, Eisenhower to War Department, 8 February 1943," cited in Coles and Weinberg, *Civil Affairs*, 160.

62. "Memo for the President, drafted by Haskell, Assistant Director, Civil Affairs Division," dated "early March," cited ibid., 165.

63. "Msg. Roosevelt to Churchill, 14 April 1943," cited ibid., 167.

64. Hearst, "Evolution of Allied Military Government," 32–34.

65. Ibid., 43.

66. Sherwood, *Roosevelt and Hopkins*, 356.

67. The army believed this was in contrast to the British system, in which civil affairs operations were closely guided by political authorities in London. See Coles and Weinberg, *Civil Affairs*, 162.

68. Marshall to Eisenhower message, cited ibid., 169.

69. Before the invasion, a "holding area" and temporary school were set up in Algeria in June.

70. Coles and Weinberg, *Civil Affairs*, 240.

71. Hearst, "Evolution of Allied Military Government," 59.

72. Coles and Weinberg, *Civil Affairs*, 248–49. See also "Msg., Rennell, CCAO, 15th Agp to MGS, AFHQ, 24 Sept 1943," ibid., 253.

73. Information here and quotes are from ibid., 249, 250, 254, 256.

74. AMGOT first had six divisions: legal, financial, public safety, public health, enemy property, and civilian supply and resources. It was then streamlined into four: military, political, economic and administrative, and communications.

75. Henry Adams, "Allied Military Government in Sicily, 1943," *Military Affairs* 15, no. 3 (Autumn 1951): 162.

76. US Dept. of State, *FRUS: 1943*, vol. 2, 423–25.

77. This term comes from the French word for "purification," *épuration*. It is used in some of the literature to describe the weeding out of Nazi and Fascist officials during World War II. For more on this process in Italy, see Roy Palmer Domenico, *Italian Fascists on Trial, 1943–1948* (Chapel Hill: University of North Carolina Press, 1991).

78. AMGOT Plan, cited in Coles and Weinberg, *Civil Affairs*, 383. There was disagreement between the British and the Americans on how far to go in this process. Roosevelt favored removing all Italians from high positions, while Churchill was willing to take some risks, as he believed it would be a mistake to "flood all these places with hundreds of British and American gauleiters, however well-meaning and trained they may be." See "Draft Msg., Roosevelt to Churchill, 19 Jun 43 and Msg. Churchill to Roosevelt, 10 Jun 43," cited in Coles and Weinberg, *Civil Affairs*, 173.

79. Benson and Neufeld, "American Military Government," 122–23, 125. It took about five months after the July proclamation to standardize screening questions. Eventually the king passed Royal Decree 159 to deal with all phases of Fascist activity.

80. Memo cited in Coles and Weinberg, *Civil Affairs*, 386.

81. Friedrich, *American Experiences in Military Government*, 122.

82. Miller, *United States and Italy*, 132–34.

83. Sir Winston Leonard Spencer Churchill, *Second World War*, vol. 5, *Closing the Ring* (New York: Houghton Mifflin, 1951), 64.

84. US Dept. of State, *FRUS, 1943: Conferences at Washington and Quebec*, 1276–78.

85. Coles and Weinberg, *Civil Affairs*, 340.

86. "Ltr., McCloy to Hopkins, 30 September 1943," cited ibid., 344.

87. "Ltr., Stimson to Hull, 5 June 1944," cited ibid., 366.

88. Ibid., 369.

89. "Min of Mtg in McCloy's Office with Assistant Secretary of State Acheson and others, 23 March 1944," ibid.

90. "Finance Div, AMGOT HQ, Rpt, May 43-Nov 43, Spofford Rpt," cited ibid., 346.

91. Information in this section if from a series of cables reprinted ibid., 375–82.

92. The first three proclamations were the announcement of the occupation, a statement on war crimes, and one on currency and exchange. Hearst, "Evolution of Allied Military Government in Italy," 45.

93. Ibid., 51.

94. "Lt. Col Walter Doherty, Chief of Public Safety, AMG, Fifth Army, Rpt. for May 1944," cited in Coles and Weinberg, *Civil Affairs*, 283.

95. "Rennell Rpt., CCAC Memo for Info No.5," cited ibid., 203.

96. Ltr, Hilldring to Gen Holmes, DACofS, G-5, SHAEF, 21 Mar 44, cited ibid., 358.

97. Information from documents cited ibid., 400–3. These documents are (1) "Spofford Rpt."; (2) "Ltr. Col. Spofford, CSO, Hq, AMG, to Rgnl CAO's, 26 October 1943, ACC Files, 10000/100/999"; (3) "Review of Educational Activities, prepared by Educational Adviser, Hq, AMG, 4 Nov 1943, ACC files, 10000/154/317"; and (4) "Educat. Div and Subcom., AMG/ACC, Rpt., Sept 43–Feb 44, Spofford Rpt., ex Y-14."

98. Bertram D. Hulen, "U.S. Policy Faces Vital Test; Soviet May Seek Free Hand," *New York Times*, October 8, 1947, cited in Miller, *United States and Italy*, 237. See also broader discussions about the importance of aid to Europe in the context of the Marshall Plan in US Dept. of State, *FRUS, 1947: The British Commonwealth, Europe*, vol. 3, 216–19.

99. US Dept. of State, *FRUS: 1948: Western Europe*, vol. 3, 849.

100. Miller, *United States and Italy*, 214–15.

101. See NSC Memorandum, "Position of the United States with respect to Italy," NSC 1/1, in US Dept. of State, *FRUS: 1948*, vol. 3, 724–46. See also US Dept. of State, *FRUS: 1947*, vol. 3, 478–81, for discussions about the need to bolster Italy before the Marshall Plan came into effect.

102. US Dept. of State, *FRUS: 1947*, vol. 3, 889–92. Another NSC document, NSC 1/2, discussed American strategy toward Italy in early 1948. See US Dept. of State, *FRUS: 1948*, vol. 3, 765–69.

103. Stefano Luconi, "Anticommunism, Americanization, and Ethnic Identity: Italian Americans and the 1948 Parliamentary Elections in Italy," *Historian* 62, no. 2 (2000): 286.

104. Criticism in Benson and Neufeld, "American Military Government," 122.

105. "Moscow Declaration in U.S. Senate Committee on Foreign Relations," in *A Decade of Foreign Policy: Basic Documents 1941–1949*, Senate Document 123, 81st Cong. (Washington, DC: GPO, 1950), 9–11.

106. In 1942 Roosevelt asked the State Department to consider options for postwar Germany. Philip Mosely, "Dismemberment of Germany: The Allied Negotiations from Yalta to Potsdam," *Foreign Affairs* 28, no. 3 (April 1950): 488. Also, in September 1942, Robert Murphy became General Eisenhower's adviser for civil affairs.

107. At the September 1944 Quebec Conference, American representatives discussed "which armies would be where and what kind of administration should be developed" in Germany. Sherwood, *Roosevelt and Hopkins*, 417.

108. The EAC began its work in January 1944. It was created to settle questions about enemy and smaller allied states. The British believed it should have a broad mandate; the US view was more circumspect, with some officials arguing that it was unwise to settle postwar issues as the war was being fought. Mosely, "Occupation of Germany," 581. The State-War-Navy Coordinating Committee, created in 1944, included military and civilian planners. Papers originating in the SWNCC were referred to the JCS for military input before being given final approval. See *Department of State Bulletin*, November 11, 1945, 746.

109. A March 1943 note from Hull to Roosevelt described the treatment of Germany and served as the foundation for the final Moscow Conference paper. Hull, *War Memoirs*, 1284–85.

110. Clark, "Conflicts over Planning."

111. Morgenthau, "Postwar Treatment of Germany," 126. His plan was called "Program to Prevent Germany from Starting a World War III."

112. Hull called the plan "blind vengeance" and added that Secretary McCloy and General Hilldring shared his views. Hull, *War Memoirs*, 1605–7. Some War Department officials were concerned that occupation costs would be very high if Germany were stripped bare. Morgenthau criticized the War Department for deciding issues of national policy at the "technical military level." Morgenthau, "Postwar Treatment of Germany," 125–26.

113. It was drafted by the Cabinet Committee, consisting of the secretaries of war, state, and the treasury.

114. This issue is somewhat confusing, as some scholars maintain that JCS 1067 was "harsh" toward Germany. See Ziemke, *U.S. Army in the Occupation*, 208–14, and Clark, "Conflicts over Planning," 212. However, there is also evidence that army leaders viewed JCS 1067 as more reasonable than Morgenthau's plan.

115. References to JCS 1067 in this paragraph are from a copy of the directive reprinted in Friedrich, *American Experiences in Military Government*, 382.

116. Some, such as General Clay, believed that though JCS 1067 allowed for economic rehabilitation, it did not go far enough. See "Interview with General Lucius D. Clay," by Col. R. Joe Rogers, January 24, 1973, *Senior Officers Debriefing Program*, US Army Military History Research Collection, Carlisle Barracks, PA (May 1975), third interview, 4.

117. McCreedy, "Planning the Peace," 734. McCreedy makes this point in footnote 68.

118. Murphy, *Diplomat among Warriors*, 227–28. Murphy cites an October 1944 memo from Roosevelt to Hull describing the president's reluctance.

119. "Memo from FDR to Secretary Hull on October 24, 1944," referred to in Sherwood, *Roosevelt and Hopkins*, 819, and Hull, *War Memoirs*, 1621.

120. Mosely, "Occupation of Germany," 588, 593. Mosely was political adviser to the US Delegation to the European Advisory Commission from 1944 to 1945. See also Fleet Adm. William D. Leahy, *I Was There: The Personal Story of the Chief of Staff to Presidents Roosevelt and Truman* (New York: Whittlesey, 1950), 197.

121. Mosely, "Occupation of Germany," 585. Mosely compared the CAD's attitude to "Soviet negotiators in their more intransigent moods."

122. Roosevelt's views cited in Ziemke, "Formulation and Initial Implementation," 31.

123. US Army, *Planning for the Occupation of Germany*, Occupation Forces in Europe Series, 1945–1946 (Frankfurt, Germany: Office of the Chief Historian, European Command, 1947), 97, cited in McCreedy, "Planning the Peace," 735.

124. In theory, army officials in Europe focused on operational details, while Washington planners focused on the broader strategic issues. Zink, *American Military Government*, 42–43.

125. Information about COSSAC/Rankin is from Frederiksen, *American Military Occupation*, 1.

126. Ibid., 2.

127. Zink, "American Military Government Organization," 331. In August 1944, the US Group, Control Council replaced the GCU. The former had twelve major divisions

roughly corresponding to the ministries in the German central government. See *Department of State Bulletin*, May 13, 1945, 901. See also Clark, "Conflicts over Planning," 234.

128. Zink, "American Military Government Organization," 310.

129. Some considered the division stagnant because it was not a TOE unit and could not control officer or enlisted personnel grades. Ibid., 72. The ECAD consisted of special units to handle civil affairs throughout Europe, three operating regiments, and a training and reception regiment. The ECAD lasted for nineteen months; initially, it had eighteen hundred officers and four thousand enlisted attached to it. Col. H. M. Pendleton, "The European Civil Affairs Division," *Military Review* 26, no. 1 (April 1946): 49, 50.

130. Ziemke, *U.S. Army in the Occupation*, 66–69.

131. Frederiksen, *American Military Occupation*, 4–5.

132. The Crimea Conference also outlined policies that were later developed at Potsdam. See Pollack and Meisel, *Germany under Occupation*, 1–2.

133. Frederiksen, *American Military Occupation*, 2–3.

134. Eclipse had circulated at SHAEF HQ after June 1944. "Memorandum Number 4, 'Airlift Plan,' 4 April 1945, in Eclipse Appreciation and Outline Plan," cited in McCreedy, "Planning the Peace," 729.

135. These earlier plans were Rankin and Talisman. Ziemke, *U.S. Army in the Occupation*, 164–65. See also Friedrich, "Three Phases of Field Operations," 239.

136. Frederiksen, *American Military Occupation*, 6, and Ziemke, *U.S. Army in the Occupation*, 165.

137. Information in this paragraph is from US Dept. of the Army, *Civil Affairs* (Provost Marshal General's *Training Packet No. 51*), 16.

138. The four Allied commanders in chief constituted the Control Council; a political adviser assisted each chief. See US Dept. of the Army, US Army Infantry School, "Theory and Operation of Military Government," 155–56. See also *Department of State Bulletin*, February 18, 1945, 214.

139. JCS 1067 is reprinted in Friedrich, *American Experiences in Military Government*, 381–402. There is some question of JCS 1067's "control" over Eisenhower, since as supreme commander, AFE, he reported through the Combined Chiefs of Staff (CCS) and not the JCS. The CCS did not formally adopt JCS 1067, though its civil affairs committee drafted a directive (CCS 551) in early 1944 that gave Eisenhower much of the same authority over military government. See "CCS 551, Directive for Military Government in Germany Prior to Defeat or Surrender, 28 April 1944," cited in Ziemke, "Formulation and Initial Implementation," 32–33.

140. *Department of State Bulletin*, May 13, 1945, 901.

141. "Interview with General Lucius D. Clay," *Senior Officers Debriefing Program*, 26.

142. Zink, *American Military Government in Germany*, 27.

143. "Eisenhower's Proclamation No. 2, and Memos to Commanding Generals from General Eisenhower, 5 October 1945, 2 November 1945, and 20 December 1945," in Pollack, Meisel, and Bretton, *Germany under Occupation*, 119–20 and 126–30.

144. Text of statement on cooperation in the Allied Control Council in US Dept. of State, *Axis in Defeat*.

145. US Dept. of the Army, US Army Infantry School, "Theory and Operation of Military Government," 154, and Zink, "American Military Government Organization," 335–37.

146. See Zink, *American Military Government*, 2, and US Dept. of the Army, US Army Infantry School, "Theory and Operation of Military Government," 153.

147. "Msg, Smith to Hilldring, 6 Feb 44," in Coles and Weinberg, *Civil Affairs*, 674.

148. US Dept. of the Army, US Army Infantry School, "Theory and Operation of Military Government," 154.

149. The ECAD still controlled military government officers' pay and promotions, which created tensions. Zink, "American Military Government Organization," 341.

150. Ibid., 343.

151. Hadsel, "Reflections of the U.S. Commanders," 152.

152. "Interview with General Lucius D. Clay," *Senior Officers Debriefing Program*, 28.

153. SHAEF's views described by Ziemke, *U.S. Army in the Occupation*, 156. He cites the SHAEF memo "Office of CoS, to Hqs, Agps 21,12,6, sub: Directive for Military Government of Germany Prior to Defeat or Surrender, 9 Nov 44, in AFHQ G-5, Directives."

154. "Interview with General Lucius D. Clay," *Senior Officers Debriefing Program*, 2.

155. "Letter from Clay to McCloy, 16 Sept 45," cited in Ziemke, *U.S. Army in the Occupation*, 403.

156. For more on the army's reluctance, see John Gimbel, "Governing the American Zone of Germany," in Wolfe, *Americans as Proconsuls*, 92–93.

157. Assistant Secretary of War McCloy, "Our Military Government Policy in Germany," *Department of State Bulletin*, September 2, 1945, 310–11.

158. This is Clay's characterization. See "Min, US Gp CC, Staff Meeting of Division directors, 22 Jun 45," cited in Ziemke, *U.S. Army in the Occupation*, 401.

159. President Truman approved a Byrnes memo clarifying that the State Department should deal with the policy aspects of the occupation while the War Department dealt with its "executive and administrative aspects." "Memorandum of 30 August 1945," in US Dept. of State, *FRUS: 1945, European Advisory Commission*, vol. 3, 957–58.

160. "HQs, ETOUSA, Organization for Military Government of the U.S. Zone, 13 May 45, in SHAEF G-2, GBI/CI/CS/322," cited ibid.

161. "Cable, Secret, Urgent 29325, Eyes Only, General Dwight D. Eisenhower to General George C. Marshall, 26 October 1945, Eisenhower Cable Files, National Archives," cited in Gulgowski, *American Military Government*, 149–50. Gulgowski added that Secretary of the Army Paterson supported Eisenhower but that Secretary Byrnes believed the army had the better organization for governance.

162. "Ltr. SHAEF G-5 to CG's, 7 Dec 44," cited in Ziemke, *U.S. Army in the Occupation*, 163.

163. "Letter, Gen. Eisenhower to President Truman, 26 October 1945," cited in Gulgowski, *American Military Government*, 192.

164. "Interview with General Lucius D. Clay," *Senior Officers Debriefing Program*, 5.

165. Friedrich, *American Experiences in Military Government*, 382.

166. Clay, *Decision in Germany*, 16–18.

167. Murphy wrote that Lewis Douglas, one of Clay's financial advisers, said this. See Murphy, *Diplomat among Warriors*, 251.

168. Oral history interview with Lucius D. Clay, July 16, 1974, by Richard McKinzie, online at the Truman Presidential Library and Museum: https://www.trumanlibrary.org/oralhist/clayl.htm.

169. Hadsel, "Reflections of the U.S. Commanders," 152. Other recollections in this paragraph are from this account, 150–53.

170. "Interview with General Lucius D. Clay," *Senior Officers Debriefing Program*, 7.

171. Zink, "American Military Government Organization," 348.

172. Friedrich, "Denazification, 1945–1946," in Friedrich, *American Experiences in Military Government*, 262–69.

173. Ziemke, "Improvising Stability and Change," 61, 63. Information about denazification laws in the rest of the paragraph from the same source. Clay's first law was Military Government Law No. 8.

174. "Interview with General Lucius D. Clay," *Senior Officers Debriefing Program*, 18.

175. Ibid., 26.

176. Hadsel, "Reflections of the U.S. Commanders," 152.

177. Ziemke, "Improvising Stability and Change," 64.

178. "Interview with General Lucius D. Clay," *Senior Officers Debriefing Program*, 32.

179. Zink, "American Military Government Organization," 346–47.

180. Office of Military Government for Germany, "Status Report on Military Government of Germany: US Zone," March 15, 1946, 1, NA, RG 260.

181. Ziemke, "Formulation and Initial Implementation," 35.

182. Plischke, "Denazification Law and Procedure," 821. Plischke was the author of the denazification plan later adopted by USFET and drafted regulations that consolidated rules from various documents. He was also a historian for the office of the US High Commissioner for Germany.

183. Zink, *American Military Government*, 152–53.

184. JSC 1067 focused on measures that army forces could take to support military operations in Germany and had assumed that the United States would inherit a robust rather than a paralyzed economy. Fainsod, "Development of American Military Government Policy," 43.

185. Ziemke, "Formulation and Initial Implementation," 37. In May 1946, Secretary of State Byrnes also offered a twenty-five-year treaty guaranteeing German demilitarization and disarmament if Germany were unified.

186. "Interview with General Lucius D. Clay," *Senior Officers Debriefing Program*, 35.

187. Ibid., 16.

188. John Gimbel, *The American Occupation of Germany: Politics and the Military 1945–1949* (Stanford, CA: Stanford University Press, 1968), 1.

189. Unless otherwise noted, quotes and data from this section are from Clay, *Decision in Germany*, 263–80.

190. Ziemke, "Improvising Stability and Change," 60.

191. Ibid.

192. *United States Zone Constabulary Trooper's Handbook*, HQ, US Zone Constabulary, APO 46, 1st ed. (February 15, 1946), 8. Available at http://carlisle-www.army.mil/usamhi/Sampler/const46/0005.htm.

193. Plischke, "Denazification Law and Procedure," 812, 813. Before February 1946, arrests averaged four hundred to five hundred per day.

194. *Status Report on Military Government of Germany*, US Zone, Office of Military Government for Germany (March 15, 1946), 2.

195. For discussion of basic court system established in Germany, see Clay, *Decision in Germany*, 246–48.

196. Plischke, "Denazification Law and Procedure," 823–24.

197. See the copy of his memorandum that outlined this plan and was accepted by the Americans, British, and French at the 1947 London conference, in Clay, *Decision in Germany*, 398–400.

198. "Relations between the American Forces of Occupation and the German People," *State Department Bulletin*, December 2, 1945, 885.

199. McCloy's comments on General Clay from McCloy, "From Military to Self-Government," 117–18.

200. By the London conference in late 1947, it was clear that the Soviet attitude would prevent any unification. Clay, *Decision in Germany*, 394.

201. *Department of State Bulletin* 17, no. 437 (November 1947): 936–41, cited in Ziemke, "Formulation and Initial Implementation," 44.

202. Acheson, *Present at the Creation*, 338.

203. Some studies related to the occupation of Japan include Mayo, "American Wartime Planning"; US Dept. of the Army, *Reports of General MacArthur*; Martin, *Allied Occupation of Japan*; Hille, "Eighth Army's Role"; Dower, *Embracing Defeat*; and Borton, "United States Occupation Policies in Japan."

204. Martin, *Allied Occupation of Japan*, 5.

205. Mayo, "American Wartime Planning," 7–21.

206. "Joint War Plans Committee Directive JWPC 264/D, 22 August 1944, 'Occupation of Strategic Positions upon Japanese Withdrawal, Collapse or Surrender,'" cited in Boose, "Portentous Sideshow," 4.

207. An early version of Blacklist, MacArthur's plan to occupy Japan, first appeared in May 1945. A more final version, which will be discussed later in this chapter, appeared in July 1945. See US Dept. of the Army, *Reports of General MacArthur*, 2.

208. Mayo, "American Wartime Planning," 465; see notation in footnote 78. See also US Dept. of State, *FRUS: 1945*, vol. 6, 497–515, and US Dept. of the Army, *Reports of General MacArthur*, 2. MacArthur assumed he would have to impose terms on the Japanese.

209. "GHQ USAFPAC, Basic Outline Plan for 'Blacklist' Opns (2d ed), 25 Jul 45 (TS)," cited in US Dept. of the Army, *Reports of General MacArthur*, 2.

210. The CAD asked the State Department about the nature of Japan's government, economic issues, and the final form of the occupation. See Mayo, "American Wartime Planning," 25. Assistant Secretary of War McCloy supported the idea of a constitutional monarchy for Japan. McCloy, "From Military Government," 114–15.

211. Final versions of these papers are reprinted in US Dept. of State, *FRUS, 1944*, The Near East, South Asia, and Africa, the Far East, vol. 5, 1198–1285. Guidance on key economic issues was absent since disagreements remained over how to treat Japan.

212. Mayo, "American Wartime Planning," 21.

213. Papers originating in the SWNCC were referred to the JCS for the military point of view before final approval was given. The JCS contributed military views and issued SWNCC directives to the Supreme Commander for the Allied Powers. See Dept. of State, *Bulletin*, November 11, 1945, 746. See also Borton, "United States Occupation Policies in Japan," 250–257, and Mayo, "American Wartime Planning for Occupied Japan," 4. And JCS, "Basic Directive for Post Surrender Military Government in Japan Proper," reprinted in Martin, *Allied Occupation of Japan*, 122–50.

214. "U.S. Initial Post-Surrender Policy," *Department of State Bulletin*, September 23, 1945, 4423–26.

215. Immediately following Japan's surrender, Secretary of State Byrnes announced that that SCAP would have authority over the existing Japanese government, including the emperor. See *Historical Survey of World War II CA/MG Operations of the United States*, Provost Marshal General School, Military Government Department, HRC 388.5, Civil Affairs and Military Government, folder 1 of 2, 44, archived at the Military History Institute.

216. Blacklist specifically delegated authority to commanders on the ground. See US Dept. of the Army, *Reports of General MacArthur*, 4.

217. Many American officials were caught by surprise. See Robert Murphy, *Diplomat among Warriors*, 280. On September 2, 1945, the emperor announced the surrender to the Japanese people and commanded them to obey the orders of SCAP.

218. MacArthur's HQ envisioned some nine military government groups and thirty-three companies assigned to the Sixth Army and six military government groups and eighteen companies assigned to the Eighth Army. See Braibanti, "Administration of Military Government," 252. There were around 644,000 men in the Sixth and Eighth Armies. See US Dept. of the Army, *Reports of General MacArthur*, 6.

219. Data from Boutrese, Taylor, and Maass, "American Military Government Experience," 320.

220. US Dept. of the Army, *Reports of General MacArthur*, 198.

221. SCAP is used to refer to the occupying authority in Japan. The twelve sections were (1) Economic/Scientific, (2) Civil Information and Education, (3) Natural Resources, (4) Public Health and Welfare, (5) Government, (6) Legal, (7) International Prosecution, (8) Civil Communications, (9) Statistical and Reports, (10) Counter-Intelligence, (11) Civil Intelligence, and (12) Diplomatic Section. See US Dept. of State, *Occupation of Japan*, 15. See also *Historical Survey of World War II CA/MG Operations*, 46–47.

222. Hille, "Eighth Army's Role," 11.

223. Combat troops in normal command channels were used only for special missions that were "beyond the means of military government teams." For example, they surveyed Japanese national elections. Ibid., 14.

224. *Historical Survey of World War II CA/MG Operations*, 47. Military government teams were named after prefectures—for example, the Ibaraki Military Government Team.

225. Braibanti, "Administration of Military Government," 250, 256, 259. He reported that only some two thousand military government personnel were actually in the prefectures. Many of the staff positions could be filled by specially certified civilian employees. Only some positions, such as commander, adjutant, and executive, and other administrative offices were excluded from civilians. There is a map of Japan's prefectures and the six groups, twenty-four companies, and twenty-eight detachments assigned to them as of January 1946 in US Dept. of the Army, *Reports of General MacArthur*, 197.

226. Braibanti, "Administration of Military Government," 253.

227. Thirteen prefectures were designated minor; eighteen were "intermediate," and twelve were considered "major." Military government teams were then tailored to these needs, and the number of personnel in each team was adjusted according. Teams generally had several staff functions: commerce, industry, procurement, health, money and banking, adjutants, and natural resources. Braibanti, "Administration of Military Government," 254–55.

228. US Dept. of the Army, US Army Infantry School, "Theory and Operation of Military Government," 158–60.

229. *Historical Survey of World War II CA/MG Operations*, 48.

230. Braibanti, "Administration of Military Government," 267.

231. *Historical Survey of World War II CA/MG Operations*, 48.

232. Borton, "United States Occupation Policiesin Japan," 257. The commission contributed to delays in getting answers to important questions, such as the level of industry and reparations.

233. Martin, *Allied Occupation of Japan*, 9.

234. Fearey, *Occupation of Japan*, 7.

235. Kazuo Kawai, *Japan's American Interlude* (Chicago: University of Chicago Press, 1960), 18.

236. MacArthur, *Reminiscences*, 281–82.

237. "U.S. Initial Post-Surrender Policy for Japan," 423.

238. The Combined Chiefs of Staff transmitted a message to General MacArthur on September 6, 1945, stating that he should exercise his authority through Japanese governmental structures. US Dept. of State, *Occupation of Japan*, 73. For more on the army in supervisory role, see "GHQ USAFPAC, Opns Instns No. 4, 15 Aug 45 (S), Amendment No. 12, Doc. App. IV," cited in US Dept. of the Army, *Reports of General MacArthur*, 27. One SCAP section was devoted to reporting compliance by the Japanese government. See *Historical Survey of World War II CA/MG Operations*, 47.

239. US Dept. of the Army, *Reports of General MacArthur*, 194.

240. Braibanti, "Occupation Controls in Japan," 215.

241. Braibanti, "Administration of Military Government," 259.

242. *Historical Survey of World War II CA/MG Operations*, 46.

243. Boutrese, Taylor, and Maass, "American Military Government Experience," 343.

244. Williams, "Completing Japan's Political Reorientation," 1456. Williams was chief of the Government Section's Legislative Division during the occupation.

245. Some criticized this relationship because of the close interests between occupier and the existing government. See John M. Maki, "Japan: Political Reconstruction," *Far Eastern Survey* 16 (April 9, 1947): 75, and also Ulmer, "Local Autonomy in Japan," 46–65, for criticisms of the Allied approach.

246. Boutrese, Taylor, and Maass, "American Military Government Experience," 341–42. This quote and the next are from the same source, 262, 264.

247. Ibid., 344.

248. Martin, *Allied Occupation of Japan*, 56–57.

249. Ibid., 53–55. A SCAP "purge" directive of January 1946 ordered the removal of key persons during the war. The directive called for the removal/exclusion of "undesirable" persons from public office. See reprint of directive in US Dept. of State, *Occupation of Japan*, appendix 21, 112–16.

250. US Dept. of State, *Occupation of Japan*, 112–16, 19.

251. Ulmer, "Local Autonomy in Japan," 50–51.

252. *Historical Survey of World War II CA/MG Operations*, 51.

253. Braibanti, "Administration of Military Government," 274, on polling places.

254. US Dept. of State, *Occupation of Japan*, 26

255. Some believed that many officials previously appointed by Tokyo were restored to power. See Martin, *Allied Occupation of Japan*, 70

256. SCAP Directive, January 12, 1946, in US Dept. of State, *Occupation of Japan*, 136.

257. Information about the new constitution in this paragraph is from Masland, "Postwar Government and Politics," 570.

258. MacArthur's statement in "SCAP, *Summation of Non-Military Activities in Japan*, no. 1 (Sept.–Oct. 1945)," cited in Masland, "Postwar Government and Politics," 570.

259. MacArthur, *Reminiscences*, 314.

260. Ulmer, "Local Autonomy in Japan," 52–53. See also *Historical Survey of World War II CA/MG Operations*, 49.

261. US Dept. of State, *Occupation of Japan*, 19.

262. Ibid., 244.

263. The trials, for many reasons, were controversial. See Dower, *Embracing Defeat*, 450–52.

264. Braibanti, "Administration of Military Government," 269.

265. Fearey, *Occupation of Japan*, 20. SCAP worked on these issues until October 1949.

266. Dower, *Embracing Defeat*, 447.

267. *Historical Survey of World War II CA/MG Operations*, 49.

268. James H. Buck, "The Japanese Self-Defense Forces," *Asia Survey* 7, no. 9 (September 1967): 597–613.

269. Williams, "Completing Japan's Political Reorientation," 1468.

270. U.S. Initial Post Surrender Policy for Japan, 425. See also the JCS Basic Directive of November 1945 that called for policies permitting a wide distribution of income and wider ownership of the means of production. See Eleanor Hadley, "From Deconcentration to Reverse Course in Japan," in Wolfe, *Americans as Proconsuls*, 141.

271. U.S. Initial Post Surrender Policy for Japan, 426.

272. R. Vernon and C. Wachenheimer, "Dissolution of Japan's Feudal Combines," *Department of State Bulletin* 17 (July 13, 1947): 55–60.

273. Martin, *Allied Occupation of Japan*, 77.

274. Report by Kennan in US Dept. of State, *FRUS: 1948*, vol. 6, 697–706, and also Kennan, *Memoirs*, 381–84.

275. For an excellent discussion of these debates in Washington, see the chapter on William H. Draper in Schonberger, *Aftermath of War*, 161–97.

276. "MacArthur to Department of the Army, 24 October 1947," Stimson Papers, Yale University, New Haven. Cited in Schonberger, *Aftermath of War*, 172.

277. Schaller, *Altered States*, 15.

278. Directive reprinted in appendix of Martin, *Allied Occupation of Japan*. Also available at http://www.ndl.go.jp/constitution/e/shiryo/01/036/036tx.html.

279. For information on policies toward labor, see David Flath, *The Japanese Economy* (London: Oxford University Press, 2000), esp. chap. 4 on Japan's postwar recovery.

280. Dower, *Embracing Defeat*, 245–46.

281. Martin, *Allied Occupation of Japan*, 87.

282. MacArthur, *Reminiscences*, 312–13. See also Martin, *Allied Occupation of Japan*, 89. The policy had critics too, with George Kennan noting that not all land was actually resold to tenants. See his *Memoirs*, 387.

283. MacArthur, *Reminiscences*, 313.

284. Wildes, *Typhoon in Tokyo*, 238, and MacArthur, *Reminiscences*, 313.

285. Zook, "Educational Missions to Japan and Germany," 3.

286. Zook, "Summary of the Report," 20–26. See also Martin, *Allied Occupation of Japan*, 59.

287. MacArthur, *Reminiscences*, 312. Dower, *Embracing Defeat*, 247.

288. Boutrese, Taylor, and Maass, "American Military Government Experience," 342. SCAP asked Japan's Ministry of Health and Social Affairs to complete a full report on the state health care system. Data, however, was poor and inaccurate. Wildes, *Typhoon*, 208–9, 211.

289. SCAP inspired the Daily Life Security Law—the first comprehensive welfare law in Japan. Hille, "Eighth Army's Role," 15–16.

290. Record of conversation with MacArthur, "Sir Alvary Gascoigne to Foreign Office, March 4, 1947," and MacArthur press conference, March 17, 1947, both noted in Schaller, *Altered States*, 1.

291. MacArthur quote cited in Masland, "Postwar Government and Politics," 565.

292. SWNCC 381, the State Department plan, and SWNCC 384, the army plan, both proposed a multiyear aid program to provide Japan with raw materials and capital for the renewal of industry. These ideas were incorporated into the Economic Recovery in Occupied Areas program passed by Congress in June 1948. See SWNCC 360, 381, 384 files, Records of the State, War, Navy Coordinating Committee, NA, RG 353, as cited in Schaller, *Altered States*, 262n16.

293. Schonberger, *Aftermath of War*, 171. See also page 166 for discussion of Draper's memo to MacArthur on this subject.

294. Fearey, *Occupation of Japan*, 11.

295. Schonberger, *Aftermath of War*, 237.

296. NSC 49, "Strategic Evaluation of United States Security Needs in Japan," in US Dept. of State, *FRUS: 1949*, vol. 7, 774–79.

297. "Dulles to Sebald, July 27, 1951," in US Dept. of State, *FRUS: 1951*, vol. 6, 1226–27, cited in Shaller, *Altered States*, 39.

298. Dower, *Embracing Defeat*, 75.

299. Works on Korea include Schnabel, *Policy and Direction*; Taylor, "Military Government Experiences"; Harry G. Huppert, "Korean Occupational Problems," *Military Review*, no. 29 (December 1949): 9–16; McCune, "Occupation Politics in Korea"; Bertram Sarafan, "Military Government: Korea," *Far Eastern Survey* (November 20, 1946): 349–52; Borton, "Occupation Policies in Japan and Korea"; Roger Dingman, "Strategic Planning and the Policy Process: American Plans for War in East Asia, 1945–50," *Naval War College Review* (November–December 1979): 4–21; and Hoag, "American Military Government in Korea."

300. In 1946 George McCune, a State Department official in charge of Korean affairs, wrote that US policy had always been to give Korea its own democratic government. McCune, "Occupation Politics in Korea," 36. See also US Dept. of State, *FRUS: 1944*, vol. 5, 1224–28.

301. US Dept. of State, *FRUS: 1943, The Conferences at Cairo and Tehran*.

302. US policymakers grew increasingly concerned with Soviet intentions and believed that it would be useful to have US military forces stationed there. See US Dept. of State, *FRUS: 1945*, vol. 6, 556–80. Secretary of State Stimson suggested to Truman that at least a token force of US soldiers be stationed in Korea during the trusteeship period. See US Dept. of State, *FRUS: 1945, The Conference of Berlin (The Potsdam Conference)*, vol. 2, 631. The other two were the occupations of Japan and China. Schnabel, *Policy and Direction*, 10.

303. David I. Steinberg, *The Republic of Korea: Economic Transformation and Social Change* (Boulder, CO: Westview, 1989), 40.

304. Taylor, "Military Government Experiences in Korea," 356–60.

305. Primary source documents affirm this; cited in Boose, "Portentous Sideshow," 4, 116.

306. Information about Blacklist in General Staff of MacArthur, *Report of General MacArthur*, vol. 1, supplement, cited in Kang, "United States Military Government in Korea," 2. Also see MacArthur, *Reminiscences*, 261. Portions of Baker-Forty reprinted in Hoag, "American Military Government in Korea," 516–20.

307. Hoag, "American Military Government in Korea," 97.

308. "HQ, XXIV Corps, Baker-Forty, Field Order 55," in US Army Military Government in Korea Records, Federal Record Center, Kansas City, MO, 3, cited in Kang, "United States Military Government in Korea," 4.

309. US Dept. of State, *FRUS: 1944*, vol. 5, 1190–94.

310. The State Department responded in May 1944 with twenty-four papers—all but three on Japan. See Hoag, "American Military Government in Korea," 22.

311. US Dept. of State, *FRUS: 1945, Conferences at Malta and Yalta*, 770. State Department planners had discussed the idea of a trusteeship at least since 1942, when the Division of Far Eastern Affairs discussed the issue. See Matray, "End to Indifference," 184–85. The State Department's Inter-Divisional Area Committee on the Far East advocated strengthening a trusteeship with a partial or full military occupation upon Japan's departure. See Jun, "State Making in South Korea," 85. See also SWNCC 176/8 in US Dept. of State, *FRUS: 1945*, vol. 6, 1074.

312. In addition, the United States, Great Britain, the Soviet Union, and China agreed to divide Korea at the thirty-eighth parallel upon Japan's surrender, with the northern portion to be occupied by Soviet forces and the southern half by American troops.

313. "Memo, Office of Far Eastern Affairs for Hull," in US Dept. of State, *FRUS: 1944*, vol. 5, 1234.

314. "Draft Memorandum to the Joint Chiefs of Staff," n.d., in US Dept. of State, *FRUS: 1945*, vol. 6, 1037.

315. Hoag, "American Military Government in Korea," 85

316. There was a Joint Army-Navy Intelligence Survey on Korea, but it focused more on tactical conditions for combat rather than on the establishment of a military government. See Taylor, "Military Government Experiences," 357.

317. Appendix "B" discussion, in US Dept. of State, *FRUS: 1945*, vol. 6, 1098–99.

318. Ibid.

319. Blacklist had actually designated Gen. Joseph Stilwell to serve as commander of the Korean occupation. See Boose, "Portentous Sideshow," 6–7. Also see Jun, "State-Making in South Korea," 94, on other commanders considered to head the occupation.

320. Statement by President Truman, September 18, 1945, in *Decade of American Foreign Policy*, 676.

321. Kang, "United States Military Government in Korea, 1945–1948," 5.

322. "History of United States Army Military Government in Korea," Statistical Research Division, USA Military Government in Korea, Special Staff of US Army, Historical Division, No author, n.d. Marked first draft, incomplete, 18.

323. See full text in US Dept. of State, *FRUS: 1945*, vol. 6, 1073–91.

324. Cha, "Search for a 'Graceful Exit,'" 72, and Hoag, "American Military Government in Korea," 188.

325. "Memo by acting chairman, SWNCC, SWNCC 176/4, September 10, 1945," in US Dept. of State, *FRUS: 1945*, vol. 6, 1044–45.

326. Hoag, "American Military Government in Korea," 117.

327. MacArthur's request was a mere three weeks before the landing of US troops. See request in US Dept. of State, *FRUS: 1945*, vol. 6, 1037. For Hodge's concerns, see Schnabel, *Policy and Direction*, 14.

328. "Experiences of a Staff Officer, HQ, XXIV Corps in the Occupation of Korea, September–November 1945, Former Acting Chief of Staff, 24th Corps, Folder: WWII Misc. Kenneth C. Strother, HQ XXIV Corps, Memoir, August–November 1945," 5, located at the US Army Military History Institute.

329. Meade, *American Military Government*, 48.

330. Information about G-2's activities from *History of the United States Armed Forces in Korea*, compiled under the supervision of chief historian Harold Larsen, Tokyo and Seoul, XXIV Corps G-2, Historical Section, manuscript in the Office of the Chief of Military History, Washington, DC, 1/1:21–24, 1/1:51–61, and 3/5:10, cited in Jun, "State-Making in South Korea."

331. "Memo, political advisor in Korea (Benninghof) to Sec State, 29 September 1945," in US Dept. of State, *FRUS: 1945*, vol. 6, 1064.

332. "Experiences of a Staff Officer," 5, 14.

333. Trip referenced in "Political Advisor in Korea (Benninghof) to the Secretary of State," September 26, 1945, in US Dept. of State, *FRUS: 1945*, vol. 6, 1059. He noted that two weeks since the landing, "this headquarters has not even entered into discussions with the Russians on a number of urgent subjects."

334. Taylor, "Military Government Experiences," 359–60. Even in late August, the State Department considered options for a joint civil administration of Korea. See "Draft memorandum to the Joint Chiefs of Staff," Washington, DC, n.d., in US Dept. of State, *FRUS: 1945*, vol. 6, 1038.

335. The military government structure initially mirrored elements of the organization that Japan had put in place in Korea. The eight secretariats were General Affairs, Foreign Affairs, Intelligence and Information, Personnel (Korean), Army Administration, Property Custodian, Planning, and Accounts. The nine bureaus were Finance, Mining and Industry, Agriculture and Commerce, Public Safety, Public Health, Education, Justice, Communication, and Transportation. See Daugherty and Andrews, *Review of U.S. Historical Experience*, 400.

336. *Historical Survey of World War II CA/MG Operations*, folder 1 of 2.

337. Telegram from Hodge's political adviser Benninghof to the secretary of state, September 15, 1945, in US Dept. of State, *FRUS: 1945*, vol. 6, 1052.

338. Meade, *American Military Government*, 77.

339. *Historical Survey of World War II CA/MG Operations*, folder 1 of 2, 40.

340. Taylor, "Military Government Experiences," 361.

341. Sometimes the Japanese administrator would be retained as an adviser if needed.

342. "Memo from Hodge to General of the Army MacArthur at Tokyo, 24 September 1945," in US Dept. of State, *FRUS: 1945*, vol. 6, 1056.

343. Koreans from Japan and North Korea had to be repatriated.

344. "'Report on Repatriation August 15, 1945–September 1 1946,' HQ XXIV 20 September 1946, AGO: 14.33, HIST Files," cited in Hoag, "American Military Government," 136.

345. SWNCC 176/8 guided overall reconstruction policy. Also known as "Basic Initial Directive to the Commander in Chief, U.S. Army Forces, Pacific, for the Administration of Civil Affairs in Those Areas of Korea Occupied by U.S. Forces" (originally SWNCC 176/3), in US Dept. of State, *FRUS: 1945*, vol. 6, 1073–91.

346. *History of the Occupation of Korea: August 1945–May 1948*, 3 vols., prepared in 1948 by historians of XXIV Corps, vol. 1, chap. 1, Center of Military History, cited in Schnabel, *Policy and Direction*, 14. Another analyst noted that Korea was the "one country in the Pacific Theater over which real military government was established, [and the] only important area occupied by American troops for which some study or preparations had not been made." See Taylor, "Military Government Experience," 355. This sentiment is repeated in other accounts. See Bertram D. Sarafin, "Military Government: Korea," *Far Eastern Survey* (November 20, 1946): 350.

347. Daugherty and Andrews, *Review of U.S. Historical Experience*, 401. See also *Historical Survey of World War II CA/MG Operations*, folder 1 of 2, 40.

348. Meade, *American Military Government*, 78.

349. "Statement by the President on the Liberation of Korea, September 18, 1945," *American Presidency Project*, http://www.presidency.ucsb.edu/ws/?pid=12352. See also US Dept. of State, "Memorandum for the President, Proposed Statement on Korea, September 14, 1945," http://www.trumanlibrary.org/whistlestop/study_collections/korea/large /documents/pdfs/kr-1–2.pdf. MacArthur initially supported this course and instructed Hodge to make maximum use of the Japanese governmental machinery in Korea. "History of United States Army Military Government in Korea," 18. The State Department also supported this policy but then reversed its position. See US Dept. of State, *FRUS: 1944*, vol. 5, 1228–30.

350. Draft JCS message to MacArthur in September 10, 1945, "Draft message to General of the Army Douglas MacArthur," in US Dept. of State, *FRUS: 1945*, vol. 6, 1045. This message also contains the SWNCC warning that the retention of Japanese "has already had an unfortunate effect on our position in Korea."

351. *Historical Survey of World War II CA/MG Operations*, folder 1 of 2, 41.

352. US leaders consistently pointed out that the division was due to military necessity as opposed to having any political logic. See Truman, *Memoirs*, 445, 521–22, and also Acheson, *Present at the Creation*, 449.

353. Meade, *American Military Government*, 3.

354. US Dept. of State, *FRUS: 1946*, vol. 8, 713–14. The State Department reportedly influenced Truman to turn down the War Department's requests.

355. Meade, *American Military Government*, 60.

356. Daugherty and Andrews, "Review of U.S. Historical Experience," 404.

357. "Assistant Secretary of War McCloy message to Under Secretary of State Acheson, November 13, 1945," in US Dept. of State, *FRUS: 1945*, vol. 6, 1123.

358. "LTG Hodge to General of the Army Douglas MacArthur, at Tokyo, November 2, 1945," in US Dept. of State, *FRUS: 1945*, vol. 6, 1106. To this end, some censorship was allowed. See SWNCC 176/8, ibid., 1081.

359. See section III of what is known as the Soviet-Anglo-American Communiqué, December 27, 1945, contained in a document called "Interim Meeting of Foreign Ministers of the United States, the United Kingdom and the USSR, Moscow, December 16–26, 1945." Reprinted in *A Decade of American Foreign Policy*, accessed online at http://avalon .law.yale.edu/20th_century/decade19.asp.

360. For the difficulties of this process, see "Meetings of the Joint Commission for Korea, May 21–Oct 18, 1947," in *Decade of American Foreign Policy*, 677–79.

361. "Hodge telegram to War Department through CINCAFPAC Tokyo, November 20, 1945," NA, RG 59, General Records of the Department of State, confidential file, box 212, cited in Cha, "Search for a 'Graceful Exit,'" 122

362. See "Basic Initial Directive to the Commander in Chief" (SWNCC 176/8), 1075–76.

363. Hoag, "American Military Government," 227–28.

364. Some 85 percent of the personnel had been Japanese. See Meade, *American Military Government*, 132.

365. SCAP, *Summation of Non-Military Activities in Japan*, no. 4, January 1946, cited in Hoag, "American Military Government in Korea," 227.

366. George M. McCune, *Korea Today* (Cambridge, MA: Harvard University Press, 1950), 25–26.

367. See "Basic Initial Directive to the Commander in Chief" (SWNCC 176/8), 1075–76.

368. MPs were then charged with enforcing military regulations and guarding government property. Meade, *American Military Government*, 119–20.

369. Hoag, "American Military Government," 233.

370. Sawyer, *Military Advisors in Korea*, 5. See also SCAP, *Summation of Non-Military Activities*, no. 1, part V, 12, and Hoag, "American Military Government," 233.

371. Sawyer, *Military Advisors in Korea*, 17

372. In the first year of the occupation, debate took place over the appropriate form and strength of a Korean defense forces. See ibid., 10, 29.

373. "RAD CS 562.66, CINCFE to DA 22 Oct 1947," cited in Schnabel, *Policy and Direction*, 33. MacArthur advocated a smaller, police-type force of some twenty-five thousand but noted that it might be advisable to set up national defense forces. He was resistant to helping with the creation of a field army in the South not so much for strategic regions, but because of concerns that US troops were already overextended in the region. See Schnabel, *Policy and Direction*, 31, and Ridgway, *Korean War*, 11.

374. Gene M. Lyons, *Military Policy and Economic Aid: The Korean Case, 1950–1953* (Columbus: Ohio State University Press, 1981), 163. The JCS hoped to postpone a decision until US-Soviet negotiations over the provisional government were complete. See Sawyer, *Military Advisors in Korea*, 12–13. Generals Hodge and MacArthur and Brig. Gen. Lawrence E. Schick, provost marshal general of XXIV Corps, supported stronger defense forces for Korea but wanted Washington guidance. See "MacArthur to Eisenhower, 26 November 1945," in US Dept. of State, *FRUS: 1945*, vol. 6, 1136–37. See also Schnabel, *Policy and Direction* , 32.

375. Sawyer, *Military Advisors in Korea*, 10, 17. See also Hermes, "Survey of the Development," 62.

376. Sawyer, *Military Advisors in Korea*, 15

377. Meade, *American Military Government*, 190–201, focuses on agriculture issues.

378. Information about public health from ibid., 219–24, unless otherwise noted.

379. Information from ibid., 213–18.

380. For a statement of US policy after the 1945 Moscow Conference, see "Memorandum by the U.S. Delegate at the Moscow Conference, December 17, 1945," in US Dept. of State, *FRUS: 1945*, vol. 2, 641–43. The Soviets did not respond to specific US proposals in

August 1947 that urged each zone to hold elections for a legislature. Zonal legislatures would then choose a national legislature that would then work with a provisional government to negotiate the withdrawal of all occupying forces from Korea. See "United States Proposals Regarding Korea," part of letter from Acting Secretary Robert Lovett to Soviet foreign minister Vyacheslav Molotov, August 29, 1947, in *Department of State Bulletin*, September 7, 1947, 473–75.

381. "BG Lerch letter to Hodge, July 27, 1947," cited in Cha, "Search for a 'Graceful Exit,'" 205.

382. "Report by the NSC on the Position of the United States with Respect to Korea, April 2, 1948," in US Dept. of State, *FRUS: 1948*, vol. 6, 1164–69.

383. Truman message to Congress, *Department of State Bulletin*, June 19, 1949, 781–83.

384. Cha, "Search for a 'Graceful Exit,'" 204.

385. Hodge told the State Department that information he sent from the "Korean hot spot" was "based on fact and not theory." See Hoag, "American Military Government," 358. For Hodge's views, see "Telegram, Political Advisor to Sec State, 26 May 1946," in *FRUS: 1946*, vol. 8, 685–89.

386. "JCS, Memo to Marshall on 'The Interest of the U.S. in Military Occupation of South Korea from the Point of View of Military Security of the U.S.,' September 24, 1947," NA, RG 218, "Records of the United States Joint Chiefs of Staff, 1942–1953," geographic file, box 130, cited in Cha, "Search for a 'Graceful Exit,'" 231.

387. "Hodge to Marshall, June 23, 1948," in US Dept. of State, *FRUS: 1948*, vol. 6, 1220. See also "Butterworth Memorandum to Marshall and Lovett, August 17, 1948," in US Dept. of State, *FRUS: 1948*, vol. 6, 1227. See also the memo by the Special Inter-Departmental Committee on Korea outlining US government policy at the time, in US Dept. of State, *FRUS: 1947*, vol. 6, 608–18.

388. "Report by the Special Ad Hoc Committee to the SWNCC, April 21, 1947," in US Dept. of State, *FRUS: 1947*, vol. 1, 725–33.

389. "BG C. V. R. Schuyler, Chief of Plans and Policy Group, P&D Division, the Army Department, Memo to Blum, January 2, 1948," NA, RG 218, geographic file, box 130, and "Far Eastern Subcommittee of the SANACC, Report on 'U.S. Policy in Korea,' January 15, 1948," both cited in Cha, "Search for a 'Graceful Exit,'" 245.

390. "Lovett, telegram to the American Embassy in Moscow, September 16, 1947," in US Dept. of State, *FRUS: 1947*, vol. 6, 790.

391. Sawyer, *Military Advisors in Korea*, 34.

392. "Memorandum by the Secretary of State to President Truman, Subject: Proposed Appointment of Appointment of Mr. John J. Muccio as Ambassador to Korea, April 27, 1948," cited in US Dept. of State, *FRUS: 1949, The Far East and Australasia*, vol. 7, document 123.

393. "Hodge telegram to Marshall, February 22, 1948," in US Dept. of State, *FRUS: 1948*, vol. 6, 1127. As early as 1946, Hodge pressed Washington for a clear statement of economic aid to any emergent Korean provisional government. See "Political Advisor to Sec State," in US Dept. of State, *FRUS: 1946*, vol. 8, 630–32.

394. *Historical Survey of World War II CA/MG Operations*, 42.

395. Sawyer, *Military Advisors in Korea*, 37.

396. Information in this paragraph is from Sawyer, *Military Advisors in Korea*, 38, 187.

397. See recollections of Dean Rusk, assistant secretary of state for Far Eastern affairs, in US Dept. of State, *FRUS: 1945*, vol. 6, 1039.

398. Oral history interview with Lucius D. Clay, July 16, 1974, conducted by Richard McKinzie. See also Clay, *Decision in Germany*, 53.

399. General Administrative Instruction No. 1, cited in Fainsod, "Development of American Military Government Policy," 30.

400. See Vernon, "Civil Affairs and Military Government," 29–30. Vernon was an instructor at the Command and General Staff School. See also US Dept. of the Army, US Army Infantry School, "Theory and Operation of Military Government," 140, 150–155. Information about both forms of organization is from these two sources.

401. "Interview with General Lucius D. Clay," *Senior Officers Debriefing Program*, 22.

402. Vernon, "Civil Affairs and Military Government," 29.

403. US Dept. of the Army, US Army Infantry School, "Theory and Operation of Military Government," 153.

404. Ibid., 154.

405. Working through Italian administrators produced mixed results, depending on the particular agency involved. Indirect rule seemed to work better in some of the older agencies, while newer agencies tended to need closer supervision. Benson and Neufeld, "American Military Government in Italy," 118–20.

406. Coles and Weinberg, *Civil Affairs*, 232, 233.

407. Braibanti, "Occupation Controls in Japan," 217. These official reports are called *Monthly Summation of Non-Military Activities* and were produced by SCAP. Braibanti also notes that many of the trained military government specialists departed Japan in the summer of 1946, leaving Eighth Army personnel to deal with occupation duties.

408. "Guide to Civil Affairs and Military Government Records in the Adjutant General's Records Center," Washington, DC, November 1952, 2. Copy in US Army Center of Military History.

409. Swarm, "Impact of the Proconsular Experience," 400.

410. *Military Government Journal and Newsletter*, April 1952, vol. 4, 2. Later the first head of the army's new civil affairs and military government division, Maj. Gen. William Marquat, continued to work closely with the independent MGA to institutionalize civil affairs within the army. The association had close ties to Congress. See the *Military Government Journal and Newsletter*, January 1953, 1. See also the Marquat memo urging his staff to join the MGA: "Memorandum for All Personnel from MG William F. Marquat, 18 November 1952," NA, RG 319, Civil Affairs and Military Government Administrative Office, 1952–54, decimal file 080–091 Korea, box 5, folder 080 Korea.

411. Fahey, "Overall U.S. Politico-Military-Complex" (the Fahey Report); "Memorandum by the Secretary of State to President Truman, Subject: Proposed Appointment of Appointment of Mr. John J. Muccio as Ambassador to Korea, April 27, 1948," cited in US Dept. of State, *FRUS: 1948, The Far East and Australasia*, vol. 6, document 123. This copy of the Fahey Report contains a memorandum for the secretary of the army summarizing Fahey's points. The report itself was completed in February 1951. It is also reprinted in Wing, *Civil Affairs / Military Government*, 173–77.

412. Wing, *Civil Affairs / Military Government*, 73.

413. Army General Order 37 of April 13, 1952, created the new office. See ibid., 27.

414. "Col. Strom Thurmond, Commanding 360th MG Area HQ, 'Comments and Recommendations on Civil Affairs / MG Organization and Operations,' December 1953, to the Secretary of the Army," NA, RG 319, 1952–54, 300.6–310.1, box 11, folder 310.1, Administration and Organization, 8.

415. Hunt, *Military Government of Occupied Germany*, 56–57.

416. "Address of Franklin L. Orth, Deputy Assistant Secretary of Defense for the Army, Manpower and Reserve Forces, to the Washington Chapter of the Military Government Association on November 20, 1954," NA, RG 319, box 5, folder 080.

417. Thurmond, "Comments and Recommendations," 16. Thurmond argued that civil affairs reservists were "uniquely" qualified owing to their job expertise in civilian life.

418. By about 1950, there were some forty-seven hundred personnel in these seventy reserve units. See Swarm, "Impact of the Proconsular Experience," 401.

419. "Memo, Clay, Dir of Materiel, ASF, for the Dir of Personnel, ASF, 31 May 43," cited in Coles and Weinberg, *Civil Affairs*, 79. Note that Clay, who held this view, went on to be Germany's military governor.

420. There is a sense of this from reading old MGA newsletters and accounts of their annual conferences, which cite speakers and their civilian jobs. The first officers of the MGA, for instance, were received by President Truman in the Oval Office in April 1947. See Eli Nobleman, "A Brief History of the Civil Affairs Association," which is available on the association's website at http://www.civilaffairsassoc.org/history.htm.

421. Transcript of interview conducted by Dr. Richard Stewart, May 2, 1993, Civil Affairs / Military Government Interviews, Fort Bragg, NC, located in USASOCOM Archives, cabinet 3, drawer 5, transcripts M-Z, folder Nobleman/Oravetz, Oral History Interview 1993.

422. Swarm, "Impact of the Proconsular Experience," 404.

423. Despite the fact that in the civil affairs community civilian jobs were supposed to be matched to their military functional specialties, data on such matching was very hard to come by in the early years. In 2003 and 2004, this started to change, with a requirement for the military reserves as a whole to collect data on reservists' civilian occupations. Author telephone interview with Dr. Glenn Gotz, February 7, 2005. Gotz was then a research analyst at the Institute for Defense Analysis and an expert on the reserves. His work was instrumental in urging the DOD to begin collecting key data on reservists, such as their civilian occupations. See Glenn A. Gotz, *Strengthening Employer Support of the Guard and Reserve* (Alexandria, VA: Institute for Defense Analysis, January 2003).

424. With the emergence of nuclear weapons, strategists and analysts were examining ideas such as limited war, the belief being that we could not afford to conduct large-scale war owing to the threat of nuclear annihilation. See Robert E. Osgood, *Limited War: The Challenge to American Strategy* (Chicago: University of Chicago Press, 1957), 1–2. See also Gacek, *Logic of Force*, 16.

# FOUR

# THE COLD WAR

## ILLUSIVE LESSONS

DESPITE THE SUCCESSES of the World War II military governments, the army did not institutionalize approaches to transforming the political order in states against which it would fight. Although a new reserve structure had emerged in 1949 to recruit and retain civil affairs soldiers, three trends characterized the army's attitude toward governance operations during the post–World War II period. First, despite the strategic value of governance operations during the war, army officials tended to consider civil affairs operations as tactical-level challenges. Within the army's regular, conventional force structure, the predominant view held that civil affairs units played important combat-service-support functions by ensuring that the civilian population did not interfere with military activities. Second, reservists making the case for the importance of civil affairs tended to emphasize the "specialness" of these units. While this reflected a natural desire to record their experiences and build a lasting constituency for civil affairs missions, it further separated civil affairs from the regular army. The army's placement of the majority of civil affairs units in the reserves following the war formalized this separation.[1] Third, as the Cold War intensified, the army began to pay attention to "new forms" of warfare, and governance operations became more closely associated with tasks related to low-intensity conflict and nation building, a tendency that was reinforced by the eventual inclusion of civil affairs assets into the USSOCOM organization.

A recurring debate about the merits of specialization for civil affairs–type functions unfolded during this period. As the civil affairs community evolved and grew, a central argument it made was that the military could not expect to "produce" experts in key civilian specialties, and thus, the civil affairs reservists who held these specialized jobs in "civilian life" could be called on to tap into these skills in a military contingency. However, with the development of approximately twenty army reserve functional specialties,[2] it became clear that it would be difficult to perfectly match each one with civilian practitioners. The May 1957 army manual for civil affairs acknowledged that "in assigning personnel to CAMG [Civil Affairs/Military Government] duties it must be recognized that there is a scarcity of individuals qualified to conduct various CAMG functional specialties" and that consideration must also be given to age, military experience, and physical qualifications.[3]

Such arguments about specialization tended to further separate governance missions from the regular army's role during wartime. These arguments tended to downplay the fact that thousands of regular army officers conducted governance missions throughout World War II. A comprehensive study conducted for the army in 1955 concluded that the army's almost "total reliance on the reserve for civil affairs and military government in tactical, logistical and area commands . . . suggest strongly that the immediacy of CA/MG needs in the event of general war has not been fully recognized by the army."[4] And at times, the emphasis on specialized civil affairs skills could create problems. In 1965, in the Dominican Republic, active-duty army officers complained in an after-action report that civil affairs personnel were "unfamiliar with team equip[ment], personnel, unit SOP [standard operating procedures] and CA mission."[5]

Several constituencies continued to emphasize the combat-service-support function of civil affairs operations, such as ensuring that civilians remain out of harm's way and not interfere with military activities. Maj. Gen. John H. Hilldring, then the chief of the army's CAD, remarked that that was "the beginning and end of our involvement in this business."[6] The 1952 graduates of the military government course at Camp Gordon, Georgia, were reminded of "the importance of assuring that our military operations are not impeded by civil disturbances."[7] Early civil affairs doctrine described civil affairs operations as "obtaining for a military commander essential civilian support, reducing civilian interference with military operations and assisting in the attainment of his political-military objectives."[8] In 1959 the army's vice chief of staff reaffirmed that, "simply stated," the role of civil affairs and military government "may be said to be unchanged from what it has been in the past . . . that of relieving interference from the civilian population."[9] Furthermore, the school's placement under the control of the PMG—who was primarily responsible for military police training—reinforced the army's tendency to view governance-related activities as narrow, rule-of-law-related tasks rather than having a strategic-level connection to the final political order of a state.

But others did advocate a broader approach to civil affairs. For example, a prominent report commissioned by the secretary of the army in 1951, the so-called Fahey Report, viewed civil affairs and military governance functions as political and military requirements both "during and after combat."[10] Fahey observed that for the army, "lessons learned the hard way within the politico-military-economic area must be flagged again and again." He observed that the US military "had a propensity to shy away from political and economic considerations—in fact all matters not traditionally associated with combat" and resolved that a sound organizational approach overcoming "traditional military propensities" must be established. Another report at the time concluded that the army should establish a career pattern for civil affairs and military government.[11]

A broader appreciation of civil affairs tended to exist within the emerging special operations community. During the 1960s and 1970s, some proponents in the army argued that civil affairs units were assets to be used in "nonregular warfare," such as contingencies in Latin America and Southeast Asia, and that civil affairs units were valuable instruments for "military civic action" or "nation building."[12] This thinking reflected an important shift away from thinking about civil affairs as combat-service-support elements in conventional war to assets that could be used in low-intensity conflicts in order to undercut political support for an enemy's forces and mobilize the support of indigenous populations.[13] Military civic action included the use of military forces in peacetime to accomplish humanitarian missions in countries around the world—a sort of Peace Corps in camouflage. Civil affairs units could be designated for military civic action and used to reach out to local communities to help establish the legitimacy essential to success in low-intensity conflict. Some nation-building or military civic action tasks were similar to those undertaken during governance operations in war, such as the reconstitution of a nation's police and defense forces. However, military civic action was not specific to wartime and could occur during peacetime as well. Since military civic action was primarily within the realm of special operations forces, even this broader view of civil affairs reinforced the traditional separation between governance operations and conventional war. Although reserve civil affairs units were linked to conventional units, their utility was seen within the context of low-intensity-conflict-type situations and unconventional warfare.[14]

The Vietnam War and its aftermath marked an important turning point for the army and reinforced the tendency to discount the role of civil affairs within the *regular* force. As the political, social, and economic development (nation building) of South Vietnam received growing US attention and resources from 1966 onward, US pacification and nation-building efforts became increasingly uncoordinated and rife with problems. The legacy of Vietnam—and the failure of the pacification efforts there—resulted in a determination by many civil and military leaders to approach the political complexities of war by creating an entirely new structure to address these issues and the forms of warfare that emerged from counterinsurgencies. The post-Vietnam decision to specialize training and thinking related to the political component of war in a separate special operations community was an effort to redress US weaknesses in fighting "the other war" that emerged in Vietnam, but it also increased the tendency to view these operations as separate and distinct from regular warfare.

The inclusion of civil affairs within the congressionally mandated USSOCOM in 1987 codified the trend toward specialization and separation of governance operations from "regular war" and general-purpose forces. Congress created USSOCOM after years of bitter debate between special operations advocates and more "conventional" DOD proponents. The special operations community argued for a new command to provide more focused attention to the problems and challenges associated with unconventional warfare.[15] Civil affairs was one of several special missions assigned to the new command. Civil affairs units would serve as combat-service-support elements to special operations forces and also retain their combat-service-support role to general forces.[16] An army subordinate command, the US Army Civil Affairs and Psychological Operations Command, was established to provide forces, resources, and equipment related to civil affairs and psychological operations (PSYOPS) in support of regional commanders, joint task forces, and State Department assets around the world. At the time, about 96 percent of the command's approximately ten thousand personnel were in the reserve, with one active-duty civil affairs unit, the Ninety-

Sixth Civil Affairs Battalion (Airborne) (with six companies), based at Fort Bragg, North Carolina.

Two main points of view regarding the inclusion of civil affairs assets in the special operations community emerged. Some believed that integration would increase awareness of civil affairs because the new command could serve as an advocate and urge other commands to make use of civil affairs assets.[17] JCS chairman Adm. William J. Crowe supported the assignment of all civil affairs (and PSYOPS) units to the new command, arguing that they would be better supported.[18] However, other officials, such as the undersecretary of defense for policy, Fred Iklé, warned that shifting civil affairs units to the new USSOCOM would undercut the fact that they supported conventional warfare as well.[19] The inclusion of civil affairs assets in the new command also separated the training of these units from their respective services' training and doctrine commands.[20] This reinforced the separation of civil affairs from the regular army by reinforcing their separateness from the active component.

## THE KOREAN WAR

Although in the immediate post–World War II years the regular army did not sustain a strong interest in governance-related activities, the army's first major Cold War engagement, the Korean War, brought them again to the forefront of the war effort.[21] Governance operations during this conflict were a lesser-known but important part of the army's efforts to restore order and stability to ravaged South Korea. From the start of the war, US political and military leaders recognized that two opposing armies would clash in combat but that the war's final outcome would hinge on the political system that prevailed. The objective of the war was to prevent the spread of the totalitarian Communist system from the North to the South. US forces had withdrawn from South Korea in 1948, leaving it politically, economically, and militarily weak. Although the World War II military government had succeeded in transitioning Korea from Japanese control into an independent state, Lt. Gen. John R. Hodge's World War II efforts to stabilize South Korea by strengthening non-Communist forces had fallen short.[22] Throughout the earlier military government period, the US policy community debated how to strengthen the South against an internal or external Communist takeover. They debated how long American troops should remain in Korea, as well as the appropriate level of military and economic aid. And throughout this experience, the US Army played an active role mediating among local political parties and the international and Washington-based policy communities. Although by 1948 the United States had conceded that a political division of the peninsula would take place, many in the South continued to oppose the creation of a separate republic, viewing it as a barrier to unification.[23] But some army leaders also expressed concern that in the long run, the "costs of our retreat from Korea would be far, far greater than any present or contemplated appropriations to maintain ourselves there."[24]

Despite army efforts during the World War II military government period to augment the South's small constabulary forces and equip them with heavier weapons, South Korean defenses remained weak.[25] Through 1949, the United States, led by army advisers with the Koreans, sought to augment and strengthen South Korean defenses by building up an internal police and defense organization, which, ideally, would deter an attack by the North.[26] Although the NSC supported this effort and agreed to continue some military aid to the South, the amount was not enough to offset Korean economic weaknesses or to fully supply the emerging Korean defense force.[27]

Before the invasion, Syngman Rhee pleaded with Secretary of State John Foster Dulles for more positive US action to try to avoid a "hot war" on the peninsula.[28] Although US political and military leaders were well aware of the South's vulnerability, Washington had written Korea out of its defense plans.[29] A report to the JCS warned of the need to shore up the South against an invasion, which would likely "result in communist domination."[30] The JCS did not believe the South could defeat an attack but remained unwilling to divert troops from elsewhere in Asia to bolster the ROK. The Central Intelligence Agency (CIA) agreed that it would be tough to prevent eventual Communist control over the peninsula—even with some US military and economic assistance.[31]

In the end, however, constrained resources and growing commitments and concerns elsewhere in the world militated against a long-term US presence in Korea. In early 1947, the US Congress decided to cut military spending, and legislators expressed concern about the high ratios in the army of officers to enlisted men and of civilians to military personnel—ratios that were closely linked to occupation duties.[32] Secretary of Defense James Forrestal complained about the "drain upon Army resources in the form of occupation troops" and lamented that the occupation in Korea was a "source of unceasing complaint from parents of the enlisted men who were unhappy, dissatisfied and bored."[33] By June 1950, supply and service to Korean combat units was conducted only on a subsistence basis.

On June 25, 1950, North Korean forces surprised the South Korean army at dawn, marching toward the capital of Seoul. One American officer in the region stated that this looked like "the real thing."[34] Several hours later, North Korean forces had captured the town of Kaesong, forty miles west of Seoul and home to the First Division of the South Korean army. The United States responded by pushing a resolution through the UN's Security Council calling for military assistance to South Korea in order to repel the armed attack and restore international peace and security in the area. The Soviet Union had been boycotting the council at the time and thus could not veto the resolution. President Harry Truman dispatched US land, air, and sea forces to Korea, hoping to restore the thirty-eighth parallel as the demarcation line on the peninsula and to restore peace based on a liberal democratic system. The president initially limited Gen. Douglas MacArthur to the use of air and sea support only, calling the US response a "police action" and avoiding the term "war."[35] Truman hoped to avoid committing US ground forces, believing that the United States could be challenged elsewhere in the world by "the communists."[36]

As the war progressed, Washington's aims expanded. In the fall of 1950, President Truman acknowledged that a significant rehabilitation program for Korea would likely be necessary.[37] Following the Inchon landing on September 15, 1950, UN and ROK forces drove north and crossed the thirty-eighth parallel. Washington contemplated the establishment of a new political order across the entire peninsula, and the JCS instructed General MacArthur to destroy the North Korean army and establish a foundation for the unification of Korea under Syngman Rhee. The army anticipated that governance operations would likely be required to achieve unification, and army planners actually drew up procedures for the occupation of the North.[38] The UN endorsed these broader goals with a resolution recommending the establishment of a "unified, independent, and democratic government in the sovereign state of Korea."[39]

Given the South's weakness at the outset of the war, it was not surprising that the army would be directly engaged in key political and economic programs throughout the course of the war. As the war progressed, the North's forces destroyed much of the South's political and economic infrastructure. A critical part of the army's mission as combat unfolded was to ensure that deteriorating political and economic conditions among the South Koreans did not undermine combat operations and did not jeopardize the overall goal of achieving a democratic political order in the South. Political leaders in Washington directed MacArthur to make sure that army commanders arranged civil affairs agreements so that MacArthur's overall mission could be accomplished.[40]

### Developing an Organization for Governance

Three themes relevant to governance operations dominated the early and later phases of the war in Korea. First, the US Army was determined to retain unity of command over governance operations in the theater. Second, interagency squabbling over control of civil assistance programs and the scope of such programs took place throughout the war. Third, US forces in Korea faced the simultaneous challenge of engaging in combat *and* governance operations throughout the war, illustrating the interconnectedness of the two phases.

The United States assumed leadership over the United Nations Command (UNC) in Korea. Serving as its commander in chief (CINCUNC), General MacArthur decided that Lt. Gen. Walton H. Walker's Eighth Army, which had been occupying Japan, should lead the South Korean army in the war.[41] Army leaders in the theater tried to clarify lines of authority between the UNC (which effectively represented US Army forces) and a newly established UN agency, the United Nations Korean Reconstruction Agency (UNKRA).[42] UNKRA had been created to fill a gap left by the collapse of the Economic Cooperation Administration (ECA), which had been created in 1949 as the United States transitioned from its World War II military government in Korea. Owing to a lack of funding, the ECA was phased out, but the withdrawal of ECA personnel had left a gap that was filled, by necessity, with army personnel.[43] This created tensions between the army and the UN, which was also supervising economic rehabilitation in the region. The US military maintained that military conditions in 1951 did not permit a transfer of operational responsibilities to the UN and that working through UNKRA would result in an unacceptable division of responsibilities in the wartime theater. The army argued that as long as hostilities continued, there could be no divided responsibility.[44] The army did not want to assume responsibility for governance missions indefinitely and agreed that, eventually, UNKRA should acquire greater control over civil administration.[45] But it believed that a transfer of power should occur as combat ended and only with the CINCUNC's approval.

The United States sponsored two UN resolutions providing the Eighth Army with initial guidance on governance operations. These resolutions, combined with a directive from President Truman, essentially gave the Eighth Army responsibility for all civil assistance activities and set the stage for the future reconstruction of Korea.[46] The Civil Assistance Command was established within the Eighth Army to direct governance-related tasks. General MacArthur gave General Walker "complete and overall responsibility for the provision of necessary supplies and equipment to prevent disease, starvation and unrest among the civilian population in Korea."[47] The Eighth Army's effort to manage governance tasks—its determination to seek unity of command—was due to the belief that governance operations could contribute to the success of combat operations.[48]

Many army leaders viewed reconstruction inextricably linked to their combat efforts. Maj. Gen. Lyman Lemnitzer, the deputy army commander for civil affairs in Korea, maintained that stability was "absolutely vital to a healthy military situation in Korea" and that a "strong Korean government [able to] stand on its own feet [was] manifestly important to us all."[49] The commanding general of the UN Civil Assistance Command Korea (UNCACK), Brig. Gen. W. E. Crist, made it clear that preventing disease, starvation, and unrest was critically important, though secondary to the mission that must "constantly be borne in mind"—that of support for military operations.[50] Maj. Gen. William Marquat, head of the army's CAD, believed that rehabilitation in Korea was "an end in itself" and that the commander should devote a great deal of attention to marshaling resources at his disposal to build up the economy of the country."[51]

Army proposals envisioned greater UNKRA involvement only if UN personnel remained under the operational control of the commanding general of the Eighth Army.[52] Not surprisingly, the State Department opposed army efforts to control UNKRA personnel. State was determined to keep the conflict "internationalized" through UNKRA oversight.[53] Eventually, a compromise in the army's favor was reached, with the secretary of defense agreeing to allow UNKRA to commence relief efforts if its programs remained "subject to the exigencies of military necessity as determined by General [Matthew] Ridgway."[54] As CINCUNC, Ridgway created a staff in UNC headquarters that provided supervision over civil assistance and economic aid.[55] The army's insistence on military necessity had prevailed.

This headquarters staff was focused on developing policy and overall supervision. But the Eighth Army developed an organization for the conduct of governance operations in its forward combat areas by creating a special staff section for civil affairs and working through its own civil affairs and military government channels. Corps- and division-level civil assistance teams worked in the field with local ROK representatives.[56] After the first few months of the war, UNCACK was established, assuming many of the Eighth Army's responsibilities for governance-related tasks in rear areas—as far forward as the corps rear boundaries of the Eighth Army.[57] UNCACK's structure paralleled the Republic of Korea's government, to facilitate the coordination of activities.[58] It placed advisers in ROK ministries and bureaus and supervised ten field teams.[59] Although UNCACK was supposed to advise and supervise the ROK government, in practice it functioned much more as an operating agency. The prevailing view of army personnel in UNCACK was that "if you wanted to get something done here you have to go out and do it yourself."[60]

UNCACK was organized along territorial lines, patterned after national and local governments. It provided each Korean province and Seoul with a civil assistance team, each containing about twenty individuals who included officers, some civilians, and enlisted personnel.[61] These teams implemented policies ordered by the headquarters and the government in each province. Advisers, headquartered in Seoul, provided advice to Korean ministers of agriculture, social affairs, public health, transportation, communications, and others. Since a South Korean government existed, unlike the situation in some of the army's previous experiences with governance operations, the army did not completely run Korean administrative structures. Eventually, a Korean Civil Assistance Command (KCAC) replaced UNCACK. KCAC functioned as a major command of the UNC, placing the civil assistance mission at a higher command level than previously.[62] By the spring of 1953, the military situation in Korea had become sufficiently stabilized to allow for a consideration of longer-range programs for economic rehabilitation.[63]

## Reconstruction

Despite the army's efforts to retain unity of command in the theater, competing lines of authority emerged between three entities: the government of South Korea, Eighth Army troops, and UN authorities. Organizations related to governance operations changed several times during the war to deal with these competing authorities. The existence of a functioning South Korean government placed the army, technically, in an advisory and supervisory role, reinforcing the army's traditional preference for "indirect control" over governance tasks. However, complicating the army's mission was the requirement of balancing its activities with the wishes of South Korean government officials, who were, understandably, often resistant to US leadership.[64] In addition, the army received expert advice from civilians in the State Department and other agencies. Ultimately US political and military leaders recognized that establishing a foundation for a US departure would require that the South have a reasonable chance of defending itself against a future attack and that it regain enough political and economic stability to counter and withstand pressures from the North.

Thus, many army leaders regarded the reconstruction of Korea's national defense forces as a central part of the war effort, not only to reduce the immediate burden on US forces but also for the longer-term security implications in the region.[65] Yet US advisers faced formidable problems as they tried to create a more effective South Korean fighting force. Most units were poorly trained, with a weak understanding of how to use their weapons and little experience with hostile fire.[66] By the fall of 1952, the JCS had approved a South Korean army and marine force of up to 463,000 men, but they admitted that to supply and equip such forces would mean diverting supplies from US forces elsewhere in the world.[67] To meet the demand created by these larger numbers, US advisers within KMAG increased to almost two thousand.[68] Overall, US Army efforts in this area were relatively successful. A training command—the Replacement Training and School Command—was established to send South Korean forces to the United States for artillery and infantry training. By early 1953, over six hundred Koreans had been trained in US schools. In addition, the new command established indigenous schools for training infantry, artillery, and technical officers. Eventually ROK forces worked in every sector and made up nearly three-quarters of frontline troops by the end of 1952.[69]

Economic problems in Korea were also closely linked to combat operations, since the course of the war depended to some degree on the ability of South Korea to maintain a functioning economy. The ROK's ability to sustain its own forces would reduce the burden on the United States. The US Army faced the dual challenge of rebuilding Korea's industrial base and managing its fiscal weaknesses. Korea faced severe inflation, a significant shortage of raw materials, and a limited supply of foreign exchange. Basically, the army sought to keep South Korea afloat so that it would be able to provide defense forces to assist the UN in combat. Army personnel negotiated with the government of South Korea to allow the UNC to maintain control over economic concerns, and by the spring of 1951, army leaders had drafted a comprehensive economic agreement, including plans for the rehabilitation of agriculture and industry.[70] Soldiers, working through the UN, rehabilitated key industries, surveyed important segments of the industrial sector such as mining, assessed energy supplies, and rebuilt rail lines and ports to improve transport.[71] They helped to build thousands of individual homes, improve water production and supply, and grow power production by rehabilitating electric power plants and allocating power to key industries. By determining which industries would be supplied with power, army personnel helped to determine what commodities should be produced.[72]

In the spring of 1952, the president sent a mission to South Korea to negotiate an agreement with the government. Six out of its eight members were army or DOD representatives. This group, called the Meyer mission, reaffirmed UNC control over the Korean economy but allowed for an eventual takeover of economic matters by UNKRA and the ROK "within 150 days after the end of hostilities."[73] A Combined Economic Board (CEB) was created to serve as a forum for the exchange of South Korean and US views. The US representative to the board was an active-duty army officer, Maj. Gen. Thomas W. Herren, who also served as the deputy commander for civil affairs for the Eighth Army. Later, as the combat phase of the war came to an end, an NSC memorandum on aid for Korea gave the CINCUNC responsibility for an integrated program of aid as a "basis for Korean relief, rehabilitation, and stabilization."[74] The directive gave him overarching power over economic aid and coordination until "such date as the Unified Command" would determine. It established an economic coordinator, with the rank of minister, on the CINCUNC's staff and gave the coordinator wide authority.

Army personnel also improved public welfare and education. The Unified Command in Korea managed the flow of millions of refugees throughout the war.[75] The initial challenge of safeguarding refugee health and controlling disease ended up expanding into a broad program for the entire South.[76] The Eighth Army's civil assistance section distributed health supplies and offered advice to Korean authorities.[77] Within months after the UNC initiated an inoculation and health program, some twenty-six million people received immunizations; incidences of diseases dropped 96 percent in a year.[78] In addition, UNCACK purified water supplies, improved sanitation procedures, and undertook widespread DDT dusting.[79] Villagers received instruction on public health, local cleanup campaigns took place, and since civilian hospitals were no longer functioning in parts of the South (having been seized by the ROK army), UNCACK established "basic medical units" around the country.[80] As the war ended, KCAC became the operating agency for the Korean health system and focused on its continuing long-term rehabilitation. The UNC also restored educational facilities to a point where normal schooling could be resumed. Although the State Department believed that education was an ideal focus area for the UN because the UN insisted on working through its own supply channels, US commanders argued that responsibility could not be delegated because it was linked to the accomplishment of the military mission.[81]

US forces also worked to restore the South's self-sufficiency in food production.[82] Following the North's invasion, land cultivation in the South dropped to two-thirds of prewar levels, and the importation of fertilizer (which had been substantial) came to a standstill. The army expended funds to import fertilizer, and through the resettlement of DPs and the cultivation of new areas of land, land under cultivation increased. US military and UN officials also rehabilitated South Korean fisheries, providing raw materials for fisheries to allow greater production of nets and ice. Shipbuilding facilities were also restored.[83]

It is important to keep in mind that throughout these efforts, whether working through Eighth Army organizations or later KCAC, civilian policy experts provided the military with important advice. The army did not tackle problems of economic policy alone but did serve as the key implementing agency.[84] President Truman appointed Henry R. Tasca as an expert economic adviser to the military. His job was to compile economic information collected by the military and UNKRA and to develop a plan that the president could present to Congress for approval.[85] The Tasca mission recommended a bilateral, billion-dollar program of defense support and reconstruction to last four or five years. The report argued for improving agricultural and industrial production to build up a self-sustaining Korean economy. In addition, a defense support program would be administered through the Mutual Security Administration.

One feature of reconstruction efforts in Korea was the discomfort of other government agencies, especially the State Department, regarding the army's central role in reconstruction. General Marquat traveled to Korea in the summer of 1952 to try to find ways to develop a joint UNC/UNKRA rehabilitation program in order to use funds most effectively. He and other army leaders hoped to avoid a situation whereby the military's funds were limited but its responsibilities increased. The army preference had been to control the procurement and distribution of supplies in an effort to preserve unity of command in the implementation of aid programs. However, the State Department and others in Washington were eager to see a reduced army role, and eventually Congress agreed that, by December 1952, army funds for economic reform should be reduced, effectively forcing the army to cooperate with UNKRA in order to finance key relief projects.[86]

## Departure

Combat operations in Korea ended on July 27, 1953, after a year of protracted and bitter armistice negotiations.[87] After three years of conflict, US political leaders had narrowed their objectives and accepted that reunification of the peninsula would not be possible.[88] The United States revised its aims to accept an honorable withdrawal of US forces, the creation of a stronger South Korean army (to provide security for the new government), and an economic aid package to foster stability. Despite fierce fighting and diplomatic sparring with the UN over control, the army accomplished a substantial program of political and economic reconstruction in South Korea.[89]

As armistice negotiations took place, a key US objective was the continued development and implementation of governance operations to ensure South Korea's rehabilitation and economic growth. On the eve of the armistice, President Dwight Eisenhower warned that all that had been won "by this valiant struggle could be imperiled and lost by an economic collapse" and asked Congress to appropriate $200 million from "the savings in expenditures from the DOD that resulted in the cessation of hostilities."[90] President Eisenhower and President Rhee agreed to a mutual security pact following the armistice, long-term economic aid, and the immediate distribution of millions of dollars of food once the armistice was signed.[91] The United States hoped to leave South Korea strong enough to ensure its own survival and serve as a bulwark against further Communist expansion in the Far East.

With the support of the NSC and the president, Congress approved the creation of the Office of the Economic Coordinator (OEC) to provide US relief and defense support. C. Tyler Wood served in this new role, coordinating the UNC, other UN agencies, and the South Korean government. His focus was on areas such as the rehabilitation of industries, fisheries, mining, education, housing, and flood control, as well as some public health projects. After the cease-fire was signed, Wood continued to coordinate UNKRA and KCAC activities. KCAC lasted until November 1955, with some of its personnel going to the OEC. By 1957 the OEC had become a self-supporting agency, staffed mainly by civilians rather than army personnel.[92]

The Korean War illustrated the army's ad hoc approach to governance operations. In this case, three years had passed between the end of the World War II governance experiences in Korea and the reconstruction undertaken during the Korean War. Yet there was surprisingly little connection between the two operations. Civil affairs activities in Korea in 1951 were handicapped by a lack of information. According to one study at the time, a disproportionate amount of time had to be spent collecting basic information through the early months of the war because the detailed statistics collected by the military government from 1945 to 1948 were unavailable to Eighth United States Army Korea (EUSAK) forces.[93] The governance operations conducted during the Korean War reinforced some of the patterns that emerged during World War II—and that would appear later as well.

Army leaders insisted throughout the conflict that military necessity required control over all activities in the theater that could interfere with combat operations. At the same time, civilians—particularly the State Department and UN—expressed discomfort over the military having such a large role. In addition, governance and combat operations occurred simultaneously in Korea, reinforcing the fluidity of these different aspects of the war. Even during the early stages of the war as the UNC engaged in heavy combat, army personnel conducted governance operations in forward and rear areas. After UNC forces entered North Korea in October 1950, they actually remained for three months and developed a program for how they would rehabilitate the North.[94] The plan anticipated that General MacArthur would assume the post of military governor, dissolve the Communist government, rebuild the economy, and then organize elections and eventually oversee the withdrawal of non-Korean military forces. A UN resolution at the time affirmed that the United States would have full responsibility for civil administration in the North. Overall, the terms of the US withdrawal were closely linked to the completion of governance operations in Korea since the United States hoped to leave behind a viable state.[95] Although the United States did not undertake a full-fledged occupation in Korea, it assisted the South Korean government with the development and implementation of policies designed to improve its defense forces, strengthen its economy, and create conditions for political stability.

# THE DOMINICAN REPUBLIC

The US intervention in the Dominican Republic in 1965 began with a clear set of political objectives shaping the course of the intervention as well as troop activities. The immediate objective of the United States was to protect American citizens in the island nation, but Washington's strategic goal was to replace its Communist government in order to offset the possible emergence of "another Cuba."[96] In his memoir, President Lyndon Johnson wrote that from the day he took office, he had been concerned about the fate of the Caribbean country.[97] The US intervention in the Dominican Republic and US strategic objectives there involved, de facto, the recognition that governance operations would be integral to the achievement of the stated political goals of the intervention.

For several years before the invasion, the United States had supported the administration of Dominican president Juan Bosch, who had assumed power in 1962. However, Bosch's government was weak and failed to implement promised reforms, leading to a military coup led by Donald Reid y Cabral. Following the coup, the US withheld recognition of the new government and ended some of its aid programs.[98] However, it reversed these steps after the Reid government announced that it would allow free elections by September 1965. The newly appointed US ambassador, William T. Bennett, arrived in Santo Domingo in March 1964 ready to encourage the development of a viable democratic system that could hold free elections and sustain economic development. Soon after the new ambassador's arrival, however, unrest on the island began to increase, as Communist rebel leaders hoped to disrupt upcoming scheduled elections. The rebels succeeded in arresting the Dominican chief of staff and orchestrating a countercoup against the Reid regime. Reid, lacking the support of key Dominican military officials, resigned. José Rafael Molina Ureña then declared himself provisional president and the head of new "constitutionalist" (Communist) government. Loyalist planes began attacking the presidential palace, pushing the Dominican Republic to the brink of civil war.

President Johnson grew increasingly concerned about the fate of Americans on the island. In response, the JCS ordered US naval vessels off the Dominican shore to prepare for the evacuation of US citizens.[99] President Johnson characterized the situation as "grave" and hoped that order could be restored and a peaceful settlement of internal problems could be reached.[100] Ambassador Bennett recommended that Washington consider armed intervention to restore order, reporting that the Communists would likely come to power and that Washington should prevent "another Cuba from arising out of the ashes of this uncontrollable situation."[101] At the same time, some in the State Department expressed concerns regarding the international impact of such an intervention. Despite the opposition of most of his military and civilian advisers, including the chairman of the JCS, Gen. Earle Wheeler, the president personally decided to intervene to quell the political unrest, according to Gen. Bruce Palmer, who was to command the US forces in the Dominican Republic.[102]

On April 28, President Johnson ordered about five hundred marines to the Dominican Republic to protect American lives and property. Two days later, a thousand more arrived.[103] The JCS named the operation Power Pack. Marine and army airborne units landed in two separate bridgeheads that were eventually linked together.[104] Although initially the president stressed the narrow focus of the intervention—the protection of American citizens and stopping "the wholesale killing of hundreds and even thousands" of Dominicans— these objectives broadened shortly after US troops arrived on the island.[105] The president explained that it had been his desire "all along" to encourage a cease-fire between the Communist rebels and the loyalist forces, facilitate the evolution of a stable and broad-based government, and make an "appropriate contribution to the necessary reconstruction of that country." Thus, the US military entered the capital, Santo Domingo, with the mission of establishing a constitutional government in the Dominican Republic, preventing a military dictatorship, and reigning in the political power of the Communists.[106] President Johnson's stated political aims implicitly required the conduct of governance operations by the US military.

## Developing an Organization for Governance

Although General Palmer was warned on the eve of his departure for the Dominican Republic that the mission of US forces "is expected to be broadened" to prevent a Communist takeover of the country, he arrived with relatively little information to assist him in achieving this objective.[107] Palmer later revealed that, on the eve of the invasion, American forces "were all starting out at the same zero base."[108] The early period of the US intervention was characterized, as many previous governance operations, by the military's development of arrangements in the theater to manage the requirements of combat as well as political tensions. Off-the-shelf plans had existed (e.g., CINCLANT OPLAN 310/2) but were from a family of relatively outdated contingency plans that had been developed for the entire region. The lack of planning for noncombat operations in the Dominican Republic was not surprising given that overall planning and coordination problems beset the intervention.[109]

The two principal units in the intervention were the Eighty-Second Airborne Division and the Fourth Marine Expeditionary Brigade. By mid-May, some twenty-three thousand American troops had landed.[110] Two key objectives dominated military operations during this initial period: establishing an overland link to connect marine and army forces and creating a safe corridor for US troops through the city of Santo Domingo. On May 2, the Eighty-Second Airborne Division was "turned loose" to establish a corridor and link up with the marines. Within a few days, army forces achieved this objective.

General Palmer's staff was initially consolidated into Headquarters, US Forces Santo Domingo. The headquarters of XVIII Airborne Corps served as the senior headquarters for US forces in the Dominican Republic, while the headquarters of the Eighty-Second Airborne Division played a tactical role. Thus, the senior military headquarters were separate from the tactical commander directing operations.[111] General Palmer preferred this setup because it relieved the tactical commander of "the onus" for decisions dictated by political considerations. Palmer's headquarters staff included a G-5 officer in charge of civil affairs. However, since the troops from the Eighty-Second Airborne ended up conducting many governance tasks and since civil affairs reservists from the Forty-Second Civil Affairs Company were attached to the Eighty-Second, oversight of governance operations ran through the tactical chain of command. The Forty-Second Civil Affairs Company established its headquarters in the same building occupied by Headquarters, US Forces Dominican Republic.[112] The civil affairs company was organized along functional teams and worked through the Eighty-Second Airborne's combat and combat-service-support units.

General Palmer faced two immediate concerns related to governance operations: first, meeting the immediate needs of the populace and, second, improving the intelligence available about political events in the country. As one expert later observed, "hurried planning, poor intelligence, inadequate briefings, and unfounded rumors created in the combat soldiers' minds a simplistic perception of what would confront them once they arrived."[113] On the eve of the intervention, General Palmer admitted, "The truth was that no one had a handle on what was going on in Santo Domingo."[114] In an effort to improve the intelligence available, Special Forces troops established six detachment sites in the countryside to assist with aid programs and gather information.[115] To redress the lack of knowledge, teams were dispatched to the countryside to "take the pulse" of the country and gauge the level of political support held by the rebels outside the capital area. Moreover, communication from the Dominican Republic to the United States was unreliable and rebels controlled key telecommunications centers. This hampered the exchange of political guidance from Washington to General Palmer.[116] After the first few days of the intervention, it became increasingly apparent that more civil affairs, military police, intelligence, and other specialists would be needed.[117] Initial relief efforts led by Eighty-Second Airborne troops made food, water, and medical care available to the inhabitants—tasks that continued for months.

Although the United States maintained its neutrality going into the invasion, once in the theater US forces faced the need to manage violence between political factions and to protect embassies from rebel forces.[118] Given the intense political situation, an early governance-related challenge was the control over and the dissemination of information. Within days of the invasion, the First Psychological Warfare Battalion arrived and put out a powerful mobile broadcast to the population to explain the purpose of the US invasion and to counter rebel broadcasts.[119] General Palmer also appreciated the importance of developing information programs so that his troops would understand the reasons they were there in the first place.[120]

## Reconstruction

Although the intensity and scale of combat that the US Army faced in Korea was obviously much greater, in the Dominican Republic it engaged in governance tasks amid political unrest and uncertainty. US forces sought to stabilize fighting among rebel groups, while US and international political leaders tried to hammer out a framework to achieve a political settlement for the country. Given ongoing fighting among rebel and loyalist forces in Santo Domingo, General Palmer and his staff were immersed in balancing political requirements and providing for the security of US troops, US officials, and Dominican civilians. It was one of the army's premier combat units—the Eighty-Second Airborne Division—that conducted many governance-related tasks to restore stability and allow the country to begin functioning again. Members of that unit were confused at times, with one soldier remarking, "We would hand out food to the people one minute and then be engaged in a fire-fight with the same ones the next," and wondering why his unit was cleaning the streets since, "Hell, we came here to fight."[121]

Several circumstances made reconstruction in the Dominican Republic difficult. Many of the facilities to be rebuilt were located in rebel territory, increasing the vulnerability of US personnel to sniper fire.[122] In addition, political constraints forced army personnel to work under strict rules of engagement as they rebuilt essential services and tried to defend themselves. Furthermore, unlike other governance operations (such as in Korea and later Panama), US forces did not have a defined relationship with the Dominican government and thus had limited power over the implementation of programs. Nevertheless, from June to October 1965, a fairly extensive program of political and economic reconstruction in the Dominican Republic took place.[123]

Political considerations demanded the involvement of the Organization of American States (OAS), which had established its own peacekeeping force, the Inter-American Peace Force (IAPF). General Palmer served as deputy commander of the IAPF.[124] With the backing of the United States, the OAS took the lead in working out arrangements for a provisional government and free elections.[125] Army officials were not involved in the negotiations leading up to the first political settlement, but they played a role in brokering between political factions on the ground. Army officers worked closely with Dominican military leaders to facilitate the departure of key military leaders from the country, which was one prerequisite for a cease-fire.[126] In addition, once Dr. Héctor García Godoy assumed the presidency of the new provisional government, the international peacekeeping force offered its support and no longer served as a "neutral" peacekeeping force.[127] However, the government became increasingly weak, and thus, General Palmer and his aides played active roles in managing the political fallout, trying to prevent further instability, which could risk future elections. General Palmer also sought to prevent still-active rebel groups from creating an autonomous political zone in Santo Domingo.[128] Overall, the army played a key role in trying to neutralize Dominican political forces that aimed to undermine the OAS's negotiated agreements.[129]

US Army forces also restored the nation's indigenous police and security forces.[130] Dominican police units were instructed to treat captured rebels decently and to improve public safety. In addition, with the political agreement to demilitarize Santo Domingo, US Army personnel created a special national police force to assist the Eighty-Second Airborne with demilitarizing the capital.[131] Although the Forty-Second Civil Affairs Company had established a legal team, its main focus was internal to the army, rather than having an external focus on the country's legal system. Although no overall plan for economic or industrial reform in the Dominican Republic existed, army personnel became involved in these issues on an ad hoc basis, with the cooperation of the State Department. Members of the Forty-Second Civil Affairs Company's economic team met with bankers in an effort to restore the country's financial operations. Civil affairs and Eighty-Second Airborne personnel also completed a survey of the local economic and banking situation.[132] Army personnel helped to complete property-ownership surveys for local civilians, and a civil affairs labor team worked with a local Dominican employment agency to identify local applicants for jobs. A public welfare team linked to the Eighty-Second Airborne worked with various nongovernmental organizations to coordinate and improve food distribution. The US Agency for International Development (USAID) had developed a plan determining food requirements for families, but it was the army's public welfare team that played a critical role in implementing the plan.

Army personnel also addressed longer-term problems such as sanitation, health care reform, and the medical system.[133] Medical units of the Eighty-Second provided a great deal of aid to Dominican civilians, establishing civil medical assistance teams to treat them. By the end of the operation, field hospitals had seen some fifty-four thousand outpatients. In addition, with their attached civil affairs units, troops of the Eighty-Second purified the water supply in order to prevent epidemics from breaking out. Although the existing Pan American Health Organization was supposed to focus on these tasks, army personnel actually ended up implementing many of the programs. In the realm of education, army involvement was limited—troops helped to get schools up and running following the invasion. A public education team gathered information about the status of schools, established plans for their openings, and coordinated the removal of troops near school areas. The team also monitored the longer-term plans of the Ministry of Education.

### Departure

Within a month after the first arrival of US troops, officials in Washington began to lay the groundwork for their eventual withdrawal. In mid-May, senior officials from Washington, including Deputy Secretary of Defense Cyrus Vance, arrived in the theater to assess the situation. Army officers were immersed in politics as the occupation wound down, though at times General Palmer felt the he had been excluded from key negotiations.[134] Civilian leaders in Washington hoped to involve regional actors, especially the OAS, in finding a solution to the crisis. President Johnson wanted the OAS to "share in the responsibility" for allowing free elections to take place.[135] A special OAS committee, chaired by US ambassador Ellsworth Bunker, eventually succeeded in installing a provisional government led by García Godoy. The agreement also included a timetable for elections and clarified the power of elected officials. By June 1966, elections were held, with over 1.3 million Dominicans voting for Joaquín Balaguer.

This intervention illustrated that general army combat troops—in this case, the men and women from the Eighty-Second Airborne Division—played an important role in overseeing many governance tasks. With the relatively limited involvement of specialized civil affairs units in the intervention, mainly the Forty-Second Civil Affairs Company, army tactical troops had no choice. Furthermore, despite the heavy involvement of the State Department and the OAS, there were certain political tasks that US Army officers remained directly involved with, such as negotiating with Dominican generals over their departure from the country. US forces also supervised—and often completely ran—most of the aid programs. In addition, the United States funded several OAS programs designed to keep the Dominican government running.

The US intervention in the Dominican Republic resulted in the establishment of a stable government. Following the US withdrawal, free elections were held every four years, and Balaguer served as president for twelve years. While the army did not establish a military government in the Dominican Republic, through its close supervision over existing Dominican government structures, it played a key role in stabilizing the situation once formal combat ended so that a new provisional government could assume power and elections could take place.

## PANAMA

In December 1989, US political leaders initiated Operation Just Cause,[136] with the political objective of replacing the corrupt government of Gen. Manuel Noriega with one more compatible to US interests.[137] As the chairman of the JCS, Colin Powell, later recalled, "We were going to eliminate Noriega *and* the PDF [Panamanian Defense Forces]. If that succeeded, we would be running the country until we could establish a civilian government and a new security force."[138] The US Army served as the key instrument in the transition from the Noriega government to a new authority and new administrative structures in Panama.

Relations between the United States and Panama had been strained for several years before the invasion. US congressional committees had begun to link the Noriega government to drug trafficking and other problematic activities, and Noriega began to be considered an embarrassment to the United States.[139] Contingency planning for the operation in Panama had begun in the summer and early fall of 1989.[140] Following a series of increasingly hostile encounters between US forces based in Panama and the PDF, the JCS issued an order to begin to expedite planning for an intervention.[141] Gen. Frederick Woerner, commander of the US Southern Command (SOUTHCOM), initially drew up plans that included recommendations for resolving the political situation in Panama.[142] He believed that a key component of an intervention would involve the restoration of the Panamanian government following the defeat of the PDF. Woerner insisted that attention be paid to planning for the aftermath of the attack.[143] Thus, the relatively clear political objectives at the outset of the conflict, and the acknowledgment that a new role for the Panamanian army would need to emerge, suggested that preinvasion planning did to some degree address the need to conduct governance operations.

There were three main phases related to planning for Panama: the buildup period, designed to try to "encourage" changes in Panama's government without an intervention; the planning for the invasion itself; and the planning for the restoration of government following combat operations.[144] General Woerner and his director of operations, Brig. Gen. Marc A. Cisneros, led the early planning for a massive buildup of US forces, which aimed to deter Panamanian leaders enough to encourage an overthrow of Noriega by the PDF.[145] This buildup plan included a consideration of civil-military issues that would arise after a change in government there.[146] The combat plan for Panama called for an "all out assault" with the deployment of a massive force of some 22,500.[147] The combat plan, Blue Spoon, called for the creation of Joint Task Force (JTF) Panama under XVII Airborne Corps and reaffirmed several political objectives of the war, including the defeat and restructuring of the PDF and the establishment of a US-approved government.[148]

SOUTHCOM developed Blind Logic, the plan for the civil-military portion of the operation, in conjunction with members of the 361st Civil Affairs

Brigade, which was attached to SOUTHCOM.[149] The planners assumed that no civilian government would be in place in Panama and recommended the establishment of a military government for about thirty days after the end of combat. After that period, the State Department, through the US embassy, would assume control over civil operations. A key constraint during the planning for this reconstruction period, according to General Woerner, was the desire to keep planning secret; concerns about leaks precluded Woerner and his staff from working with the State Department.[150] Thus, Woerner believed that SOUTHCOM was hampered in its ability to address detailed reconstruction issues such as the nature of the occupation or the complexities of transforming the PDF. On the other hand, perceived constraint on coordinating with the State Department revealed that the army was able to develop the rudiments of such a plan itself. A basic plan for governance-related tasks was completed but was then shelved until after the invasion.[151]

### Developing an Organization for Governance

Although the army had done some advance thinking about the civil affairs component of Operation Just Cause (e.g., Blind Logic), this advance preparation did not preclude several challenges from emerging during the early phases of the invasion. First, the army still had not developed an organization to conduct governance-related tasks. After the replacement of General Woerner by Gen. Maxwell Thurman as SOUTHCOM commander, planners placed less emphasis on governance-related issues, and some argued that this shift resulted in a poor integration of the combat and postcombat phases of the invasion.[152] General Thurman had received briefings on combat plans for Panama, but he apparently did not focus much attention on posthostility issues.[153] Two months before the invasion, efforts by some army planners to urge SOUTHCOM to focus greater attention on civil restoration issues had only limited success.[154] Furthermore, because the Joint Staff had not approved the civil-military plans before the invasion (attesting, it seems, to its secondary status), the plan was not formally incorporated into XVIII Airborne Corps's plans.[155] Thus, although US military and political leaders had acknowledged the political challenges they would likely face in Panama, as in previous governance operations they approached issues related to the implementation of such operations in an ad hoc manner.

A second challenge during this period was the problem of maintaining security—earlier planning had not adequately addressed the issue. As US forces landed in Panama on December 20, 1989, a complete breakdown of civil order occurred, requiring US forces to respond. Blind Logic had not anticipated the implications of the collapse of the PDF, and widespread looting and disorder challenged the ability of the army's military police units to manage crowds and restore stability.[156] This was heightened by concerns over the safety of American citizens still living in Panama after the Canal Zone was turned over in 1979. For some, this disorder was not surprising. JTF Panama initially believed that it would not play a primary role in restoring law and order, since this was considered a job for the new government of Guillermo Endara.[157] Such instability, however, once again underscored the connection between the combat phase of the intervention and the transition to a desired political outcome. Third, coordination between the army and State Department regarding governance issues remained undefined. As noted earlier, military planners had planned for governance-related tasks with little or no involvement from the State Department; later, however, the State Department expressed frustration with the army's lead role in such matters.[158] Nevertheless, many military officers did not feel that they would be able to execute the existing plan for governance operations (Blind Logic) without greater coordination with the State Department and other US government organizations.[159]

Although President George H. W. Bush announced that General Noriega's capture marked the achievement of US objectives in Panama, many challenges still remained.[160] Life did not "return to normal," and fairly extensive governance operations began.[161] As combat ended, a reorganization of US forces took place to address the challenge of restoring democracy in Panama and restructuring its security structures. With the president's announcement, the JCS asked General Thurman to terminate Just Cause and begin to execute the plan for governance operations, now renamed Promote Liberty. It is important to keep in mind that the operational organization and specific steps necessary to implement Promote Liberty had not been worked out before the arrival of the invading US Army forces.[162] There was still no clear policy on whether civil government in Panama would exist, what would replace the PDF, or what would be the state of Panama's economic and social infrastructure.[163] With the distinct separation between the combat and reconstruction phases, army personnel scrambled to develop command-and-control arrangements for arriving civil affairs personnel who were assigned nation-building tasks. Initially, army plans had called for the creation of a military governor to restore order; the May 1989 elections in Panama, however, provided an alternative government that was, in fact, used.[164] Until a new organization was created that had control over civil affairs, projects and activities were duplicated, and there was no clear focal point of effort.[165]

In an effort to streamline operations related to governance operations, the army created a new civil-military operations task force staffed by about twenty-five reservists and commanded by US Air Force brigadier general Benard Gann.[166] The original governance plan, Blind Logic, anticipated that General Gann would control the new task force, with the commander of the 361st Civil Affairs Brigade serving as his deputy.[167] However, General Thurman initially decided to place the US embassy (though understaffed) in control of the civil-military operations task force. This decision resulted in divided and unclear lines of authority but perhaps reflected his view that the army's role in the reconstruction phase should be reduced. Initially members of the task force were unsure about whether they reported directly to General Gann or through the tactical commander of the JTF, Gen. Carl Stiner. Eventually the task force emerged as the primary organization for governance-related tasks, and Gann reported to the commander in chief, US Southern Command (CINCSO).[168] This arrangement left Gann pulled in a variety of directions—by the SOUTHCOM staff, the US Army South (one of the component commands under SOUTHCOM), and the commander of the Seventh Infantry Division.[169]

In Panama, a mixture of territorial and tactical control over governance operations emerged. The civil-military operations task force included three deputies, each heading a civil affairs team organized along functional areas.[170] These areas included health, safety, refugee assistance, public works and utilities, transportation/communication, and sometimes, a finance section.[171] Initially each team was deployed to three different areas: Panama City, Colón, and David. To supplement this territorial arrangement at the request of the government of Panama, the civil-military task force assigned civil affairs personnel to each government ministry.[172] Ten ministry-level support teams and four ministry planning teams worked with regional governments in Panama.[173] However, given there were initially few elected officials in the Panamanian government, personnel from the civil-military operations task force essentially ran the government of Panama during this early period.[174]

Many viewed this early civil-military organization as flawed. General Gann's task force was only one among many with oversight over governance tasks. The task force was not adequately staffed (owing to the decision not to call up the reserves) and lacked a clear chain of command.[175] Whereas in previous governance operations tactical officers generally demanded full control over all operations in the theater, in Panama the JTF did not exert full control over governance tasks even though combat was still ongoing.[176] In sum, there appeared to be two separate but related organizations for governance operations in Panama: those under the more traditional combat control of JTF Panama and those under the civil-military chain, through the civil-military operations task force.[177]

## Reconstruction

As major combat operations came to an end, key tasks facing the US Army included the reestablishment of law and order, the management and protection of DPs, and the reconstruction and reform of Panamanian government institutions. In undertaking these tasks, two main challenges confronted the army: first, the problem of how to manage ongoing civil unrest and, second, the need to create an army organization to guide political and economic reconstruction. After the initial civil-military operations task force was up and running, the army tried to improve its ability to conduct governance activities. Gen. James Lindsay, commander in chief of USSOCOM and a supporting commander in chief to General Thurman, believed that the restoration plan "was not built around the kind of organization that was needed . . . to transition from war to peace."[178] Lindsay deployed a senior civil affairs specialist to evaluate how to set up an organizational structure.[179] These efforts resulted in the creation of the Military Support Group (MSG) to replace and consolidate the various organizations then working on governance tasks and replace the civil-military operations task force.[180] Owing to concerns about control and unity of command, army officers advocated an entirely military structure for the MSG, as opposed to one that would work formally through interagency channels.[181] Essentially the MSG revealed a deliberate effort by the army to retain unity of command by keeping all elements, such as civil affairs, PSYOPS, special operations forces, and combat-service-support elements, under one command. Furthermore, General Thurman chose a cavalry officer to head this group, as opposed to a Special Forces or civil affairs officer.[182] The MSG fell under the tactical control of Joint Task Force Panama, which in turn reported to CINCSO.

The MSG conducted "nation building operations to ensure that democracy, internationally recognized standards of justice, and professional public services are established and institutionalized in Panama."[183] It focused on

undertook many governance tasks, working through a regular tactical chain of command. Civil affairs personnel in the theater were always limited in number, and within days the army commander realized that there would not be enough civil affairs personnel or engineers for the rebuilding effort.[204] SOUTHCOM requested more volunteers to perform temporary tours of duty in Panama to work on governance-related tasks, including public health administrators, medical supply specialists, sanitary engineers, doctors and nurses, drug enforcement experts, law experts, and prison administrators.[205] Because President Bush had not ordered a reserves call-up, these needs were met by requests for civil affairs volunteers.[206] Within a week, more than seven hundred civil affairs officers and soldiers volunteered to go to Panama.[207]

Although civil affairs personnel and units played important roles in Panama, governance duties were not exclusive to them. Two-person civil affairs teams from the army's only active-duty civil affairs battalion, the Ninety-Sixth, were attached to maneuver battalions and assisted combat units with restoring order.[208] Civil affairs soldiers from the Ninety-Sixth had jumped with army rangers and worked to coordinate among military intelligence, military police, and ground force commanders, as well as to protect against civilian interference with the tactical operations.[209] After securing the main airport and working to preventing the PDF from taking hostages, civil affairs teams, together with regular tactical forces, translated, served as liaisons to local governments, determined where help was most urgently needed, and assisted commanders in taking care of a huge refugee population.[210]

US troops assessed the "shape" of towns and cities using several categories: the reliability of the mayor, the presence of drugs, and the state of the PDF, of sanitation, and of medical, banking, and business facilities.[211] The objective was to determine when infantry troops could be pulled out, allowing some Special Forces troops to focus on local redevelopment. Although there was no format "for [doing] these kinds of things," one brigade commander explained, "We did what people would normally do: improvise."[212] Civil affairs personnel, assisted by Special Forces troops, distributed food and tons of medical supplies.[213] In addition, US troops detained PDF infantry at their barracks and at the airport and conducted field interrogations.[214] Civil affairs troops from the Ninety-Sixth stabilized the airport and served as airport managers, engineers, and immigration and customs officials, as Panamanians sought to evacuate the area. As in previous governance operations, the army managed thousands of DPs. Following the arrival of combat troops, a camp for DPs was established at a high school, and an ad hoc arrangement allowed for the care of some five thousand people until members of the Ninety-Sixth could take over and run the camp. The challenge of running a these types of camps was similar to that of running a small city.

Civil affairs personnel assigned to the Panama's Ministry of Public Works helped evaluate the long-term needs of that office.[215] In the public health and welfare sectors, civil affairs personnel engaged in massive cleanups of cities and assisted with restoring Panama's medical system. Plans for these operations were not developed in advance, so civil affairs units worked ad hoc, hiring people off the streets to assist, sometimes paying them with meals.[216] One civil affairs sergeant later recalled that "the place was just a habitat for every form of virus, fungus, disease, germ you could imagine."[217] The three sewage pumps of the city of Colón were broken, leaving sewage running through the streets.[218] Humanitarian assistance teams helped to coordinate with the Red Cross and monitored Panama's emergency food and medical system.[219] Civil affairs teams also tracked medical supplies going into Panama from humanitarian assistance programs such as Project Hope, determined immunization requirements, and assessed the overall state of Panama's public health system. National Guard engineering units fixed roads, schools, and ports and undertook other projects. In addition, civil affairs teams assessed the state of schools, roads, and utilities throughout the country.

During the Panama operation, the army adhered to its traditional preference for "indirect control" over existing administrative structures. In Panama, the situation was relatively straightforward because the new Endara government had been elected and thus was a government through which the army could work to reform administrative structures. Indeed, President Endara requested the assignment of army personnel to provide advice to Panamanian ministries. As in previous governance operations, army teams in Panama served as advisers, not managers.[220] Army personnel worked with the Ministries of Education, Commerce, and Plans and Finance, as well as with the Office of the Presidency.[221] To the State Department's annoyance—due to its inability to duplicate the army's personnel resources and maintain a presence throughout the Endara government—US military personnel served as the primary interlocutors in many Panamanian government offices.[222]

## Departure

As the United States prepared to deploy US troops out of Panama, US military and political leaders considered the prospects for the future stability of the country. Key elements of the original US plan, such as the standing up of a new Panamanian army, had not yet been completed, and some US officials argued that troops should remain until at least a new Panamanian defense structure was in place.[223] Many argued that the United States was not merely reconstructing damage from the war effort (since the war itself was quite short) but was rectifying years of economic weaknesses cause by a corrupt dictator and US economic sanctions.[224] Thus, the United States sought to ensure that Panama receive a substantial economic aid package.

As US troops began to withdraw in early 1990, army personnel played important roles in assessing some of the nonmilitary needs of the country. These assessments helped to shape US follow-on assistance to Panama and, in effect, to shape and achieve broader US objectives there. Civil affairs personnel remained in the country to advise on some economic issues. They prepared ten nation-building assessments, which provided data that was used for developing a congressional aid program.[225] Even as the last elements of the active-duty civil affairs battalion, Company C, returned to Fort Bragg, some civil affairs reservists and some XVIII Airborne Corps troops remained to continue governance tasks. These reservists finalized a nationwide list of two hundred projects designed to improve quality of life and developed a strategy for coordinating these projects through US military channels and the Panamanian government.

In early January 1990, a State Department team traveled to Panama to discuss future economic assistance, and on January 25, 1990, the president announced a program worth over one billion dollars. Despite these efforts and the efforts of the Bush administration to secure the funds for Panama, Senate majority leader George Mitchell would not support an increased aid program until the president produced a "meaningful" long-term plan.[226] Two bills were submitted to Congress in early 1990 with the objective of jump-starting the Panamanian economy, although in the end aid was delayed, and the United States was criticized for the slowness of the aid package.[227] Eventually Congress passed the Urgent Assistance Act for Panama in February 1990, providing over forty-three million dollars for immediate aid and police support, with much of the funding for other programs delayed.[228]

Several issues emerged during the invasion of Panama that proved consistent with the army's other governance experiences in war. The army had planned for both combat and governance operations in Panama—for the latter, the civil-military operations plan called Blind Logic existed. But it received considerably less attention, and most military and civilian leaders gave little thought to the operational steps that would be necessary to tackle the difficult governance-related missions that the army would face. As in previous wars, the close linkage between these two phases became apparent quickly. In fact, at one point, facing the need to restore stability as combat ended and reconstruction began, General Thurman asked that troops designated for governance missions be allowed to operate using rules of engagement from the combat phase of the operation.[229] The separate plans suggested that governance tasks were separate from the broader war effort,[230] despite the fact that three out of six of the strategic objectives included in the final JCS execute order would have required, de facto, the conduct of governance operations to achieve them: the removal of Noriega and his cronies from power, the creation of a PDF responsive to and supportive of a democratic government in Panama, and the installation of a freely elected government.[231] Thus, governance operations were integrally linked to war from the start.

In addition, the intervention revealed the common problem of civil-military coordination and the tensions associated with control over governance tasks. The State Department's desire to retain control over them, due to political concerns, conflicted with its operational limitations. By the same token, although the army initially hoped to coordinate with the State Department and other executive departments but was precluded from doing so too early in the planning phases, lest information leak out.[232] Although there was some effort to encourage interagency involvement in the reconstruction of Panama, given the understaffed embassy and the weak Panamanian government, US military forces exerted real control in the theater.[233] Furthermore, somewhat to the chagrin of State Department officials, US military personnel served as effective liaisons with the Panamanian government—despite the view of many in the State Department that the US military's closeness to the Endara government was not appropriate.[234] The new US ambassador, Deane Hinton, was opposed to using the military for governance tasks. He specifically scaled back plans for more civil affairs personnel, since "this was a free country with a democratic government and you didn't do it that way."[235]

While a common view of Operation Just Cause is that better interagency coordination was needed, events might have unfolded more effectively if the army's organization had retained unity of command from the start.[236] The view that more interagency involvement was necessary before governance operations could begin arguably weakened the effectiveness of some efforts. Analysts tended to point to the lack of interagency coordination, yet in the end, US troops did what they believed necessary, often unsure of the limits of their authority.[237] Relatively short tours of duty were another problem in Panama. The decision not to call up the reserves meant that volunteers performed many of the governance tasks, despite the fact that their temporary tours of duty averaged around thirty-nine days. As a result, by late January around half of the 146 civil affairs personnel had already turned over.[238] On the other hand, as noted throughout this narrative, combat forces undertook and accomplished many governance tasks—albeit often under the leadership of key civil affairs experts or well-connected and well-informed army foreign area officers—suggesting once again that governance tasks were not solely within the domain of specialized civil affairs experts.

Final assessments of the US intervention in Panama were mixed. Many criticized the United States for its failure to fully stabilize the situation before the bulk of US troops departed. The preinvasion period (e.g., US economic sanctions) and the invasion itself had economic costs for Panama, and some argued that the United States did not do enough to rectify the situation. And by August 1991, despite promises of substantial economic assistance, Panama had only received some $150 million in aid.[239] An irony related to the invasion and its aftermath is that although it was considered in hindsight an example of the use of overwhelming superiority—a conflict in which the philosophy of the US commanders was to emphasize the principle of mass—governance operations were a key component of this war and central to the achievement of US strategic objectives.

## CONCLUSIONS

While diverse, the governance operations conducted by the US Army in Korea, the Dominican Republic, and Panama also contained many similarities. Political and military leaders began US involvement with the knowledge that attention would need to be paid to the resulting political order and that the US Army would likely play a key operational role in the restoration of political and economic order and in establishing the foundations for new governments. In Korea and Panama, the army worked through existing, albeit weak, governmental structures, with the ostensible support of the government in place. In the Dominican Republic, the army played a key role in bringing a new government to power. The army served as a key operational link for ensuring that these strategic objectives were accomplished.

Each of the three cases examined here involved political objectives that aimed to change or reconstitute specific governments. In Korea and the Dominican Republic, other actors were involved (the UN and the OAS), although their involvement did not dilute the army's central role in accomplishing governance tasks. In Korea, elements of the UN relief teams, such as the Public Health and Welfare Detachment, were organized as integral parts of the Eighth Army's fighting units. In the Dominican Republic, the OAS supported US troops through the creation of the IAPF. Although a Brazilian general led this force, it was in reality closely aligned with US leaders. Civil instability combined with army concerns about retaining unity of command— or, at the very least, control over their troops in a theater of war—meant that the army was really the only institution capable of accomplishing the governance challenges that unfolded during the course of these three conflicts.

Despite the army's extensive governance operations during the Cold War, stereotypes and misunderstandings regarding civil affairs persisted throughout the period. Even after the Korean War, a common belief held that "all too frequently, men who were involuntarily assigned to civil affairs groups . . . failed to earn their keep . . . [, leading] many to conclude that civil affairs units and staff were havens for incompetents."[240] Civil affairs proponents argued that the army needed to take "take steps to impress commanders and staff officers with the importance of civil affairs and military government" so that they could understand how civil affairs could affect the success of military operations.[241] An army consultant at the time reported that many army officers had "complex misunderstandings" as to the relationship between civil affairs and "more traditional military responsibilities."[242] Former civil affairs officers as well as active-duty officers from the army's CAMG Division realized that "the CA/MG operation often has been looked upon as an activity outside the traditional combat role of the Army," resulting in a civil affairs organization that has been "purely temporary and secondary" and is kept apart from "normal" army activities.[243]

The governance operations examined in these cases did not duplicate the more extensive military government models in Germany, Japan, Italy, or Korea during and after World War II. The scale of those efforts was much greater. Nevertheless, just as in Japan and Italy during World War II, the Korean War and Operation Just Cause involved extensive army efforts to work through existing sovereign governments, with the army providing varying degrees of supervision and control. Though to a lesser degree, as in the

World War II cases, army troops faced similar types of challenges—including establishing a foundation for holding local and then national elections, restoring basic security, and restarting schools and hospitals. Even with the involvement of international actors, such as the OAS in the Dominican Republic and the UN in Korea, the army was heavily involved in brokering among political actors in the theater.

Developments during the Cold War years generally reaffirmed and formalized the separation between governance tasks and the regular army. Ironically, Korea and Panama came to be best known as classic cases of conventional war or examples of the successes associated with the use of overwhelming force. Panama became the first case to exemplify the emergent "Powell Doctrine," articulated by JCS chairman General Powell in 1990 as the need to use overwhelming military force to achieve victory. Yet both the Korean War and the invasion of Panama revealed the central role played by governance operations. The "lesson" of Panama became the determination to use overwhelming military force to achieve one's objectives because "decisive force ends wars quickly and in the long run saves lives."[244] Although Powell had made clear the need for clear political objectives from the start of a conflict, the operational link between the two—the achievement of the political objectives and the use of decisive force—was not fully developed or internalized by the army. Some of the central lessons regarding Panama seemed to be overshadowed by the Powell Doctrine, despite the fact that the army's governance experiences there—such as its role in the reconstruction of the PDF and the creation of an MSG to oversee implementation of key reconstruction tasks—reaffirmed the relationship between political consolidation and war and would be relevant to future conflicts as well. An irony of the Powell Doctrine is that while it emphasized the need to identify political objectives clearly and apply full military force to meet them, it focused on the combat use of these forces, failing to make the operational link between the use of military forces to achieve the political-military objectives of the war.

# NOTES

1. Army reservists who participated in the World War II governance operations produced much of the postwar writing on civil affairs and often served as an informal lobbying group, seeking to build a constituency within the army to give permanence to civil affairs organizations. The MGA was created in 1947 and evolved into today's Civil

Affairs Association. The principal purpose of the association "is and has been for over 50 years, the maintenance and enhancement of the Civil Affairs capabilities required by the Armed Forces of our Nation in war and peace." Cited in "A Brief History of the Civil Affairs Association," by Col. Eli E. Nobleman, chairman emeritus of the association's executive committee, n.d., unpublished paper in possession of the author. See also fact sheet published by the Civil Affairs Association, located at http://www.civilaffairsassoc .org/#!helping-to-secure-victories-page-2/rjmvg.

2. These military government specialties were developed in the 1947 version of US Dept. of the Army and Dept. of the Navy, *FM 27-5*. These included legal, public safety, food and agriculture, price control and rationing, and arts and archives.

3. Dept. of the Army, *Field Manual 41-10*, 14.

4. Wing, *Civil Affairs / Military Government*, 3.

5. "Lessons Learned re: Preparation for CA Unit Deployment to USARPAC, CO 95th CA Gp, Report prepared by Bernard J McCune, Maj, Arty, Commanding, 11 Feb 1966," in US Army Special Operations Command Archives, cabinet 2, drawer 2, folder: CA / Dominican Republic 1965.

6. Cited in Coles and Weinberg, *Civil Affairs*, 154.

7. "Address by BG Patrick H. Tansey, Chief of the Supply Division, Department of the Army, to 7th Military Government Group," *Military Government Journal and Newsletter* 4, no. 4 (April 1952): 1 (an MGA publication). In addition to training courses offered at Camp Gordon, civil affairs reservists created training courses at universities around the country. Courses at Georgetown University included some on differences between the East and the West and on the "Christian ideal v. the materialistic ideal." See the draft syllabus for "Occupation Administration" at Georgetown University, January 26, 1953, NA, RG 319, Army Staff 1952–54, box 1, decimal number 000.4–000.8, folder CAMG Educational Institutions.

8. Barrett, "Updating Civil Affairs Doctrine," 51.

9. Quote cited in Fahey, "Overall U.S. Politico-Military-Complex." Also known as the Fahey Report in the literature.

10. Ibid.

11. Stolzenbach and Kissinger, *Civil Affairs in Korea*, 137.

12. Military civic action has been defined as training indigenous military forces to undertake projects that are useful to the local population, such as education, training, and public works. See US Dept. of the Army, *Field Manual 41-10*, 3–2, 1–6.

13. Rudolph C. Barnes, "Civil Affairs, A LIC Priority," *Military Review* (September 1988): 39.

14. The army made an effort in the 1960s, through the new Army Security Assistance Force (SAF), to integrate elements of civil affairs, Special Forces, and psychological operations with a regional orientation. See Lord et al., *Civil Affairs*, 44.

15. A good description of the debate about the creation of the command is in Marquis, *Unconventional Warfare*, 107–69.

16. Lord et al., *Civil Affairs*, 41.

17. Ibid., 40.

18. US Readiness Command, "Report on Mission and Deactivation," 43–44, cited in Marquis, *Unconventional Warfare*, 156. For overview of whole debate, see pages 156–59.

19. Marquis discusses Iklé's arguments in *Unconventional Warfare*, 156.

20. Ibid., 6.

21. Within the broader literature on the Korean War, there are few sources related to the political and economic activities undertaken by the army there. Good general sources are Stueck, *Road to Confrontation*; Sandler, *Korean War*; Hermes, *Truce Tent and Fighting Front*; and Ridgway, *Korean War*. Sources with more specific information about the governance aspects of the war include Stolzenbach and Kissinger, *Civil Affairs in Korea*; Lyons, *Military Policy and Economic Aid*; Sawyer, *Military Advisors in Korea*; and Schnabel, *United States Army in the Korean War*; Wood et al., *Civil Affairs Relations*.

22. Stueck, *Road to Confrontation*, 76.

23. Lyons, *Military Policy and Economic Aid*, 15.

24. "Minutes of Meeting of Secretaries of State, War, and Navy, 29 January 1947," cited in Stueck, *Road to Confrontation*, 75.

25. As noted in the previous chapter, the United States initially agreed to create a constabulary force for the ROK of up to fifty thousand men. Army advisers (KMAG) were sent to achieve this goal. Later the US agreed to augment this constabulary with National Defense Forces, though the latter remained weak and numbered only some 114,000 at the time of the invasion. Schnabel, *United States Army in the Korean War*, 34, and Hermes, *Truce Tent and Fighting Front*, 62.

26. "*Mutual Defense Assistance Program Fact Sheet*," Dept. of State Publication 3836, General Foreign Policy Series, April 25, 1950.

27. Sawyer, *Military Advisors in Korea*, 96–101. The rest of information about defense forces is from this source.

28. Sandler, *Korean War*, 50.

29. General MacArthur's Far East Command reported that Pyongyang had a D-day set for mid-1950. Cited ibid., 43. See also Schnabel, *United States Army in the Korean War*, 62.

30. "Report of the Joint Strategic Survey Committee to the Joint Chiefs of Staff, JCS 1483/50, 30 January 1948," cited in Schnabel, *United States Army in the Korean War*, 33.

31. Sandler, *Korean War*, 41.

32. Ibid., 77.

33. See Millis, *Forrestal Diaries*, 265.

34. "War Is Declared by North Koreans," *New York Times*, June 25, 1950.

35. Truman, *Memoirs*, 336–37. For point about police action, see Mossman, *Ebb and Flow*, 13.

36. See Truman, *Memoirs*, 341

37. This was discussed during Truman's trip to Japan to meet with MacArthur. Ibid., 366.

38. For more on the occupation plan, see "RAD W 93721, DA to CINCFE 10 October 1950," cited in Schnabel, *United States Army in the Korean War*, 219–20.

39. "UN Doc A/1435," quoted in Dept. of State Publication 4263, Far East Series 44, U.S. Policy in the Korea Conflict, 17–18, cited in Mossman, *Ebb and Flow*, 18.

40. "DA Directive to CINCFE, 6 July 1950," cited in Stolzenbach and Kissinger, *Civil Affairs in Korea*, 59.

41. Mossman, *Ebb and Flow*, 15.

42. See "Message from CINCUNC Tokyo Japan to the Department of the Army, Washington, DC, 1 April 1951," reprinted in Stolzenbach and Kissinger, *Civil Affairs in Korea*, 92.

43. Wood et al., *Civil Affairs Relations*, 12.

44. Ibid. Later in the war, army leaders expressed concern that a transfer of control to UNKRA (and the diversion of funds to UNKRA) would leave the army with fewer resources. Memorandum by the chief of staff, US Army, "Responsibilities for Economic Assistance in Korea," reprinted in Stolzenbach and Kissinger, *Civil Affairs in Korea,* 113–14.

45. "Memo of Understanding between UNC and UN Korean Reconstruction Agency, 21 Dec 51," cited in Hermes, *Truce Tent and Fighting Front,* 217.

46. Initially the army was to use the existing ECA and ensure that ECA activities were consistent with military needs. However, the ECA was not deemed suitable for the wartime effort. "Message from the Department of the Army (DA) to the Commander in Chief Far East (CINCFE), 6 July 1950," reprinted in Stolzenbach and Kissinger, *Civil Affairs in Korea,* 59–60. Truman's directive of September 29, 1950, cited in Lyons, *Military Policy and Economic Aid,* 47. See also the memo of October 1, 1950, cited in Stolzenbach and Kissinger, *Civil Affairs in Korea,* 63.

47. "CINCFE Directive to CG Eighth Army," reprinted ibid., 67.

48. Gen. Mark Clark, commander in chief of Army Forces in the Far East, believed that in order to prosecute the war effectively, it was a matter of "military expediency" that "unrest, disease and starvation" be eliminated. Clark, *From the Danube to the Yalu,* 144.

49. Thomas W. Herren Papers, box labeled "Report Unified Command Commission to the ROK, 1952," binder "Briefing Conference on ROK for Unified Command Commission to the ROK," Tokyo, April 9–12, 1952, GHQ, UN Command, Office of the Assistant Chief of Staff, G-5, Civil Affairs, US Army Military History Institute Archives.

50. Thomas W. Herren Papers, ibid., section 4 of binder "Remarks of BG W. E. Crist, CG UNCACK, at Briefing UC Mission to the ROK," Tokyo, April 9, 1952, GHQ, UN Command.

51. Statement of Maj. Gen. William Marquat before a subcommittee of the Committee on Appropriations, House of Representatives, 83rd Cong., 1st sess., Department of the Army Appropriations for 1954, 613–14, cited in Lyons, *Military Policy and Economic Aid,* 137.

52. "Message from CINCUNC Tokyo Japan to the Department of the Army, Washington, DC, 1 April 1951," reprinted in Stolzenbach and Kissinger, *Civil Affairs in Korea,* 93.

53. Technically, UNKRA functioned under the UN Commission for the Unification and Rehabilitation of Korea (UNCURK).

54. "Letter from Secretary of Defense to Secretary of State, 3 July 1951," reprinted in Stolzenbach and Kissinger, *Civil Affairs in Korea,* 118.

55. *Far East Command,* January 1, 1947, to June 30, 1957, 28

56. Maj. William B. Koons, "Civil Assistance in Korea," *Army Information Digest* 8 (February 1953): 15. Koons was an infantry officer and the assistant public information officer of UNCACK. See also the chart after page 324 in Cowdrey, *United States Army in the Korean War.*

57. *Far East Command,* January 1, 1947, to June 30, 1957, 28. See also *Yearbook of the United Nations 1951* (New York: UN Dept. of Public Information, 1952), 231.

58. Koons, "Civil Assistance in Korea," 15.

59. Divisions were Personnel and Administration, Operations, Supply, ROK Administrative Affairs, and ROK Economic Affairs. See chart 3, Cowdrey, *United States Army in the Korean War,* following page 324.

60. Stolzenbach and Kissinger, *Civil Affairs in Korea,* 36.

61. Information in this paragraph about UNCACK teams and how they function is from Mrazek, "Civil Assistance in Action," 31. Mrazek was an assistant to the deputy commander and chief of staff of the Korea Civil Assistance Command.

62. *Far East Command*, January 1, 1947, to June 30, 1957, 30.

63. Ibid.

64. Lyons, *Military Policy and Economic Aid*, 116–17.

65. Washington and the Far East Command HQ were in agreement that this was important. And when General Clark took over for Ridgway, he remarked that the bigger the ROK army, the better he would like it. See Hermes, *Truce Tent and Fighting Front*, 64. Clark comment in "Memo, Moorman for CofS 26 May 52," cited ibid., 67.

66. Ridgway, *Korean War*, 18.

67. "Memo Bradley for Secy Defense 26 Sept 52," cited in Hermes, *Truce Tent and Fighting Front*, 342–43.

68. Ibid., 346.

69. Ridgway, *Korean War*, 218. Not everyone was pleased about the buildup of the ROK army, arguing that it diverted resources from broader reconstruction efforts. See Lyons, *Military Policy and Economic Aid*, 150.

70. Ibid., 63.

71. Mrazek, "Civil Assistance in Action," 33, 34.

72. The activities discussed previously are outlined in "EUSAK Directive on Industrial Rehabilitation, Memo from EUSAK to the Commanding Officer, UNCACK, 8 July 1951," reprinted in Stolzenbach and Kissinger, *Civil Affairs in Korea*, 120–23.

73. Text of Meyer Mission May 24, 1952, Dept. of State Publication 4895 (Washington: GPO, 1953), cited in Lyons, *Military Policy and Economic Aid*, 117.

74. Memorandum reproduced ibid., 265–67.

75. Estimates were around five million refugees, more than in World War II. See *Far East Command*, 29.

76. Early in the war, a UN Public Health Survey team traveled to assess the situation. Many members of this original survey team stayed on in the region to assist Eighth Army forces.

77. Cowdrey, *United States Army in the Korean War*, 323.

78. Mrazek, "Civil Assistance in Action," 32. Cowdrey also notes that in 1951 typhoid, smallpox, and typhus claimed over twenty-four thousand lives in the South and in 1952 fewer than six hundred. See Cowdrey, *United States Army in the Korean War*, 327.

79. *Far East Command*, 29.

80. Cowdrey, *United States Army in the Korean War*, 323, 326.

81. Lyons, *Military Policy and Economic Aid*, 113.

82. Information about food production from Mrazek, "Civil Assistance in Action," 32.

83. "EUSAK Directive on Industrial Rehabilitation, Memo from EUSAK to the Commanding Officer, UNCACK, 8 July 1951," reprinted in Stolzenbach and Kissinger, *Civil Affairs in Korea*, 122.

84. In addition to more formal reconstruction efforts, American servicemen began to share food and clothing with needy Koreans. See Daugherty and Andrews, "Review of U.S. Historical Experience," 437. In November 1953, Gen. Maxwell Taylor, commander of the Eighth Army and UN forces in Korea, formalized these hundreds of independent initiatives into Armed Forces Assistance to Korea (AFAK). AFAK efforts continued beyond the armistice period, into 1957. ROK forces took over unfinished projects, but the Eighth Army

continued to supervise. As of March 1957, thousands of projects had been completed, including schools, hospitals, churches, orphanages, dams, irrigation systems, and farm resettlement projects. See *Far East Command*, January 1, 1947, to June 30, 1957, 46.

85. Information about the Tasca mission and aid is from Lyons, *Military Policy and Economic Aid*, 177–79 and 189–91. Portions of Tasca's report were reprinted in *State Department Bulletin* 29, no. 741 (September 7, 1953): 313–15.

86. Lyons, *Military Policy and Economic Aid*, 127–28, 133. Information in the rest of this paragraph is also from this source, 134, 141, 150.

87. Armistice talks took place for almost the latter two years of the war. Four major topics were negotiated: POW disposition (repatriation issues), the demarcation line and demilitarization zone, the establishment of supervisory organs to carry out the armistice, and steps needed to restore stability in the postarmistice period. See Sandler, *Korean War*, 241–42. For more on the talks, see Hermes, *Truce Tent and Fighting Front*, 171. The North Koreans hoped to eliminate all foreign forces from Korea if possible. Although they themselves were building up their own army, the North Koreans were concerned about US assistance in expanding the ROK's army.

88. "NSC 48/5 'United States Objectives, Policies and Courses of Action in Asia,' 17 May, 1951," reprinted in *FRUS: 1951, Asia and the Pacific*, vol. 6, 33–63.

89. This contrasts a bit with most of the World War II cases, in which there was at least some extended period of peace during which the focus could be on reconstruction.

90. "Message from the President to the Congress Requesting Legislation for the Rehabilitation and Economic Support of the Republic of Korea, July 27, 1953," reprinted in Lyons, *Military Policy and Economic Aid*, 259.

91. *Far East Command*, January 1, 1947, to June 30, 1957, 31.

92. Ibid., 45

93. Stolzenbach and Kissinger, *Civil Affairs in Korea*, 28

94. US forces ended up administering Pyongyang for six weeks. A military government was set up. See Lyons, *Military Policy and Economic Aid*, 199. The UN resolution was probably due to the fact that the UN had little affection for authoritarian South Korean president Rhee. Rhee was upset by the resolution. See Sandler, *Korean War*, 107. On this issue of military government in the North, see also "RAD W 94093, DA to CINCFE 12 Oct 1950," cited in Schnabel, *United States Army in the Korean War*, 220.

95. Lyons, *Military Policy and Economic Aid*, 196–97.

96. John Bartlow Martin, *Overtaken by Events: The Dominican Crisis from the Fall of Trujillo to the Civil War* (Garden City, NY: Doubleday, 1966), 661, and Ball, *Past Has Another Pattern*, 329.

97. Johnson, *Vantage Point*, 188.

98. Since the end of 1958, the US military assistance program totaled some $3.4 million. When the United States renewed diplomatic relations in 1962, a new military assistance agreement was signed, and it was designed to improve the military's capabilities as a stabilizing force in the country. See *Case Study of Civil Affairs Operations: Low Intensity Conflict; The Dominican Republic 1965*, US Army John F. Kennedy Special Warfare Center, Fort Bragg, NC, no. 4728/5386 (October 1981), 23.

99. Palmer, *Intervention in the Caribbean*, 23

100. Johnson, *Johnson Presidential Press Conferences*, 303.

101. Bennett cable quoted in Johnson, *Vantage Point*, 197. See also *Case Study of Civil Affairs Operations*, 39, and Yates, *Power Pack*, 183.

102. Palmer, *Intervention in the Caribbean*, 3–4.

103. *Case Study of Civil Affairs Operations*, 74.

104. Ibid., 41.

105. Johnson, *Johnson Presidential Press Conferences*, 311, and the next quote is from this source too.

106. *Case Study of Civil Affairs Operations*, 18, 20.

107. Wheeler memo to Palmer in Palmer, *Intervention in the Caribbean*, 6.

108. Information about plans and quote is from ibid., 31, 9.

109. Yates says that throughout the war the JCS was kept out of key meetings in which President Johnson and his advisers discussed military matters related to the invasion. See Yates, *Power Pack*, 174.

110. *Case Study of Civil Affairs Operations*, 74. The study says that by May 1 these troops were in country; Palmer's account says that this number was arrived at by May 10. Palmer, *Intervention in the Caribbean*, 76.

111. Information about organization is from ibid., 155.

112. Information in this paragraph is from "Memorandum to Commanding General, United States Forces Dominican Republic, Subject: U.S. Stability Operations in the Dominican Republic, from the HQ, 42d Civil Affairs Company, APO New York 09478, 1 November 1965," located in the US Army Special Operations Command Archives, cabinet 2, drawer 2, folder Civil Affairs, Dominican Republic 1965. See also *Case Study of Civil Affairs Operations*, 42, 45, as well as Yates, *Power Pack*, 135.

113. Yates, *Power Pack*, xi.

114. Palmer quotes and statements from *Intervention in the Caribbean*, 8, 56, 148.

115. Greenberg, *1965 Dominican Republic Intervention*, 51.

116. There are several references in his book on his and his staff's ignorance of events in theater.

117. Yates, *Power Pack*, 99. He says that Palmer was frustrated because he could not get the air force to transport these people to him.

118. Palmer discusses the need to keep embassies safe. See Palmer, *Intervention in the Caribbean*, 49–51.

119. Yates, *Power Pack*, 137

120. Greenberg, *1965 Dominican Republic Intervention*, 49.

121. Quote cited in Yates, *Power Pack*, 133.

122. Sniper fire in fact accounted for most of the American casualties during the intervention. Yates discusses the difficulties of working under conditions dominated by sniper fire and writes that this was one reason why the State Department did not insist on leading some of these efforts. Yates, *Power Pack*, 122–26, 136.

123. Palmer, *Intervention in the Caribbean*, 56–57.

124. Ibid., 70–74. Only six OAS member states volunteered to send troops to the peacekeeping force. Palmer at first wanted command, but Washington demanded that a Latin American head it. Palmer still controlled all US forces in the Dominican Republic.

125. The United States wanted the imprimatur of international participation, partially to help avoid the perception that we were imposing our "own brand of military solution or political solution." Johnson, *Johnson Presidential Press Conferences*, 311.

126. Palmer, *Intervention in the Caribbean*, 60–63.

127. Its neutrality was always questionable. A key issue was whether to support the loyalists or the Communists. Some US officials preferred outright support of the loyalists

(such as Palmer). The OAS's involvement complicated matters and forced a more "balanced" approach. Palmer, *Intervention in the Caribbean*, 80.

128. Ibid., 115–18.

129. For instance, General Palmer and the Eighty-Second's commander, Gen. Jack Deane, personally urged a key Dominican general officer, Elias Wessin y Wessin, to leave the country and not impede progress in the ongoing political negotiations. Palmer, *Intervention in the Caribbean*, 103.

130. *Case Study of Civil Affairs Operations*, 50–51.

131. Palmer, *Intervention in the Caribbean*, 111.

132. Yates, *Power Pack*, 135.

133. Information in this paragraph is from three sources. Regarding the public welfare team, see "Memorandum to Commander, U.S. Forces Dominican Republic." Regarding medical reform, see Darrell G. McPherson, *The Role of Army Medical Services in the Dominican Republic Crisis of 1965* (Washington, DC: Dept. of the Army, Office of the Surgeon General, n.d.), 6, 41, 44–46, http://www.history.army.mil/books/contingency/domrep/, and *Case Study of Civil Affairs Operations*, 45–46. Regarding sanitation, see Yates, *Power Pack*, 33, and *Case Study of Civil Affairs Operations*, 45–46. Regarding the educational team, see *Case Study of Civil Affairs Operations*, 52.

134. Palmer, *Intervention in the Caribbean*, 88

135. Johnson, *Vantage Point*, 201–2.

136. Studies include Yates, "Joint Task Force Panama"; Taw, *Operation Just Cause*; Thurman and Hartzog, "Simultaneity"; Shultz, *In the Aftermath of War*; and Millet, "Aftermath of Intervention."

137. One of Bush's objectives was the restoration of Panamanian democracy. See Bush, "Panama: Decision to Use Force," 194–95. See also Gray and Manwaring, "Panama: Operation Just Cause," 41, 46.

138. Powell, *American Journey*, 424.

139. Comment of Gen. Fred Woerner, who in the fall of 1989 was the commander of SOUTHCOM. Phone interview with author, October 29, 2004.

140. Ibid.

141. "Operation Just Cause: Lessons Learned; Volume 1, Soldiers and Leadership," Bulletin No. 90-9, Center for Army Lessons Learned, US Army Combined Arms Command, Fort Leavenworth, KS, 10, http://www.globalsecurity.org/military/library/report/1990/90-9/9091toc.htm.

142. Gray and Manwaring, "Panama: Operation Just Cause," 48. These plans were called Fissures / Fissures II.

143. Buckley, *Panama: The Whole Story*, 222–23. Also Fishel interview with General Woerner, cited in Fishel, *Civil-Military Operations*, 29, and author interview with Woerner, October 29, 2004.

144. These phases are all referred to, in varying degrees, in the main works cited in this section. In addition, they were reconfirmed in my interview with General Woerner on October 29, 2004.

145. This phase was called Elaborate Maze. See Cole, *Operation Just Cause*, 7, and Yates, "Operation Cause in Panama City," 65.

146. Fishel, *Civil-Military Operations*, 30–33. The names for the governance planning changed several times. First, it was known as Krystal Ball, then Blind Logic, and when it began, Promote Liberty.

147. Russell Wason, "Bush's Big Gamble in Panama," *Newsweek*, January 1, 1990, 21, cited in Gacek, *Logic of Force*, 278. Operation Just Cause is generally cited as an example of the use of massive force. See the Gacek book as well as Molly Moore and Rick Atkinson, "Despite Problems, Invasion Seen as Military Success," *Washington Post*, December 29, 1989.

148. Cole, *Operation Just Cause*, 9, 35, and Lawrence A. Yates, *The U.S. Military Intervention in Panama: Origins, Planning, and Crisis Management, June 1987–December 1989*, Contingency Operations Series (Washington, DC: Center of Military History, US Army, 2008), 90.

149. In addition to Fishel, see Greenhut and Grey, "Civil Affairs in Operation Just Cause," 28.

150. Comments by Woerner to author, October 29, 2004.

151. Krystal Ball was shelved until after the presidential elections. See Shultz, "Post-Conflict Use of Military Forces," 148.

152. Several authors make this point. For example, see ibid., 148.

153. Thurman later recalled that he had not "spent five minutes on BLIND LOGIC during his briefing as incoming CINC" and that in retrospect he should have spent more time on restoration issues. Shultz interview with Thurman, May 29, 1992, cited in Shultz, "Post-Conflict Use of Military Forces," 148–49. See also Fishel, *Civil-Military Operations*, 53.

154. Gray and Manwaring, "Panama: Operation Just Cause," 50.

155. Blind Logic was sent to the JCS for approval on the eve of the invasion. Fishel, *Civil-Military Operations*, 61.

156. Gray and Manwaring, "Panama: Operation Just Cause," 51.

157. This was articulated in Blue Spoon, later called OP-Plan 90–2. Fishel, *Civil-Military Operations*, 70.

158. Gray and Manwaring, "Panama: Operation Just Cause," 48

159. Fishel, *Civil-Military Operations*, 57.

160. His capture occurred after prolonged State Department negotiations with the Vatican embassy in Panama, where Noriega sought refuge.

161. Thurman said that Blind Logic had anticipated that life would return to normal in Panama, which was not the case. See Shultz, "Post-Conflict Use of Military Forces," 149.

162. Crane and Terrill, *Reconstructing Iraq*, 16–17.

163. Shultz, "Post-Conflict Use of Military Forces," 149.

164. Yates, "Operation Just Cause," 19.

165. Meyer, "Civil Affairs in Panama," 16.

166. Three hundred more reservists arrived over the next few weeks. See Welton, "Expertise in Reserve," 2.

167. Fishel, *Civil-Military Operations*, 34. It was unusual that J-5 planners had responsibility for execution. Some analysts believe this revealed the low priority of postconflict planning. See comment by Shultz, "Post-Conflict Use of Military Forces," 152.

168. Gann also oversaw three deputies, each of whom oversaw teams that were responsible for specific functional areas. See chart in Fishel, *Civil-Military Operations*, 67, 74. Gann also had a special staff officer serving as special liaison between the army and the Panamanian government.

169. Meyer, "Civil Affairs in Panama," 28.

170. The discussion of organization is from information in Fishel, *Civil-Military Operations*, 69.

171. Ibid., 67; Welton, "Army Reservists Serve in Panama Operation," *Army Reserve Magazine*, no. 2 (1990): 4; and Meyer, "Civil Affairs in Panama," 14.

172. Shultz, "Post-Conflict Use of Military Forces," 158.

173. Welton, "Army Reservists Serve in Panama Operation," 19.

174. Fishel, *Civil-Military Operations*, 66.

175. Shultz, "Post-Conflict Use of Military Forces," 155.

176. As described in previous cases, this did not always make civil affairs personnel happy. They argued that decision making was hampered by the need to work through a tactical chain of command, as opposed to their own structure. At least in the early stages, this preserved unity of command. When combat ended, this organization could shift to a more governance-focused staff, as it did in many of the World War II cases.

177. See chart in Fishel, *Civil-Military Operations*, 74.

178. Comment attributed to General Lindsay in Shultz interview with Col. Harry Youmans, August 2, 1992, cited in Shultz, "Post-Conflict Use of Military Forces," 157.

179. Information in the paragraph is from Fishel, *Civil-Military Operations*, 74–76. For a similar discussion, see Shultz, "Post-Conflict Use of Military Forces," 156–57.

180. The MSG came into force on January 17, 1990. See Shultz, *In the Aftermath of War*, 34, and Fishel and Downie, "Murky World of Conflict Termination," 70.

181. As noted earlier, given the embassy's weakness, interagency "interference" was not a problem, although the arrival of the new ambassador did create more tensions. See Schultz, "Post-Conflict Use of Military Forces," 158, and Fishel and Downie, "Murky World of Conflict Termination," 69.

182. Fishel, *Civil-Military Operations*, 245.

183. Shultz, *In the Aftermath of War*, 33.

184. Shultz, "Post-Conflict Use of Military Forces," 157.

185. Shultz, *In the Aftermath of War*, 35, 38.

186. This statement is from "Memorandum for Commander in Chief, U.S. Southern Command, From Col. Harold Youmans, Subject: Need for a Training and Support Organization, 8, January 1990," cited in Shultz, *In the Aftermath of War*, 34.

187. Donnelly et al., *Operation Just Cause*, 355.

188. Shultz, *In the Aftermath of War*, 41–42.

189. For a detailed account of the US actions to restore Panama's police forces, see Fishel and Downie, "Taking Responsibility for Our Actions?" 66–77.

190. "USCINSO OPERATIONS ORDER 6–88 (BLIND LOGIC) Declassified document," 2, cited in Shultz, "Post-Conflict Use of Military Forces," 153.

191. Gray and Manwaring, "Panama: Operation Just Cause," 45.

192. Fishel and Downie, "Taking Responsibility for Our Actions?" 67.

193. This was not an ideal situation, owing to the questionable loyalty of former PDF individuals, but because of necessity it was chosen. Fishel and Downie, "Taking Responsibility for Our Actions?" 67. See also Cole, *Operation Just Cause*, 53. By December 23, some four to five thousand PDF soldiers had asked to join the new government. See Donnelly et al., *Operation Just Cause*, 352.

194. Dandar, "Civil Affairs Operations," 129.

195. Cole, *Operation Just Cause*, 68.

196. To "civilianize" the force, however, a Department of Justice program, the International Criminal Investigation Training Assistance Program, helped to teach civilian methods of training and control. See Fishel and Downie, "Taking Responsibility for Our Actions?" 69.

197. Gray and Manwaring, "Panama: Operation Just Cause," 55. This act was later amended to allow an exception for the reconstitution of civilian police authority and capability in the postconflict restoration.

198. Fishel and Downie, "Taking Responsibility for Our Actions?" 68, 70–71. They criticize the poor quality of weapons provided to the Panamanian Public Force.

199. Fishel, *Civil-Military Operations*, 71.

200. Sullivan, "Future U.S. Role in Panama," 158.

201. Meyer, "Civil Affairs in Panama," 24, and Greenhut and Grey, "Civil Affairs in Operation Just Cause," 34.

202. Such as the penal colony on Coiba Island. See Donnelly et al., *Operation Just Cause*, 363.

203. Ibid., 374.

204. Crane, "Lure of Strike," 15–16.

205. Welton, "Expertise in Reserve," 3.

206. Blind Logic anticipated that the 361st Civil Affairs Brigade would be called up. See Greenhut and Grey, "Civil Affairs in Operation Just Cause," 29.

207. "Panama Operations and USARSOC Activation," *Civil Affairs Journal and Newsletter* (November–December 1989): 7. Other accounts note that the number grew to thousands of possible volunteers. See Greenhut and Grey, "Civil Affairs in Operation Just Cause," 29.

208. "Operation Just Cause: Lessons Learned," 22.

209. Comments of Maj. Harold E. Williams, commander of Company A, Ninety-Sixth Civil Affairs Battalion, in Greenhut and Grey, "Civil Affairs in Operation Just Cause," 29. Only fifteen active-duty civil affairs personnel from the Ninety-Sixth had deployed with the initial troop movement. See Meyer, "Civil Affairs in Panama," 7. Meyer was the executive officer, 321st Civil Affairs Group, based in San Antonio, TX. He was previously the operations officer of the 432nd Civil Affairs Company in Green Bay, WI. Members of the Ninety-Sixth were to provide direct support to the tactical elements of JTF Panama. Shortly thereafter, the first twenty-five civil affairs and PYSOPS soldiers arrived with second and third groups, totaling some 175 arriving by the end of January.

210. US Dept. of the Army, *Operation Just Cause: Lessons Learned*, vol. 2, *Operations*, 52.

211. Donnelly et al., *Operation Just Cause*, 356.

212. Comment by Second Brigade commander Col. Linwood E. Burney, cited ibid., 355.

213. Cole, "Operation Just Cause," 66.

214. Information in remainder of paragraph is from Greenhut and Grey, "Civil Affairs in Operation Just Cause," 29–32, and Meyer, "Civil Affairs in Panama," 18–19.

215. Greenhut and Grey, "Civil Affairs in Operation Just Cause," 30.

216. Quote and comment by SFC Cecil Roper (platoon sergeant), Company B, Ninety-Sixth Civil Affairs Battalion, cited in "Joint Task Force South in Operation Just Cause," Oral History Interview, JCIT 049, Dept. of the Army, XVIII Airborne Corps, Fort Bragg,

NC, and the US Army Center of Military History, Washington, DC. A copy of this tran-script can be found at http://www.army.mil/cmh-pg/documents/panama/jcit/JCIT49.htm

217. Quote and comment by SFC Roper, ibid.

218. Donnelly et al., *Operation Just Cause*, 374.

219. Medical information is from Meyer, "Civil Affairs in Panama," 17, 23, 24, and from Greenhut and Grey, "Civil Affairs in Operation Just Cause," 33, 36.

220. Greenhut and Grey, "Civil Affairs in Operation Just Cause," 32.

221. Meyer, "Civil Affairs in Panama," 26.

222. Shultz recounts several statements by the ambassador to Panama, Deane Hinton, about the military's close relationship with the Republican Party. See Schulz, *In the After-math of War*, 61–62.

223. This was the US ambassador's argument. See Cole, "Operation Just Cause," 67–68.

224. By the time of the invasion, Panama had $6 billion of foreign debt and a gross domestic product that had declined 25 percent since 1987. See Sullivan, "Future U.S. Role in Panama," 162.

225. The information about civil affairs activities in this paragraph is from Dandar, "Civil Affairs Operations," 129–30.

226. Watson and Tsouras, *Operation Just Cause*, chronology, 225.

227. Fishel, *Civil-Military Operations*, 108.

228. Gray and Manwaring, "Panama: Operation Just Cause," 55.

229. Cole, *Operation Just Cause*, 47.

230. See comments on compartmented planning by Gen. Wayne A. Downing, former commander in chief, USSOCOM, in letter to the editor, *Military Review*, February 1994, 64.

231. The other stated objectives were (1) freedom of transit through the canal, (2) freedom from PDF abuse and harassment, and (3) freedom to exercise US treaty rights and responsibilities. See "Message from CJCS, DTG 1823252Z December 1989, Subject: Exe-cute Order," cited in Bennett, "Just Cause and Principles of War," 3.

232. Greenhut and Grey, "Civil Affairs in Operation Just Cause," 32. This point was also made by General Woerner during the October 29, 2003, interview with author.

233. Fishel, *Civil-Military Operations*, 9.

234. Fishel interviews with State officials, cited ibid., 72.

235. Quoted in Donnelly et al., *Operation Just Cause*, 376.

236. See, for example, Shultz, *In the Aftermath of War*, 42, and Fishel and Downie, "Murky World of Conflict Termination," 77.

237. Fishel and Downie, "Murky World of Conflict Termination," 77.

238. Dandar, "Civil Affairs Operations," 129.

239. Taw, *Operation Just Cause and Low Intensity Conflict*, 29.

240. Daugherty and Andrews, "Review of U.S. Historical Experience," 445.

241. Stolzenbach and Kissinger, "Civil Affairs in Korea," 137.

242. Fahey, "Overall U.S. Politico-Military-Complex," 2.

243. "Memo to Lt. Col. Nicolson, From: OCAMG, 4 March 1954, Subject: Civil Affairs / Military Government Organization and Operations," NA, OCMAG Administration and Organization, file box 11 300.6–310.1, folder 310.1.

244. Powell, *My American Journey*, 434.

## FIVE

# AFGHANISTAN
# AND IRAQ

## LESSONS IGNORED

ON SEPTEMBER 11, 2001, nineteen men driven by a perverse Islamist ideology flew two planes into the World Trade Center buildings in New York City, one plane into the Pentagon, and a fourth into a field in Pennsylvania. The terrorists murdered 2,996 people and set off a series of military and political reactions around the world that continue to reverberate today. In response to the 9/11 attacks, the United States launched an offensive campaign against the Taliban regime in Afghanistan in October 2001 and, less than two years later, attacked the regime of Saddam Hussein in Iraq in March 2003. Both invasions revealed the consistent problem with the American way of war: the difficulty of integrating combat operations with the operational challenges of consolidating military gains to accomplish political goals. Because of many of the same civil-military tensions present in previous American wars, the conflicts in Iraq and Afghanistan revealed the "missing middle"—the gap between combat operations and the steps required to achieve stability, forge a sustainable outcome, and permit the withdrawal of US military forces.

US planning for the interventions in Iraq and Afghanistan did not, for the most part, connect combat requirements with desired political end states. Throughout both conflicts, policy disagreements over the political outcomes created organizational disarray and uncertainty, weakening US and allied influence over the course of events. Regarding Iraq, uncertainty about how to establish the foundations for a post-Saddam government and disagreements over the type of US organization best suited to oversee a transition to that government undermined unity of effort and created opportunities for adversaries. In contrast to Iraq, owing to international consensus there was a clear road map for a political transition to a post-Taliban Afghan government. However, the political process and military strategy in Afghanistan were disconnected; the initial US and allied military strategy focused narrowly on counterterrorism (CT) rather than a comprehensive effort to support political consolidation throughout Afghanistan. In addition, the stabilization activities in Afghanistan were mired in a complex alphabet soup of disconnected and often competing organizations.

# AFGHANISTAN

As the war in Afghanistan began, US political leaders anticipated problems of governance. Washington initially limited its political objective to the removal of Osama bin Laden, the founder of al-Qaeda and architect of the 9/11 attacks, who had been living in Afghanistan with Taliban support since 1996, and the toppling of bin Laden's sponsor, the Taliban regime led by Mullah Muhammad Omar. When President George W. Bush announced US military strikes against al-Qaeda training camps and Taliban military installations, he explained that these were carefully targeted actions designed to disrupt the use of Afghanistan as a terrorist base of operations.[1] This narrow goal, however, was short-lived, and US political objectives quickly expanded from ousting the Taliban to support for the reconstitution of a new Afghan government. US leaders recognized, albeit belatedly, that shaping a new regime was necessary to prevent the use of Afghanistan as a terrorist sanctuary in the future.

Three main lines of effort related to governance operations developed in Afghanistan: political, security, and reconstruction. All were disconnected, overlapping, and fragmented among many state and international actors. Political negotiations to reconstitute the Afghan political system, principally through the Bonn Process, constituted the first line of effort. Security operations constituted the second line of effort. These military-led security operations vacillated between CT measures and broader stabilization efforts. Military-led stabilization operations first focused on Kabul and were designed to provide a stable foundation for the new Afghan government. Those efforts eventually expanded throughout the country to support, at the local level, projects designed to gain the confidence of the Afghan people and prevent popular support for the Taliban, which had, by 2002, already begun to regenerate across the border in Pakistan with the assistance of the Pakistani intelligence organization Inter-Services Intelligence (ISI). CT operations in Afghanistan first focused on high-value targets such as the leaders of al-Qaeda and the Taliban. Later these operations also targeted commanders of the Haqqani network and Gulbuddin Hekmatyar's Hezb-e Islami Gulbiddin (HIG), which, together with former Afghan leader Mullah Omar's Quetta Shura Taliban, formed the three main armed opposition groups to the new Afghan state. The third line of effort was the civilian-led (primarily UN and donor country) state building and reconstruction in which the UN and coalition countries endeavored to rebuild or create national institutions such as the army and police, the judiciary, the Ministry of Finance, the Ministry of Health, the Ministry of Transportation, the Ministry of the Economy, and the Ministry of Education.

There has yet to be a complete account of the complexity of the governance challenges across Afghanistan.[2] The following provides a broad overview of these three lines of effort and illustrates that problems encountered in Afghanistan had antecedents in previous US experience. Efforts in Afghanistan paralleled the observations about reconstruction and stabilization problems in Vietnam by Robert Komer, a key architect of and participant in the COIN strategy there: There was no integrated approach to unify the disparate and conflicting efforts on the ground.[3] As in previous operations discussed in this book, problems of organization for governance operations hampered the achievement of US objectives. In Afghanistan the problem was particularly acute, given the utter lack of state capacity and the eventual involvement of eighteen NATO nations; non-NATO allies such as Japan, South Korea, and Australia; the UN; nongovernmental organizations (NGOs) with diverse goals; and many other US and international agencies. One analyst noted that at one point the NATO-led command was responsible for more than forty-five international coalition force members, each with its own rules of engagement.[4] There was no agreed-upon concept of operations for governance operations, no central authority, and neither a common concept of operations nor synchronicity among the various chains of command, countries, or agencies. The politically preferable concept of unity of effort—as opposed to unity of command—dominated.

Yet, in practice, even unity of effort was ephemeral. Across the three lines of effort (political, security, and reconstruction), changes in leaders and individuals, command relationships, and organizations made the continuity necessary to address problems nearly impossible to achieve. Different actors diagnosed problems again, reshaped efforts already under way, or started new projects. If one were to draw a picture of these relationships, it would look like a web. But not only would the threads of this web be extraordinarily complex to follow— they would change color and direction regularly. Moreover, the disconnect between funding cycles in Washington and actual requirements made it very challenging for the United States to develop long-term plans and to follow through on promises. The fact that the Afghan government itself was divided by competing factions further complicated governance operations.

## Political and Military Lines of Effort

On October 7, 2001, the United States and its British ally launched Operation Enduring Freedom, a military campaign designed to topple the Taliban regime through the use of air strikes, special operations forces (SOF), and CIA operators to support anti-Taliban Afghan groups on the ground. SOF and CIA operators facilitated air strikes to help Northern Alliance and other anti-Taliban forces advance on Taliban positions. One official US Army history called these forces a "surrogate ground army that proved quite effective when provided some coordination elements and air power assistance."[5] Two months later, the Taliban government fell.

As the United States launched its first strikes against the Taliban regime, a political line of effort in Afghanistan also began, with the Bonn Conference in October 2001. Under the auspices of the UN special representative of the secretary-general for Afghanistan, Lakhdar Brahimi, the conference established the Afghan Interim Authority (AIA) to govern the country after the fall of the Taliban. The Bonn participants forged a coalition of leaders in Afghanistan who would share power and govern. Afghan delegates included representatives from the three main anti-Taliban groups (the Northern Alliance, the Rome Group, and the Cyprus Group). A US State Department official, Ambassador James Dobbins, who had overseen nation-building efforts in Somalia, Haiti, Bosnia, and Kosovo, led the US delegation. Four main regional powers (Pakistan, India, Iran, and Russia) participated as well.

Just two months later, on December 5, 2001, the Bonn participants signed an agreement and developed a road map and timetable for the creation of a new constitutional order and national elections. Thus, from October to December 2001, US military and political objectives were closely intertwined, with the United States engaged in combat operations and intense political negotiations, with both aligned to bring down the Taliban and reconstitute a new and inclusive Afghan government. By early December, military operations had defeated the Taliban government, and a few weeks later the AIA took office in Kabul. It paved the way for a *loya jirga* in June 2002. Following a tradition that dated back hundreds of years, this grand assembly gathered representatives from across the country to make important political decisions. Through the summer of 2002, districts across Afghanistan chose delegates to the *loya jirga*, and the delegates chose Hamid Karzai to lead Afghanistan as interim president. He and a constitutional committee drafted a new constitution, which was approved by a reconvened *loya jirga* in January 2004. Nine months later, in October 2004, millions of Afghan men and women voted in Afghanistan's first presidential election and elected Hamid Karzai as president.

But even as the AIA took power in December 2001, the problem of how ongoing military operations should support the new government emerged. The situation in early 2002 posed two fundamental challenges. First, insurgents, assisted by the ISI, had already begun to regroup. To address this immediate problem of terrorists gathering in the east, the United States launched Operation Anaconda in March 2002, with the goal of destroying Taliban and al-Qaeda forces concentrated in the Shahikot Valley. Originally planned as a three-day offensive for which only light resistance was anticipated, the battle instead lasted about two weeks. Eventually US forces called in substantial numbers of air strikes as US soldiers and Afghan militia fought against the enemy in rugged terrain.[6]

Second, a leaked CIA report warned that Afghanistan could succumb to violent chaos if US and coalition partners did not act to mitigate tribal and ethnic tensions and competitions among rival warlord organizations.[7] The special presidential envoy to Afghanistan, Zalmay Khalilzad, believed that the challenge was to "prevent a return to warlordism."[8] Yet coalition military operations remained focused on raids associated with more narrow CT objectives, as competing militias began to infiltrate Afghanistan's nascent security forces and its Ministry of the Interior (MOI) and Ministry of Defense (MOD). Although Operation Anaconda had succeeded in clearing the area of insurgent forces, many of the enemy escaped to Pakistan. US military operations focused exclusively on the enemy in remote areas did not address the larger problem of how to consolidate combat gains and harden Afghanistan against the regenerative capacity of the Taliban. At this time, there was still little debate among officials in Washington about how to shift from predominantly CT raids to a more comprehensive strategy that would align combat operations with stabilization efforts. Such a shift would require a new operational plan and more troops.

Concurrent to US-led combat operations, the UN authorized the establishment of the International Security Assistance Force for Afghanistan (ISAF) in December 2001. Originally the UN called it a "coalition of the willing," and its role was narrow: It would comprise about five thousand troops from eighteen countries and would deploy just to Kabul to maintain security and to support the AIA. Thus, by 2002, two separate military missions—a US-led coalition and an ISAF mission (led first by the United Kingdom and then Turkey)—operated in Afghanistan under distinct military commands, a division that became more pronounced as ISAF's mission expanded beyond Kabul to the rest of the country.

By the end of 2002, ISAF's initial focus on Kabul became a point of contention as civilian and military officials debated the evolution of the war. Two fundamental arguments unfolded. Some State Department officials argued for a larger peacekeeping force of about twenty-five thousand—in contrast to ISAF's five thousand or so troops in Kabul. They believed that more forces were required to fight insurgents and foster security so that key political steps—such as holding elections—could unfold with a reduced chance of violence. They argued that the United States and its allies needed to shift from an exclusive focus on the hunt for Taliban and al-Qaeda leaders to a broader effort that recognized the requirements of improving security across the country. Ambassador Dobbins, supported by Special Envoy Khalilzad (who would later serve as the US ambassador in Kabul), argued that it would be "irresponsible" to think that "Afghanistan could be secured adequately by Afghans in the immediate aftermath of a twenty-three-year civil war."[9]

Other senior US officials continued to view the problem as primarily a terrorism situation, rather than one stemming from a contest for political power and control of the Afghan state. They tended to separate the targeting of terrorists from the need to undertake stabilization tasks and to see the campaign as an opportunity to validate the theory that new technologies had revolutionized warfare and allowed for more of a "light footprint."[10] An official army account noted that in early 2002, when American troops still numbered around five thousand, US commanders believed that they were operating under an informal force cap of around seven thousand personnel.[11] Secretary of Defense Donald Rumsfeld was reluctant to provide US support to a larger stabilization force. While he acknowledged the importance of security, he argued against expanding ISAF and believed that the emphasis should be on helping Afghanistan "develop a national army so that they can look out for themselves over time."[12] The problem, of course, was time. The creation of the Afghan National Army (ANA) would not occur overnight. Stabilization efforts were necessary in the near term to support the political process and prevent the resurgence of insurgent forces as the Afghan security forces grew. The development of a strong ANA and stabilization measures needed to occur simultaneously. But there were ongoing debates about the time it would take to build a new and effective ANA, as well as disagreements about the size of such a force. The mismatch between ambitious objectives and the desire to limit the size and scope of the coalition effort persisted as the Taliban regenerated power and began to regain control of territory and populations in Afghanistan.

Moreover, reluctance to involve US forces in a larger stabilization mission was consistent with the Bush administration's wariness about nation building. As a presidential candidate in 2000, Bush had expressed the view that American troops should not be involved in nation building. Two years later, in the midst of the war in Afghanistan, the White House maintained that the president continued to believe that "the purpose of the military is to be used to fight and win wars, and not to engage in peacekeeping."[13] This thinking among top civilian (and military) leaders was consistent with the lack of operational planning for *how* a desired political objective—the establishment of a capable Afghan government—would actually be accomplished.

Eventually, a change of course occurred. In May 2003, Secretary Rumsfeld announced a shift from "major combat activity" to stability and stabilization activities and projected that ISAF troops would expand. (By the end of October 2009, ISAF would have an estimated seventy-one thousand troops from forty-two countries, with the twenty-eight NATO members providing the core of the force and the largest deployment of over thirty-four thousand from the United States.[14]) In August 2003, NATO assumed command of the ISAF mission and eventually oversaw the expansion of the force to the north, west, south, and east of the country.[15] Over time, a different NATO member led each regional command, which corresponded, roughly, to Afghanistan's main regions. The ISAF expansion sought to implicitly recognize that wider stabilization measures would be required in order to achieve the political goals set forth at Bonn.

As this expansion took place, ISAF and US-led coalition forces operated under different rules of engagement (ROEs). The ROEs differentiated between coalition forces, which were prosecuting the "war on terror," and ISAF forces, which focused on the stabilization mission. This distinction allowed NATO nations with political sensitivities to limit their involvement to stabilization activities, as opposed to combat operations. This distinction was one example of the extremely complex array of national caveats that limited the activities of various national forces and that, in turn, undermined their ability to adapt to the evolving conflict in Afghanistan.[16]

The creation of ISAF as a separate organization to address stabilization treated the problems of stabilization and consolidation as distinct from combat operations. In the theater, however, stabilization challenges stemmed mainly from the instability generated by the Taliban and other insurgent groups. This artificial separation between political and security efforts sought to make the Afghan mission attractive to a broad range of international actors, many of whom were wary of CT or COIN operations. But it also made it quite hard to integrate stabilization efforts into the overall campaign plan—a requirement for achieving a sustainable outcome.

In addition, as in other conflicts, US soldiers found themselves conducting governance tasks by necessity early in the conflict, well before "real" guidance emerged. For example, the soldiers in Combined Joint Task Force 180 (CJTF-180) had been meeting local leaders, interacting with local populations, and undertaking reconstruction projects, such as the digging of wells, despite the ambivalence concerning US forces engaging in stabilization missions and laborious approval and funding processes for emerging governance tasks.[17] Moreover, CJTF-180 and the Combined Joint Special Operations Task Force (CJSOTF) empowered some local leaders at the expense of others through support for their militias and the awarding of contracts for logistics and reconstruction. The Taliban took advantage of the exclusionary political economies that the United States and ISAF unwittingly created, portraying themselves as patrons for tribes and leaders who considered themselves losers in the post-Taliban order.

Against the backdrop of this expanded and broader stabilization mission, the United States reconsidered its command arrangements. As in previous wars, thinking about how to integrate governance tasks as combat operations unfolded did not occur in advance. Until October 2003, CJTF-180 provided the command structure for Operation Enduring Freedom, controlling all US forces in the theater. It had wide geographic responsibilities—Afghanistan, parts of Tajikistan, parts of Uzbekistan, and parts of Pakistan. And although its mission then expanded to stabilization, it remained responsible for the tactical operations of SOF and conventional forces. In addition, Central Command (CENTCOM) also had responsibility for SOF operations through the new CJSOTF, which included not only US units but also SOF units from allied countries. To add to this complexity, separate "black" SOF activities were taking place under SOCOM's command. (SOCOM had global SOF capabilities that could and did deploy into Afghanistan.)[18] Combat activities were not always well synchronized or consistent with the political design underpinning stabilization efforts. Indeed, US commands were not only divided between the two types of security missions (i.e., counterterrorism and stabilization), but they were also divided *within* these missions since there were diverse authorities directing the varied counterterrorism efforts.

In the summer of 2003, the United States improved its command structure. US Army general John P. Abizaid assumed command of CENTCOM and created a headquarters in Kabul to improve the synchronization of strategic political-military issues. This new command, Combined Forces Command–Afghanistan (CFC-A), would now serve as the higher headquarters for the original CJTF-180. CFC-A coordinated efforts among regional strategic partners, members of ISAF, the UN, the Afghan government, and numerous other actors involved in political-military activities. US Army lieutenant general David Barno led the new command, which quickly grew from six to around four hundred joint service and coalition members.[19] Military operations for CFC-A continued to be led by a subordinate headquarters located in Bagram.

This shift recognized the need for an alignment of tactical theater command priorities with broader governance and consolidation issues. Barno wanted to shift from an "enemy centric approach," which emphasized raids against enemy forces, to one that would isolate the Taliban and its allies from the Afghan people.[20] Before the development of the formal US COIN doctrine (which would be implemented in 2007 under the direction of US Army general David Petraeus and US Marine Corps general James Mattis), Barno developed a "five-pillar" approach for Afghanistan: to defeat terrorism and deny sanctuary, enable Afghan security structures, sustain area ownership, enable reconstruction and good governance, and engage regional states. Barno argued that "interagency and international unity of purpose" was essential to achieving those goals. And he moved his office onto US embassy grounds in order to facilitate integrated civil-military cooperation. The move reflected a growing appreciation among Washington policymakers that the conflict had "moved from a major combat activity to a period of stability and stabilization and reconstruction activities."[21]

Despite a consistent emphasis on "unity of purpose" throughout Barno's tenure, his efforts to work closely with the US embassy did not outlast him. Several years later, when US Army general Stanley McChrystal conducted his assessment of the situation in Afghanistan, he identified better unity of effort as one of two principal areas that warranted a "dramatic shift." The United States struggled to achieve this objective within its own government, let alone among the dozens of other actors in Afghanistan. By then, the NATO-led ISAF had taken over all combat and stabilization efforts in the country. And even though a US four-star general led ISAF, the integration of military and civilian efforts remained decidedly uneven. This was largely because each NATO nation was effectively designing its own "comprehensive" strategy for Afghanistan. As General Barno later observed, over "two dozen comprehensive approaches" were under way, leading to a breakdown of integration and wasted and overlapping resources.[22]

As CFC-A's role in Afghanistan expanded (even though in the summer of 2003 US troops were actually drawing down, owing to the pressure to shift to Iraq[23]), newly created provincial reconstruction teams (PRTs) further complicated the stabilization landscape. In 2003 US Army lieutenant general Dan McNeill, the commander of Coalition Forces Afghanistan, established these civil-military teams to address stabilization and reconstruction requirements in the field. The early PRTs were based on more modest civil-military operations teams that had been composed of around six reservists (mainly civil affairs personnel) who had been working from US military bases to rebuild schools, wells, and other damaged infrastructure.[24] PRTs were designed to improve stability in an area by helping to build the capacity of the host nation. Under General Barno's leadership, the PRT model expanded, but the teams differed in size, structure, and manning depending on each country's involvement.[25] A US team might be composed of fifty to one hundred people, led by a military officer (typically a lieutenant colonel). It initially stressed force protection and small, quick-impact reconstruction and assistance operations. Civilians on the team included specialists from the State Department, USAID, the Department of Agriculture, and the Department of Justice. The British PRT model was similar to the US model in size but stressed security reform efforts, while German PRTs strictly separated the military and civilian functions of the teams. At various points throughout the war, more than two dozen PRTs operated in Afghanistan with great variation.

With the expansion of PRTs around the country, tensions arose around the issue of whether predominantly military teams should even be leading reconstruction tasks. Pressure grew in Washington to increase civilian presence on the PRTs. Although the PRTs were supposed to be integrated civil-military teams, the US model, according to one expert, featured a complement of seventy-nine American military and three civilian government representatives.[26] The State Department hoped to grow the number of US civilians in Afghanistan from 320 to 1,000 by 2010.[27] As in other wars, however, there was no significant civilian operational capacity to deploy to a war zone on a large scale.

In addition, many international NGOs were skeptical of the military's role, questioning the "motivations" of assistance activities since they were not "delivered according to the core principles of: the primacy of the humanitarian imperative; the independence of humanitarian aid: [sic] and the impartial provisioning of aid."[28] This type of reflexive "neutrality" was common among large NGOs operating in Afghanistan. This was problematic because the United States sought to partner with NGOs, even though many refused to work with the US military. Indeed, in 2002 the US Army's Peacekeeping and Stability Operations Institute (PKSOI) had discussed the idea of "wholesale aid distribution," which would rely on civilian networks to provide aid across the country. Yet relationships among military forces, the UN, and the NGOs were not always collaborative at the operational and strategic levels, though "accommodations occurred at the tactical level." CENTCOM's approach favored providing support to NGOs conducting humanitarian assistance so that the coalition could "continue its campaign against international terrorism."[29] The United States thus relied on key outside entities—many of which had different priorities—to conduct operations central to its mission in Afghanistan.

While sensible on paper, the PRT model in practice reflected many of the problems of previous experiences with divided authorities and illustrated the familiar US ambivalence as to whether these missions were a core part of the war effort. Initially, the PRTs deployed across the country reported through chains of command *different* from those of the coalition's maneuver units in the same geographic area or "battlespace."[30] Yet PRTs were often on the front lines of the continuum between combat and stabilization because the villages that they operated in were often contested. As in the past, dual chains of command created conflicting lines of authority, which in turn obstructed the implementation of initiatives, programs, and activities critical to the achievement of US and ISAF goals.

Disconnected stabilization efforts in Afghanistan suffered further following the invasion of Iraq. As General Barno later observed, CENTCOM was under enormous pressure *not* to commit additional resources to Afghanistan.[31] The requirements for Iraq were straining the active army, which had to find ways to stretch its forces. For example, the army could no longer afford to continue assigning active-duty units to the Afghan National Security Force (ANSF) training mission and instead gave this critical reconstruction task to a range of National Guard units, many of which did not have sufficient experience or training for this mission. Also, the United States relied more on a multinational model, which meant employing NATO forces whose capabilities and willingness to accept risk varied widely. To make matters worse, the insurgency escalated dramatically in late 2005 and early 2006. Afghan and international forces had increasing difficulty maintaining security in the east and south. As the insurgency grew stronger, the United States could reinforce operations only on the margins.

When President Barack Obama assumed office in January 2009, one of his first major national security decisions was how to pursue the war in Afghanistan. The view in the White House was that that United States did not have a strategy. One of the first presentations to Obama's national security team, made by army lieutenant general Douglas Lute (who had been the White House special coordinator for Afghanistan since 2007), said that the United States did not have a "strategy that you can articulate or achieve."[32] Thus, in the first days of his presidency, Obama asked Bruce Riedel, a former CIA officer with deep knowledge of the region, to lead a review. Riedel, serving as an independent scholar at the Brookings Institution, had been critical of President Bush's "half-hearted" efforts in Afghanistan. His review argued that the United States should adopt a more fully resourced COIN strategy that would (1) reverse Taliban gains and secure the population, particularly in the most contested southern and eastern regions; (2) provide Afghan national security forces with the training and the mentoring needed to expand rapidly and ultimately take the lead in providing security; and (3) provide a secure environment to enable governance and development efforts to take root and grow. The Riedel review emphasized not just the military aspects of the war but also the need to "provide the kind of civilian support that this mission has always needed."[33]

General McChrystal, who had assumed command of ISAF in 2009, completed his own assessment of requirements in Afghanistan. From his perspective, improving security was essential to achieving durable improvements in governance and development. McChrystal outlined three options: eighty thousand additional troops to conduct a COIN campaign throughout the country, forty thousand troops to reinforce the south and east simultaneously, or ten to fifteen thousand troops to train Afghan forces.[34] Earlier, he had argued that success was possible but that it was not merely about "trying harder" or about additional resources; it was also about an "urgent need" for a change in strategy and in how "*we think and operate*."[35] McChrystal rejected the incrementalism that characterized American strategy, observing that "incremental decisions to provide forces over time are not the same as a clear decision up front that facilitates effective force employment."[36] His emphasis was on a campaign to secure the population and to speed up the training of Afghan security forces, including closer partnering with Afghan forces until they were able to secure populations in contested areas.

In the end, the president decided in December 2009 on an "escalate then exit strategy" of thirty thousand additional troops.[37] He effectively rejected McChrystal's concern about incremental escalation and set an arbitrary deadline of eighteen months for the withdrawal of troops. He explained that the goal would be to use these additional forces to reverse some of the Taliban's momentum and that they would allow the United States to accelerate "handing over responsibility to Afghan forces." Obama would now focus on three elements: a military "effort to create conditions for a transition; a civilian surge that reinforced positive action; and an effective partnership with Pakistan." Obama justified the articulation of a time frame as a way to inject a "sense of urgency in working with the Afghan government." But he did not address the fact that such a publicly announced timeline raised doubts about American determination. In essence, the president equated strategic restraint with tactical restraint. By rejecting the use of force to overwhelm and defeat enemy forces, he not only emboldened the enemy but also encouraged in friends and neutrals a tendency to hedge their bets and consolidate power in advance of post-ISAF Afghanistan. This short-term mentality frustrated reform efforts and drove unchecked corruption and organized-crime activity that perpetuated state weakness.

Even with additional troops, therefore, there was no fundamental commitment to consolidation. The White House began to back away from its already limited approach by not following through with a commitment of resources required for the so-called surge recommended by his military advisers. With that thirty-thousand-troop increase, it was not possible to *simultaneously* secure the south and the east—it now would be done sequentially. And with the arbitrary deadline set by the president, this sequential approach was also effectively undercut. Top White House officials, including Vice President Joe

Biden, advocated avoiding reconstruction and population protection and instead focusing on disrupting the Taliban, improving the ANA, and pursuing reconciliation with the Taliban.[38] By 2011 President Obama had announced that most major US goals had already been achieved.[39] The US mission would change from combat to support. It would start to withdraw ten thousand troops, with thirty-three thousand back in the United States by June 2012. Essentially, by mid-2011 the US had shifted back toward a CT approach, reinforcing the pattern throughout the course of the intervention since early 2002 that had shifted between CT and stabilization. Fundamentally, there was never an overarching campaign plan to link the two operational approaches and connect them to other lines of effort and strategic objectives.

## State Building

State building represented a third line of effort in Afghanistan. Initially, it was predominantly led by the UN but involved many national country efforts as well. After decades of war, years of Taliban rule, and extreme poverty, virtually all of the institutions of a functioning state had been destroyed, including most of Afghanistan's health and educational systems, the courts, the parliament, and much of its civil service. Women and girls, who made up the majority of the population, had been denied the right to education and to work. In the spring of 2003, President Karzai, seeking support for reconstruction, hoped that the country could develop the "institutions that will provide it with the administration that it needs."[40]

At the January 2002 Tokyo donors' conference, eight nations and various international actors gathered to consider Afghanistan's reconstruction needs. As one observer noted, donors were more eager to fund some tasks over others: While support for "schools and hospitals" were "safe bets," support for armies and police were less politically popular in donor countries.[41] The division of donor efforts proved to be problematic. Dobbins later criticized the effort: "No nation, including most notably the United States, made the effort necessary to get these institutions up and running. Neither were lead nations able to secure significant support for their programs from other donors, for few wanted to accept another government's oversight." Dobbins later observed that having liberated Afghanistan, the United States was proposing to provide Afghans the same amount of assistance they would have received had they remained under the Taliban.

In April 2008, President Karzai approved the Afghan National Development Strategy (ANDS), which was soon also endorsed by the international community. Three broad pillars constituted the plan: security, governance, and economic and social development. It also specified eight subpillars, seventeen sectors, and six cross-cutting issues. Efforts to help the Afghans carry out the ANDS were hampered by an extraordinarily complex array of donor organizations, different requirements across the regions of Afghanistan, and lack of human capital. Not only were civilians constantly under fire, but the entire reconstruction effort was also characterized by divisions of authority and resources over different sectors. It was bureaucratic anarchy, with no one in charge or providing order to the overall effort. Perhaps even more than the military combat and stabilization problems described previously, unity of effort was virtually impossible to achieve simply because it was almost impossible for one actor or organization to know all of the other actors involved in seeking to improve a particular sector. In 2009 key US officials admitted that they were still searching for ways to refocus international assistance in a way that was "more coordinated and more rational."[42]

All of the actors underestimated the scale of the task. There was virtually nothing left of the Afghan state: Ministries were empty shells destroyed by twenty-five years of war, and most basic infrastructure was absent. There was a persistent inability to scale particular tasks and to resource them. There was neither an overarching picture of the situation nor an effective information-management system or other means to track programs undertaken by various entities in Afghanistan.[43] Moreover, the programs and actions of major donors were carried out by an array of contractors and NGOs, with varying degrees of expertise, commitment, and effectiveness. No one had a clear sense of how many other private companies or individuals were involved in various aspects of reconstruction (and many were mainly providing security to workers). Overall, this country-led model of reconstruction was fragmented and deeply flawed.

In addition, to make progress more quickly, donors tended to focus on opening their own management office at the expense of building local institutions through local actors. The vast majority of economic and security assistance bypassed the government, with nations and international organizations finding it more expedient to work through NGOs and contractors.[44] This hollowed out an already weak Afghan government since most capable personnel went to work for contractors and international NGOs, who could pay more and who controlled more resources. The Afghan minister of finance and later, president, Ashraf Ghani, denounced this pattern of creating "parallel structures" to the Afghan government. From the US perspective, Secretary of War Marcy's instructions during the Mexican-American War—to work through existing administrative structures—would have been equally apt in Afghanistan over 150 years later.

Moreover, there was no serious planning related to sustainment.[45] This gap, combined with myriad complex regulations, made it difficult if not impossible to correct problems that were identified on the ground. Even though the military emphasized "mission command"—the need to devolve authority to lower levels—this was not a philosophy that dominated in the civilian-led reconstruction efforts. Indeed, the modern contingencies of Afghanistan and Iraq differed from those in the past. While General Wood in Cuba could, in the absence of guidance, figure out what was needed and work to fix it, the US government was inflicting constant and often crippling regulations, reducing the flexibility of operators. Congress established the Office of the Special Inspector General for Afghanistan Reconstruction (SIGAR) to provide oversight and address contracting abuses but focus was on how much money was spent rather than on how projects and spending contributed to the mission as a whole. Moreover, regulations were so complex it was extremely difficult to respond to local circumstances. Thus, for example, even though a road project was under way and in use by local Afghans and coalition forces, DOD regulations did not allow for commanders' funds—from the Commander's Emergency Response Program (CERP)—to be used for the maintenance and sustainment of the road (and other infrastructure projects), even though fixes were needed.[46] And although state-building efforts were primarily led by civilians, US soldiers were involved from the start on the tactical level, working with locals on the actual implementation of specific initiatives decided in Kabul, Washington, and the capitals of coalition forces. As the level of violence in Afghanistan grew, through 2009 (and beyond), gains across most of the ANDS pillars and sectors were limited owing to security issues and a lack of governing capacity to manage programs.[47]

As in previous wars, one of the most important components for longer-term stabilization and political consolidation was the shift to local security forces. The creation of the ANA and the Afghan National Police (ANP) was central to the long-term success of the central government. Without a national army and local police forces, the country would not be able to the fight the insurgency or create the local conditions for security to prevent the growth of insurgent strongholds. This was recognized at Bonn, where participants had agreed that the ANA would be a volunteer force numbering no more than seventy thousand.

The challenges were immense. The United States and its allies needed to start a program essentially from scratch. Three fundamental problems weakened the effort. First, there was a mismatch between stated US preference to shift more responsibility for stability and security to the ANA and actual resources applied to this goal. In mid-2002 US Army Special Forces began training ANA personnel. At the time, the plan was for around 2,500 new recruits to complete training by the end of 2002. The DOD intended to train up to 14,400 Afghan troops by the end of 2003 at a cost, including establishing a general staff and a headquarters staff, of about $135 million.[48] In 2002 the objective was to support an ANA of 70,000. But the ability of the ANA to reach this goal was seriously hampered by difficulties in finding qualified candidates, by critical equipment shortages, and by shortfalls in trainers.[49]

This goal remained unchanged until 2006, even though by then Afghanistan was in the midst of a serious insurgency and war.[50] In 2006 Afghan defense minister Abdul Rahim Wardak maintained that the assessment of seventy thousand for the ANA had been "unrealistically low" and had underestimated the threat, which was then exploited by enemy forces.[51] Violence escalated through 2005 and 2006. In 2008 the ANA reached the seventy-thousand threshold, but it was clear that, overall, Afghan security force end strength remained too low. The ISAF commander at the time, General McNeill, stated that ANA and ANP troop numbers would not be sufficient to allow for a US drawdown until 2011.[52] In 2008 a Government Accountability Office (GAO) report called on the Defense and State Departments to develop detailed plans for completing and sustaining the ANSF, since there was poor interagency planning and no sustainable strategy for the development of the forces.[53] Regarding police forces, it took until fiscal year 2004 to start providing more serious funding for Afghan police. Given the lead time required to train and equip such units, results would not be visible until fiscal year 2006.[54] By 2008, although an investment of over $6 billion had been made, no police unit was considered fully capable.[55] Eventually, in March 2009, President Obama promised to increase ANA forces to 134,000 and police forces to 82,000. Overall, the United States kept changing its plans regarding ANA (and then ANP) force numbers, even though in many cases the reasons were unclear.[56] It was not until the McChrystal review in 2009 that a proposal was designed to build Afghan forces sufficiently to meet the threat level.

McChrystal proposed a combined ANA and ANP force of 400,000; the president later approved a plan for only 352,000.

Similar to the political and economic reconstruction tracks, the security track was beset by divided authorities. So not only were Afghanistan's indigenous problems formidable but the international efforts in the area of building security forces alone were also complex and divided among NATO, US, Afghan, and lead-country priorities. The lead nation concept, developed in early 2002, divided the problem of security-sector reform among several countries. It addressed home-country priorities, not necessarily requirements on the ground. The United States served as the lead for the Afghan army; Germany focused on the national police forces; the United Kingdom focused on counternarcotics; Japan led disarmament, demobilization, and reintegration (DDR); and Italy focused on the justice system. Not only did these divisions undercut the linked nature of all of these tasks, but they also resulted in a lack of common procedures and priorities among the coalition forces, as well as constant rotations of new people. It is hard to imagine that this approach could produce a cohesive system.

Despite the promise of the Bonn process, which successfully fostered cooperation among Afghans, the United States, and NATO countries, operational approaches were never able to connect disparate efforts in Afghanistan. Without unity of command, unity of effort never took hold and, quite simply, failed as an operational concept in wartime. Yet, because of political constraints—made immutable by the attitudes and historical understanding of civilian and military leaders—concepts and strategies that might have prioritized unity of command could not be or were not put into place. Most civilian and military officials did not accept that stability and reconstruction were fundamental to the war effort—indeed, coalition partners insisted that they could or would do only bits and pieces of various reconstruction tasks, depending on their domestic political proclivities. The United States, in the midst of an ongoing war, persisted in transferring responsibility for coordination on "all things Afghanistan" to the State Department. Even key officials such as Ambassador Dobbins expressed "serious doubts" about the workability of an arrangement whereby the State Department would take the lead for activities where most of the assets were bound to come from the DOD. But instead of a military lead, even his view was that the White House needed to take more responsibility.[57] There was a consistent and fundamental reluctance to allow the military to take the lead in areas that were directly linked to the success of the war effort as a whole. And the strategic vacillation between CT and stabilization never allowed for the necessary consolidation of gains. As the United States intervened in Iraq, despite a common refrain that Afghanistan and Iraq were different conflicts—and indeed the specifics of each were different—many of the same constraints that hampered the US ability to undertake governance tasks emerged in both wars.

# IRAQ

Two months after 9/11, President George W. Bush directed army general Tommy Franks, the commander of CENTCOM, to begin planning for the removal of Saddam Hussein from power in Iraq. US leaders identified regime change in Iraq as a key strategic goal if Saddam did not agreed to destroy his weapons of mass destruction (WMDs). This objective was not new. The 1991 Gulf War had pushed Iraqi troops out of Kuwait but stopped short of removing the Saddam regime. Since then, the United States and the international community had remained concerned about Iraq's WMD program. In January 1998, then–secretary of state Madeleine Albright stated that the US saw no alternative to using military force against Iraq if Baghdad did not comply with UN efforts to end its WMD development program.[58] A few months later, President Bill Clinton approved the bipartisan Iraq Liberation Act, which stated that the US would "support efforts to remove the regime headed by Saddam Hussein" and "promote the emergence of democratic government" there. Even after Operation Desert Fox, which involved air strikes against WMD sites, the Iraqi leader remained intransigent, and high-level policy debates continued in Washington about whether to continue to contain the regime or to replace it.[59] In his 2002 State of the Union address, President Bush described an "axis of evil" and identified Iraq as a continuing state supporter of "terror" that was developing chemical, biological, and nuclear weapons. A few months later, Congress passed a joint resolution to authorize US force against Iraq, setting the stage for Operation Iraqi Freedom (OIF).

US civilian and military leaders articulated five objectives for OIF: to demonstrate that the United States aspired to liberate, not occupy or control, Iraq; to eliminate Iraq's WMDs and related facilities; to eliminate its terrorist infrastructure; to safeguard its territorial unity; and to begin the process of economic and political reconstruction.[60] Despite these stated goals, the planning for and implementation of the stabilization of Iraq was disconnected and ad hoc. Although US civilian and military leaders considered regime change a goal, they failed to develop a concomitant operational (and resourced) plan for how to reconstitute an Iraqi regime and stabilize the country. Five years after the invasion, the inspector general for Iraq observed that the United States had not "developed a legislatively sanctioned doctrine or framework for planning, preparing and executing contingency operations in which diplomacy, development and military action all figure."[61] This disconnect created the conditions for a political vacuum of power that violent actors quickly filled, generating a competition that set the conditions for the emergence of a tenacious and deadly insurgency.

Several elements of American denial syndrome emerged during the course of the war. Despite considerable work by military planners, military and civilian actors tended to reinforce the separation between combat operations and those tasks associated with stabilization. The regional combat commander at the time, General Franks, later wrote that "you [the civilian bureaucracy] pay attention to the day after and I'll pay attention to the day of."[62] Even well after US forces were engaged, US military and civilian leaders did not resource the requirements for the political consolidation of combat gains nor did most fully understand the operational problems of this challenge. Yet, as in the past, the need to restore basic order and undertake some reconstruction arose in tandem with combat operations. And the military was the only agency with the scale and the logistical capacity to carry out these tasks. The phased approach to the war separated combat operations (Phase III) from postwar stabilization (Phase IV) and reinforced the view that "postwar" problems were not integral to the war itself.[63] Thus, as American troops arrived in Baghdad, a vacuum of authority arose, since the restoration of security did not fall squarely into the realm of what American troops perceived to be part of their mission.

As in previous governance operations, dual command structures emerged, adding complexity to an already difficult mission set. In Iraq, this dichotomy reflected contentious policy differences over how to rebuild an Iraq government and the timeline for doing so. As in the past, political concerns about military control over governance functions contributed to the decision to avoid ceding full operational control of these tasks to the military, leading to a tendency to rely on civilian capabilities that never materialized. In effect, a strange hybrid organization was created whereby *civilian* DOD organizations had oversight over reconstruction, but in reality these civilian-led and civilian-staffed organizations lacked the resources and capabilities to accomplish the missions in a conflict zone. Moreover, the military forces in the theater were not subordinated to these civilian leaders. The lack of unity of command, one of the most enduring principles of war, created serious operational problems and undermined US efforts from the start.

Elements of this denial syndrome can be seen in four main phases of the war: (1) the planning phase, which lasted from approximately November 2001 to March 2003; (2) the arrival of US forces in March 2003 until dissolution of the US civilian governing body (the Coalition Provisional Authority [CPA]) in June 2004; (3) the transition to Iraqi sovereignty, which was marked by the growing insurgency, from June 2004 to January 2007; and (4) the surge period, which began in early 2007 and ended with the complete withdrawal of American forces from Iraq in 2011.

*Planning for War*

Before the March 2003 invasion, at least four related but disconnected planning efforts considered the problem of how to remove Saddam from power and install a new government in Iraq. Civilians led three of these planning efforts, and the military led a fourth. First, on the civilian side, in the summer of 2002 the NSC created the Executive Steering Committee (ESG) to plan for a new Iraqi regime. The ESG coordinated among senior officials and their staffs at the State Department, the DOD, and the Office of the Vice President, and various intelligence agencies. Despite the attempt to create an integrated planning apparatus, it was a loose structure that did not include the full range of activities or actors, nor did it exert unifying control or direction over participants. Indeed, ESG meetings were not always attended by every agency, nor did the same representatives attend meetings, reducing continuity.[64] Second, the State Department led the Future of Iraq Project, involving US experts and Iraqi nationals. This effort examined sixteen areas of transition and resulted in volumes of papers.[65] It was supplemented by planning processes at USAID and other agencies. Third, the Office of the Secretary of Defense created within its Near East Bureau the Office of Special Plans, which developed ideas for political and military aspects of Iraq policy.

Fourth, in addition to these civilian initiatives, CENTCOM developed the overarching military campaign plan for Iraq, called 1003-V.[66] General Franks affirmed that success would be a "destroyed" regime followed by the creation of an "acceptable provisional/permanent government."[67] CENTCOM's subordinate command, the Combined Forces Land Component Command (CFLCC), developed the land component of this plan, called Cobra II. Both 1003-V and Cobra II outlined four phases of operations: deter and engage, seize the initiative, decisive operations, and the transition to a post-Saddam government. This last phase, which the military referred to as Phase IV, meant the range of activities required to stabilize and reconstruct Iraq.[68] Army officers who later completed an extensive study of OIF observed that there was an "incorrect belief that stability and support operations took place only after major offensive and defensive combat had ended, and that full spectrum operations meant the sequential *instead* of simultaneous use of offense, defense, and stability operation."[69] Top military leaders such as Gen. Peter Pace, the chairman of the JCS, believed that the consideration of the political aspects of a conflict were "outside his lane."[70] The deputy director for military affairs of the JCS echoed this view, acknowledging that CENTCOM was "not resourced to [do] military administration."[71]

Using World War II as a guide, staff-level military planners thought through details of Phase IV. CENTCOM's 1003-V plan anticipated that the postcombat phase would involve three stages: (1) a military-led stabilization of Iraq, (2) oversight to a joint task force, and (3) transition from US authorities to Iraqi leaders. The plan assumed that the United States would work through existing Iraqi organizations (an assumption also held by many US policymakers) and that US forces might be required to undertake an occupation lasting up to two years. War games had shown that because the "joint campaign was specifically designed to break all control mechanisms of the regime," instability would likely ensue and that planners would thus need to allocate "adequate resources to quickly re-establish postwar control throughout Iraq."[72] Through this war gaming, planners realized that "Phase IV was becoming more and more complex" and would require even more detailed consideration.[73] Despite these reasonable predictions, these plans were not resourced or linked in a meaningful way to the main military campaign plan or to the evolving civilian plans and organizations.

Across these civilian and military efforts, serious policy disagreements unfolded over how the United States should reconstitute a new Iraqi state and over the timeline for a transition. Some argued that a transfer of sovereignty to Iraq should take place at the earliest possible time. This was, in a sense, an application of the Afghan model, where the Bonn process established the AIA within weeks of the US intervention. A quick transfer in Iraq would require advance preparation or the rapid development of a Bonn-like political process after Baghdad fell. Others, however, believed that a significant period of time would be required before a transfer of authority to a new Iraqi government would be possible and that a US occupation would be required. This included some CENTCOM planners.

President Bush failed to make a clear decision before the war. Thus, his January 2003 National Security Presidential Directive 24 essentially codified a muddled middle ground. It designated the DOD as the lead agency for the reconstruction of Iraq but did so through the creation of the new, civilian-led Office for Reconstruction and Humanitarian Assistance (ORHA), which would be responsible for reestablishing basic services, "reshaping the Iraqi military," and supporting the transition to Iraqi-led authority "over time." But the DOD did not give the new planning office adequate resources or authorities to accomplish these ambitious goals. A civilian, Jay Garner, was placed in charge of ORHA. Notably, however, Garner was a retired army general officer who had overseen humanitarian and security efforts in the Kurdish region of northern Iraq after the Gulf War. With ORHA, the DOD would technically *not* be conducting a military occupation, since military forces did not run through ORHA's chain of command. Thus, from the start, two military and civilian chains of command existed within the DOD, and a "continual battle" ensued over "who worked for whom."[74] There was a clear aversion to giving the military unity of command. According to one authoritative report, Garner suggested putting himself and Army lieutenant general David McKiernan (then the CFLCC commander) under CENTCOM's authority because Garner acknowledged that he "didn't own any helicopters, and I didn't own any fuel, and I didn't own any trucks."[75]

At the same time, President Bush had tasked Special Envoy Khalilzad to lead a political process to foster discussions among Iraqi groups opposed to Saddam. These included organizations such as the Iraqi National Congress, which was composed of exiles. It also included Kurdish leaders. Khalilzad convened conferences in London, Turkey, and northern Iraq before the invasion and in Nasiriya and Baghdad afterward, to advance thinking about the selection of leaders for an Iraqi Interim Authority. This process, however, was never brought to fruition.

In the three months between the creation of ORHA and the start of the war, Garner had to "build an organization, develop interagency plans across the administration, coordinate them with CENTCOM and the still undetermined military headquarters that would assume the military lead in post-Saddam Iraq, and deploy his team to the theater." Garner later observed that it "proved to be an almost impossible set of tasks."[76] He was right. According to ORHA officials, the organization "never had enough people," and individual agency plans were done in vertical stovepipes without much interrelationships to other agencies.[77] One ORHA official observed that "no lessons seem to have taken hold from the recent nation-building efforts in Bosnia or Kosovo, so we in ORHA felt as though we were reinventing the wheel."[78]

The decision to create ORHA revealed several elements of American denial syndrome. It reflected the traditional US ambivalence about military oversight over governance tasks. Bush, supported by Rumsfeld, had appointed a "civilian" (albeit a retired general) in charge of governance in Iraq at the time that military planners still assumed that a military occupation was likely. And CENTCOM itself did not want to conduct occupying duties. One military planner observed that CENTCOM never "wanted to have military administration and the Joint Staff and OSD [Office of the Secretary of Defense] had not decided what it would look like."[79] But, as in the past, military necessity prevailed, since the United States faced the practical problem of how to exert control in the theater given that only the military had the required manpower. And as in the past, ambivalence about overseeing governance operations translated into uncertainty about how to transition from combat operations to organizations that could oversee and implement stabilization activities. Even as the various Phase IV plans were being written, the kind of headquarters organization that should emerge remained undetermined. A vacuum developed: The military was not tasked with governance operations, and ORHA lacked the capacity to conduct them as well.

## War and Occupation

On March 20, 2003, the US Army (V Corps) and the US Marine Corps (the First Marine Expeditionary Force) initiated OIF. Coalition air forces had struck a wide range of Iraqi political and military targets in advance, and within three weeks coalition forces toppled Saddam's government and secured Iraq's oil fields. The military historian John Keegan called the offensive "a lightning campaign" that was so complete in its results that it was almost "unprecedented."[80] The speed of Iraq's collapse, however, meant that the problem of stabilization emerged quickly. Later several defense analysts would observe that because the combat phase of the war succeeded so quickly, US forces were not able to "control events throughout some semblance of a transition to stability operations," and the United States quickly lost influence.[81] This was not helped by the fact that US troop numbers were dropping as instability grew. From a high of around 148,000 US troops in May 2003, US troop strength dropped to about 121,000 by the fall of 2003 and to 108,000 by January 2004.[82]

As US troops departed Iraq and the Iraqi security forces (ISF) collapsed and were dissolved, the United States faced the interrelated problems of how to address the emerging political and security vacuums of power and how to begin the complicated process of reestablishing governing institutions. US policy leaders remained undecided about the kind of new governing structures to support and how to ensure representation by Iraqi political, ethnic, and religious communities within these new organizations. Some US officials began to realize that it could take "more than six months to cede power to an Iraqi-led civilian authority."[83]

Amid this uncertainty, the United States continued to change its own organizations in Iraq. The DOD abruptly disbanded ORHA after only a few weeks and replaced it with the CPA in May 2003. The CPA would govern Iraq until a transition to a new Iraqi government took place. As with ORHA, US leaders were reluctant to install a military occupation. Secretary Rumsfeld had decided there should be a civilian administrator to oversee governance and reconstruction (e.g., the CPA) and a separate military commander responsible for security. Thus, the president tapped a former ambassador, Paul Bremer, to lead the CPA, in effect establishing a civilian governor as the senior civilian official in charge of all policy efforts. Bremer insisted on full control of the planning for a new Iraqi state. As a result, the political process led by Khalilzad abruptly ended. Bremer instead pursued an indefinite US occupation of Iraq, although the CPA as a civilian agency lacked the capacity to staff and run effective governance operations. Bremer did not have control over military forces, which remained under the command of CFLCC (and then Combined Joint Task Force 7 [CJTF-7]). Overall, the CPA's ability to undertake activities in Iraq was fundamentally limited by fact that it was understaffed and was not an "expeditionary" organization that could implement plans and connect tactical accomplishments to strategic goals. The CPA lacked the capability to secure areas and establish security and the conditions for reconstruction and stability tasks.

The CPA floundered. Bremer had not played a role in the prewar planning efforts and, when he assumed his role, acknowledged that "we were far from identifying honest, energetic, and patriotic Iraqis who could govern post-Baathist Iraq."[84] He did not have a plan for effecting a political transition and creating an inclusive government among distrustful Iraqis. The minority

Sunnis who had been favored under Saddam, felt disenfranchised by the shift in power to the Shi'ites and by US plans to place the latter, who represented 60 percent of the population, in a more powerful political position.[85] Kurdish political parties wanted to achieve autonomy and pursed a recidivist agenda at the expense of Arab and Turkmen populations in the north. Over time, the Sunni Arabs and Turkmen began to back insurgents because they believed that they could protect their interests only through violence. What started as a localized, decentralized hybrid insurgency coalesced, supported by foreign fighters who arrived in greater numbers. This gave rise to al-Qaeda in Iraq (AQI).

One of the most controversial decisions of the war exacerbated these security problems. On May 23, 2003, CPA Order No. 2 disbanded Iraq's military, security, and intelligence infrastructure. The directive reflected a "perfect storm" of dysfunction rooted in the "dual authority problem," which led to improvised and disconnected decisions. While the US military had assumed that it would work *through* existing Iraqi security structures (a view that other senior officials such as National Security Adviser Condoleezza Rice shared), the CPA disbanded those institutions without considering the consequences.[86] The United States did not have enough forces to fill the growing security vacuum, which Sunni Arab insurgents and Shi'a militias began to fill. CPA Order No. 2 also revealed a lack of an understanding of the internal situation in Iraq, since the plan was to build a small Iraqi army focused on external security (e.g., in regard to Iran) as opposed to a force able to address Iraq's burgeoning internal instability. Finally, Bremer's order highlighted the operational weaknesses of US civilian organizations in the country. Although the CPA had formal authority for reconstituting the ISF, it had none of the resources or expertise to accomplish this goal. Yet at the same time, Bremer and DOD officials rejected the CJTF-7's efforts to assist with the training mission.[87] With the disbanding of the Iraqi military, a US official later observed that "we [had] made 450,000 enemies on the ground."[88]

The violent actions of Iran-backed militias exacerbated fears among the Sunni population. By early 2004, Sunni insurgents controlled the city of Fallujah, and the uprisings of Shi'a groups led by religious extremist Muqtada al-Sadr against coalition troops in Baghdad, Najaf, and Karbala made the prospect of a strengthening insurgency and a sectarian civil war increasingly likely. The insurgents sought to compel the United States to withdraw from Iraq and to recapture political power that the Sunnis had lost to the Shi'a Arabs and Kurds. In this context, Bremer began to rethink the timelines associated with the transfer of authority back to Iraq and sought to expedite such a transfer to quell growing unrest.

The policies and actions of the CPA exacerbated the interconnected problems of insurgency and sectarian tensions. To begin a shift to Iraqi authority, the CPA created the Interim Governing Council (IGC), composed of twenty-five representative members of the Iraqi body politic: Shi'ites, Sunni Arabs, Kurds, Assyrians, and Turkmen. The IGC, however, suffered from a lack of political legitimacy, with most viewing it as a puppet of the CPA that had little capacity to deliver results to the Iraqi people.[89] The United States formally committed to turning sovereignty over to an interim Iraqi government by July 1, 2004. The UN, Iraqi leaders, and the CPA created a road map for transition to Iraq rule. They adopted the Transitional Administrative Law in March 2004, which set forth a timetable for a transition: Elections would be held for a transitional National Assembly by the end of January 2005, a constitution would be drafted by August 2005 and then put to a national referendum by October 2005, and national elections for a full-term government would take place by December 15, 2005.[90]

Through the winter and spring of 2004, sectarian violence continued to grow throughout the country, reflecting a growing insurgency and increasing distrust among Iraqi Sunni and Shi'a groups. Under Abu Musab al-Zarqawi, AQI took advantage of that distrust and formed tactical alliances with many Baathists and disenfranchised Sunni Arabs. The growing violence undercut the CPA's ability to undertake its work. Because of the lack of security and its dependency on military forces, which were outside Bremer's chain of command, the CPA's reach was fundamentally limited. Military commanders set the rules for transportation. The CPA's missions would often be "scrubbed" if the military could not provide the requested convoys.[91] Critics argued that the CPA made promises that it could not keep. In one of many examples, it had agreed to provide equipment to local police in Anbar Province, but the aid did not come through, thus undermining the credibility of US troops operating in the region.[92] The CPA also tended to focus on "big ticket projects" that had long lead times and therefore did not affect ordinary Iraqis. Maj. Gen. Ray Odierno, at the time the commander of the army's Fourth Infantry Division, observed that if coalition authorities could not start "paying" those who were sitting on the fence, through their inclusion in reconstruction efforts, "we might as well arrest them right now."[93]

The US emphasis on civilian control without concomitant attention to the CPA's operational weaknesses had strategic effects. It fundamentally reduced early reconstruction successes. And because of the lack of civilian capacity, the military was pulled into reconstruction projects quickly. By the fall of 2003, in order to build support among Iraqis, the military tackled hundreds of reconstruction projects. Units such as the 101st Airborne Division carried out school repairs, road and water projects, the repair of buildings such as police stations, and the construction of small Iraqi army training and operating bases. This was undertaken with CERP funds. CERP allowed soldiers to respond to reconstruction needs more flexibly, since it was not tied to normal government purchasing rules. General Petraeus and others would emphasize that in Iraq, "depending on the situation, money can be more important than real ammunition."[94] CERP reflected the growing view among senior officers that you can't "shoot yourself out of an insurgency" and that "bureaucracy kills."[95] Many later criticized CERP efforts for not being linked to more sustainable projects. Yet it would have been difficult to have connected local successes to the broader operating landscape in the absence of a campaign plan linking the reconstruction part of the war to the fighting effort.

Complicating civilian and military reconstruction efforts was that fact that there were confusing *military* combat lines of effort as well. One general officer later observed that "we had all these transitions of organizations and command and control—CENTCOM, CFLCC, V Corps, CJTF-7—on top of a transition in the campaign from Saddam to post Saddam" and that was "not how we would plan normally."[96] Three different coalition military commands and four separate military campaign plans existed since early 2003.[97] When the Phase III combat phase "ended," new personnel transitioned in quickly, with top leadership changes at both CENTCOM *and* CFLCC. General Abizaid now commanded CENTCOM, while army lieutenant general Ricardo Sanchez replaced General McKiernan as the commander of the US-led CJTF-7, which commanded all coalition forces in Iraq. CJTF-7 had initial responsibility for providing "security, law and order," securing WMD sites, eliminating terrorist infrastructure, and providing emergency humanitarian relief. Sanchez would observe that he had arrived in theater "stunned" to "find that there had been a complete lack of Phase IV post-invasion planning by the administration and the military."[98]

In fact, however, as previously noted, CENTCOM and CFLCC planners had developed plans for Phase IV, but these plans were not resourced or operationalized and were often replaced. An early CFLCC Phase IV planning team had identified key challenges that would likely emerge and identified lines of operation to deal with these problems—security, rule of law, governance, administration, infrastructure recovery, perception, humanitarian assistance—but this effort became so complex that CLFCC initiated a new plan, called Eclipse II.[99] Eclipse II referred to the Eclipse plan for the US military governance of Germany after World War II. However, Eclipse II was then replaced when the new CJTF-7 commander, General Sanchez, initiated his own efforts. The CJTF-7 plan sought to neutralize destabilizing influences in order to "create a secure environment in direct support of the CPA" and to "concurrently conduct stability operations" in order to set the conditions for a transfer of authorities.[100] These Phase IV planning efforts remained apart from the overarching military campaign plan. It was never clear what troops would be used to implement the tasks identified in the various plans.

As the date for the transfer of sovereignty to the Iraqi Interim Authority approached, US policy suffered from several contradictions. The United States sought to transfer responsibility to a new Iraqi authority, but the dismantling of the ISF meant that a new government would not have the capacity to provide security. In addition, the rising violence meant that it would take longer to prepare a new Iraqi army to provide security. Yet the US had not created programs capable of building the ISF rapidly and at sufficient scale. Nonetheless, amid a growing insurgency, political pressure continued to grow in Washington for a reduction in US forces. High-level officials dispatched to Baghdad warned the CPA that "politics were not going to permit" a longer US presence in Iraq.[101] And in late 2004, the Defense Science Board report warned that the US military lacked sufficient personnel to meet the nation's "current and projected" commitments.[102]

### Transition to an Iraqi Sovereignty

As power shifted formally to the Iraqi Interim Authority in June 2004, Ayad Allawi became Iraq's interim leader. He would govern the country until the January 2005 national elections. The US role shifted from an occupying power to one that would support a host government through its new embassy in Baghdad. The new US ambassador, John Negroponte, established US-Iraqi diplomatic relations for the first time since January 1991 and led an embassy of over one thousand. The United States was now operating in a "normal" bilateral relationship.[103] In reality, of course, this was far from the case, given the presence of around 130,000 US troops and US efforts to rebuild the ISF and other institutions from the ground up.[104]

With this transition, the United States continued to pursue two lines of effort: political and military. On the political side, the main effort consisted of pressing Iraqis to create an inclusionary government and to undertake reconstruction efforts to help the new Iraqi state establish normalcy. However, when the Sunni Arabs largely boycotted the January 2005 elections, this effort faltered because the new government was dominated by Shi'a Arab Islamist parties and the Kurds. Under Prime Minister Ibrahim al-Jaafari, sectarian conflict escalated.

The military line of effort focused on two objectives. The coalition sought to suppress the growing insurgency and to transition security responsibilities to the ISF. Two subordinate commands were established under army general George W. Casey Jr.: Multi-National Corps–Iraq (MNC-I), to focus on day-to-day operations, and Multi-National Security Transition Command–Iraq (MNSTC-I), which would be commanded by General Petraeus. MNSTC-I would build and train the ISF (both police and army) with the goal of "leaving Iraq able to secure its streets, its borders and its Citizenry without Coalition help."[105] MNSTC-I was also charged with developing the MOD and the MOI, both critical parts of a new security force. One of the first steps Petraeus took was to replace with military personnel many of the US contractors who had been doing most of the training. Petraeus was succeeded by army lieutenant general Martin Dempsey, who commanded as MNSTC-I from September 2005 to June 2007. Under Dempsey's tenure, force generation improved: By 2007 the Iraqi army had grown to almost 195,000, while the police reached close to 242,000 men. In addition, the use of foreign military sales accelerated the flow of military equipment to the ISF.[106]

The political and military tracks were closely linked. Absent enough US forces and reliable ISF forces to keep the violence at bay, political progress would remain difficult to achieve. And without an inclusionary government that was trusted by Iraq's three main groups (Kurds, Shi'ites, and Sunnis), the cycle of violence would escalate. Ambassador Negroponte and General Casey, his military counterpart, recognized that security and political progress were mutually reinforcing. But there was still a disconnected view of the problem. In an interview at the time, Negroponte commented that "George [Casey] has the lead on the purely military part," while he would take the lead on the "political and reconstruction pieces," but that both were "intertwined," since if coalition forces "go into one of these towns, clear them of rebels, but don't have the other pieces in place, it'll be a Pyrrhic victory. So it is a combined thing."[107] However, in fact there was no "purely military part" to the problem—Casey's troops were very much involved in the day-to-day problems of reconstruction and politics, and the State Department was fundamentally limited in its ability to conduct reconstruction and governance-related missions given the security problems throughout the country.

This division was reflected in the operational arrangements for reconstruction, which fell under two separate chains of command with overlapping authorities. Concurrent with the transfer of sovereignty to Iraq and the appointment of Negroponte as ambassador, National Security Presidential Directive 36 created the Iraq Reconstruction Management Office (IRMO) in the embassy to provide strategic direction to reconstruction efforts, as well as the Project and Contracting Office (PCO) to manage the specific projects. It directed the State Department to control IRMO and the DOD to oversee the PCO. Thus, the directive institutionalized dual authority over critical reconstruction efforts. State controlled strategy, while the operational plan to accomplish specific tasks was largely in the DOD's hands, through its oversight of troops and contracting authorities. In addition, the DOD controlled about 87 percent of the five major funds allocated for Iraq's reconstruction.[108] One of the early directors of the PCO did not even believe that he reported to IRMO.[109] The directive gave State the lead for all US activities except for military operations and the development of the ISF, which fell under DOD's lead. This reinforced the dual-authority problem throughout the war.

In the field, embedded PRTs were microcosms of the civil-military disconnects at the operational and strategic level. The PRT idea had been exported from Afghanistan in order to bring integrated civil-military reconstruction efforts to the Iraqi countryside. Ten teams were deployed to assist provincial governments with developing a capability to govern, promote increased security and rule of law, and spur political and economic development.[110] But like most other efforts to integrate civil-military resources, in practice the effort did not achieve its potential. Disagreements about command-and-control relationships delayed team deployments for a year. The Office of the Special Inspector General for Iraq Reconstruction (SIGIR) later observed that "coaxing the Departments of State and Defense to set the terms of their first major operational collaboration in Iraq required a herculean effort that touched off frequent arguments between MNF-I [Multi-National Force–Iraq], the embassy, and Washington." The agreements that described how the reconstruction teams would function did not allow the teams to "work for the military" except if security was involved.[111] Yet working on governance and economic matters required mobility, even though the State Department's culture created serious restrictions on movements. Regional security officers (RSOs) imposed severe restrictions on travel by State civilians. One former PRT official noted that State civilians had to find ways around such restrictions because, as a PRT civilian explained, if "left to the RSO, our mission would have failed."[112] As in the past, civilians were hampered by their inability to operate under fire and could only accomplish their missions when protected by the military. Later Negroponte would admit that although the US embassy had "moved into the reconstruction phase," it was actually still "in a conflict phase."[113]

Negroponte's political line of effort aimed to ensure that the January 2005 elections took place with minimal violence, and through the summer of 2004 his military counterpart, General Casey, developed plans to support this goal.[114] The January 2005 elections did take place, despite a boycott by many Sunni Arabs. Jalal Talabani, the Kurdish leader of the Patriotic Union of Kurdistan, became president, and Ibrahim al-Jaafari, the leader of the Shi'a Islamist Dawa Party, became prime minister of the transitional government. In the midst of the intensive Iraqi political transition, after just nine months the president called Negroponte back to Washington to take over as the director of national intelligence. A new US ambassador, Zalmay Khalilzad, arrived in Baghdad in June 2005. (He himself was pulled away from the important and highly relational-based work of forging political progress in Afghanistan.) At both the tactical and strategic levels, US approaches toward key personnel changes were perhaps best reflected by young officer who later wrote about the challenges of "getting past the first cup of tea" and of the "Lazy Susan style rotation of American leadership."[115] This highlighted a problem throughout both wars in Iraq and Afghanistan—a lack of continuity

Khalilzad continued the effort of mediating between Kurdish, Shi'a, and Sunni leaders. He sought to foster a national compact of political groups and communities that could agree on a national-unity government, encourage broad participation in the December 2005 elections, and work on issues that divided the country. One focus was on identifying parts of the Sunni Arab insurgency that could be reconciled. Almost a year later, Sunnis did turn out for elections to the National Assembly, and Khalilzad declared that it looked like "a first step toward politics breaking out in the region."[116] Although he acknowledged that the transition would be difficult, the US goal remained to create a "multi-ethnic, multi-sectarian democratic Iraq that will be unique in this part of the world, where traditionally the dominant ethnic or sectarian group has sought to suppress others."[117]

Some of this apparent progress on Iraq's political transition was undermined by shifting drivers of violence. Despite changes in the character of the conflict that jeopardized the entire effort, the United States remained determined to get the Iraqi Transitional Government "to begin to accept the counterinsurgency lead."[118] There was no countrywide approach to the population security necessary to rebuild political trust with the Sunni minority population and reduce popular support for insurgents. Increasing sectarian violence limited the prospects for political progress. Through 2005 and 2006, key ministries in Iraq, including the powerful MOI and many of its security forces, were viewed as parties in what had become a civil war. For example, Minister of the Interior Bayan Jabr ran death squads and militias, many of which were connected to the Islamic Revolutionary Guards of Iran. These death squads operated under the cover of Iraqi police uniforms. Atrocities abounded and, along with AQI mass murders of Shi'ites, accelerated the cycle of sectarian violence. In November 2005, front-page news stories focused on an American raid that discovered 173 mostly Sunni prisoners whom the MOI held secretly and tortured in a bunker.[119] During this period, Shi'a and Sunni death squads operated throughout Baghdad, intent on cleansing previously integrated neighborhoods.[120] The chaotic environment associated with sectarian violence served the interest of AQI as well as the Shi'a Islamist militias. The actions of Shi'a militias actually strengthened AQI. By the end of 2005, the semiannual MNF-I Campaign Progress Review observed that the level of insurgent attacks and the capacity for "spectacular acts of terrorism" remained "stubbornly high."[121]

Senior military leaders remained focused on the transition to Iraqi forces. New command arrangements reflected that priority. In the summer of 2004, MNF-I replaced General Sanchez's CJTF-7. General Casey assumed command of MNF-I, which was to provide theater-strategic and operational-level command and control for all coalition forces in Iraq and direct support to the coalition political authority and the emerging Iraqi government. MNF-I was tasked to coordinate, synchronize, and deliver security, economic, diplomatic, and information operations with the US embassy and the new Iraqi government, leaving tactical combat operations to its subordinate headquarters.[122]

On paper MNF-I's new campaign plan emphasized full-spectrum COIN operations to isolate extremists and to train and equip the ISF. It replaced the phase construct of "offensive operations" and "stability operations" used in the CJTF-7 plan with the simultaneous conduct of offensive, defensive, and stability operations. The plan described four lines of operation (LOOs): security, governance, economic development, and strategic communications. In light of the level of violence, security became the leading priority.[123]

But in practice, although US troops were increasingly faced with the need to tamp down the growing insurgency, these efforts were not integrated into a countrywide COIN campaign plan. As Kalev Sepp, a member of the Iraq Study Group, observed, the strategy "did not talk about what you had to do to defeat an insurgency. It was not a counterinsurgency plan."[124] Casey's priority was to transition to Iraqi-led operations, not to defeat the insurgency. By the spring of 2006, Casey argued that the longer the United States continued to "bear the main burden of Iraq's security," the more it lengthened the time that the Iraqi government had to "take the hard decisions about reconciliation and dealing with the militias" and the more likely it was that they would "continue to blame us for all of Iraq's problems."[125] Later, critics would maintain that Casey was more focused on withdrawal than victory and was, therefore, inured to the shift in the conflict from an insurgency to a sectarian civil war that undermined the legitimacy of security forces essential to effective transition.

As in previous governance operations, the US military was faced with the need to rebuild local security forces. No institutionalized knowledge, however, was carried over from those previous experiences, and the Iraq effort started essentially from scratch. The effort of building capable and legitimate security forces was beset by the usual interagency rivalries and divisions, made more complicated in Iraq because of the initial US decision to divide the training of the army and the police. Also, both efforts were disconnected from justice- and rule-of-law-related reforms until 2007. Even during the earlier CPA days, the US military fought for control of decisions related to Iraqi police. At that time, General Odierno believed that the US military should have been entrusted with key decisions related to the police, since not only was the security of American soldiers jeopardized by poor decisions but the United States also lost key windows of opportunities as a result of the divided authorities.[126] The divisions of responsibility between the police and the army reflected US bureaucratic priorities as opposed to actual security requirements. In reality, the missions of the two were fundamentally linked. Iraq was facing a civil war, and both security arms had to be professionalized, trusted, and shaped into effective forces.

The MNSTC-I program increased the pace of ISF training and focused on rebuilding tactical skills among Iraqi forces. By the end of August 2006, the goal was that some 75 percent of Iraqi army battalions and brigades would lead COIN operations, with coalition forces playing only training and supporting roles.[127] A key part of the effort involved the embedding of military transition teams into Iraqi army and police units. Many units lacked the willingness to improve or professionalize, owing to infiltration by militias and political groups determined to capture institutions and use them to advance narrow interests. Police forces were a particular concern as Shi'a Islamist militias used them in sectarian-cleansing campaigns in Baghdad and other mixed sectarian areas.

Without a comprehensive counterinsurgency effort, US commanders in the field had to develop strategies to deal with the insurgency themselves. Soldiers were directly involved with politics, and they began to adapt and apply new approaches to respond to the growing violence and to understand the politics driving that violence. In 2005 a well-known example unfolded in the northwestern city of Tal Afar, where US Army colonel H. R. McMaster's Third Armored Cavalry Regiment (ACR) applied classical COIN techniques.[128] About 75 percent of the city's two hundred thousand people were Sunnis, and about 25 percent Shi'ites. Al-Qaeda was determined to foment sectarian violence, and terrorists employed brutal tactics to control the populace. In response, a purely Shi'a police force responded with extrajudicial killings that perpetuated a cycle of fear and violence. As McMaster arrived, he explained that the purpose of his operation was to "secure the population so that we can lift the enemy's campaign of intimidation and coercion and to allow economic and political development to proceed here and to return to normal life."[129] His campaign emphasized the simultaneous application of offensive, defensive, and stability operations. Defeating al-Qaeda fighters was just one effort in a larger campaign to reform and build security forces, reconstruct the city, restore services, and most important, build confidence between the city's communities. McMaster and his regiment worked with Iraqi leaders to address the political drivers of violence and reduce popular support for Sunni insurgents and Shia militias. Tal Afar illustrated that effective COIN requires unity of effort between the military and police and that security must be connected to courts and prisons as well.

Another example of initiative taken by combat commanders took place in 2006 in Ramadi. Col. Sean MacFarland's First Brigade Combat Team of the US Army's First Armored Division arrived in May 2006, after initially relieving McMaster's Third ACR in Tal Afar. In Ramadi, insurgents operated openly, using violence to control local tribes. The tribes, according to Mac-Farland, "had adopted a passive posture, not wishing to antagonize a powerful

Al-Qaeda presence in and around Ramadi."[130] The challenge was to introduce sufficient Iraqi and US forces to secure the city and thereby enable the tribes to oppose al-Qaeda. Without the support of locals, any security gains would be temporary. US soldiers had to convince tribal leaders to rejoin the fight against the al-Qaeda insurgents. As tribes broke with al-Qaeda, in what became known as the "Anbar Awakening," they agreed to work with US troops, which reinforced MacFarland's efforts to operate within the city and among the people. The approach succeeded, and the city became a place where citizens could again walk the streets.[131]

But the successes of Tal Afar and Ramadi were not linked to a broader campaign plan that might have allowed a consolidation of these accomplishments across the country. The military as a whole had not shifted to a population-security model, and there were not enough troops to consolidate local gains around the country. The internal political "glue" of Iraq remained fragile, and insurgents continued to undermine prospects for a new unity government. Al-Qaeda–linked groups, Shi'a militias, Iranian-backed militias and actors, and criminal gangs continued to foment sectarian violence. By the late summer of 2006, the CENTCOM commander warned that Iraq was on the verge of civil war.[132]

Amid the security crisis, a new prime minister, Nouri al-Maliki, came into office, heading a national unity government. Though this marked important progress, the level of violence remained unabated. Sunni and Shi'a legislators accused each other of supporting terrorists and militias. Even though the ranks of the ISF were growing, their effectiveness was uneven.[133] Police forces, especially in Baghdad, had militia components, and some units took direction from militia leaders. Factions within the ISF fed the growing conflict, and in many respects, as the SIGIR later observed, MNF-I faced a moving target: As it trained and equipped the ISF, it was feeding the sectarianism in the country.[134] Although by the fall of 2006 some three hundred thousand ISF personnel had been trained and equipped, experts observed that many of them had deserted, were on unauthorized leave, were not operational, or had died in the ongoing violence. Sunnis left in large numbers because of Shia domination of many units and because AQI controlled much of the Sunni population and threatened the families of those who served in the ISF.

Thus, from the summer of 2004 through the fall of 2006, the United States was not able to consolidate its gains across Iraq. The military focus on transition was incompatible with the increasing sectarian violence and the inability of the ISF to reduce the violence. The push toward transition did not account for the timing and difficulty of creating a new ISF capable of maintaining security and achieving a trusted status among the populace. President Bush summed up the US strategy: "As the Iraqis stand up, we will stand down." But as one analyst put it, the president was describing a withdrawal plan rather than a strategy.[135] Weak security, in turn, was exploited by insurgents and sectarian militias—many of which were supported and fostered by outside powers such as Iran. The violence made it harder to achieve progress on the political front, where US political efforts also suffered from a lack of continuity, thus making it difficult to build trust among Iraqi political leaders. By the end of 2006, the US effort to turn over responsibility for security to the Iraqis was failing. National Security Adviser Stephen Hadley summarized the situation: "We could not clear and hold. Iraqi forces were not able to hold neighborhoods, and the effort to build did not show up. The sectarian violence continued to mount, so we did not make the progress on security we had hoped. We did not bring the moderate Sunnis off the fence, as we had hoped. The Shia lost patience, and began to see the militias as their protectors."[136]

## The Surge

President Bush's decision to deploy more troops to Iraq in January 2007 formally reversed and rejected the transition approach that had dominated US policy in Iraq since June 2004. He changed the US approach after a consideration of the findings of three main strategy reviews that took place in the fall of 2006. A review by the independent and bipartisan Iraq Study Group issued seventy-nine specific recommendations and ultimately argued that unless Iraq made "substantial progress" toward an Iraqi-centric approach to security and rebuilding, the US presence in the country should be reduced. In contrast, a closely held review by the chairman of the Joint Chiefs of Staff, Marine Corps general Peter Pace, argued for only a modest increase in forces. And an internal White House review led by National Security Adviser Hadley, with input from a range of outside experts, determined that an increase in the number of troops in Iraq was required and recommended increasing numbers to 150,000 by 2007. In the end, the president overruled his senior military advisers and adopted the recommendations of the reviews that argued for more troops and a change in strategy. President Bush stated that additional US troops would give the Iraqi government "the breathing space it needs to make progress in other critical areas."[137]

The surge involved not only the deployment of five additional brigades but also a shift to a new strategy that emphasized population security and sought to establish the security conditions that would allow for the growth of a more inclusive Iraqi government. It recognized that a transition to Iraqi forces would need to take place, but by emphasizing population security and providing the troops necessary to accomplish this goal, it also acknowledged the intertwined nature of the problem. Population security would lay the groundwork for a political accommodation between Iraq's warring factions that would, in turn, remove support for al-Qaeda and Shia militias. Only after that accomplishment would the US transition to Iraqi control.

The plan for the "new way forward" unfolded in several steps. Initially the goal was to reduce violence in Baghdad. As one military expert explained, "chaos in the capital" made a negotiated political compromise impossible. If a safe space in Baghdad could be created, the hope was that the national leaders of Iraq's Sunnis, Shi'ites, and Kurds could afford to take the risks inherent in compromise.[138] Accordingly, General Odierno, now commanding MNC-I, and General Petraeus, the MNF-I commander, focused on improving security in Baghdad by defeating insurgents in the surrounding areas, referred to as "belts," and by focusing on population security within the city itself. Odierno focused on the Baghdad belts and support zones that had "always been the generator of violence."[139] Before 2006, the coalition had not made control of the belts a priority, thus allowing enemy forces to project forces and funnel supplies into the city.[140] As the military analyst Kim Kagan observed, the earlier focus had been on AQI's safe havens inside Baghdad but had largely ignored the ones outside the city. In addition to measures to secure communities through the use of concrete barriers, the surge strategy called for getting more US troops into local communities. With the additional troops, an approach of "clear, hold, build" took over, allowing US forces to retain control over areas that had been cleared of insurgents.[141] Military operations were conducted to support the political objective of forging a political accommodation across sectarian and ethnic communities. As forces broke the cycle of violence physically, they targeted "irreconcilables" such as AQI terrorists and Iranian-backed militia leaders while brokering cease-fires and mediation between factions.

Petraeus became MNF-I commander in February 2007, and soon afterward Ambassador Ryan Crocker arrived to lead the US embassy. During this period, even though civil-military command arrangements remained divided, dual-authority tensions dissipated because Crocker and Petraeus worked so well together. The general and the ambassador commissioned a joint strategic assessment team that delivered a civil-military operational plan that synched population security and stabilization efforts to the desired outcome of the war. One reporter of the conflict likened it to the "miniature version of the Pentagon Papers" that was a "merciless chronicling of problems that needed fixing under Petraeus."[142] Although organizational structures remained flawed, Petraeus and Crocker fostered unity of effort through a well-conceived plan and force of personality. Civil-military fusion cells integrated previously disconnected programs, plans, and initiatives.

The growth in the quantity and quality of the ISF was also a key development that contributed to the success of the surge. Indeed, orchestrating an accelerated growth of the ISF—both military and police—in size, capability, and confidence contributed significantly to the success of counteroffensive operations.[143] US Army lieutenant general James Dubik, who commanded MNSTC-I from June 2007 until July 2008, later observed that the responsibility for defeating an insurgency rested not only with US troops but with indigenous forces as well, since "passing on an active insurgency to weak indigenous forces is a failing strategy."

This shift was significant. During the early days of the CPA, there had been virtually no operational plan for how to rebuild the ISF. The earliest efforts, led by army major general Paul Eaton in May 2003, were nested in the CPA but had minimal resources. He led a group of about five individuals called the Coalition Military Assistance Team (CATT), which was in charge of building the ISF. It initially had only four trainers. Eaton's team was essentially an "orphan in the military system."[144] Five years later, however, important improvements had been made, setting a foundation for the surge to take place. Dubik oversaw the accelerated generation and training of the ISF, which had built on the needs identified by General Odierno, the operational commander in Iraq, and by Dubik's MNSTC-I predecessor, General Dempsey. In addition, he worked closely with the Iraqis and NATO. The Iraqi minister of defense, the chief of the Iraqi Joint Forces, the minister of the interior, and the commanding general of the Iraqi National (now Federal) Police all made significant contributions, as did the NATO Training Mission–Iraq. The funding plan intertwined ISF funds with those of the MOD and MOI, and the NATO contingent conducted both staff training and, through the Italian Carabinieri, much-needed leadership training for the Federal Police. As Dubik later explained, "In spending our money in a complementary way, we could accomplish more, faster."

One of Dubik's first steps was to reverse the false dichotomy that had taken hold. This was that MNF-I's job was to fight the war, while MNSTC-I's role was to transition to Iraqi control by training and equipping the ISF. Instead, in reality, *both* MNF-I and MNSTC-I were "in the security business," and as Dubik observed, the challenge both commands faced was akin to "building an aircraft while in flight." Dubik led an important conceptual shift that recognized the reality that the US fight against the insurgency and the preparation of Iraqi forces to provide local security (police) and to fight better (military) were intertwined missions: Success depended on both being conducted simultaneously.

Dubik's approach emphasized that there were no separate "MNSTC-I priorities" and that, as a result, MNSTC-I should abandon its separate campaign plan and accept the overall plan developed by Crocker and Petraeus. The MNSTC-I goal was to generate new units and replenish units already formed and fighting "when, where, and at the pace the operational commander needed them," which also required that it expand the output of Iraq's training bases. If Iraqi forces could be trained and deployed to contribute to the counteroffensive, the "end result would ultimately be the indirect effect we all sought: transition of security responsibility to Iraqi control." Dubik's MNSTC-I developed a disciplined plan that focused on spending and growth, new units and replacements, partner units, and embedded advisers. Overall, he refocused the mission from transition to security, from training and equipping to enterprise, and from quality-versus-quantity to sufficiency.

The surge and new strategy delivered results. A more effective civil-military effort, combined with AQI's brutality and innate Iraqi resistance to Iranian subversion, reduced popular support for sectarian extremists and helped to bring communities together. The Anbar Awakening of Sunni tribes initiated during Colonel MacFarland's operations in Ramadi spread across Sunni areas into the Baghdad belts and beyond. Actions by the Iranian-influenced militia of Muqtada al-Sadr in Baghdad, Najaf, Karbala, and Basra triggered a strong response by Nuri al-Maliki that led some to hope for a new period of nonsectarian, inclusive governance. Violence dropped precipitously, with a significant reduction in daily security incidents by 2009.[145] When General Odierno replaced General Petraeus as MNF-I commander in September 2008, US officials were optimistic but guarded. Secretary of Defense Robert Gates reflected on this success, observing that "19 months ago, darkness had descended" in Iraq, "merchants of chaos were gaining strength," and at that time most questioned whether a new strategy could make a "real difference."[146] He concluded that a new strategy did make a difference, with attacks falling to their lowest point in four years and eleven of eighteen provinces turned over to the ISF. Yet supporting the fragile political accommodation would require an active and sustained US effort to consolidate gains and prevent the return of large-scale communal violence.

# CONCLUSIONS

Robert Komer might just as well have commented on the wars in Iraq and Afghanistan when he observed that "the way in which the counterinsurgency response was organized and managed greatly influenced how it was carried out and even led to reshaping the response itself from what was originally intended." He described the real-life constraints "largely inherent in the typical behavior patterns" of the US institutions involved in the conflict, "which made it difficult for them to cope with an unfamiliar conflict environment and greatly influenced what they could and could not, or would and would not, do."[147] The problems were cognitive as well as structural and organizational. He did not call it American denial syndrome, but that is what it was.

In Afghanistan and Iraq, all of the features of American denial syndrome emerged and seriously undermined the ability of the United States to achieve strategic success. Clearly other factors, such as internal struggles for power and resources, malign interference by hostile neighbors, and corruption, were important drivers of the difficulties encountered. Nonetheless, many problems were self-generated and limited US ability to respond to and consolidate military gains. US decisions related to reconstruction and stabilization in both countries compounded the difficulty of achieving sustainable security in Iraq and Afghanistan and created serious obstacles to the achievement of US goals.

The need for simultaneous efforts to defeat enemy organizations and consolidate gains was lost on civilian and military leaders in both conflicts. In Iraq, consistent with past experiences, the early emphasis on phased operations separated combat from political stabilization. And in Afghanistan, the vacillation between CT-centric approaches and stabilization did not account for the need to extend military operations beyond conducting raids against the enemy to security efforts essential to achieving political outcomes, such as securing populations and developing capable and legitimate security forces. The belief that a phase would be "completed" before beginning a new one encouraged a myopic fixation on killing and capturing terrorists and insurgents. Indicative of the failure to consider military operations as integral to consolidation was the US declaration that the end of major combat operations in Iraq had arrived, illustrated by the "mission accomplished" sign that greeted President Bush as he arrived on the USS *Abraham Lincoln* in May 2003. That failure, the military's emphasis on transition, and the absence of a comprehensive counterinsurgency plan left many soldiers wondering why, if the "war is supposed to be over," they were still being shot at.[148]

The idea of a "postwar" phase contributed to the illusion that civilians could retain and execute more control than was in fact realistically possible during an ongoing armed conflict. Washington spread responsibility for reconstruction and stabilization among dozens of actors. None had complete authority over their mission or control over the resources needed to accomplish it. The "unity of effort" that predominated on paper remained weak in practice and could never, in reality, substitute for an operational concept. There was no coordination across civilian and military organizations on even some of the most important decisions—such as how to reconstitute security in the theater. Regarding security forces, General Dubik acknowledged that no single organization, headquarters, or agency could do all that was necessary but that a "single organization should be given the responsibility for developing police and law enforcement systems."[149] Partnerships are key but must operate under a unity-of-action model.

The political stabilization on which strategic success depended was not considered fundamental to the war effort. Good ideas met with resistance, and without unity of command there was often no one to champion those ideas. For example, with respect to Iraq, the Joint Staff developed important insights concerning political consolidation in a war game (Prominent Hammer II). The recommendation that emerged from the game was to create a three-star headquarters staffed by civilian experts to oversee the reconstitution of the Iraqi army and the restoration of basic services. Another idea advanced by then–director of the Joint Staff General Abizaid was to use the army's III Corps to oversee Iraqi reconstruction.[150] But in the end, no unified headquarters existed to direct a war effort that combined combat operations and reconstruction tasks. As in previous governance operations, this command transition had not been well thought out. Moreover, bureaucracy undermined missions that were also beset by poor planning and flawed command structures. Procedures, such as contracting rules, designed for nonconflict environments were applied in a war environment, making it impossible for actors to respond quickly to evolving needs.[151] Commanders, frustrated by their inability to act quickly enough to effect local drivers of conflict, warned repeatedly that "bureaucracy kills."[152]

The historical reluctance to put the military in charge of governance-related missions reappeared, despite the fact that no civilian organization existed with the capability to accomplish reconstruction tasks in wartime. Although officials tried to create umbrella organizations to tie together the various initiatives, numerous planning efforts were conducted in parallel, not as part of an integrated campaign plan that identified the resources and capabilities needed to implement requirements. Planning, said a former State Department official, "never got to the point where things were in place that could be implemented."[153] As in the past, soldiers found themselves trying to make sense of a situation that required both reconstruction and combat efforts. Lt. Col. Scott Rutter, then commander of the US Army's Second Battalion, Seventh Infantry, Third Infantry Division, which helped take the Baghdad airport, stated, "We knew what the tactical end state was supposed to be at the end of the war, but we were never told what the end state, the goal was, [sic] for the postwar." He observed that his unit was faced with making decisions on its own, from "everything from how to deal with looters to whether and how to distribute food."[154]

In Afghanistan, as in other conflicts, some senior military leaders believed that they could avoid the politics of the conflict. General Franks explained that while the United States supported the interim government in Afghanistan, "we were not going to be picking sides between groups."[155] And the US did not even focus intelligence sufficiently to understand political competitions for power and resources with which multiple groups, including many hostile to US interests, were engaged. Those competitions extended beyond the physical battleground and carried over into governmental institutions and security forces. As the former director of national intelligence Dennis Blair observed later, the United States lacked intelligence about the power structures inside the country and other basic information.[156] It was, as in previous conflicts, impossible for the military to remain apart from the "politics on the ground" in both countries. Without understanding the nature of political competitions, however, US programs and actions often strengthened rather than weakened adversaries. And when soldiers began to understand how to mobilize groups whose interests aligned with those of the United States, they were often frustrated when civilian leaders rebuffed or did not take seriously their recommendations to cooperate with certain groups. Early outreach by Sunni leaders before the Iraqi insurgency coalesced and gained strength is just one example.[157]

American denial syndrome undermined key US efforts from the start and perpetuated the belief that governance operations were not an integral part of war. This directly affected both the planning processes before both wars and the campaign plans that emerged during them. This was a view that appeared consistently throughout the Bush and Obama administrations and was later supported by a sometimes strident literature that saw reconstruction tasks as a distraction from the military's core task of winning conventional conflicts. Such articles often portrayed proponents of COIN as part of a "hubristic plan to manage the international system."[158]

These critics failed to understand the operational implications of the political drivers of the conflicts and their interactions with combat operations. And top policy leaders consistently underestimated the time it would take and the types of organizational arrangements needed to consolidate political gains. In 2003 Rumsfeld contrasted Iraq and Germany after World War II. He pointed out that "within two months, all major Iraqi cities and most towns had municipal councils—something that took eight months in postwar Germany. Within four months, the Iraqi Governing Council had appointed a cabinet—something that took 14 months in Germany."[159] President Obama may have been right when he observed that "since World War II, some of our most costly mistakes came not from our restraint, but from our willingness to rush into military adventures without thinking through the consequences." But he himself did not apply that admonition to his decision making: He did not understand the requirements of consolidation in wartime.

# NOTES

1. George W. Bush, *Decision Points* (New York: Random House, 2010), 184.

2. The closest might be the quarterly reports published since 2008 by the Special Inspector General for Afghanistan Reconstruction. The National Defense Authorization Act (P.L. 110–181) established SIGAR to understand better the use of US funds in Afghanistan.

3. Komer, *Bureaucracy Does Its Thing*, ix.

4. Greentree, "Bureaucracy Does Its Thing," 10.

5. Neumann et al., *Operation Enduring Freedom*, 45.

6. Kugler, *Operation Anaconda*, 1.

7. Michael Gordon, "C.I.A. Warns That Afghan Factions May Bring Chaos," *New York Times*, February 21, 2002.

8. Marcella Bombardieri, "US Advisers Mulled to Aid Peacekeeping: Afghan Warlords Threaten Process, Bush Envoy Says," *Boston Globe*, February 25, 2002.

9. See interviews with Jones, *Graveyard of Empires*, 110.

10. On this point and the persistence of this thinking, see Leon Wieseltier, "Welcome to the Era of the Light Footprint: Obama Finally Finds His Doctrine," *New Republic*, January 29, 2013.

11. Wright et al., *Different Kind of War*, 191.

12. Michael Gordon, "U.S. Backs Increase in Peacekeepers for Afghanistan," *New York Times*, August 30, 2002, http://www.nytimes.com/2002/08/30/world/us-backs-increase -in-peacekeepers-for-afghanistan.html.

13. Ari Fleisher quoted in Jones, *Graveyard of Empires*, 113.

14. Vincent Morelli and Paul Belkin, *NATO in Afghanistan: A Test of the Transatlantic Alliance*, (Washington, DC: Congressional Research Service, December 3, 2009), 1. See also "Secretary Rumsfeld Joint Media Availability with President Karzai," Department of Defense News Transcript, May 1, 2003, http://www.defenselink.mil/transcripts/transcript .aspx?transcriptid=2562.

15. Institute for the Study of War, *Report on the Expansion of ISAF*, n.d., http://www .understandingwar.org/international-security-assistance-force-isaf#sthash.PWSnZHo2 .dpuf.

16. Collins, *Understanding War in Afghanistan*, 64.

17. Wright et al., *Different Kind of War*, 223.

18. Defense Secretary Donald Rumsfeld had directed SOCOM take the lead in planning and leading US global counterterrorism operations, rather than supporting other combatant commands, as it had in the past. It used its global assets and deployed them around the world, including in Afghanistan. For a description of special operations forces deployed around the world, including Afghanistan, see "Posture Statement of Admiral William McRaven, United States Navy, Commander, United States Special Operations Command, before the 113th Congress, Senate Armed Services Committee, Emerging Threats and Capabilities Subcommittee," http://www.armed-services.senate.gov/imo/media /doc/McRaven_03-11-14.pdf.

19. Wright et al., *A Different Kind of War*, 243.

20. The information in this paragraph about Barno's approach is from Barno, "Fighting the Other War," 32–44.

21. "Secretary Rumsfeld Joint Media Availability with President Karzai."

22. Quote is from author interview with David Barno conducted on January 22, 2016.

23. See Ballard et al., *From Kabul to Baghdad*, chap. 5.

24. Pamela Constable, "Courting Afghanistan Brick by Brick: Expanded Civil-Military Program Aims to Win Hearts and Minds," *Washington Post*, December 8, 2002.

25. See Perito, *U.S. Experience with Provincial Reconstruction Teams*, 2–3.

26. Ibid., 1.

27. Special Inspector General for Afghanistan, Report to the US Congress, April 30, 2010, https://www.sigar.mil/pdf/quarterlyreports/2010-04-30qr.pdf, 9.

28. Gerard McHugh and Lola Gostelow, *Provincial Reconstruction Teams and Humanitarian Military Relations in Afghanistan* (London: Save the Children, 2004), https://docs .unocha.org/sites/dms/Documents/Save%20the%20Children-%20PRTs%20and%20Human itarian%20Military%20Relations%20in%20Afghanistan%20(2004).pdf.

29. US Central Command, "Operation Enduring Freedom: Humanitarian Assistance (HA) Strategic Concept," briefing slides, November 12, 2001, cited in Flavin, *Civil Military Operations*, 17.

30. Barno, "Fighting the Other War," 43. In an interview with the author, Barno explained that he had recognized that this was a problem and that by March 2004 he had made improvements, asking them to report through the maneuver brigade–level HQ.

31. Ballard et al., *From Kabul to Baghdad*, 112.

32. Recollection of Tom Donilon (later President Obama's national security adviser), quoted in David Sanger, "Charting Obama's Journey to a Shift on Afghanistan," *New York Times*, May 19, 2012.

33. See "White House Press Briefing by Bruce Riedel, Amb. Richard Holbrooke, and Michelle Flournoy, On the New Strategy for Afghanistan and Pakistan, March 27, 2009," https://www.whitehouse.gov/the-press-office/press-briefing-bruce-riedel-ambassador -richard-holbrooke-and-michelle-flournoy-new-.

34. McChrystal, *My Share of the Task*, 345.

35. "August 2009 COMSAF Review," http://media.washingtonpost.com/wp-srv/politics /documents/Assessment_Redacted_092109.pdf?sid=ST2009092003140.

36. McChrystal, *My Share of the Task*, 287.

37. Term used in Baker, "How Obama Came to Plan." See also McChrystal, *My Share of the Task*, 361.

38. Baker, "How Obama Came to Plan."

39. "Remarks by the President on the Way Forward in Afghanistan," White House, Office of the Press Secretary, June 22, 2011.

40. "Secretary Rumsfeld Joint Media Availability with President Karzai."

41. The information in this paragraph is from Dobbins, *After the Taliban*, 120–24.

42. "Statement by Amb. Richard Holbrooke, Special Envoy to Afghanistan, at Press Briefing by Bruce Riedel, Ambassador Richard Holbrooke, and Michelle Flournoy on the New Strategy for Afghanistan and Pakistan," White House, Office of the Press Secretary, March 27, 2009, https://www.whitehouse.gov/the-press-office/press-briefing-bruce-riedel -ambassador-richard-holbrooke-and-michelle-flournoy-new-.

43. This point and the next are discussed in SIGAR, "Quarterly Report to the United States Congress," October 30, 2009, 7, 4, https://www.sigar.mil/pdf/quarterlyreports/2009 -10-30qr.pdf.

44. Collins, *Understanding War in Afghanistan*, 76.

45. See also Government Accountability Office report on the problem of the Afghan government's lack of capacity to maintain US-funded infrastructure projects: "Statement of Charles Michael Johnson Jr., Director, International Affairs and Trade, Testimony before the Subcommittee on State, Foreign Operations, and Related Programs, Committee on Appropriations," in *Afghanistan Development: USAID Continues to Face Challenges in Managing and Overseeing U.S. Development Assistance Programs* (Washington, DC: GAO, July 15, 2010), GAO-10-932T, http://www.gao.gov/assets/130 /124994.pdf.

46. The April 30, 2010, SIGAR report described how US officials inspected a twenty-eight-kilometer road project in Kapisa Province that would connect the provincial capital to a smaller town (Nirjab). The construction of the road was going fairly well, with the Afghan contractor having completed about 60 percent of the work. The road was used for local traffic as well by coalition vehicles. https://www.sigar.mil/pdf/quarterlyreports/2009 -10-30qr.pdf.

47. Ibid.

48. Briefing slides prepared by the National Defense University, for the DOD J-5, June 2002, cited in Katzmann, *Afghanistan: Current Issues*, 12.

49. GAO, *Afghanistan Security: Further Congressional Action May Be Needed to Ensure Completion of a Detailed Plan to Develop and Sustain Capable Afghan National Security Forces*, GAO-08-661, June 2008, http://www.gao.gov/new.items/d08661.pdf, 4.

50. Cordesman et al., *Winning in Afghanistan*, 43. Unless otherwise noted, information about ANSF force levels and funding is from this monograph, 43–47.

51. Comment made by General Wardak to NATO Parliamentary Assembly. See "Press Conference by Afghan Minister of Defence, Abdul Rahim Wardak, and Ambassador Adam Kobieracki, March 13, 2006," NATO Headquarters, Online Library, http://nato.int/docu/speech/2006/s060313b.htm.

52. Katzmann, *Afghanistan: Postwar Governance*, 34.

53. GAO, *Afghanistan Security*, 3.

54. Cordesman et al., *Winning in Afghanistan*, 45.

55. GAO, *Afghanistan Security*, 68

56. Cordesman et al., *Winning in Afghanistan*, 110.

57. Dobbins, *After the Taliban*, 118.

58. Thomas W. Lippman, "Albright, Cohen to Deliver Tough Message; Trips to Reinforce U.S. Will to Use Force If Iraq Doesn't Comply with Weapons Inspections," *Washington Post*, January 28, 1998.

59. See Feith, *War and Decision*, 200–12, for a good description of these debates among Bush administration officials.

60. Feith and Grossman testimony before the Senate Foreign Relations Committee on February 11, 2003.

61. Office of the Special Inspector General for Iraq Reconstruction, *Hard Lessons*, 338.

62. Franks, *American Soldier*, 441.

63. I make this point in my 2003 article "War and the Art of Governance," *Parameters* 33, no. 3 (Autumn 2003): 85–94.

64. Dobbins, *After the Taliban*, 107.

65. "Memorandum from SECSTATE WASHDC (State 130333) To: Special Embassy Program —Priority, Subject: Future of Iraq Expert Working Groups, July 8, 2002," https://nsarchive.gwu.edu/NSAEBB/NSAEBB163/iraq-state-01.pdf.

66. An excellent discussion of this can be found in Col. Kevin Benson's account "OIF Phase IV: A Planner's Reply to Brigadier Alwyn Foster," *Military Review* (March–April 2005), http://www.au.af.mil/au/awc/awcgate/milreview/benson.pdf. Benson served as the C/J5 (planner) to the Third US Army / Combined Forces Land Component Command and developed a range of plans for CFLCC from before operations began in March 2003 until July 2003. In addition, clarifications and additional information are from the author's interview with Colonel Benson in February 2016.

67. Gordon and Trainor, *Cobra II*, 67.

68. Phase IV is in Joint Doctrine JP 5.0

69. Wright et al., *On Point II*, 66. Emphasis is mine.

70. Linda Robinson, *Tell Me How This Ends: General David Petraeus and the Search for a Way Out of Iraq* (New York: PublicAffairs, 2008), 27.

71. Rear Adm. Carlton B. Jewett, quoted in Gordon and Trainor, *Cobra II*, 141.

72. Interview with Lt. Col. Steven Peterson, the chief of intelligence planning within CENTCOM's C-5, in Nora Bensahel, Olga Oliker, Keith Crane, Rick Brennan Jr., Heather S. Gregg, Thomas Sullivan, and Andrew Rathnell, *After Saddam: Prewar Planning and the Occupation of Iraq* (Washington, DC: RAND, 2008), 12.

73. See Col. Kevin Benson, "OIF Phase IV: A Planner's Reply to Brigadier Alwyn Foster," *Military Review* (March–April 2006): 62.

74. Quote is from Mike Fitzgerald, the army colonel in charge of CENTCOM's war plans, in SIGIR, *Hard Lessons*, 39.

75. Garner quoted ibid., 39.

76. Wright et al., *On Point II*, 71.

77. Charles Ferguson interview with Garner and other members of ORHA, cited in Charles Ferguson, *No End in Sight* (New York: PublicAffairs, 2008), 72, 79.

78. Rieff, "Blueprint for a Mess."

79. Gordon and Trainor, *Cobra II*, 139.

80. John Keegan, *The Iraq War* (New York: Knopf, 2004), 1.

81. Ballard et al., *From Kabul to Baghdad*, 87.

82. "American Forces in Iraq and Afghanistan," interactive troop strength chart, *New York Times*, June 22, 2011, http://www.nytimes.com/interactive/2011/06/22/world/asia/american-forces-in-afghanistan-and-iraq.html?_r=0.

83. Paul Wolfowitz quoted in Eric Schmitt, "Plans for Policing a Postwar Iraq," *New York Times*, April 9, 2003, http://www.nytimes.com/2003/04/09/international/worldspecial/09POLI.html.

84. Bremer, *My Year in Iraq*, 9.

85. For a good discussion of the growing political polarization and insurgency in Iraq, see Malkasian, "Counterinsurgency in Iraq," 241–59.

86. Rice had anticipated that Iraqi "institutions would hold," including security institutions. See her quoted in Gordon and Trainor, *Cobra II*, 142.

87. Wright et al., *On Point II*, 168.

88. Rieff, "Blueprint for a Mess."

89. This report is critical of the IGC for reflecting more of the CPA's desires rather than Iraqi views: http://www.crisisgroup.org/en/regions/middle-east-north-africa/iraq-iran-gulf/iraq/017-governing-iraq.aspx.

90. Katzman, "Iraq."

91. Quoted in Rieff, "Blueprint for a Mess."

92. Account of Col. David Teeples in Gordon, *Endgame*, 25.

93. Odierno quoted in Gordon, *Endgame*, 26.

94. See quote in Dan Murphy, "The GI's Weapon of Choice in Iraq: Dollars," *Christian Science Monitor*, January 29, 2004, http://www.csmonitor.com/2004/0129/p01s04-woiq.html. See also this point made by Gen. David Petraeus, "Learning Counterinsurgency: Observations from Soldiering in Iraq," *Military Review* (January–February 2006): 3.

95. Marine colonel John A. Koenig, quoted in Dana Hedgpeth and Sara Cohen, "Money as a Weapon," *Washington Post*, August 11, 2008. The second quote is from unnamed senior commander cited in Thom Shanker, "The Reach of War: Washington: Iraq Commanders Warn That Delays in Civil Projects Undermine Military Mission," *New York Times*, October 17, 2004.

96. McKiernan interview in Wright et al., *On Point II*, 195.

97. The information in this paragraph is from ibid., 161–63.

98. Ricardo S. Sanchez, *Wiser in Battle: A Soldier's Story* (New York: HarperCollins, 2008). See chap. 1.

99. See Steven W. Peterson, "Central but Inadequate: The Applications of Theory in Operation Iraqi Freedom," National Defense University, National War College, Fort Lesley J. McNair, Washington, DC, 2004, 5, http://www.dtic.mil/dtic/tr/fulltext/u2/a441663.pdf. The information in this paragraph is from Wright et al., *On Point II*, 72, and the author's conversations with former CFLCC planner Kevin Benson.

100. CJTF-7 Briefing slides, September 30, 2004, cited in Wright et al., *On Point II*, 163.

101. "Frontline" interview with Robert Blackwill, http://www.pbs.org/wgbh/pages /frontline/yeariniraq/interviews/blackwill.html. Rumsfeld was also pressing for giving more responsibility to the ISF, which numbered around sixty thousand at that time. See Douglas Jehel with David E. Sanger, "The Struggle for Iraq: Occupation Foes; Iraquis' Bitterness Is Called Bigger Threat that Terror," *New York Times*, September 17, 2003, http://www.nytimes.com/2003/09/17/world/struggle-for-iraq-occupation-foes-iraqis -bitterness-called-bigger-threat-than.html.

102. Mark Mazzetti, "U.S. Military Is Stretched Too Thin, Defense Board Warns," *Los Angeles Times*, September 30, 2004.

103. The information about "normal" functions of the embassy and the relationship between it and the military is from Dale, *Operation Iraqi Freedom*, 47.

104. Troop numbers in Amy Belasco, *Troop Levels in the Afghan and Iraq Wars, FY2001-FY2012: Cost and Other Potential Issues* (Washington, DC: Congressional Research Service, July 2, 2009), 9.

105. Quoted in Kagan, *Surge*, 29.

106. The information about Dempsey's tenure is from Hammes, "Raising and Mentoring," 310.

107. Bradley Graham, "U.S. Officials Build a Powerful Partnership in Iraq," *Washington Post*, November 30, 2004.

108. These included the Iraqi Security Forces Fund (over $20 billion), CERP funds (around $4 billion), and contracting for the Iraq Relief and Reconstruction Fund (almost $21 billion). See the summary in SIGIR, *Learning from Iraq*, 38.

109. SIGIR, *Hard Lessons*, notes this about Charlie Hess, 166.

110. The information in this paragraph is from SIGIR, *Hard Lessons*, 241–45.

111. US Institute of Peace (USIP), Association for Diplomatic Studies and Training, Iraq PRT Experience Project, interview #1, interviewed by Sam Westgate, initial interview on February 8, 2008, http://www.usip.org/sites/default/files/file/resources/collections /histories/iraq_prt/1.pdf. This is part of a larger oral history project conducted by USIP; from 2009 to 2011, USIP interviewed two hundred returning government, military, and NGO representatives who had served on provincial reconstruction teams in Iraq and Afghanistan.

112. USIP, Association for Diplomatic Studies and Training, Iraq PRT Experience Project, interview #48, interviewed by Marilyn Greene, initial interview on September 23, 2008, http://www.usip.org/sites/default/files/file/resources/collections/histories/iraq _prt/48.pdf.

113. SIGIR, *Hard Lessons*, 166.
114. Wright et al., *On Point II*, 175.
115. J. Andrew Person, "Getting Past the First Cup of Tea," *Small Wars Journal* 6, no. 1 (February 4, 2010): 11. Person's article won an honorable mention in the SWJ Writing Contest.
116. Ellen Knickmeyer and Jonathan Finer, "Iraqi Vote Draws Big Turnout of Sunnis," *Washington Post*, December 16, 2005.
117. Gilmore, "Ambassador Khalilzad."
118. George Casey and John Negroponte, "Joint Mission Statement: A Plan for the Year Ahead; Transition to Self Reliance," Memorandum, February 7, 2005, cited in Brennan et al., *Ending the U.S. War*, 39.
119. John F. Burns, "Torture Alleged at Ministry Site outside Baghdad," *New York Times*, November 16, 2005, http://www.nytimes.com/2005/11/16/world/middleeast/torture-alleged-at-ministry-site-outside-baghdad.html?_r=0.
120. For an account of the sectarian evolution of the MOI and the ethnic cleanings it perpetuated, see Joel Rayburn, *Iraq after America: Strongmen, Sectarians, Resistance* (Stanford, CA: Hoover Institution Press, 2014), 76–91.
121. "MNF-I, Campaign Progress Review, June 2005–December 2005, Baghdad, December 20, 2005," cited in Brennan et al., *Ending the U.S. War*, 41.
122. The MNF-I information here and in the next paragraph is from Wright et al., *On Point II*, chap. 4. The plan was named Operation Iraqi Freedom; Partnership: From Occupation to Constitutional Elections.
123. "MNF-I, Campaign Plan: Operation Iraqi Freedom," cited in Brennan et al., *Ending the U.S. War*, 34–35.
124. Sepp is quoted in Ballard et al., *From Kabul to Baghdad*, 143.
125. Sanger et al., "Chaos Overran Iraq Plan."
126. See his comments in Gordon and Trainor, *Cobra II*, 491.
127. Numbers and goal from Khalilzad and Casey, "Path to Success."
128. Information from this paragraph is from Maj. Jay B. Baker, "Tal Afar 2005: Laying the Counterinsurgency Groundwork," *Army*, June 2009, 61–68, http://www.ausa.org/publications/armymagazine/archive/2009/6/Documents/Baker_0609.pdf.
129. "U.S. Department of Defense, Office of the Assistant Secretary of Defense (Public Affairs), Press Briefing on Overview of Operation Restoring Rights in Tall Afar, Iraq, News Transcript, Army Col. H. R. McMaster, commander of the 3rd Armored Cavalry Regiment, Tuesday, September 13, 2005," http://www.globalsecurity.org/military/library/news/2005/09/mil-050913-dod01.htm.
130. Information about this account is from Maj. Niel Smith, US Army, and Colonel Sean MacFarland, US Army, "Anbar Awakens: The Tipping Point," *Military Review* (March–April 2008): 43.
131. Megan K. Stack and Louise Roug, "Fear of Big Battle Panics Iraqi City," *Los Angeles Times*, June 11, 2006.
132. Hearing before the Senate Armed Services Committee, Washington, DC, August 2, 2006, http://www.washingtonpost.com/wp-dyn/content/article/2006/08/03/AR2006080300802.html.
133. Information about the ISF is from Anthony H. Cordesman, "Iraq's Sectarian and Ethnic Violence," 32–35, http://www.comw.org/warreport/fulltext/061214cordesman.pdf.

134. SIGIR, *Hard Lessons*, 202.

135. Andrew Krepinevich, "How to Win in Iraq," *Foreign Affairs* (September/October 2005): 87–104.

136. Sanger et al., "Chaos Overran Iraq Plan."

137. "President's Address to the Nation, the White House, President George W. Bush, Office of the Press Secretary, January 10, 2007," https://georgewbush-whitehouse.archives.gov/news/releases/2007/01/20070110-7.html.

138. Stephen Biddle, "Iraq after the Surge," testimony before the Committee on Armed Services Oversight and Investigations Subcommittee, US House of Representatives, 110th Cong., 2nd sess., January 23, 2008.

139. Anne Tyson, "Commanders in Iraq See 'Surge' into '08," *Washington Post*, May 9, 2007.

140. Information from this paragraph is from Kagan, *Surge*, 30–32.

141. "Multinational Force Iraq (MNF-I) Press Conference with Gen. David Petraeus, Topic: Ongoing Security Operations," Combined Press Information Center, Baghdad, Iraq, March 8, 2007. He said, "Importantly, Iraqi and coalition forces will not just clear neighborhoods, they will also hold them to facilitate the build phase of the operation and help Baghdad's residents realize aspirations beyond survival."

142. Michael Gordon, *Endgame*, 356.

143. This is the point that Lt. Gen. James Dubik, USA (Ret.), makes in Dubik, *Building Security Forces*. Unless otherwise noted, information about the ISF here and in the next three paragraphs is from this source, as well as from e-mail exchanges and interviews conducted by the author with Dubik on April 6 and 15, 2016.

144. Hammes, "Raising and Mentoring Security Forces," 306.

145. SIGIR, *Learning from Iraq*, 92.

146. Quotes from Gates speech at the change of command of MNF-I from army general David Petraeus to army general Raymond Odierno, quoted in Jim Garamone, "Odierno Assumes Command of Coalition Forces in Iraq," American Forces Press Service, September 16, 2008, http://www.army.mil/article/12470/Odierno_assumes_command_of_coalition_forces_in_Iraq/.

147. Komer, *Bureaucracy Does Its Thing*, vi

148. Williams and Chandrasekaran, "U.S. Troops Frustrated."

149. Dubik, *Creating Police and Law Enforcement Systems*, 12.

150. Gordon and Trainor, *Cobra II*, 140–41.

151. Ambassador Negroponte appealed for greater flexibility in the application of federal acquisition regulations. He identified twenty federal acquisition regulations that needed to be waived in order for him to conduct critical reconstruction-related tasks.

152. Thom Shanker, "Iraq Commanders Warn That Delays in Civil Projects Undermine Military Mission," *New York Times*, October 17, 2004.

153. Robert Perito quoted by Rieff, "Blueprint for a Mess."

154. Rieff, "Blueprint for a Mess."

155. Elliott, "Battle over Peacekeeping."

156. Thom Shanker and Peter Baker, "Obama Sets New Afghan Strategy," *New York Times*, March 26, 2009, www.nytimes.com/2009/03/27/washington/27prexy.html?_r=0.

157. Derek Harvey, memo, "Sunni Outreach to the Governing Council and the CPA," October 2003, cited in Gordon, *Endgame*, 35.

158. Tierney, "Backlash against Nation-Building," 16.

159. "Beyond Nation Building," remarks by Secretary of Defense Donald H. Rumsfeld, Intrepid Sea-Air-Space Museum, New York City, February 14, 2003, http://www.defense link.mil/speeches/2003/sp20030214-secdef0024.html.

# CONCLUSIONS

AMONG HIS MANY observations and reflections about World War II, Winston Churchill wrote that it was "not possible in a major war to divide military from political affairs. At the summit, they are one."[1] Beneath the summit too, politics continue to shape the character of a war, from its tactics and operations to its wartime organizations. This book has shown that in virtually all of its experiences with war, the United States has faced the problem of how to consolidate combat successes into a desired political end state. It has shown how ground forces, usually soldiers, have been the critical operational link to achieve America's political objectives in wartime and set a foundation for the development of longer-term strategic outcomes. When done well, as in the World War II cases of Germany, Japan, and Italy, lasting strategic successes have resulted. When done poorly, the failure to consolidate gains resulted in protracted conflicts, increased costs, higher causalities, and the loss of public support for the effort. Governance operations are central to strategic success in war. Despite the need for these operations, American civilian and military leaders have been reluctant to think through, operationalize, and resource efforts needed to consolidate political gains in war. Civilian and military leaders consistently refused (or failed) to make consolidation an integral part of campaign planning from the start.

When criticized concerning the US Army's unpreparedness for aspects of the intervention in Iraq, former secretary of defense Donald Rumsfeld made the oft-quoted observation that "you go to war with the Army you have." The question is, *why* do we have the army we have? The case studies in this book explain why, despite having to consistently grapple with the problem of reconstituting political order during and following combat, US political and military leaders resisted taking the steps needed to institutionalize the lessons of governance operations. The army remained reluctant to embrace these operations as an integral part of war. And US political leaders reinforced that reluctance and remained hesitant to allow military forces to serve as the main instrument for political consolidation. Civilian and military reluctance to acknowledge the requirement for governance operations as a fundamental dimension of war has resulted in a denial syndrome that precludes effective war planning and perpetuates unpreparedness for this aspect of war. This book has described the denial syndrome as fundamentally a problem of civil-military relations. Improving US planning for and outcomes in future interventions will require a fundamental change in the way that the United States plans for war. The five recommendations presented here will require overcoming this denial syndrome in order to prepare the army and the nation for the demands of future armed conflict.

First, if we are to achieve our strategic objectives in a conflict, American policymakers must accept that the political dimension is indispensable *across the full spectrum* of war. Policymakers must appreciate the complexity of politics as they relate to *all* wars and recognize that governance tasks are not separate from "conventional" war. Governance operations and combat operations often occur simultaneously, with the defeat of the enemy forces in rear areas requiring a consolidation of the political situation while remaining troops continue to fight. In Iraq in 2003, for example, US Army forces vacated the southern portion of the country as it continued the offensive to Baghdad. In the meantime, Shi'a Islamist militias under Iranian control began to execute consolidation tasks, greatly complicating coalition efforts to forge a political settlement consistent with US interests. Eight years into the wars in Iraq and Afghanistan, the then secretary of defense Leon Panetta admitted that there did not appear to be a sustained vision of how to address the political problems of reconstruction. Tellingly, he still saw the problem as distinct from war proper, observing that the US "military was in Iraq to fight a war. They were not USAID. That's not their role."[2] Although the policy and academic literature on COIN, small wars, and low-intensity conflict acknowledged, to varying degrees, the importance of governance tasks and their relationship to the achievement of desired political outcomes, this connection was not made for war as a whole. In Vietnam this artificial distinction was crystallized in the division that emerged between the "regular war" and "the other war."[3]

Yet many of the specific activities associated with pacification in Vietnam, such as rebuilding security forces, were not very different from many of the governance tasks undertaken by the army in its "regular wars." Given this separation, policymakers tended to view governance tasks as those to be conducted by specialized units, such as the army's civil affairs units, which were located primarily in the reserve (and later in the special operations community). The push toward specialization—a view held by civil affairs proponents—tended to place governance missions further away from the regular, conventional force structure and perpetuated unpreparedness for the tasks essential to prevailing in war.

The January 2015 Defense Strategic Guidance document suggests that the tendency to separate politics from war remains. It asserts that US forces would "no longer be sized to conduct large-scale, prolonged stability operations."[4] This ignores the reality that the requirements for consolidation are a part of war. It suggests that troops can depart a conflict on a predetermined schedule without creating opportunities for the enemy and risking the reversal of combat gains. Certainly, responsible leaders do not deliberately seek to "prolong" the commitment of military forces. Yet, paradoxically, the propensity not to plan or size forces for stability operations increases the possibility of "prolonged operations." Because war is inherently political, wars of *all* kinds involve fighting in deeply political terrain. And because wars are fundamentally human endeavors, wars do not end until one's enemies are convinced that they have been defeated.

Second, given the centrality of politics to war, the United States must realize that unity of command is essential to operational and strategic success in war. A flawed view of the nature of war and politics in Washington combined to dictate organizations, rather than the operational requirements on the ground. The United States adopted what might be called a "divide and fail" model that prevented unity of command over critical parts of the war effort that needed to be integrated to order to achieve objectives. Because most policymakers did not consider the consolidation of political gains an integral part of war, they created dual and often competing chains of command to conduct governance tasks.

Lack of unity of command is a long-standing problem. During World War II, General Eisenhower remarked that he was "having as much trouble with civilian forces behind aiding us as I am with the enemy in front of us."[5] A senior official writing to President Roosevelt lamented that much more was needed than "the mere addition of another authority with broad, vague powers of coordination and integration" and that it was the "confusion in the basic war jobs—the multiplicity of operating agencies—which complicates the task."[6] Years later Robert Komer observed that the "diffusion of authority and fragmentation of command" that characterized the US pacification effort in Vietnam "did much to explain why it proved so hard for so long to . . . convert our overwhelming superiority in manpower and resources into operational results."[7] Today the situation remains dishearteningly similar. Absent unity of command in Iraq and Afghanistan and given the myriad actors in each theater, it became virtually impossible to coordinate, track, or direct resources to lines of effort on which political outcomes depended. Unity of effort became the catchphrase to emphasize the need for improved coordination. But unity of effort is not an effective operational concept in war, and no integrated campaign plan linked these important dimensions of the wars (combat and politics) until very late in both conflicts. Even then, lack of unity of command made the execution of those plans wholly dependent on personalities and relationships between key civilians and military leaders. The 2004 National Military Strategy document recognized that "winning decisively will require synchronizing and integrating major combat operations, stability operations and significant post-conflict interagency operations to establish conditions" favorable to the United States.[8] Command arrangements, however, did not reflect that imperative.

Third, although civilians formulate and drive policy, they must give the army operational control over governance operations in war. To achieve this, two interrelated obstacles need to be overcome. First, policymakers must acknowledge that civilian organizations are not capable of operating in conflict zones in sufficient scale over time. This is because civilians are neither prepared nor predisposed to operate in dangerous environments. The military's advantages in this area extend beyond the ability operate in a violent environment: They include scale, logistics, communications, and experience managing larger institutions. When the army established its first school of military government in 1942, it did so recognizing that it was the "sole agency capable of initiating the reconstruction process."[9] Not much has changed since then. Military control over governance operations was considered a necessary (but ideally short-term) endeavor. Gen. Lucius Clay, as military governor in Germany, expressed the hope that the occupation would not last long but realized that it would be difficult for the army to leave quickly because no organization except the army had the capacity to take over. He thus worked to build an organization that could "be transferred bodily to a civil branch of government."[10] Civilians such as John McCloy, who later became the civilian high commissioner in Germany, initially rejected the oversight job in 1945, believing it was too *early* for civilians to lead events in the theater. Ironically, in recent years there seemed to be a fundamental misunderstanding of role of civilian administrators in the past. Paul Bremer said that he had used the German model for his CPA role and that he had studied "the handover of state institutions during the 1945–52 occupation of Germany."[11] But McCloy assumed his post much later in the war, after General Clay had accomplished key governance tasks.

Years later, similar problems emerged in Iraq and Afghanistan. In 2004 the State Department created an office to address the need to grow and integrate more civilians into efforts to stabilize conflict zones. Political leaders, including President Bush, commented that civilian agencies needed to "step up to the task,"[12] since more civilian expertise was needed to "win the peace."[13] Although many dedicated civil servants and Foreign Service officers volunteered, the State Department was never able to deploy enough civilians. At the time, close to half of the State Department positions required in Iraq had to be filled by military personnel.[14] The 2012 Defense Strategic Guidance continued to advance the view that in conflict situations, the United States would seek to "emphasize non-military means" and "reduce the demand for significant US force commitments to stability operations." This underscores the myth that there are significant nonmilitary, deployable capabilities in sufficient scale that have the training and skills necessary to undertake sustained operations in insecure environments. The very fact that "stability" is in question in a particular contingency gives pause to this idea and remains wishful thinking.

Second, these persistent concerns are rooted in an American political culture that makes policymakers uncomfortable with placing the military in charge of governance-related tasks. American officials often acknowledged that the military was best equipped to undertake such tasks in conflict zones, but at the same time they expressed hesitancy about placing the army squarely in charge. One analyst, Carnes Lord, explains this as an American unease with creating a Roman precedent of "proconsuls" and giving army leaders a "proconsul" role.[15] In Iraq, General Franks realized the efficiency inherent in military control but also recognized that such "pluses" were outweighed by the perceived political drawbacks, since "civilian control of government has long been an American value."[16] Civilians led ORHA and then the CPA but had no real operational capabilities to accomplish critical governance tasks. With this model, Washington took the "politically correct" decision rather than one that would have allowed greater operational efficiency.

Fourth, American leaders must not be seduced by the idea that they can achieve policy objectives from afar by kinetic means alone. Technology is an important element of the military's differential advantage over potential enemies, but it cannot deliver victory. Winning requires consideration of the political outcome of the war. The so-called CT approach is a modern-day version of strategic bombing theory. It ignores the drivers of conflict and the conditions (e.g., state weakness and civil war) that allow terrorist organizations to operate or to control territory, populations, and resources. Favored by the Obama administration, a CT approach seeks "quick and easy" outcomes that avoid the uncomfortable fact that air strikes destroy but do not reclaim territory, secure, or rebuild.[17] We need to look only to Libya and the sectarian civil war across the Middle East for recent evidence of how raids by drones and special operations forces are insufficient to defeat enemy organizations and address the causes of violence. CT is a powerful operational capability that can kill individuals and degrade organizations at the tactical level (ideally in a way that advances a broader political strategy), but it can never, and has never, had strategic effects on its own. Army leaders such as H. R. McMaster have pointed out that it is a "conceit" to think that "lightning victories" can be achieved by "small numbers of technologically sophisticated American forces capable of launching precision strikes against enemy targets from safe distances." Such theories were initially applied to the wars in Afghanistan and Iraq, clouding our understanding of the conflicts and delaying the development of effective strategies.[18]

Fifth, the United States, especially the military, must have some standing capabilities and organizations that are prepared to conduct key governance tasks. The army must be large enough to conduct operations of sufficient scale and for ample duration to consolidate gains. But just the size of the army is insufficient. The army's view of what constitutes its fundamental competencies must expand to include the broad range of activities necessary to achieve sustainable political outcomes in war. The army must reject the narrowly circumscribed view of the profession of arms as the "management of violence" and reconsider its persistent hope that, in the next war, civilians will generate the capability to take over governance tasks. And army leaders must recognize that, in the past, efforts to escape the difficult and often unglamorous tasks associated with consolidation by deliberately avoiding preparation have failed and only served to make those tasks more difficult.

The army faced remarkably similar governance-related challenges in all of its interventions. Army personnel played key roles in rebuilding local police forces to assist combat troops with the maintenance of law and order as well as bolster the stability and security of that particular country. Soldiers oversaw local and/or national elections and often negotiated with new members of governing elites. In many earlier cases, army personnel were directly involved in the development of new constitutions, which were then submitted to the local populace for a referendum. Army personnel oversaw or worked to rebuild the judicial and legal systems of countries and undertook improvements in public welfare infrastructure, including the health care, educational, and often, sanitation systems of countries. Army personnel often oversaw economic and industrial reform programs and tried to improve and stabilize the immediate situation to ensure adequate food supplies. Because those wide-ranging efforts are a consistent part of consolidation, developing and retaining expertise in key areas makes sense. If the army fails to do so, it is likely to experience the same difficulties it has experienced historically. The cost of failing to build those capabilities is not only greater in time and money but also leads to the protraction of armed conflict and greater casualties. It is necessary to avoid what an officer now in Iraq (dealing with the crisis of ISIS) observed: "It is as if the lessons we learned from 2003–2011 in Iraq have been wiped clean."[19]

Unless the United States considers the problem of order from the start of a conflict, worse outcomes are likely. Obviously no one wanted Iraq to turn into a protracted large-scale COIN campaign. It seems clear that the failure to prepare for the reestablishment of political order after the collapse of the Hussein regime in Baghdad allowed what was initially a localized, decentralized, hybrid insurgency to coalesce over time. The presence of US regular forces unable to restore political stability despite their advantages in firepower created a vacuum of power that the insurgents exploited. Policies that exacerbated the fears of the minority population and initially ineffective efforts to generate security forces tied to rule of law created more opportunities for Sunni insurgents—who later allied with AQI. Weak governance, corrupt security forces, and the absence of rule of law also allowed Iran-sponsored militias to subvert state institutions and establish control of territory and resources, conditions that set conditions for the large-scale communal violence of 2006–9. Presumably, a better understanding among civilian leaders of the deeply political dimension of war might give them pause before they decide to enter one. But once a decision is made, they should have confidence that the force being deployed is prepared fully for all kinds of contingencies. This requires preparation, not wishful thinking. As one prominent strategist put it, after over fourteen years of undertaking stabilization and governance challenges in Iraq and Afghanistan, "we have never been able to never do this again."[20]

Despite the remaining obstacles to the adoption of these recommendations, the army has made progress toward fundamentally rethinking the role of governance operations in war. This progress has occurred at the tactical, operational, and strategic levels. The army's concept of "unified land operations" advances the idea that military operations are a combination of offensive, defensive, and stability tasks.[21] Its manual *Stability Operations* (which is currently being updated) explains that restoring basic order and rebuilding institutions provides the "foundations for enduring peace and stability." It elevated stability operations to a status equal to that of offense and defense in war.[22] Perhaps most important, army documents that drive decisions about how to educate and train soldiers have introduced the term "consolidate" to describe the importance of translating combat successes into political gains.[23] These documents explain that soldiers will need to undertake several types of operations—offense, defense, and stability—at once. In this vein, the army is also playing a leading role advancing the view that the "phasing" construct used to plan for wars should be rethought and that campaign plans must consider the continuum of conflict. A goal is to replace the flawed phrase "postwar" with the concept of consolidation and the need to support combat gains with political and economic measures that lead to the accomplishment of desired aims.

Army leaders have also expanded the concept of combined arms—which traditionally focused on combining various kinetic capabilities such as firepower and airpower—to include the integration of efforts "critical to consolidating gains and ensuring progress toward accomplishing strategic objectives."[24] These might include tasks such as building security forces, restoring essential services, and facilitating political and economic development. Finally, the army has also adopted a new warfighting function, called "engagement."[25] Warfighting functions are important because they drive the kind of training and education soldiers receive. Before 2014, there were six: mission command, movement and maneuver, intelligence, fires, sustainment, and protection. The adoption of the new warfighting function recognized that the existing six did not adequately capture the full range of army experiences during wartime and that a new one was needed to describe the lessons of Iraq and Afghanistan.

## FINAL THOUGHTS

These are important steps forward, but American denial syndrome remains powerful. The goal of a statesman must be to avoid war. But there will be times when war will be necessary to protect American interests. As Henry Kissinger has observed, "Conflicts within and between societies have occurred since the dawn of civilization."[26] And with the decision to go to war, American forces must understand and influence the populations among whom the war is fought. Military intervention also requires American leaders to develop a strategy that defines what that intervention seeks to achieve and how all the elements of national power are to be combined to accomplish wartime goals. Because the cause of conflict most often entails political competitions for power, resources, and survival, accomplishing wartime goals requires the consolidation of military gains politically. Violence removes and destroys but does not reconstruct. In recent conflicts a failure to reconstruct in the wake of apparently successful military operations has perpetuated rather than reduced threats to national and international security.

Shortly after the US-led coalition bombing in Libya and the death of its dictator, Muammar Qaddafi, Secretary of State Hillary Clinton observed, "We came, we saw, he died,"[27] a pronouncement that sounded eerily like George Bush's announcement of "victory" as American troops entered Baghdad in April 2003. We do ourselves an enormous disservice to think that we can "come, kill, and leave." It is an opprobrious waste of lives if nothing better results. In the United States, elected civilian leaders take the decision to intervene in a country, and it is their responsibility to understand the factors—political, military, social, and economic—that are likely to *reduce* the success of an intervention and that may thus give pause *before* committing to war.

As the cases in this book have shown, the problem of political consolidation following war is intertwined with debates about "nation building," the "export of democracy," and "state building." During the World War II period, officers worried that "our military government plans have been attacked as unprecedented, un-American, imperialistic, grandiose and personally ambitious."[28] Similar concerns are voiced today. Scholars argue that it is "time to lay to rest the 100-year-old Wilsonian drive to democratize the world."[29] The highly respected development economist William Easterly criticized military efforts to conduct stability operations as "social engineering," which, "if put into practice," creates "delusions" of excessive ambition and generates the "excessive use of military force, which kills real human beings."[30] Partly owing to such concerns, there is often pressure to strike enemy targets from afar. This technology-centric approach to war is rooted in an understandable concern about sacrificing American lives but also in the deep ambivalence about thinking through the relationship between violence and political order.

Such arguments, however, leave us with several uncomfortable questions. Without some idea of what one wants to leave behind—and how to create a certain order—war is disconnected from politics and becomes a purely destructive act. Fighting wars requires a connection to political order to fulfill the moral and practical requirement to establish a just end and baseline of stability following combat operations. This does not mean that the United States must *impose* its system or engage in elaborate state building. It does mean that the United States, multinational partners, and local actors must work together to establish a sustainable baseline of stability such that people can proceed to reconstruct their lives. While countless debates have unfolded over the immorality and wrongheadedness of war, what is the morality of leaving behind chaos? Oxford University's Paul Collier has estimated that the cost of a failing state over the entire history of its failure, for itself and its neighbors, is $100 billion, not counting civil wars or the horrors generated by disorder. Because threats to security emanate from disorder in areas where governance and rule of law are weak, defeating enemy forces and networks requires integrated efforts that aim to strengthen institutions that are essential to sustainable security. Knowing what you are getting into and preparing for it does not make you more prone to war; it ensures that you are prepared better for its demands and are able to achieve an outcome worthy of the cost and sacrifice that are inherent in armed conflict. An emphasis on early and effective consolidation activities as a part of a campaign can shorten a war.

During the entire period of President Obama's time in office, he oversaw two wars in which success hinged on the problem of consolidation. Nonetheless, he apparently embarked on new operations without thinking about the centrality of how to consolidate combat successes. On October 20, 2011, the day that Qaddafi was killed, Obama announced that we had "achieved our objectives." Three years later, he regretfully spoke of the "lesson I had to learn that still has ramifications to this day." While he affirmed that the intervention was "the right thing to do," he acknowledged that he had "underestimated the need to come in full force" and that there had to be a "much more aggressive effort to rebuild societies that didn't have any civic traditions." He explained that that was "a lesson that I now apply every time I ask the question, 'Should we intervene, militarily? Do we have an answer [for] the day after?"[31] That question, astonishing after well over a decade of war in Iraq and Afghanistan, sadly suggests that American denial syndrome persists. And that the themes explored in this book remain salient today.

# NOTES

1. Winston Churchill, *The Second World War: The Grand Alliance*, vol. 3 (Houghton Mifflin, 1986), 24.

2. Office of the Special Inspector General for Iraq, *Learning from Iraq*, 21.

3. See Hunt, *American Struggle*, esp. chap. 3, and Krepinevich, *Army and Vietnam*; Sorley, *A Better War*. The latter book is devoted to explaining the shift in strategy after the replacement of Gen. William Westmoreland by Gen. Creighton Abrams, who believed that the key to winning the war lay in the "hamlets and villages of South Vietnam." See p. 10. Another study is Komer, *Bureaucracy at War*.

4. Defense Strategic Guidance, January 2012, http://archive.defense.gov/news/Defense _Strategic_Guidance.pdf.

5. Swarm, "Impact of the Proconsular Experience," 399.

6. James E. Webb, director of the Bureau of Budget for FDR, February 6, 1943, WDCSA files 386 Africa, 1942, reproduced in Coles and Weinberg, *Civil Affairs*, 60.

7. Komer, *Bureaucracy at War*, 81.

8. Chairman of the Joint Chiefs of Staff, *The National Military Strategy of the United States of America: A Strategy for Today; a Vision for Tomorrow*, 2004, http://archive.defense .gov/news/Mar2005/d20050318nms.pdf.

9. See "Memo, Wickersham, Comdt, SMG, for PMG, 17 June 1942," cited in Coles and Weinberg, *Civil Affairs*, 12.

10. Oral history interview with Lucius D. Clay, July 16, 1974, conducted by Richard McKinzie, online at the Truman Presidential Library and Museum, http://www.truman library.org/oralhist/clayl.htm. See also Clay, *Decision in Germany*, 53.

11. Michael Hirsh, "Endgame: How Will We Know When We Can Finally Leave?" *Washington Post*, September 26, 2004. Hirsh interviewed Bremer for this article. And to further make this point: I was contacted in the spring of 2003 by officials in the Office of the Secretary of Defense who were inquiring about the relationship between John McCloy and Lucius Clay. The sense from my conversation was that there was not a clear under-

standing that General Clay had done most of the reconstruction as military governor and that McCloy was the civilian administrator later.

12. Former Secretary of Defense Gates stated that President Bush had made this statement when he addressed a meeting of the National Security Council. See Thom Shanker and David Cloud, "Military Wants More Civilians to Help in Iraq," *New York Times*, February 7, 2007, http://www.nytimes.com/2007/02/07/washington/07military.html ?pagewanted=all.

13. Stabilization and Reconstruction Civilian Management Act of 2004 (S 2127, 108th Cong.), http://www.gpo.gov/fdsys/pkg/BILLS-108s2127rs/pdf/BILLS-108s2127rs.pdf.

14. Ibid.

15. Lord, *Proconsuls*, 229–30.

16. See General Franks's comments in his book *American Solder*, 422.

17. I make this point in "Six Seductive Stories That Undercut the Army," *War on the Rocks*, October 9, 2015.

18. H. R. McMaster, "The Pipe Dream of Easy War," *New York Times*, July 21, 2013, http://www.nytimes.com/2013/07/21/opinion/sunday/the-pipe-dream-of-easy-war.html ?_r=0.

19. As told to retired US Army colonel Derek Harvey, former CENTCOM planner in Iraq. Used with his permission here.

20. From remarks made by Dr. Conrad Crane, US Army Historian, Strategic Studies Institute, Army War College, at the army-sponsored July 2015 Historical Lessons Learned Conference in Laurel, MD.

21. Stability Operations are now a core mission, as noted in Army Doctrinal Publication 1, *The Army*, October 2012, 1–3, http://www.apd.army.mil/Search/ePubsSearch /ePubsSearchForm.aspx?x=ADP. The army has also advanced, in conjunction with the Marine Corps, a concept of Strategic Landpower that explains that the sustainment of combat victories requires an understanding of the contested cultural, political, and economic landscape in which US troops will operate. See Strategic Landpower Task Force paper, May 2013 signed by Gen. Raymond Odierno, Gen. James Amos, and Adm. William McRaven, http://www.arcic.army.mil/app_Documents/Strategic-Landpower-White-Paper -06MAY2013.pdf.

22. US Dept. of the Army, *Field Manual 3-0: Stability Operations*, October 2008, HQ, Department of the Army.

23. US Dept. of the Army, *Army Operating Concept*, October 2014, iii, and US Dept. of the Army, *Army Capstone Concept*, TRADOC pamphlet 525-3-0, December 2009, 15, 19, 31, 32.

24. US Dept. of the Army, *Army Operating Concept*.

25. US Dept. of the Army, *Functional Concept for Engagement*, TRADOC pamphlet 525–8-5, October 2014, http://www.tradoc.army.mil/tpubs/pams/tp525-8-5.pdf. Engagement falls short of placing these activities squarely within "war proper" and discusses them more as parts of a prewar shaping phase of an interaction. Its emphasis is on how shaping events beforehand could help to avoid the outbreak of conflict. While this is certainly desirable, equally important is how governance-related tasks are an integral part of war itself. The term "consolidate" more closely links the relationship between combat and stability.

26. Henry Kissinger, *World Order* (New York: Penguin, 2014), 345.

27. Corbett Daly, "We Came, We Saw, He Died," CBS News, October 20, 2011. This report is of a news interview that Secretary of State Hillary Clinton did when she met with leaders of Libya's National Transitional Council. The written report is at http://www .cbsnews.com/news/clinton-on-qaddafi-we-came-we-saw-he-died/. A video clip is at http:// www.cbsnews.com/videos/clinton-on-qaddafi-we-came-we-saw-he-died/?lumiereId=501135 26&videoId=676582e1-8bdf-11e2-9400-029118418759&cbsId=7385396&site=cbsnews.

28. "Gullion Memo for BG Edwin Watson, Secy to the President, 6 February 1943," cited in Coles and Weinberg, *Civil Affairs*, 28. This concern was especially apparent in the 1960s, and US officials were sensitive to it. State Department officials recognized that "Latin Americans so not want a paternalistic United States deciding which particular political faction should rule their countries," and they do not want the United States to "launch itself" on a civilizing mission, no matter how good its intentions. "Remarks of Under Secretary of State for Economic Affairs Thomas C. Mann before the Annual Meeting of the Inter American Press Association at San Diego, CA, October 12, 1965," Department of State Archives, no. 241, 1.

29. Amitai Etzioni, "Democratisation Mirage," 139–56.

30. William Easterly, "J'Accuse: The US Army's Development Delusions," June 18, 2009, AIDWATCH blog, http://aidwatchers.com/2009/06/j%E2%80%99accuse-the-us-army %E2%80%99s-development-delusions/.

31. Friedman, "Obama on the World."

# SELECTED BIBLIOGRAPHY

## ARCHIVAL SOURCES

Center of Military History, Fort McNair, Washington, DC
National Archives, College Park, MD
    Record Group 165: Records of the War Department General and Special Staffs
    Record Group 260: Records of US Occupation Headquarters, World War II
    Record Group 319: Records of the Army Staff
    Record Group 332: Records of US Theaters of War, World War II
    Record Group 338: Records of US Army Operational, Tactical, and Support Organizations (World War II and Thereafter)
    Record Group 350: Records of the Bureau of Insular Affairs, 1868–1945
US Army Military History Institute (archives now within the Military History Institute of the Army Heritage Education Center, Carlisle, PA)
US Special Operations Command Archives, Fort Bragg, NC

## OTHER SOURCES

Acheson, Dean. *Present at the Creation: My Years in the State Department.* New York: W. W. Norton, 1987 (first published 1969).
"Administration Policy Decisions on Peacekeeping Operations." *Foreign Policy Bulletin* 5 (July–August 1994): 72–77.
Alger, Russell Alexander. *The Spanish-American War.* New York: Harper & Brothers, 1901.
Allen, Henry T. *The Rhineland Occupation.* Indianapolis: Bobbs-Merrill, 1927.
Ambrose, Stephen E. *Duty, Honor, Country: A History of West Point.* Baltimore: Johns Hopkins University Press, 1999.

---

Sources that appear only once in the text are not included in the bibliography. Full publication information may be found in the notes section.

"American Policy in Occupied Areas." A series of articles reprinted from the *Department of State Bulletin* of July 14, 1946, August 18, 1946, February 9, 1947, and March 9, 1947. Washington, DC: Government Printing Office (GPO). Publication #2794, n.d.

Appleman, Roy N. *South to the Naktong, North to the Yalu (June–November 1950).* United States Army in the Korean War Series. Washington, DC: Center of Military History, US Army, 1961.

Ash, Stephen V. *When the Yankees Came: Conflict and Chaos in the Occupied South 1861–1865.* Chapel Hill: University of North Carolina Press, 1995.

Bacon, Robert, and James Brown Scott, eds. *The Military and Colonial Policy of the United States: Addresses and Reports by Elihu Root.* Cambridge, MA: Harvard University Press, 1916.

Bagget, James Alex. "Emancipation, Freedmen, and the Freedmen's Bureau." In *The American Civil War: A Handbook of Literature and Research,* edited by Steven E. Woodworth. Westport, CT: Greenwood Press, 1996.

Baily, Thomas. *Woodrow Wilson and the Lost Peace.* New York: Macmillan, 1944.

Baker, George T. "Mexico City and the War with the United States: A Study in the Politics of Military Occupation." PhD diss., Duke University, 1970.

Baker, Ray Stannard. *Woodrow Wilson: Life and Letters.* 8 vols. New York: Scribner, 1931–39.

Ball, George. *The Past Has Another Pattern: Memoirs.* New York: Norton, 1982.

Ballard, John R., David Lamm, and James K. Wood. *From Kabul to Baghdad and Back: The United States at War in Afghanistan and Iraq.* Annapolis, MD: Naval Institute Press, 2012.

Barnes, Rudolph C. "Civil Affairs, a LIC Priority." *Military Review* 68, no. 9 (September 1988): 38–49.

Barno, David W. "Fighting the Other War: Counterinsurgency Strategy in Afghanistan, 2003–2005." *Military Review* 5 (September–October 2007): 32–44.

Barrett, Raymond J. "Updating Civil Affairs Doctrine and Organization." *Military Review* 54, no.7 (July 1974): 50–61.

Basler, Roy P., ed. *Collected Works of Abraham Lincoln.* 8 vols. and index. New Brunswick, NJ: Rutgers University Press, 1953.

Bauer, Jack K. *The Mexican War 1846–1848.* New York: Macmillan, 1974.

Bennett, William C. "Just Cause and the Principles of War." *Military Review* 71, no. 3 (March 1991): 2–13.

Benson, George C. S., and Mark Dewolf Howe. "Military Government Organizational Relationships." In *American Experiences in Military Government in World War II,* edited by Carl J. Friedrich. New York: Rinehart, 1948.

Benson, George C. S., and Maurice Neufeld. "American Military Government in Italy." In Friedrich, *American Experiences in Military Government.*

Benson, Kevin C., and Christopher B. Thrash. "Declaring Victory: Planning Exit Strategies for Peace Operations." *Parameters* 26 (Autumn 1996): 69–80.

Bentley, George. *A History of the Freedmen's Bureau.* New York: Octagon Books, 1970.

Berge, Dennis E. "A Mexican Dilemma: The Mexico City Ayuntamiento and the Question of Loyalty, 1846–1848." *Hispanic American Historical Review* 50, no. 2 (May 1970): 229–56.

Bergeron, Paul H., ed. *The Papers of Andrew Johnson.* Vol. 12, *February–August 1867.* Knoxville: University of Tennessee Press, 1995,

Berthoff, Rowland T. "Taft and MacArthur, 1900–1901: A Study in Civil-Military Relations." *World Politics* 5 (January 1953): 196–213.

Bethel, Elizabeth. "The Freedman's Bureau in Alabama." *Journal of Southern History* 14, no. 1 (February 1948): 49–92.

Birtle, Andrew. *U.S. Army Counterinsurgency and Contingency Operations, 1860–1941.* Washington, DC: Center of Military History, US Army, 1998.

Blaufarb, Douglas S. *The Counterinsurgency Era: U.S. Doctrine and Performance 1950 to the Present.* New York: Free Press, 1977.

Blount, James H. *The American Occupation of the Philippines, 1898–1912.* New York: G. P. Putnam's, 1912.

Boose, Donald W., Jr., "Portentous Sideshow: The Korean Occupation Decision." *Parameters* 25, no. 4 (Winter 1995–96): 112–29.

Borton, Hugh. "Occupation Policies in Japan and Korea." *Annals of the American Academy of Social Science* (January 1948): 146–55.

———. "United States Occupation Policies in Japan." *Political Science Quarterly* 62 (June 1947): 250–57.

Boutrese, Arthur, Philip Taylor, and Arthur Maass. "American Military Government Experience in Japan." In Friedrich, *American Experiences in Military Government.*

Braibanti, Ralph. "Administration of Military Government at the Prefectural Level in Japan." *American Political Science Review* 43, no. 2 (April 1949): 250–74.

———. "Occupation Controls in Japan." *Far Eastern Survey* 17 (September 22, 1948): 215–19.

Bremer, L. Paul. *My Year in Iraq: The Struggle to Build a Future of Hope.* New York: Simon & Schuster, 2006.

Brennan, Richard R., Jr., Charles Ries, and Larry Hanauer. *Ending the U.S. War in Iraq: The Final Transition, Operational Maneuver, and Disestablishment of United States Forces–Iraq.* Washington, DC: RAND, 2013.

Buckley, Kevin. *Panama: The Whole Story.* New York: Simon & Schuster, 1991.

Buehrig, Edward H. *Woodrow Wilson and the Balance of Power.* Bloomington: Indiana University Press, 1955.

Builder, Carl H. *The Masks of War: America Military Styles in Strategy and Analysis.* Baltimore: Johns Hopkins University Press, 1989.

Bullard, Robert L. "The Army in Cuba." *Journal of the Military Science Institute of the United States* 41 (September–October 1907): 152–57.

Bullard, Robert Lee. "The Citizen Soldier: The Volunteer." *Journal of the Military Service Institute of the United States* 39 (September–October 1906): 153–67.

———. "Military Pacification." *Journal of the Military Science Institute of the United States* 46 (January–February 1910): 1–24.

———. *Personalities and Reminiscences of the War.* Garden City, NY: Doubleday, Page, 1925.

Bush, George H. W. "Panama: The Decision to Use Force." *Vital Speeches of the Day* 56 (January 15, 1990): 194–95.

Butler, Benjamin F. *Butler's Book.* Boston: A. M. Thayer, 1892.

Callwell, Charles E. *Small Wars: Their Principles and Practice.* 3rd ed. New York: Free Press, 1965.

Capers, Gerald M. *Occupied City: New Orleans under the Federals, 1862–1865.* Lexington: University of Kentucky Press, 1965.

Carnes, Mary. "The American Occupation of New Mexico, 1821–1852." *New Mexico Historical Review* 14, no. 1 (1939): 34–75.

Carpenter, A. H. "Military Government of Southern Territory, 1861–1865." *Annual Report of the American Historical Association for the Year 1900.* Vol. 1. Submitted to the House of Representatives, 56th Congress, 2nd Session, Document No. 548. Washington, DC: GPO, 1901: 467–98.

Cha, Sangshul. "The Search for a 'Graceful Exit': General John Reed Hodge and American Occupation Policy in Korea, 1945–1948." PhD diss., Miami University, 1986.

Chayes, Antonia Handler, and George T. Raach. *Peace Operations.* Washington, DC: National Defense University Press, 1995.

Cimbala, Paul A., and Randall M. Miller, eds. *The Freedmen's Bureau and Reconstruction: Reconsiderations.* New York: Fordham University Press, 1999.

Clark, Colin. "U.S. Military to Scrap COIN, Focus on Pacific." *AOL Defense,* November 17, 2011.

Clark, Dale. "Conflicts over Planning at Staff Headquarters." In Friedrich, *American Experiences in Military Government.*

Clark, Mark. *From the Danube to the Yalu.* New York: Harper & Brothers, 1954.

Clarke, Dwight D. *Stephen Watts Kearny, Soldier of the West.* Norman: University of Oklahoma Press, 1961.

Clausewitz, Carl von. *On War.* Edited and translated by Michael Howard and Peter Paret. Princeton, NJ: Princeton University Press, 1989.

———. "Two Letters on Strategy." In *Understanding War: Essays on Clausewitz and the History of Military Power,* edited by Peter Paret. Princeton, NJ: Princeton University Press, 1992.

Clay, Lucius D. *Decision in Germany: A Personal Report on the Four Crucial Years That Set the Course of Future World History.* Garden City, NY: Doubleday, 1950.

Cline, Ray S. *Washington Command Post: The Operations Division.* Washington, DC: GPO, 1951.

Coakley, R. A. *The Role of Federal Forces in Domestic Disorders, 1789–1878.* Army Historical Series. Washington, DC: Center of Military History, US Army, 1988.

Coffman, Edward M. *The Hilt of the Sword: The Career of Peyton C. March.* Madison: University of Wisconsin Press, 1966.

———. *The Old Army: A Portrait of the American Army in Peacetime 1784–1898.* New York: Oxford University Press, 1989.

Cole, Ronald H. *Operation Just Cause: The Planning and Execution of Joint Operations in Panama, February 1988–January 1990.* Washington, DC: Joint History Office, Office of the Chairman of the Joint Chiefs of Staff, 1995.

Coles, Harry L., and Albert K. Weinberg. *Civil Affairs: Soldiers Become Governors.* United States Army in World War II Series. Washington, DC: Center of Military History, US Army, 1964.

Collins, James Lawton, Jr. *The Development and Training of the South Vietnamese Army, 1950–1972.* Vietnam Studies. Washington, DC: Center of Military History, US Army, 1975.

Collins, Joseph. *Understanding War in Afghanistan.* Washington, DC: National Defense University Press, 2011.

Connor, Seymour, and Odie Faulk. *North America Divided: The Mexican War, 1846–1848.* New York: Oxford University Press, 1971.

Cooke, James J. *The Rainbow Division in the Great War*. Westport, CT: Praeger, 1994.

Cordesman, Anthony H. "Iraq's Sectarian and Ethnic Violence and the Evolving Insurgency: Developments through mid-December 2006." CSIS Working Paper. Updated December 14, 2006.

Cordesman, Anthony H., David Kasten, and Adam Mausner. *Winning in Afghanistan: Creating Effective Afghan Security Forces*. Washington, DC: Center for Strategic and International Studies, 2009.

Cosmas, Graham. *An Army for Empire: The United States Army in the Spanish-American War*. College Station: Texas A&M University Press, 1994.

———. "From Order to Chaos: The War Department, the National Guard, and Military Policy, 1898." *Military Affairs* 29, no. 3 (Autumn 1965): 105–22.

———. "Military Reform after the Spanish-American War: The Army Reorganization Fight of 1898–1899." *Military Affairs* 35, no. 1 (February 1971): 12–18.

———. "Security the Fruits of Victory: The U.S. Army Occupies Cuba 1898–1899." *Military Affairs* 38, no. 3 (October 1974): 85–91.

Courtenay, William. "The Politico-Strategic Problem of Korea." *Military Review* 28, no. 7 (October 1948): 78–82.

Cowdrey, Albert E. *United States Army in the Korean War: The Medics' War*. Washington, DC: Center of Military History, US Army, 1987.

Craig, Gordon. *Germany, 1866–1945*. New York: Oxford University Press, 1978.

Cramer, Frederick H. "Reeducation of Germany: An American Experiment." *Forum* 105 (October 1945): 114–19.

Crane, Conrad D. "The Lure of Strike." *Parameters* 43 (Summer 2013): 5–12.

Crane, Conrad D., and W. Andrew Terrill. *Reconstructing Iraq: Insights, Challenges, and Missions for Military Forces in a Post-Conflict Scenario*. Carlisle, PA: Strategic Studies Institute, US Army War College Press, February 2003.

Crawford, Michael J., Mark Hayes, and Michael D. Session. *The Spanish-American War: Historical Overview and Select Bibliography*. Naval History Bibliographies, no. 5. Washington, DC: Naval Historical Center, Department of the Navy, 1998.

Cumings, Bruce. *The Origins of the Korean War*. Princeton, NJ: Princeton University Press, 1990.

Dale, Catherine. *Operation Iraqi Freedom: Strategies, Approaches, Results, and Issues for Congress*. Washington, DC: Congressional Research Service, March 28, 2008.

Dandar, Edward F., Jr. "Civil Affairs Operations." In *Operation Just Cause: The US Intervention in Panama*, edited by Bruce W. Watson and Peter G. Tsouras. Boulder, CO: Westview, 1991.

Daugherty, William E., and Andrews, Marshall. "A Review of U.S. Historical Experience with Civil Affairs 1776–1954." A Special Study of the Operations Research Office, OrO-TP-29. Bethesda, MD: Johns Hopkins University Press, 1961.

Davis, Franklin M. *Come as Conqueror: The United States Army's Occupation of Germany, 1945–1949*. New York: Macmillan, 1967.

Dawes, Charles G. *A Journal of Reparations*. London: Macmillan, 1939.

Dawson, Joseph G., III. "American Civil-Military Relations and Military Government: The Service of Colonel Alexander Doniphan in the Mexican War." *Armed Forces and Society* 22 (Summer 1996): 555–72.

———. *Army Generals and Reconstruction: Louisiana 1862–1877*. Baton Rouge: Louisiana State University Press, 1982.

————. "The US Army in the South: Reconstruction as Nation Building." Paper presented to the Combat Studies Combat Studies Institute conference "Armed Diplomacy: Two Centuries of American Campaigning," US Army Command and General Staff College, Fort Leavenworth, Kansas, August 5–7, 2003. http://usacac.army.mil/cac2/cgsc/carl/download/csipubs/ArmedDiplomacy_TwoCenturiesOfAmericanCampaigning.pdf.

————. "'Zealous for Annexation': Volunteer Soldiering, Military Government, and the Service of Alexander Doniphan in the Mexican-American War." *Journal of Strategic Studies* 19, no. 4 (December 1996): 10–36.

De Pauw, John W., and George W. Luz. *Winning the Peace: The Strategic Implications of Military Civic Action.* Westport, CT: Praeger, 1992.

Dickman, Joseph T. *The Great Crusade: A Narrative of the World War.* New York: D. Appleton, 1927.

Dobbins, James. *After the Taliban: Nation-Building in Afghanistan.* Washington, DC: Potomac Books, 2008.

Dobbins, James, John G. McGinn, Keith Crane, Seth G. Jones, Rollie Lal, Andrew Rathmell, Rachel Swanger, and Anga Timilsina. *America's Role in Nation-Building: From Germany to Iraq.* Washington, DC: RAND, 2003.

Donnelly, Thomas, Margaret Roth, and Caleb Baker. *Operation Just Cause: The Storming of Panama.* New York: Lexington Books, 1991.

Dorn, Walter L. "The Debate over American Occupation Policy in Germany in 1944–1945." *Political Science Quarterly* 72, no. 4 (December 1957): 481–501.

Dower, John W. *Embracing Defeat: Japan and in the Wake of World War II.* New York: W. W. Norton, 1999.

Dubik, James M. *Building Security Forces and Ministerial Capacity: Iraq as a Primer.* Washington, DC: Institute for the Study of War, May 2010.

————. *Creating Police and Law Enforcement Systems.* Washington, DC: Institute for the Study of War, May 2010.

————. "FM 100–5 and Counterinsurgency Warfare." *Military Review* 63, no. 11 (November 1983): 41–48.

Dufour, Charles L. *The Mexican War: A Compact History 1846–1848.* New York: Hawthorne Books, 1968.

Dunning, William A. "Military Government in the South during Reconstruction." *Political Science Quarterly* 12, no. 3 (September 1897): 381–406.

Echevarria, Antulio. *Reconsidering the American Way of War: US Military Practice from the Revolution to Afghanistan.* Washington, DC: Georgetown University Press, 2014.

————. "Transforming the Army's Way of Battle: Revising Our Abstract Knowledge." In *The Future of the Army Profession,* edited by Lloyd J. Matthews and Don M. Snider. Boston: McGraw-Hill, 2005.

Edwards, Morris Oswald. "A Case Study of Military Government in Germany during and after World War II." PhD diss., Georgetown University, 1957.

Eikenberry, Karl W. "The Challenge of Peacekeeping." *Army* (September 1993): 14–20.

Eisenhower, Dwight D. *Crusade in Europe.* Garden City, NY: Doubleday, 1950.

Eisenhower, John S. D. *Agent of Destiny: The Life and Times of General Winfield Scott.* Norman: University of Oklahoma Press, 1997.

Elliot, Charles Winslow. *Winfield Scott: The Soldier and the Man.* New York: Macmillan, 1937.

Elliott, Michael. "The Battle over Peacekeeping." *Time,* February 24, 2002.

Etzioni, Amitai. "The Democratisation Mirage." *Survival: Global Politics and Strategy* 57, no. 4 (August–September 2015): 139–56.

Fahey, Daniel Cox. "The Overall U.S. Politico-Military-Complex, and the U.S. Civil Affairs / Military Government Organization." September 16, 1953. Manuscript located in the US Army War College Library, Carlisle Barracks, PA. This copy of the Fahey Report contains a memorandum for the secretary of the army summarizing Fahey's points. The report itself was completed in February 1951. It is also reprinted in Roswell Wing, *Civil Affairs / Military Government Organization, Plans, and Training, 1953–1954,* cited below.

Fainsod, Merle. "The Development of American Military Government Policy in World War II." In Friedrich, *American Experiences in Military Government.*

Fastabend, David A. "Checking the Doctrinal Map: Can We Get There from Here with FM 100-5." *Parameters* 25 (Summer 1995): 37–46.

Fearey, Robert A. *The Occupation of Japan Second Phase: 1948–1950.* Westport, CT: Greenwood, 1950.

Feit, Edward. *The Armed Bureaucrats: Military Administrative Regimes and Political Development.* Boston: Houghton Mifflin, 1973.

Feith, Douglas. *War and Decision: Inside the Pentagon at the Dawn of the War on Terrorism.* New York: HarperCollins, 2008.

Finely, Randy. "The Personnel of the Freedmen's Bureau in Arkansas." In *The Freedmen's Bureau and Reconstruction: Reconsiderations,* edited by Paul A. Cimbala and Randall M. Miller. New York: Fordham University Press, 1999.

Finnegan, Patrick. "Operational Law." *Military Review* 76, no. 2 (March–April 1996): 29–37.

Fisch, Arnold G. *Military Government in the Ryukyu Islands: 1945–1950.* Washington, DC: Center of Military History, US Army, 1988.

Fishel, John T. *Civil-Military Operations in the New World.* Westport, CT: Praeger, 1997.

———. *The Fog of Peace: Planning and Executing the Restoration of Panama.* Carlisle Barracks, PA: US Army War College, Strategic Studies Institute, 1992.

Fishel, John T., and Richard D. Downie. "The Murky World of Conflict Termination: Planning and Executing the 1989–90 Restoration of Panama." *Small Wars and Insurgencies* 3 (Spring 1992): 58–71.

———. "Taking Responsibility for Our Actions? Establishing Order and Stability in Panama." *Military Review* 72, no. 4 (April 1992): 66–77.

Fisher, Thomas R. "Allied Military Government in Italy." *Annals of the American Academy of Political and Social Science* 267 (January 1950): 114–22.

Fitzpatrick, David J. "Emory Upton and the Citizen Soldier." *Journal of Military History* 65, no. 2 (April 2001): 355–90.

Flavin, William. *Civil Military Operations in Afghanistan: Observations on Civil Military Operations during the First Year of Operation Enduring Freedom.* Carlisle, PA: US Army Peace Keeping and Stability Operations Institute, March 2004.

Foch, Ferdinand. *The Memoirs of Marshal Foch.* Translated by T. Bentley Mott. Garden City, NY: Doubleday, Doran, 1931.

Fraenkel, Ernst. *Military Occupation and Rule of Law: Occupation Government in the Rhineland, 1918–1923.* New York: Oxford University Press, 1944.

Franklin, John Hope. *Reconstruction after the Civil War.* Chicago: University of Chicago Press, 1961.

Franks, Tommy. *American Soldier.* New York: Regan Books / HarperCollins, 2004.

Frederiksen, Oliver J. *The American Military Occupation of Germany, 1945–1953.* Historical Division, Headquarters, US Army, Europe, 1953.

Freeman, Joseph, and Scott Nearing. *Dollar Diplomacy: A Study in American Imperialism.* New York: Viking, 1925.

Freidel, Frank. "General Orders 100 and Military Government." *Mississippi Valley Historical Review* no. 32 (March 1946): 541–56.

Friedman, Thomas. "Obama on the World: President Obama Talks to Thomas Friedman about Iraq, Putin and Israel." *New York Times,* August 8, 2014.

Friedrich, Carl J. *American Experiences in Military Government in World War II.* New York: Rinehart, 1948.

———. "Three Phases of Field Operations in Germany 1945–1946." In Friedrich, *American Experiences in Military Government.*

Friedrich, Carl J., and Sydney Conner, eds. *Military Government.* Philadelphia: Annals of the American Academy of Political and Social Science, 1950.

Futrell, Robert J. "Federal Military Government in the South, 1861–1865." *Military Affairs* 15, no. 4 (Fall 1951): 181–91.

Gacek, Christopher. *The Logic of Force: The Dilemma of Limited War in American Foreign Policy.* New York: Columbia University Press, 1994.

Galula, David. *Counterinsurgency Warfare: Theory and Practice.* New York: Praeger, 1964.

Gates, John Morgan. *Schoolbooks and Krags: The United States Army in the Philippines 1898–1902.* Westport, CT: Greenwood, 1973.

Gentile, Gian. *Wrong Turn: America's Deadly Embrace of Counterinsurgency.* London: New Press, 2013.

Gilmore, Gerry. "Ambassador Khalilzad: U.S. Goals for Iraq Remain Unchanged." American Forces Press Service, Washington, DC, October, 24, 2006.

Gimbel, John. "American Military Government and the Education of a New German Leadership." *Political Science Quarterly* 83, no. 2 (June 1968): 248–67.

———. "Governing the American Zone of Germany." In *Americans as Proconsuls: United States Military Government in Germany and Japan, 1944–1952,* edited by Robert Wolfe. Carbondale: Southern Illinois University Press, 1958.

Glick, Edward B. *Peaceful Conflict: The Non-Military Use of the Military.* Harrisburg, PA: Stackpole Books, 1967.

Gordon, Michael, and Bernard Trainor. *Cobra II: The Inside Story of the Invasion and Occupation of Iraq.* New York: Pantheon, 2006.

———. *The Endgame: The Inside Story of the Struggle for Iraq, from George W. Bush to Barack Obama.* New York: Random House, 2012.

Govan, Gilbert E., and James W. Livingood. "Chattanooga under Military Occupation, 1863–1865." *Journal of Southern History* 17, no. 1 (February, 1951): 23–47.

Graber, Doris Appel. *The Development of the Law of Belligerent Occupation: 1863–1914*. New York: Columbia University Press, 1949.

Graf, Leroy P., and Ralph W. Haskins, eds. *The Papers of Andrew Johnson*. Knoxville: University of Tennessee Press, 1967.

Gray, Anthony, and Maxwell Manwaring. "Panama: Operation Just Cause." In *Policing the New World Disorder*, edited by Robert Oakley, Michael J. Dziedzic, and Eliot Goldberg. Washington, DC: National Defense University Press, 1988: 41–68.

Greenberg, Lawrence. *United States Army Unilateral and Coalition Operations in the 1965 Dominican Republic Intervention*. Historical Analysis Series. Washington, DC: Center of Military History, US Army, 1987.

Greene, Frances Vinton. *The Revolutionary War and the Military Policy of the United States*. New York: Charles Scribner's Sons, 1911.

Greenhut, Jeffrey, and Gerry Grey. "Civil Affairs in Operation Just Cause." *Special Warfare* 4, no. 1 (Winter 1991): 28–37.

Greentree, Todd. "Bureaucracy Does Its Thing: US Performance and the Institutional Dimension of Strategy in Afghanistan." *Journal of Strategic Studies* 36, no. 2 (April 2013): 261–88.

Grenville, John A. S., and George Berkeley Young. *Politics, Strategy and American Foreign Diplomacy: Studies in American Foreign Policy, 1873–1917*. New Haven: Yale University Press, 1966.

Grimsley, Mark. *The Hard Hand of War: Union Military Policy toward Southern Civilians, 1861–1865*. New York: Cambridge University Press, 1995.

Grivas, Theodore. *Military Governments in California, 1846–1850*. Glendale, CA: Arthur H. Clark, 1963.

Gulgowski, Paul. *American Military Government of United States Occupied Zones of Post World War II Germany in Relation to Policies Expressed by Its Civilian Governmental Authorities at Home, during the Course of 1944/5 through 1949*. Frankfurt/Main, Germany: Haag und Herchen, 1983.

Hadsel, Fred. "Reflections of the U.S. Commanders in Austria and Germany." In *U.S. Occupation in Europe after World War II: Papers and Reminiscences from the April 23–24 1976 Conference at the George C. Marshall Research Foundation*, edited by Hans A. Schmitt. Lawrence: Regents Press of Kansas, 1976.

Hagedorn, Hermann. *Leonard Wood: A Biography*. 2 vols. New York: Harper & Brothers, 1931.

Hamilton, Alexander [Publius]. "The Federalist VIII." In *The Debate on the Constitution: Federalist and Antifederalist Speeches, Articles, and Letters during the Struggle over Ratification*. Part 1, 334–35. New York: Library of America, 1993.

Hammes, T. X. "Raising and Mentoring Security Forces in Iraq and Afghanistan." In *Lessons Encountered: Learning from the Long War*, edited by Richard D. Hooker and Joseph Collins. Washington, DC: National Defense University Press, 2015.

Hartigan, Richard S. *Lieber's Code and the Law of War*. Chicago: Precedent, 1983.

Hayward, Edwin J. "Co-ordination of Military and Civilian Civil Affairs Planning." *Annals of the American Academy of Political and Social Science*, 267 (January 1950): 19–27.

————. "History of the Civil Affairs Division, War Department Special Staff, World War II, March 1946; Part I." Manuscript in the US Army Center of Military History.

Healy, David. *The United States in Cuba, 1898–1902: General's Politicians, and the Search for Policy.* Madison: University of Wisconsin Press, 1963.

Hearst, John A., Jr. "The Evolution of Allied Military Government in Italy. PhD diss., Columbia University, 1960.

Heneman, Harlow J. "American Control Organization in Germany." *Public Administration Review* 6 (February 1946): 1–9.

Hennessey, Melinda M. "Reconstruction Politics and the Military: The Eufaula Riot of 1874." *Alabama Historical Quarterly* 38 (Summer 1976): 12–125.

Hermes, Walter G. "Survey of the Development of the Role of the U.S. Military Advisor." Draft study, Office of Chief of Military History, US Army, n.d. Military History Institute Library, Carlisle Barracks, PA.

————. *Truce Tent and Fighting Front.* United States Army in the Korean War Series. Washington, DC: Center of Military History, US Army, 1966.

Herrera, Ricardo A. "Self-Governance and the American Citizen as Soldier, 1775–1861." *Journal of Military History* 65, no. 1 (January 2001): 21–52.

Hesseltine, William B. *Lincoln and the War Governors.* New York: Alfred A. Knopf, 1948.

————. *Lincoln's Plan of Reconstruction.* Gloucester, MA: Peter Smith, 1963.

Hille, Henry H. "Eighth Army's Role in Military Government of Japan." *Military Review* 27, no. 11 (February 1948): 9–18.

Hoag, Charles Leonard. "American Military Government in Korea: War Policy and the First Year of Occupation, 1941–1946." Draft manuscript produced under the auspices of the Office of the Chief of Military History, Department of the Army. Washington, DC: Army Military History Institute, 1970.

Holborn, Hajo. *American Military Government: Its Organization and Policies.* Washington, DC: Infantry Journal Press, 1947.

Holsten, Ned A. "Military Necessity, Humanity and Military Government." *Military Review* 36, no. 10 (January 1957): 15–21.

Hooker, Richard D., and Joseph J. Collins. *Lessons Encounter: Learning from the Long War.* Washington, DC: National Defense University Press, 2015.

Hughes, Charles E. "Secretary of State Remarks before the American Historical Association at New Haven, Connecticut, on December 29th, 1922." In Charles Dawes, *A Journal of Reparations.* London: Macmillan, 1939.

Hull, Cordell. *The War Memoirs of Cordell Hull.* Vol. 2. New York: Macmillan, 1948.

Hunt, Irvin L. *American Military Government of Occupied Germany, 1918–1920.* Report of the officer in charge of civil affairs, Third Army and American Forces Germany. 4 vols. First ed. Coblenz, 1920. Washington: GPO, 1943. http://www.history.army.mil/html/bookshelves/resmat/interwar_years/american_military_government_of_occupied_germany_1918-1920.pdf.

Hunt, Richard. *The American Struggle for Vietnam's Hearts and Minds.* Boulder, CO: Westview, 1995.

Huntington, Samuel. *The Solder and the State: The Theory and Politics of Civil-Military Relations.* 2nd ed. Cambridge, MA: Harvard University Press, 1985.

Huppert, Harry G. "Korean Occupational Problems." *Military Review* 24, no. 9 (December 1949): 9–16.

Hyman, Harold M. "Deceit in Dixie." *Civil War History* 3 (March 1957): 65–82.

Iklé, Fred Charles. *Every War Must End.* New York: Columbia University Press, 1991.

Jessup, Philip C. *Elihu Root.* New York: Archon Books, 1964; reprint of Dodd, Mead 1938 edition.

Johnson, James Turner. *Morality and Contemporary Warfare.* New Haven: Yale University Press, 1999.

Johnson, Lyndon B. *Johnson Presidential Press Conferences.* Vol. 1, *April 27, 1965.* New York: Earl M. Coleman Enterprises, 1978.

———. *The Vantage Point: Perspectives of the Presidency, 1963–1969.* New York: Holt, Rinehart and Winston, 1971.

Jones, Richard A. "The Nation Builder: Solider of the Sixties." *Military Review* 45, no. 1 (January 1965): 63–67.

Jones, Seth. *In the Graveyard of Empires: America's War in Afghanistan.* New York: W. W. Norton, 2009.

Jun, Sang-In. "State-Making in South Korea, 1945–48: US Occupation and Korean Development." PhD diss., Brown University, 1991.

Kagan, Kim. *The Surge: A Military History.* New York: Encounter Books, 2009.

Kang, Han Mu. "The United States Military Government in Korea, 1945–1948: An Analysis and Evaluation of Its Policy." PhD diss., University of Cincinnati, 1970.

Kaplan, Fred. *The Insurgents: David Petraeus and the Plot to Change the American Way of War.* New York: Simon & Schuster, 2013.

Katzmann, Kenneth. *Afghanistan: Current Issues and U.S. Policy.* Washington, DC: Congressional Research Service, October 24, 2002.

———. *Afghanistan: Postwar Governance, Security and U.S. Policy.* Washington, DC: Congressional Research Service, August 8, 2008.

———. *Iraq: Post-Saddam Governance and Security.* Washington, DC: Congressional Research Service, October 28, 2009.

Kennan, George F. *Memoirs, 1925–50.* Boston: Little, Brown, 1968.

Khalilzad, Zalmay, and George W. Casey Jr. "A Path to Success in Iraq." *Los Angeles Times,* April 11, 2006.

King, James E., Jr. *Civil Affairs: The Future Prospects of a Military Responsibility.* Staff Paper ORO-SP-55. Washington, DC: Operations Research Office, Johns Hopkins University, June 1958.

Komer, Robert W. *Bureaucracy at War: U.S. Performance in the Vietnam Conflict.* Boulder, CO: Westview, 1986.

———. *Bureaucracy Does Its Thing: Institutional Constraints on U.S.-GVN Performance in Vietnam.* RAND Report R-967-ARPA. Washington, DC: RAND, August 1972.

———. "Civil Affairs and Military Government in the Mediterranean Theater." Manuscript in the US Army Center of Military History.

———. "The Establishment of Allied Control in Italy." *Military Affairs* 13 (Spring 1949): 20–28.

Krepinevich, Andrew. *The Army and Vietnam.* Baltimore: Johns Hopkins University Press, 1986.

Kugler, Richard. *Operation Anaconda in Afghanistan: A Case Study of Adaptation in Battle.* Case Studies in Defense Transformation, no. 5. Washington, DC: National Defense University, prepared by the Center for Technology and National Security Policy, 2007.

Kyre, Martin T. "United States Army Civil Affairs Policy: An Attempt to Discover Its Predictable Ingredients." PhD diss., University of Washington, 1962.

LaFeber, Walter. *The American Search for Opportunity 1865–1913.* Cambridge History of American Foreign Relations, vol. 2. Cambridge: Cambridge University Press, 1993.

Langer, William L. "Critique of Imperialism." *Foreign Affairs* (October 1935): 102–19.

Leech, Margaret. *In the Days of McKinley.* New York: Harper & Brothers, 1959.

Licklider, Roy. "The American Way of State Building: Germany, Japan, Somalia and Panama." *Small Wars and Insurgencies* 10, no. 3 (1999): 82–115.

Liggett, Hunter. *Commanding an American Army: Recollections of the World War.* Boston: Houghton Mifflin, 1925.

Link, Arthur S. *Woodrow Wilson and the Progressive Era.* New York: Harper, 1954.

Linn, Brian. "The American Way of War Revisited." *Journal of Military History* 66 (April 2002): 502–33.

———. *The US Army and Counterinsurgency in the Philippine War, 1899–1902.* Chapel Hill: University of North Carolina Press, 1989.

Lord, Carnes. *Proconsuls: Delegated Political-Military Leadership from Rome to America Today.* Cambridge: Cambridge University Press, 2012: 229–30.

Lord, Carnes, and John R. Brinkerhoff, eds. *Civil Affairs: Perspectives and Prospects.* A study by the Institute for National Strategic Studies. Washington, DC: National Defense University, June 1993.

Luttwak, Edward. *On the Meaning of Victory: Essays on Strategy.* New York: Simon & Schuster, 1986.

Lyons, Gene M. *Military Policy and Economic Aid: The Korean Case, 1950–1953.* Columbus: Ohio State University Press, 1961.

MacArthur, Douglas. *Reminiscences.* New York: McGraw-Hill, 1964.

Malkasian, Carter. "Counterinsurgency in Iraq: May 2003–January 2007." In *Counterinsurgency in Modern Warfare,* edited by Daniel Marstan and Carter A. Malkasian. Oxford: Osprey, 2008.

Mansfield, Edward D. *Life and Services of General Winfield Scott.* New York A. S. Barnes, 1852.

March, Peyton C. *The Nation at War.* Westport, CT: Greenwood, 1970. Originally Garden City, NY: Doubleday, Doran, 1932.

Marquis, Susan. *Unconventional Warfare: Rebuilding U.S. Special Operations Forces.* Washington, DC: Brookings Institution Press, 1997.

Marstan, Daniel, and Carter A. Malkasian. *Counterinsurgency in Modern Warfare.* Oxford: Osprey, 2008.

Martin, Edwin M. *The Allied Occupation of Japan.* Stanford, CA: American Institute of Pacific Relations and Stanford University Press, 1948.

———. *Results of the Allied Occupation of Japan: An Interim Report.* American Institute of Pacific Relations, United States Paper no. 4. New York: Institute of Pacific Relations, 1947.

Masland, John W. "Postwar Government and Politics of Japan." *Journal of Politics* 9 (November 1947): 565–88.

Maslowski, Peter. *Treason Must Be Made Odious: Military Occupation and Wartime Reconstruction in Nashville, Tennessee, 1862–65.* Millwood, NY: KTO Press, 1978.

Matloff, Maurice. *American Military History.* Army Historical Series. Washington, DC: Center of Military History, US Army, 1969. Rev. ed. 1973.

Matray, James Irving. "End to Indifference: American's Korean Policy during WWII." *Diplomatic History* 2, no. 2 (1978): 184–85.

———. *The Reluctant Crusade: American Foreign Policy in Korea, 1941–1950.* Honolulu: University of Hawaii Press, 1985.

May, Ernest. *Imperial Democracy.* New York: Harcourt, Brace and World, 1961.

May, Ernest R., ed. *The Coming of War, 1917.* Chicago: Rand McNally, 1963.

———. *The World War and American Isolation, 1914–1917.* Cambridge, MA: Harvard University Press, 1959.

Mayer, Hugo E. *Operations Other Than War.* Fort Leavenworth, KS: TRADOC Analysis Center, Operations Analysis Center, February 1995.

Mayo, Marlene J. "American Wartime Planning for Occupied Japan: The Role of the Experts." In Wolfe, *Americans as Proconsuls.*

McAfee, Ward, and J. Cordell Robinson. *Origins of the Mexican War: A Documentary Source Book.* Vol. 2. Salisbury, NC: Documentary Publications, 1982.

McCaffrey, James M. *Army of Manifest Destiny: The American Soldier in the Mexican War, 1846–1848.* New York: New York University Press, 1992.

McChrystal, Stanley. *My Share of the Task.* New York: Penguin, 2013.

McCloy, John. "From Military to Self-Government." In Wolfe, *Americans as Proconsuls.*

———. "Our Military Government Policy in Germany." *Department of State Bulletin* (September 2, 1945): 310–11.

McCloy, John J. "American Occupation Policies in Germany." *Proceedings of the American Academy of Political Science* 21 (January 1946): 540–51.

McCreedy, Kenneth O. "Planning the Peace: Operation Eclipse and the Occupation of Germany," *Journal of Military History* 65, no. 3 (July 2001): 713–39.

———. *Winning the Peace: Postconflict Operations.* Fort Leavenworth, KS: Command and General Staff College, December 21, 1994.

McCune, George M. "Occupation Politics in Korea." *Far Eastern Survey* (February 13, 1946): 33–37.

McDonough, James. *Schofield: Union General in Civil War and Reconstruction.* Tallahassee: Florida State University Press, 1972.

McKitrick, Eric L. *Andrew Johnson and Reconstruction.* Chicago: University of Chicago Press, 1964.

McMaster, H. R. "The Pipe Dream of Easy War." *New York Times,* July 20, 2013.

McNaugher, Thomas. "Mission Stretch: The Army and Operations Other than War. In *The Future of the Profession,* edited by Don Snider and Gayle Watkins. New York: McGraw-Hill, 2002.

McPherson, James M. *Ordeal by Fire: The Civil War and Reconstruction.* New York: Alfred A. Knopf, 1982.

Meade, Edward Grant. *American Military Government in Korea.* New York: King's Crown Press of Columbia University, 1951

Meyer, Douglas K. "Civil Affairs in Panama: Is CA a Viable Asset for Future Conflicts?" Air War College Associate Studies. Randolph AFB, San Antonio, TX: Air University Press, November 1990. This Meyer paper was located in the USASOCOM Library, Fort Bragg, GA, cabinet 3, drawer 1, folder CA in Panama.

Mezes, Sidney Edward. "Preparations for Peace." In *What Really Happened at Paris: The Story of the Peace Conference, 1918–1910,* edited by Edward Mandell House and Charles Seymour. New York: Charles Scribner's Sons, 1921.

Miles, Nelson A. *Serving the Republic.* New York: Harper & Brothers, 1911.

———. "The War with Spain." Part I. *North American Review* 168, no. 510 (May 1899): 513–29.

Miller, James E. *The United States and Italy, 1940–1950: The Politics and Diplomacy of Stabilization.* Chapel Hill: University of North Carolina Press, 1986.

Miller, John, Jr., Owen J. Carroll, and Margaret E. Tackley. *Korea 1951–1953.* Washington, DC: Office of the Chief of Military History, Department of the Army, 1962.

Millet, Richard L. "The Aftermath of Intervention: Panama 1990." *Journal of InterAmerican Studies & World Affairs* 32 (Spring 1990): 1–15.

Millett, Allan R. *The Politics of Intervention: The Military Occupation of Cuba, 1906–1909.* Columbus: Ohio State University Press, 1968.

Millett, Allan R., and Peter Maslowski. *For the Common Defense: A Military History of the United States of America.* New York: Free Press, 1994.

Millis, Walter. *Of Arms and Men: A Study in America Military History.* New Brunswick, NJ: Rutgers University Press, 1984.

Millis, Walter, ed. *American Military Thought.* Indianapolis: Bobbs-Merrill, 1966.

———. *The Forrestal Diaries.* New York: Viking, 1951.

———. *The War Reports of General of the Army George C. Marshall, General of the Army H. H. Arnold, Fleet Admiral Ernest J. King.* New York: Lippincott, 1947.

Minger, Ralph Eldin. "Taft, MacArthur, and the Establishment of Civil Government in the Philippines." *Ohio Historical Quarterly* 70 (October 1961): 308–31.

Morgenthau, Henry, Jr. "Postwar Treatment of Germany." *Annals of the American Academy of Political and Social Science* (July 1946): 125–29.

Morrison, James. *The Best School: West Point, the Pre-Civil War Years 1833–1866.* Kent, OH: Kent State University Press, 1986.

Mosely, Philip. "Dismemberment of Germany: The Allied Negotiations from Yalta to Potsdam." *Foreign Affairs* 28, no. 3 (April 1950): 487–98.

———. "The Occupation of Germany: New Light on How the Zones Were Drawn." *Foreign Affairs* 28, no. 4 (July 1950): 580–604.

Mossman, Billy C. *Ebb and Flow November 1950–July 1951.* United States Army in the Korean War. Washington, DC: Center of Military History, US Army, 1990.

Mrazek, James E. "Civil Assistance in Action." *Military Review* 35, no. 7 (October 1955): 30–36.

Mulrooney, Virginia Frances. "No Victor, No Vanquished: United States Military Government in the Philippine Islands, 1898–1901." PhD Diss, UCLA, 1975.

Murphy, Robert. *Diplomat among Warriors.* Garden City, NY: Doubleday, 1964.

Nenninger, Timothy K. *The Leavenworth Schools and the Old Army: Education, Professionalism and the Office Corps of the United States Army, 1881–1918.* Westport, CT: Greenwood, 1978.

Neumann, Brian, Lisa Mundey, and Jon Mikolashek. *Operation Enduring Freedom: March 2002–April 2005.* Washington, DC: Center of Military History, US Army, n.d.

Office of the Special Inspector General for Iraq Reconstruction. *Hard Lessons: The Iraq Reconstruction Experience.* Washington, DC: US Independent Agencies and Commissions, February 2009.

———. *Learning from Iraq: A Final Report of the Special Inspector General for Iraq Reconstruction.* Washington, DC: GPO, March 2013.

Olcott, Charles S. *The Life of William McKinley.* 2 vols. Boston: Houghton Mifflin, 1916.

Paddock, Alfred H. *U.S. Army Special Warfare: Its Origins; Psychological and Unconventional Warfare, 1941–1952.* Washington, DC: National Defense University Press, 1982.

Paschall, Rod. "Low-Intensity Conflict Doctrine: Who Needs It?" *Parameters* 15 (Autumn 1985): 33–45.

Palmer, Bruce. *Intervention in the Caribbean: The Dominican Crisis of 1965.* Lexington: University Press of Kentucky, 1989.

Paret, Peter, ed. *Understanding War: Essays on Clausewitz and the History of Military Power.* Princeton, NJ: Princeton University Press, 1992.

Perito, Robert M. *The U.S. Experience with Provincial Reconstruction Teams in Afghanistan: Lessons Learned.* US Institute of Peace Special Report 152. Washington, DC: US Institute of Peace, October 2005.

Pershing, John J. *My Experiences in the World War.* New York: Frederick A. Stokes, 1931.

Plischke, Elmer. "Denazification Law and Procedure." *American Journal of International Law* 41, no. 4 (October 1947): 807–27.

Polk, James K. *Polk: The Diary of a President 1845–1849.* Edited by Allan Nevins. New York: Longmans, Green, 1929. Reprint, New York: Capricorn Press, 1968.

Pollack, James K., James H. Meisel, and Henry L. Bretton. *Germany under Occupation: Illustrative Materials and Documents.* Ann Arbor, MI: George Wahr, 1949.

Pomeroy, Earl S. "The American Colonial Office." *Mississippi Valley Historical Review* 30, no. 4 (March, 1944): 521–32.

Powell, Colin. *An American Journey: An Autobiography.* New York: Random House, 1995.

Ranson, Edward. "Nelson A. Miles as Commanding General, 1895–1903." *Military Affairs* 24 (Winter 1965–66): 179–200.

Rasmussen, John Curtis, Jr. "The American Forces in Germany and Civil Affairs, July 1919–January 1923." PhD diss., University of Georgia, 1972.

Richardson, James D., ed. *A Compilation of the Messages and Papers of the Presidents, 1789–1897.* 10 vols. Washington, DC: GPO: 1896–1899.

Richter, William L. *The Army in Texas during Reconstruction, 1865–1870.* College Station: Texas A&M University Press, 1987.

Ridgway, Matthew B. *The Korean War.* Garden City, NY: Doubleday, 1967.

Rieff, David. "Blueprint for a Mess." *New York Times,* November 2, 2003.

Roosevelt, Theodore. "General Leonard Wood: A Model American Military Administrator." *Outlook* 61 (January 7, 1899): 19–22.

Root, Elihu. "The American Solider." Address by the secretary of war at the Marquette Club in Chicago, October 7, 1899. In Robert Bacon and James Scott Brown. *The Military and Colonial Policy of the United States*. Cambridge, MA: Harvard University Press, 1916: 3–13.

———. "The Character and Office of the American Army." In Robert Bacon and James Scott Brown. *The Military and Colonial Policy of the United States*. Cambridge, MA: Harvard University Press, 1916: 15–25.

———. *Five Years of the War Department*. Washington, DC: GPO, 1904. (Also published as *Five Years of the War Department following the War with Spain, 1899–1903*. Washington, DC: US War Department, 1904.)

Rosenfeld, Harvey. *Diary of a Dirty Little War: The Spanish-American War of 1898*. Westport, CT: Praeger, 2000.

Royall, Kenneth C. "Civil Functions of the Army in the Occupied Areas." *Military Review* 29, no. 5 (August 1949): 37–43.

Rumsfeld, Donald. "Beyond Nation Building," Remarks delivered at the Intrepid Sea-Air-Space Museum, New York, February 14, 2003. http://www.au.af.mil/au/awc/awcgate/dod/sp20030214-secdef0024.htm.

Sandler, Stanley S. *The Korean War: No Victors, No Vanquished*. Lexington: University Press of Kentucky, 1999.

Sanger, David, Michael Gordon, and John F. Burns, "Chaos Overran Iraq Plan in '06, Bush Team Says." *New York Times*, January 2, 2007.

Sawyer, Robert K. *Military Advisors in Korea: KMAG in Peace and War*. Washington, DC: Office of the Chief of Military History, Department of the Army, 1962.

———. *United States Military Advisory Group to the Republic of Korea*. Parts 1 and 2. Washington, DC: Office of the Chief of Military History, Department of the Army, n.d.

Scales, Robert H. *Certain Victory: The U.S. Army in the Gulf War; The Official U.S. Account*. Washington, DC: Brassey's, 1997.

Schaller, Michael. *Altered States: The United States and Japan since the Occupation*. New York: Oxford University Press, 1997.

Schmitt, Hans A., ed. *U.S. Occupation in Europe after World War II: Papers and Reminiscences from the April 23–24 1976 Conference at the George C. Marshall Research Foundation*. Lawrence: Regents Press of Kansas, 1976.

Schnabel, James F. *Policy and Direction, The First Year*. United States Army in the Korean War, Washington, DC: Center of Military History, US Army, 1972.

Schofield, John M. *Forty-Six Years in the Army*. New York, 1897.

Schonberger, Howard B. *Aftermath of War: Americans and the Remaking of Japan, 1945–1952*. Kent, OH: Kent State University, 1989.

Schroeder, John H. *Mr. Polk's War: American Opposition and Dissent, 1846–1848*. Madison: University of Wisconsin Press, 1973

Scott, Winfield. *Memoirs of Lieut.-General Scott*. Vol. 2. New York: Sheldon, 1846.

Sefton, James E. *The United States Army and Reconstruction 1865–1877*. Baton Rouge: Louisiana State University Press, 1967.

Seymour, Charles. *The Intimate Papers of Colonel House.* 4 vols. Boston: Houghton, 1926–28.

Sherwood, Robert. *Roosevelt and Hopkins: An Intimate History.* New York: Harper & Brothers, 1948.

Shultz, Richard H. *In the Aftermath of War: U.S. Support for Reconstruction and Nation-Building in Panama following Just Cause.* Maxwell Air Force Base, AL: Air University Press, August 1993.

———. "Low Intensity Conflict: Future Challenges and Lessons from the Reagan Years." *Survival* (July/August, 1989): 359–74.

———. "The Post-Conflict Use of Military Forces: Lessons from Panama, 1989–91." *Journal of Strategic Studies* 16 (June 1993): 145–72.

Shultz, Richard H., and Andrea Dew. "Counterinsurgency by the Book." *New York Times,* August 7, 2006.

Simpson, Brooks D., Leroy P. Graf, and John Muldowny. *Advice after Appomattox: Letters to Andrew Johnson, 1865–1866.* Special vol. 1 of the Papers of Andrew Johnson. Knoxville: University of Tennessee Press, 1987.

Simpson, Emile. *War from the Ground Up: Twenty-First Century Combat as Politics.* Oxford: Oxford University Press, November 2012.

Sinclair, Duncan. "The Occupation of Korea: Initial Phases." *Military Review* 27, no. 4 (July 1947): 29–36.

———. "The Occupation of Korea: Operations and Accomplishments." *Military Review* 27, no. 5 (August 1947): 53–60.

Singletary, Otis A. *The Mexican War.* Chicago: University of Chicago Press, 1960.

Smith, George Winston, and Charles Judah. *Chronicles of the Gringos: The U.S. Army in the Mexican War, 1846–1848.* Albuquerque: University of New Mexico Press, 1968.

Smith, Justin H. "American Rule in Mexico." *American Historical Review* 23, no. 2 (January 1918): 287–302.

———. *The War with Mexico.* 2 vols. New York: Macmillan, 1919. Reprint, Gloucester, MA: Peter Smith, 1963.

Snider, Donald, and Gayle Watkins, eds. *The Future of the Army Profession.* New York: McGraw-Hill Primis, 2002.

Sorley, Lewis. *A Better War: The Unexamined Victories and Final Tragedy of America's Last Years in Vietnam.* New York: Harcourt, 1999.

St. Clair, Kenneth E. "Military Justice in North Carolina, 1865: A Microcosm of Reconstruction." *Civil War History* 11 (December 1965): 341–50.

Stewart, Richard W. "The United States Army and Training in Military Government and Civil Affairs." Unpublished paper, n.d, by USASOCOM historian, in author's possession.

Stimson, Henry L., and McGeorge Bundy. *On Active Service in Peace and War.* New York: Harper & Brothers, 1947.

Stolzenbach, C. Darwin, and Henry A. Kissinger. "Civil Affairs in Korea 1950–1951." Working paper. Chevy Chase, MD: Operations Research Office, Johns Hopkins University, August 1952.

Stueck, William Whitney, Jr. *The Road to Confrontation: American Policy toward China and Korea, 1947–1950.* Chapel Hill: University of North Carolina Press, 1981.

Sullivan, Mark P. "The Future U.S. Role in Panama." In *Operation Just Cause: The U.S. Intervention in Panama*, edited by Bruce W. Watson and Peter G. Tsouras. Boulder, CO: Westview Press, 1991.

Summers, Harry J. *On Strategy: The Vietnam War in Context*. Carlisle Barracks, PA: Strategic Studies Institute, US Army War College, 1981.

Sutter, Richard. "The Strategic Implications of Military Civic Action." In *Winning the Peace: The Strategic Implications of Military Civic Action*, edited by John W. De Pauw and George A. Luz. Westport, CT: Praeger, 1992.

Swarm, William. "Impact of the Proconsular Experience on Civil Affairs Organization and Doctrine." In Wolfe, *Americans as Proconsuls*.

Tansey, Patrick. "Address by BG Patrick H. Tansey, Chief of the Supply Division, Department of the Army, to 7th Military Government Group." *Military Government Journal and Newsletter* 4, no. 4 (April 1952).

Taw, Jennifer Morrison. *Operation Just Cause and Low Intensity Conflict*. Washington, DC: RAND, February 1992.

Taylor, Philip H. "Military Government Experiences in Korea." In Friedrich, *American Experiences in Military Government*.

Thackrey, Russell I. "Military Government in the Pacific: Initial Phase." *Political Science Quarterly* 60 (March 1945): 90–99.

Thomas, David Yancy. *A History of Military Government in the Newly Acquired Territory of the United States*. Studies in History, Economics and Public Law. Vol. 20, no. 2. New York: AMS Press, 1967.

Thomas, Ralph. *A History of Military Government in the Newly Acquired Territory of the United States*. Studies in History, Economics and Public Law. Vol. 20, no. 2. New York: Columbia University Press, 1904. Reprint, New York: AMS Press, 1967.

Thorndike, Rachel S., ed. *The Sherman Letters: Correspondence between General and Senator Sherman from 1837 to 1891*. New York: Charles Scribner's Sons, 1971.

Thurman, Maxwell R., and William Hartzog. "Simultaneity: The Panama Case." *Army*, no. 43 (November 1993): 16–20.

Tierney, Dominic. "The Backlash against Nation-Building." *Prism* 5, no. 3 (2015): 12–27.

Trask, David. *The War with Spain*. New York: Macmillan, 1981.

Truman, Harry S. *Memoirs: Year of Decisions, 1945*. Vol. 1, Garden City, NY: Doubleday, 1956.

Turner, Henry Smith. *The Original Journals of Henry Smith Turner: With Stephen Watts Kearny to New Mexico and California, 1846–1847*. Norman: University of Oklahoma Press, 1966.

Twitchell, Ralph Emerson. *The History of the Military Occupation of the Territory of New Mexico from 1846–1851 by the Government of the United States*. Denver: Smith-Brooks, 1909. Reprint, Chicago: Rio Grande Press, 1963.

———. *The Leading Facts of New Mexican History*. Cedar Rapids, IA: Torch Press, 1912.

Ulmer, Sidney. "Local Autonomy in Japan since the Occupation." *Journal of Politics* 19, no. 1 (February 1957): 46–65.

US Congress, Senate Committee on Foreign Relations. *A Decade of American Foreign Policy: Basic Documents, 1941–49*. Prepared at the request of the Senate Committee on Foreign Relations by the Staff of the Committee and the Department of State. Washington, DC: GPO, 1950. http://avalon.law.yale.edu/subject_menus/decade.asp.

————, 30th Cong., 1st sess. Executive Document No. 60. *Messages of the President of the United States with the Correspondence, Therewith Communicated, between the Secretary of War and Other Officers of the Government: The Mexican War.* Washington, DC: Wendell & Van Benthuysen, 1848. This source is also known as *House Executive Document 60*, 30th Cong., 1st sess.

————. 30th Cong., 1st sess. House Executive Document No. 59. *Correspondence between the Secretary of War and General Scott.* Washington, DC: Wendell & Van Benthuysen, 1848.

————. 30th Cong., 2nd sess. Executive Document No. 1. *Message from the President of the United States to the Two Houses of Congress.* With accompanying documents. Correspondence from October 1846 through April 1848. Washington, DC: Wendell & Van Benthuysen, 1848.

————. *The United States and the Korean Problem: Documents 1943–1953.* Senate Document No. 74, 83rd Cong., 1st sess., 1953.

US Department of State. "American Organizational Plans for Military Government of Germany." *Department of State Bulletin* 12 (May 13, 1945): 900–2.

————. *The Axis in Defeat: Collection of Documents on American Policy toward Germany and Japan.* Publication 2423. Washington, DC: GPO, 1943. Reprint 2005, University Press of the Pacific.

————. "Basic Initial Directive to the Commander in Chief U.S. Army Forces Pacific, for the Administration of Civil Affairs in Those Areas of Korea occupied by U.S. Forces." SWNCC 176/8. In *Foreign Relations of the United States [FRUS]: 1945,* vol. 6, 1073–91. Washington: GPO, 1969.

————. *Department of State Bulletin.* September 23, 1945.

————. *Department of State Bulletin.* November 11, 1945.

————. *Foreign Relations of the United States (FRUS),* as listed below. Volumes related to material prior to 1932 were titled *Papers Relating to the Foreign Relations of the United States.*

————. *FRUS, 1919: Paris Peace Conference.* Vol. 1. Washington, DC: GPO, 1942.

————. *FRUS, 1919: Paris Peace Conference.* Vol. 5. Washington, DC: GPO, 1946.

————. *FRUS, 1919: Paris Peace Conference.* Vol. 6. Washington, DC: GPO, 1946.

————. *FRUS, 1919: Paris Peace Conference.* Vol. 7. Washington, DC: GPO, 1946.

————. *FRUS, 1919: Paris Peace Conference.* Vol. 11. Washington, DC: GPO, 1945.

————. *FRUS, 1919: Paris Peace Conference.* Vol. 13. Washington, DC: GPO, 1947.

————. *FRUS: The Conferences at Washington, 1941–42 and Casablanca, 1943.* Washington, DC: GPO, 1968.

————. *FRUS, 1943: The Conferences at Cairo and Tehran.* Washington, DC: GPO, 1961.

————. *FRUS, 1943: Conferences at Washington and Quebec.* Washington, DC: GPO, 1970.

————. *FRUS, 1943: Europe.* Vol. 2. Washington, DC: GPO, 1964.

————. *FRUS, 1944: The Near East, South Asia, and Africa, the Far East.* Vol. 5. Washington, DC: GPO, 1965.

————. *FRUS, 1945: The Conference of Berlin (The Potsdam Conference).* Vol. 2. Washington, DC: GPO, 1960.

————. *FRUS, 1945: Conferences at Malta and Yalta.* Washington, DC: GPO, 1955.

———. *FRUS, 1945: General: Political and Economic Matters.* Vol. 2. Washington, DC: GPO, 1967.

———. *FRUS, 1945: European Advisory Commission, Austria, Germany.* Vol. 3. Washington, DC: GPO, 1968.

———. *FRUS, 1945: The British Commonwealth, The Far East.* Vol. 6. Washington, DC: GPO, 1969.

———. *FRUS, 1946: Eastern Europe, The Soviet Union.* Vol. 6. Washington, DC: GPO, 1969.

———. *FRUS, 1946: The Far East.* Vol. 8. Washington, DC: GPO, 1971.

———. *FRUS, 1947: General: The United Nations.* Vol. 1. Washington, DC: GPO, 1973.

———. *FRUS, 1947: The British Commonwealth, Europe.* Vol. 3. Washington, DC: GPO, 1972.

———. *FRUS, 1947: The Far East.* Vol. 6. Washington, DC: GPO, 1972.

———. *FRUS, 1948: Western Europe.* Vol. 3. Washington, DC: GPO, 1974.

———. *FRUS, 1948: The Far East and Australasia.* Vol. 6. Washington, DC: GPO, 1974.

———. *FRUS, 1949: The Far East and Australasia.* Vol. 7. Parts 1 and 2. Washington, DC: GPO, 1976.

———. *FRUS, 1951: Asia and the Pacific.* Vol. 6. Parts 1 and 2. Washington, DC: GPO, 1977.

———. *Occupation of Japan: Policy and Progress.* Publication 267. Far Eastern Series 17. Washington, DC: GPO, 1946.

———. "Our Military Government Policy in Germany." *Department of State Bulletin* 13 (September 2, 1945). Statements by Dean Acheson and others.

———. *Papers Relating to the Foreign Relations of the United States: The Lansing Papers, 1914–1920.* 2 vols. Washington, DC, GPO, 1939.

———. *Papers Relating to the Foreign Relations of the United States, with the Annual Message of the President Transmitted to Congress December 3, 1900.* Washington, DC: GPO, 1902.

———. "Postwar Foreign Policy Preparation, 1939–1945." Department of State Publication 3580. Washington, DC, 1949.

———. "U.S. Initial Post Surrender Policy for Japan." *Department of State Bulletin,* September 23, 1945.

US Department of the Army. *Army Capstone Concept: Operational Adaptability.* TRADOC pamphlet 525-3-0. December 2009. http://www.defenseinnovationmarketplace.mil/resources/ArmyCapstoneConcept.pdf.

———. *Army Capstone Concept.* December 2012. http://www.tradoc.army.mil/tpubs/pams/tp525-3-0.pdf.

———. *The Army Operating Concept: Win in a Complex World.* October 31, 2014. http://www.tradoc.army.mil/tpubs/pams/tp525-3-1.pdf.

———. *Civil Affairs.* Office of the Chief Historian, European Command. Occupation Forces in Europe Series, 1945–1946. Frankfurt, Germany, 1947. Reprinted as *Training Packet No. 51,* Provost Marshal General's School, n.d.

———. *Field Manual 41-10: Civil Affairs / Military Government Operations.* May 1957. Revised versions in October 1969 and January 1993.

———. *FM 100-5: Operations.* Washington, DC, June 14, 1993.

———. *FM 100-23: Peace Operations*. Washington, DC, December 1994.

———. *Military Government: An Historical Approach*. Training Packet No. 9. Provost Marshal General's School. Military Government Department for ORC Units. Conference No. 2, US Military Government in Mexico. Camp Gordon, GA, 1951.

———. *Military Government under General Winfield Scott*. Training Packet No. 58. Provost Marshal General's School, Military Government Department for ORC Units, Camp Gordon, GA. Handwritten, dated October 1960.

———. *Reports of General MacArthur: MacArthur in Japan; The Occupation—Military Phase. Vol. 1 supplement. Prepared by His General Staff*. Washington, DC: GPO, 1966.

———. *Operation Just Cause: Lessons Learned*. Vol. 1, *Soldiers and Leadership*, and vol. 2, *Operations*. Bulletin No. 90-9. Center for Army Lessons Learned, US Army Combined Arms Command, Fort Leavenworth, KS. http://www.globalsecurity.org/military/library /report/1990/90-9/9091toc.htm. There are three parts to this bulletin.

———. US Army Infantry School. "The Theory and Operation of Military Government." Infantry School Mailing List. Vol. 30, chapter 7 (April 1947).

———. *United States Army in the World War, 1917–1919: American Occupation of Germany*. Vol. 11. Washington, DC: Center of Military History, US Army, 1991.

———. *United States Army in the World War, 1917–1919: The Armistice Agreement and Related Documents*. Vol. 10. Part 1. Washington, DC: Center of Military History, US Army, 1991.

US Department of the Army and Department of the Navy. *Manual of Civil Affairs Military Government: FM 27-5*. Washington: GPO, October 1947.

———. *Manual of Military Government and Civil Affairs: FM 27-5*. Washington: GPO, December 22, 1943.

US Department of the Army and US Marine Corps. *Counterinsurgency Manual, FM 3-24*. Chicago: University of Chicago Press, 2007. Original issued December 2006.

US Department of War. *Annual Reports of the War Department for the Fiscal Year Ended June 30, 1898: Annual Report of the Major General Commanding the Army, Nelson A. Miles*. Washington, DC: GPO, November 1898.

———. *Annual Reports of the War Department for the Fiscal Year Ended June 30, 1899: Report of the Major General Commanding of the Army; Report in Three Parts*. Vol. 1. Part 2. Washington: GPO, 1900.

———. *Correspondence Relating to the War with Spain and Conditions Growing Out of the Same . . . between the Adjutant General of the Army and Military Commanders in the United States, Cuba, Porto [sic] Rico, China and the Philippine Islands from April 15, 1898 to July 30 1902*. 2 vols. Washington, DC, 1902.

———. *Final Report of General John J. Pershing, Commander in Chief American Expeditionary Forces*. Washington, DC: GPO, 1920. Found at US Army Military History Institute.

———. *Five Years of the War Department following the War with Spain, 1899–1903, as Shown in the Annual Reports of the Secretary of War, Report for 1899*. Washington, DC: GPO, 1904. This single volume brings together the annual reports of the secretary of war, covering the period from the close of the war with Spain in 1898 to the end of the year 1903. It was also published as a book of the same title authored by Elihu Root.

———. *Military Government and Civil Affairs: Field Manual 27-5*. Washington, DC: GPO, July 30, 1940.

————— *Report of the Adjutant General of the Army and Military Commanders in the United States, Cuba, Porto* [sic] *Rico, China and the Philippine Islands from April 15, 1898 to July 30 1902.* Vol. 1. Washington, DC, 1902.

—————. *Rules of Land Warfare.* FM 27-10, Washington, DC: GPO, 1940.

—————. *War of the Rebellion: A Compilation of the Official Records of the Union and Confederate Armies.* Vol. 2. Washington, DC, 1880–1901. Often cited as *Official Records.* This series can also be found at http://www.archives.gov/research/alic/reference/military/civil-war-armies-records.html.

US Government Accounting Office. *Afghanistan Security: Further Congressional Action May Be Needed to Ensure Completion of a Detailed Plan to Develop and Sustain Capable Afghan National Security Forces.* GAO-08-661. Washington, DC, June 2008.

US Korean Military Advisory Group, Public Information Office. *The United States Military Advisory Group to the Republic of Korea, 1945–1955.* Tokyo: Daito, 1955.

Utley, Robert. "The Contribution of the Frontier to the American Military Tradition." In *The American Military on the Frontier: The Proceedings of the 7th Military History Symposium, United States Air Force Academy 30 September–1 October 1976,* edited by James P. Tate. Washington, DC: Office of Air Force History, 1978: 3–13.

—————. *Frontier Regulars: The United States Army and the Indian Wars 1866–1891.* Lincoln: University of Nebraska Press, 1973.

—————. *Frontiersmen in Blue: The United States Army and the Indian, 1848–1865.* Lincoln: University of Nebraska Press, 1981.

Vernon, E. H. "Civil Affairs and Military Government." *Military Review* 26, no. 3 (June 1946): 25–32.

Waghelstein, John. "Preparing the US Army for the Wrong War: Educational and Doctrinal Failure 1865–91." *Small Wars and Insurgencies* 10, no. 1 (1999): 1–33.

Wallace, Edward S. "The United States Army in Mexico City." *Military Affairs* 13, no. 3 (Autumn 1949): 158–66.

Watson, Bruce W., and Peter G. Tsouras, eds. *Operation Just Cause: The U.S. Intervention in Panama.* Boulder, CO: Westview, 1991.

Watson, Mark Skinner. *Chief of Staff: Prewar Plans and Preparations.* Washington, DC: Center of Military History, US Army, 1991.

Weaver, Herbert, and Paul Bergeron, eds. *Correspondence of James K. Polk.* Nashville, TN: Vanderbilt University Press, 1969.

Wedemeyer, Albert C. *Report to the President: Korea.* Washington, DC: GPO, 1951.

Weigley, Russell F. *The American Way of War: A History of United States Military Strategy and Policy.* Bloomington: Indiana University Press, 1977.

—————. *A History of the United States Army.* Bloomington: Indiana University Press, 1984.

—————. *Towards an American Army: Military Thought from Washington to Marshall.* New York: Columbia University Press, 1962.

Weigley, Russell F., ed. *New Dimensions in Military History.* San Rafael, CA: Presidio, 1975.

Welton, Courtenay S., II. "Expertise in Reserve." *Civil Affairs Journal and Newsletter* 43, no. 1 (January–February 1990). This was a reprint from the original that appeared as "Reservists Equal to Task for Panama." *The Officers* (March 1990): 11–15.

Westover, John G. *Combat Support in Korea.* US Army in Action Series. Washington, DC: Center of Military History, US Army, 1987.

Wildes, Harry Emerson. *Typhoon in Tokyo: The Occupation and Its Aftermath*. New York: Macmillan, 1959.

Williams, Daniel, and Rajiv Chandrasekaran. "U.S. Troops Frustrated in Iraq." *Washington Post*, June 20, 2003.

Williams, Justin. "Completing Japan's Political Reorientation 1947–1952: Crucial Phase of the Allied Occupation." *American Historical Review* 73, no. 5 (June 1968): 1454–69.

Williams, Robert W., and Dan Caldwell. "Just Post Bellum: Just War Theory and the Principles of Just Peace." *International Studies Perspectives* 7, no. 4 (November 2006): 309–20.

Wing, Roswell B. *Civil Affairs / Military Government Organization, Plans, and Training, 1953–1954*. Technical memorandum ORO-T-273. Study conducted under contract for the Department of the Army, Operations Research Office, Johns Hopkins University, October 26, 1954.

Wolfe, Robert, ed. *Americans as Proconsuls: United States Military Government in Germany and Japan, 1944–1952*. Carbondale: Southern Illinois University Press, 1958.

Wood, Carlton L., Robert A. Kinney, and Charles N. Henning. *Civil Affairs Relations in Korea*. Chevy Chase, MD: Project Legate, Operations Research Office, ORO-T-264, Johns Hopkins University, July 16, 1954.

Wood, Leonard. "The Military Government of Cuba." *Annals of the American Academy of Political and Social Science* 21 (March 1903): 153–82.

Wooster, Robert. "The Frontier Army and the Occupation of the West, 1865–1900." Paper presented at the Combat Studies Institute Conference "Armed Diplomacy Two Centuries of American Campaigning," August 5–7, 2003. http://usacac.army.mil/cac2/cgsc/carl/download/csipubs/ArmedDiplomacy_TwoCenturiesOfAmericanCampaigning.pdf.

Wright, Donald, ed. *Vanguard of Valor: Small Unit Actions in Afghanistan*. Fort Leavenworth, KS: Combat Studies Institute Press, 2011.

Wright, Donald P., James R. Bird, Steven E. Clay, James R. Bird, Lynne Chandler Garcia, Dennis F. Van Wey, Peter W. Connors, and Scott C. Farquhar. *A Different Kind of War: The United States Army in Operation Enduring Freedom (OEF), October 2001–September 2005*. Fort Leavenworth, KS: Combat Studies Institute Press, May 2010.

Wright, Donald, and Timothy Reese, with the Contemporary Studies Operations Team. *On Point II: Transition to the New Campaign; The United States Army in Operation Iraqi Freedom, May 2003–January 2005*. Fort Leavenworth, KS: Combat Studies Institute Press, June 2008.

Yates, Lawrence A. "Joint Task Force Panama: Just Cause Before and After." *Military Review* 71, no. 10 (October 1991): 58–71.

———. "Operation Just Cause in Panama City, December 1989." In *Urban Operations: An Historical Casebook*. Fort Leavenworth, KS: Combat Studies Institute Press, 2002.

———. *Power Pack: U.S. Intervention in the Dominican Republic, 1965–1966*. Leavenworth Papers. US Army Command and General Staff College. Fort Leavenworth, KS: Combat Studies Institute Press, 1988.

Ziemke, Earl F. "Civil Affairs Reaches Thirty." *Military Affairs* 36, no. 4 (December 1972): 130–33.

———. "The Formulation and Initial Implementation of U.S. Occupation Policy in Germany." In *U.S. Occupation in Europe after World War II: Papers and Reminiscences from* the *April 23–24 1976 Conference at the George C. Marshall Research Foundation*, edited by Hans A. Schmitt. Lawrence, KS: Regents Press of Kansas, 1976.

———. "Improvising Stability and Change in Postwar Germany." In Wolfe, *Americans as Proconsuls*.

———. "Military Government: Two Approaches, Russian and American." In Weigley, *New Dimensions in Military History*.

———. *The U.S. Army in the Occupation of Germany: 1944–1946*. Army Historical Series. Washington, DC: Center of Military History, US Army, 1990.

Zink, Harold. *American Military Government in Germany*. New York: Macmillan, 1947.

———. "American Military Government Organization in Germany." *Journal of Politics* 8 (August 1946): 329–49.

———. *The United States in Germany: 1944–1955*. Princeton, NJ: D. Van Norstrand, 1957.

Zook, George F. "The Educational Missions to Japan and Germany." *International Conciliation*, no. 427 (January 1947): 3–19.

———. "Japan and Germany: Problems in Reeducation." *International Conciliation*, no. 427 (January 1947).

———. "Summary of the Report of the United States Education Mission to Japan." *International Conciliation*, no. 427 (January 1947): 20–26.

# INDEX

Operation Desert Fox, 238
Operation Eclipse, 112, 113, 114
Operation Enduring Freedom, 15, 223, 227
Operation Iraqi Freedom (OIF), 238–39, 243–44
Operation Just Cause, 194–95, 197, 205
Operation Power Pack, 189
operations other than war (OOTW), 20, 21
Operations Research Office (ORO), 23n4
Operation Torch, 96
Organization of American States (OAS), 192, 194, 207, 208, 214n124, 215n127
Otis, Elwell Stephen, 58, 59

Pace, Peter, 241, 256
Palmer, Bruce, 189, 190–92, 214n124, 215n129
Panama, 194–206; combat/reconstruction phase relationship in, 197–98, 205; conclusions and lessons from, 204–6, 208; departure from, 204–6; economic problems of, 204, 219n224; health care in, 203; interagency coordination in, 199, 205–6, 217n181; judicial system reorganization in, 201; planning for, 195–96; police and security force reorganization in, 200–201, 217n193, 218nn196–97; structure for governance operations in, 196–99; tactical force/civil affairs coordination in, 201–3; US economic aid to, 204, 206; US objectives in, 195, 197, 205, 219n231
Pan American Health Organization, 193
Panetta, Leon, ix, 8–9, 273
Patton, George S., Jr., 105
Peacekeeping and Stability Operations Institute (PKSOI), 230
peace operations, 20, 21
Perry, Benjamin F., 46
Pershing, John, 30, 67, 90n224, 153n27
Petraeus, David, 228; and Iraq, 247, 249, 257–58, 259, 270n141
Phelps, John, 43
Philippines: counterinsurgency campaign in, 59, 60; governance operations in,

57–58, 59–60, 63–64, 78; in Spanish-American War, 54, 55
police and security forces: in Afghanistan, 221–22, 235–37; in Cuba, 61–62; in Dominican Republic, 192–93; in Iraq, 244, 245, 248–49, 252–54, 255–56, 258–60; in Japan, 128; in Korea, 140, 169n373, 178, 183, 210n25, 212n65; in Panama, 200–201, 217n193, 218nn196–97; in Rhineland, 72–73
political reform and reorganization: in Afghanistan, 224; during Civil War and Reconstruction, 47; in Cuba and Puerto Rico, 61, 62, 63; in Germany, 118–19; in Iraq, 251; in Italy, 106–8; in Japan, 127–28; in Korea, 147
Polk, James K., 36, 38, 40; strategic goals of, 34–35, 41–42
Pope, John, 49
Potsdam Conference (1945), 113–14, 116, 134
Potsdam Declaration, 124
Powell, Colin, 194–95, 208
Powell Doctrine, 208
Powers, Samantha, 13n18
preventative diplomacy, 20
Proclamation of Amnesty and Reconstruction, 44, 84n89
proconsuls, 276–77
Project and Contracting Office (PCO), 250
Project Hope, 203
Promote Liberty, 197, 200, 215n146
provincial reconstruction teams (PRTs), 229–30, 250
Provost Marshal (PMG), 47, 49, 50, 98; Division of Military Government of, 153n30
psychological operations (PSYOPS), 176, 177, 191, 218n209
Puerto Rico, 55, 57, 62–63

Qaddafi, Muammar, 9, 280
Quebec Conference (1944), 111
Quetta Shura Taliban, 222

# ABOUT THE AUTHOR

NADIA SCHADLOW is a senior program officer in the International Security and Foreign Policy Program of the Smith Richardson Foundation. She plays a strategic planning role at the foundation, identifying issues that warrant further attention from the US policy community and managing programs to develop the intellectual foundation for more effective foreign and defense policies. Dr. Schadlow began her career in the Office of the Secretary of Defense and later served on the Defense Policy Board from September 2006 to June 2009. Her articles about national security have been published in the *Wall Street Journal, ForeignPolicy.com, The American Interest, Parameters, War on the Rocks, Orbis, Small Wars Journal,* and elsewhere. She holds a PhD from Johns Hopkins University's Nitze School of Advanced International Studies and is a member of the Council on Foreign Relations.